Value Creation from e-Business Models

Value Creation from e-Business Models

Edited by

Wendy L. Currie

ELSEVIER
BUTTERWORTH
HEINEMANN

AMSTERDAM • BOSTON • HEIDELBERG • LONDON • NEW YORK • OXFORD
PARIS • SAN DIEGO • SAN FRANCISCO • SINGAPORE • SYDNEY • TOKYO

Elsevier Butterworth-Heinemann
Linacre House, Jordan Hill, Oxford OX2 8DP
30 Corporate Drive, Burlington, MA 01803

First published 2004

British Library Cataloguing in Publication Data
Value creation from e-business models
   1. Electronic commerce   2. Business – Mathematical models
   I. Currie, Wendy, 1960–
   658'.054678

Library of Congress Cataloguing in Publication Data
A catalogue record for this book is available from the Library of
Congress

ISBN 0 7506 6140 2

For information on all Elsevier Butterworth-Heinemann publications
visit our website at http://books.elsevier.com

Typeset by Charon Tec Pvt. Ltd, Chennai, India
Printed and bound in Great Britain

Contents

List of Figures   vii

List of Tables   xi

Preface   xiii

Part One   e-Business Model Ontologies and Taxonomies   I

1   Value-creation from e-Business models: issues and perspectives   3
     Wendy L. Currie

2   Business models and their relationship to strategy   II
     Peter B. Seddon, Geoffrey Lewis, Phil Freeman and
     Graeme Shanks

3   A framework for codifying business models and process
     models in e-Business design   35
     Philip Joyce and Graham Winch

4   An ontology for e-Business models   65
     Alexander Osterwalder and Yves Pigneur

5   e-Business value modelling using the *e³-value* ontology   98
     Jaap Gordijn

Part Two   e-Business Markets and Strategies   129

6   A causal network analysis of e-market business models   131
     Jon Moon

7   Knowledge management and e-Commerce: when self-service
     is not the sensible solution   158
     Sue Newell and Jimmy Huang

8   Perceptions of strategic value and adoption of e-Commerce:
     a theoretical framework and empirical test   178
     Elizabeth E. Grandón and J. Michael Pearson

Part Three   e-Business Performance Measurement and
**   Value Creation**   211

9   Value creation from corporate Web sites: how different features
     contribute to success in e-Business   213
     Nils Madeja and Detlef Schoder

10 Evaluating the quality of e-Business implementation with
    E-Qual   229
    Stuart Barnes and Richard Vidgen

11 The e-sourcing opportunity: from projects and ASPs to value
    networks   253
    Leslie P. Willcocks and Robert Plant

12 Value creation in application outsourcing relationships:
    an international case study on ERP outsourcing   283
    Erik Beulen and Pieter Ribbers

Part Four   e-Business Applications and Services   311

13 NHS information systems strategy, planning and
    implementation of primary service provision   313
    Matthew W. Guah

14 A framework of integrated models for supply chain
    e-Management   335
    Charu Chandra, Sameer Kumar and Alexander V. Smirnov

15 Building out the Web services architecture: the challenge of
    software applications integration   370
    Wendy L. Currie

    About the authors   409

    Glossary of terms   417

    Index   421

List of Figures

Figure 2.1:   The relationship between the concepts 'business model', Porter's (1996, 2001) 'strategy', and a real-world firm.   13

Figure 2.2:   Evolution of 'Harvard school' thinking on strategy.   15

Figure 2.3:   Porter's (1979) five-forces model: forces governing competition in an industry.   15

Figure 2.4:   Structure of Porter and Millar's (1985) value chain diagram.   16

Figure 2.5:   An example of a Porter-style (1996, p. 73) activity system map.   19

Figure 2.6:   Comparing the work of six widely cited researchers using Pateli's (2002) six different themes of business model papers.   20

Figure 2.7:   Example e-Business model schematic based on Weill and Vitale (2001) (intended to correspond to the activity system map in Figure 2.5).   23

Figure 2.8:   Linder and Cantrell's (2000) operating business model for SupplyGenie.com   26

Figure 2.9:   Strategies and business models as abstractions of different degree of some parts of a real-world firm.   28

Figure 2.10: Comparing strategy and business models on two dimensions: abstraction and competitive focus (the dots show placement on each dimension).   29

Figure 3.1:   Business model strategic conceptual framework.   50

Figure 3.2:   The 'triple pair' process flow model of supply chain fulfilment.   52

Figure 3.3:   Schematic showing the supply chain, as depicted in the beer game.   53

Figure 3.4:   A 'supply chain network dynamic process model' drawn with *iThink* (after Chandra et al., 2002).   54

Figure 3.5:   A re-drafted depiction of Chandra et al.'s model.   55

Figure 3.6:   The triple pair model with detail for each flow process.   55

Figure 3.7:   Weill and Vitale's direct to customer business model (Weill and Vitale, 2001, p. 246).   56

Figure 3.8:   Basic 'triple pair' flow structure of direct-to-customer model.   57

Figure 3.9:   Fuller direct-to-customer model with specification confirmation and goods returns.   58

Figure 3.10: Weill and Vitale's characterisation of their FS
provider model. 59

Figure 3.11: Extension to the direct-to-customer model to
represent offer of secondary products/services
from the FS provider. 59

Figure 3.12: Product delivery and fund transfer mechanisms
added. 60

Figure 4.1: Environment, business models, strategy, process
and information systems. 68

Figure 4.2: Business model ontology. 69

Figure 4.3: Value proposition. 71

Figure 4.4: Distribution channel. 76

Figure 4.5: Channel matrix at Nokia mobile phone. 77

Figure 4.6: Customer equity and relationship. 78

Figure 4.7: Customer relationship of Orange. 83

Figure 4.8: Value configuration and activities. 86

Figure 4.9: ColorPlaza value configuration, activities, resources
and partnerships. 88

Figure 4.10: Partnership. 90

Figure 5.1: Concepts and relations of the e^3-value ontology
(global actor viewpoint). 103

Figure 5.2: Value model for a free Internet access service.
(a) the global actor viewpoint; (b) Actor a can decide
to exchange value objects with actor **b**, or actor **c**. 104

Figure 5.3: A value exchange can be in multiple transactions. 109

Figure 5.4: A value model without and with market segment.
(a) Actor **a** exchanges value objects actors b_1, b_2 or b_3,
who may value these objects differently; (b) Actor **a**
exchanges value objects with actors b_1, b_2 or b_n,
who value these objects equally. 111

Figure 5.5: Concepts and relations of the e^3-value ontology
extended for the detailed actor viewpoint. A composite
actor and an elementary actor are generalized into an
actor. 112

Figure 5.6: Value model for the free Internet case: the detailed
free Internet service provider actor view. 112

Figure 5.7: Concepts and relations of the e^3-value ontology
extended for the value activity viewpoint. 113

Figure 5.8: Value model for the free Internet case: the value
activity view. 116

Figure 5.9: UCM constructs. 118

Figure 5.10: An ontology of UCMs based on Amyot and
Mussbacher (2000). 119

Figure 5.11: UCMs applied to the global actor viewpoint. 120

Figure 5.12: UCMs applied to the detailed actor viewpoint. 120

Figure 6.1:   The EM paradox model.   146
Figure 6.2:   Process model for Company A, 'integrated
              solutions provider'.   150
Figure 6.3:   Process model for Company B, purchasing portal.   151
Figure 6.4:   Process model for Company C, vertical
              industry portal.   152
Figure 6.5:   Process model for Company D, evolutionary model.   153
Figure 6.6:   Interview variables.   154
Figure 7.1:   A contingency model of e-Commerce based on the
              knowledge requirements of activities and the
              organization's value-proposition.   174
Figure 8.1:   Theoretical framework to study perceptions of
              strategic value and adoption of e-Commerce.   189
Figure 8.2:   The revised theoretical framework.   201
Figure 10.1: Radar chart of E-Qual 4.0 subcategories for online
              bookshops (Barnes and Vidgen, 2002).   234
Figure 10.2: The E-Qual questionnaire interface (see www.webqual.
              co.uk/demonstration.htm).   237
Figure 10.3: The FSMKE site prior to redesign.   238
Figure 10.4: The FSMKE site after redesign.   238
Figure 10.5: Radar chart of E-Qual subcategories before and after
              site redesign.   244
Figure 11.1: Four sourcing options for e-development.   257
Figure 11.2: Alamo: evolving through a four-phase mixed
              sourcing path. Adapted from Research model.   262
Figure 11.3: Covisint: remodelling supply and delivery
              (early 2001).   269
Figure 11.4: Strategic e-sourcing (A) by business activity.   273
Figure 11.5: Strategic e-sourcing (B) by market comparison.   275
Figure 12.1: overview of responsibilities for ERP outsourcing
              (based on Klepper, 1995).   284
Figure 12.2: Research framework.   292
Figure 12.3: The Capabilities and (contractual) relationships
              of the investigated ERP outsourcing relationship.   295
Figure 12.4: Governance structure ERP hosting.   299
Figure 13.1: NHS structure for IS procurement.   315
Figure 13.2: The ICRS structure (adapted from DoH, 2002).   329
Figure 13.3: NHS Direct Online @ www.nhsdirect.nhs.uk.   330
Figure 14.1: Interconnectedness of topics in enterprise
              integration research.   345
Figure 14.2: An integrated supply chain management
              systems development framework.   353
Figure 14.3: An automotive supply chain enterprise
              decomposition model.   356
Figure 14.4: Illustration of an SCN dynamic process flow model.   357

Figure 14.5: The fundamental pattern.   358
Figure 14.6: Elements and interactions of control.   359
Figure 14.7: IM domain object model.   361
Figure 15.1: Three stages of software applications development
              and IT outsourcing.   374
Figure 15.2: Description and discovery processes in Web service
              architecture. *Source*: Vinoski (2002).   389
Figure 15.3: The Web services structure of J2EE and .NET.
              Source: Vawter and Roman theserverside.com   391
Figure 15.4: The flow of information within firms A and B.   398

List of Tables

Table 2.1:   Six themes of papers on business models   21
Table 4.1:   Value proposition   71
Table 4.2:   The core VALUE PROPOSITION of easyMoney.com   74
Table 4.3:   Target customer   75
Table 4.4:   Distribution channel   76
Table 4.5:   Customer equity and relationship   78
Table 4.6:   Capabilities and resource   84
Table 4.7:   Value configuration and activities   86
Table 4.8:   Partnership   90
Table 5.1:   Various value exchange types   115
Table 5.2:   Structure of a profitability sheet   122
Table 6.1:   Case study sample   136
Table 6.2:   Clustered summary table of themes   138
Table 7.1:   Different approaches to knowledge management   164
Table 8.1:   Summary of relevant factors associated with the
             adoption of different technologies   187
Table 8.2:   Hypothesized factors that create strategic value in
             e-Commerce   189
Table 8.3:   Hypothesized factors that determine e-Commerce
             adoption   190
Table 8.4:   Demographic information for Study 1   196
Table 8.5:   Measures of overall model fit   197
Table 8.6:   Standardized canonical coefficients and
             canonical loadings for perceived strategic value
             and adoption   198
Table 8.7:   Demographic information for Study 2   199
Table 8.8:   Measures of overall model fit   200
Table 8.9:   Standardized canonical coefficients and canonical
             loadings for perceived strategic value and adoption   200
Table 9.1:   Numerical results for the hypothesized effectiveness
             of the web features   224
Table 10.1: The E-Qual 4.0 instrument   232
Table 10.2: The most important qualities for users of
             Internet bookshops   234
Table 10.3: Respondent demographics and experience   239
Table 10.4: Summary of the data – mean, standard error (SE),
             and standard deviation (SD)   241
Table 10.5: Weighted scores and E-Qual indices CWQI – before
             and after redesign   242

Table 11.1   Case study organizations performance assessment   277
Table 12.1: Interviewees of the ERP outsourcing case study   293
Table 13.1: Definitions of ASP   318
Table 15.1: xSP categories   376
Table 15.2: Definitions of Web services   382
Table 15.3: Type of software application and KPA   385
Table 15.4: Phases of Web service adoption   387
Table 15.5: Differences between the two firms used in the study   396

Preface

At the height of the dot.com boom around the beginning of 2000, confidence in e-business fuelled the growth of numerous start-up firms, all claiming to offer customers a unique value proposition in this emerging and exciting market. Governments across the globe were spearheading programmes on e-business. In the UK, the government developed the role of the 'E-Envoy'. The European Union also set an extensive programme to fund e-business ('E-Society') research. Similar programmes appeared in the US, Australia, and Asia. Against the backdrop of international interest in the e-business phenomenon, I decided to visit Silicon Valley on two occasions to explore a new information systems innovation called application services provision (ASP). Like other e-business initiatives, ASP was marketed as a new revolution in business computing. My first visit in April 2000 was both exciting and stimulating. Virtually every street corner advertised a new dot.com company. Office space was difficult to find. So was skilled IT labour and expertise. Migration was taking place on a vast scale with people moving from one US state to California to take part in the new dot.com era. Similarly, people from overseas were keen to secure their H1B visas to come to Silicon Valley to work. Salary scales reached high levels with employers having to entice people to work for them by offering attractive share options. This spawned a new wave of dot.com millionaires. This *gold rush* scenario was infectious, as people left their secure jobs with established firms on the promise of earning huge salaries in the dot.coms.

During my first visit to Silicon Valley, I visited a large number of dot.coms, mainly describing themselves as ASPs. My interest was to learn about their e-business models. Several firms showed me their presentation slides for venture capital firms. These presentations were glossy and interesting, but appeared to overlook two important factors. First, they said little about their target customers. Second, they said even less about how they would generate revenues. What was apparent was that much of the content focused upon developing a 'brand' identity. To this end, a vast amount of money was spent on marketing initiatives. Trade fairs and exhibitions were rife with start-up firms featuring their products and services on platforms and kiosks, often giving away numerous small gifts in the process. Yet customers were few and far between at these events!

Between April and August 2000, the fortunes of the dot.coms changed enormously. My second visit to Silicon Valley in August 2000 was met with less 'irrational exuberance' from the dot.coms. In fact, some of the firms I visited only four months before appeared to be struggling. Most of them had only a few customers, so revenues continued to remain small or non-existent. By the end of 2000, the dot.com crash was well underway.

Having returned from Silicon Valley I was soon to learn that I had been successful in winning two UK funded research grants (EPSRC and ESRC) to study e-business models in the emerging ASP market. Whilst this was good news, I was soon to discover that several of my industrial collaborators had also gone out of business. Those that remained were suffering in the technology collapse.

As a result of the dot.com shakeout, interest tended to shift from an implicit assumption that any business, product or service prefixed with 'e' or ending in .com would be automatically successful, to one of extreme caution where the rules of the 'old economy' still prevailed. In fact, many pundits quickly dispensed with the distinction between 'old' and 'new' economies.

Having witnessed the rapid pace at which Internet start-ups were created and abandoned, academic and practitioner interest has shifted to the issue of value creation. *Value Creation from E-Business Models* is therefore intended to draw together a collection of work which links theory with practice. As opposed to a quick-fix guide for managers about the various attributes of e-business success, the book aims to encourage a deeper critical analysis of e-business models. Even the term, e-business models is problematized by some of the chapter authors to encourage the reader to conceptualize how e-business models relate to a wider industry analysis.

The book is divided into four broad sections: (1) e-Business Model Ontologies and Taxonomies; (2) e-Business Markets and Strategies; (3) e-Business Performance Measurement and Value Creation; (4) e-Business Applications and Services. Ontologies and Taxonomies attempt to classify e-business models into their component parts. This may be achieved by delineating the various characteristics and variables pertaining to specific e-business models. This section also considers the relationship between e-business models and the wider management, i.e. strategy literature. Markets and Strategies consider e-business models in the macro context of the market and the micro context of individual firm strategies. Much of the literature in these areas stems from the fields of economics and sociology. In recent years, the technology acceptance model (TAM) has been widely used to explore issues relating to user acceptance to determine the significant barriers to business performance and success of Web sites.

Performance Measurement and Value Creation are further covered in this book. The work in this area focuses upon the development of tools and techniques to evaluate the quality of e-business implementation and specific e-business models such as ASP. Indeed, the collapse of so many e-businesses has intensified interest in performance measurement and evaluation. Finally, the area of Applications and Services is important for examining particular types of e-business offerings. We consider ASP and Web Services in the UK National Health Service; supply chain e-management (SCeM) and how Web services may resolve problems of software applications integration.

While this book includes a body of work across a range of issues, themes and perspectives, much is omitted through space limitations. This contribution is aimed to give readers a broad appreciation of some of the current research and thinking on e-business models from a range of internationally respected and some less well known scholars and colleagues. More importantly, it hopes to generate fresh ideas and potentially new research areas for further study. The main audience is likely to be within the academic community (i.e. business management and information systems); specialist masters degrees; MBA modules (particularly e-business) and undergraduate degrees. Those students undertaking PhD and MPhil degrees will also find the content of immense value as many chapters contain numerous sources for further reading.

Finally, I would like to wholeheartedly thank all the chapter authors for their excellent contributions to the book.

Wendy L. Currie

Dedication

To my beloved parents, who both passed away in 2003

Part One

---

e-Business Model Ontologies and Taxonomies

1 Value creation from e-Business models: issues and perspectives

Wendy L. Currie

Over the last decade, interest in e-Business has evolved from optimistic scenarios with the explicit message in the popular press that: *If you're not an eBusiness, you're out of business*, to pessimistic scenarios pointing to the demise of the dot.coms (Cassidy, 2002) largely as a result of 'flawed e-Business models' (Hagel, 2002). The literature on e-Business models is varied with contributions focusing upon the successful examples of Amazon.com, e-bay and priceline.com from a buyer behaviour perspective (Kauffman and Wang, 2001); taxonomies of e-Business models (Timmers, 1999; Weill and Vitale, 2001); value creation from e-Business models (Amit and Zott, 2000) and e-Business model applications and services, such as application service provisioning (ASP) (Kern et al., 2002; Currie et al., 2004) and Web services (Hagel and Seely-Brown, 2001).

The concept of the business model has gained momentum in recent years, partly through the growth and interest in e-Business. Definitions of what constitutes a *business model* vary in the literature, with some running the risk of being tautological. Thus, Magretta (2001, pp. 86–87) contends that: *a good business model remains essential to every successful organization, whether it's a new venture or an established player*. Timmers (1999, p. 5) defines a business model as *'the organization (or 'architecture') of product, service and information flows, and the sources of revenues and benefits for suppliers and customers.'* Similarly, Rappa (2000, p. 1) claims that: *In the most basic sense, a business model is the method of doing business by which a company can sustain itself, that is, be profitable*. The link between the business model concept and e-Business has become explicit in recent years. Weill and Vitale (2001, p. 34) define an e-Business model as: *a description of the roles and relationships among a firm's consumers, customers, allies, and suppliers that identifies the major flows of product, information, and money, and the major benefits to participants.*

Such a broad definition poses problems in researching e-Business models. Recognizing this, Weill and Vitale (2001) deconstruct the e-Business model into eight 'atomic e-Business models'.[1] Firms may develop one or a combination of these atomic e-Business models to pursue their business strategies. There will also be variants of each atomic e-Business model, depending upon the factors outlined by the authors. Other writers suggest that the business model is a useful construct for understanding value creation from e-Business. Amit and Zott (2000, p. 1) assert that: *a business model depicts the design of transaction content, structure and governance so as to create value through the exploitation of business opportunities. We propose that a firm's business model is an important locus of innovation and a crucial source of value creation for the firm and its suppliers, partners and customers*. Similarly, Ross et al. (2001, p. 3) claim that business models demonstrate: *changes in how the firm generates revenues or manages costs*.

Treating the e-Business model as the unit of analysis is useful since it enables a deeper understanding of firm performance (Magretta, 2001), particularly at the organizational, rather than industry level. A cursory glance at the literature identifies a common thread, which is the search for successful business models. During the first phase of the dot.com era (from 1994 to 2001) the majority of the popular publications, largely from the technology sector, suggested that developing an e-Business was critical to the survival of the firm. Within the media, there was talk of the 'old economy' (bricks and mortar) versus the 'new economy' (Internet businesses), with the former often described in pejorative terms (see Rappa, 2000).

Firms, it was suggested, had little choice but to 'innovate or die'. In 1999, 3957 US companies received a total of $59.5 billion to develop e-Business inititatives. The average venture capital deal in 1999 was $15 million (Cassidy, 2002, p. 240). Many of these firms adopted a 'get big fast' (GBF) strategy (Oliva et al., 2003) by forming strategic alliances and partnerships to compete in the high velocity technology market (Eisenhardt and Martin, 2000). e-Business models became prolific. According to Timmers (1999), e-Business models developed as e-shops, e-procurement, e-mail, e-auctions and e-markets (EMs). In fact, just by prefacing anything with an 'e' seemed to imply an e-Business model existed. Taxonomies of e-Business models emerged (Timmers, 1999; Weill and Vitale, 2001). Others focused more specifically at the emergence of EMs (Bakos, 1998), value creation from e-Business (Amit and Zott, 2000; Magretta, 2001), profitability and revenue generation (Ross et al., 2001), B2B e-Commerce (Soh and Markus, 2002) and group buying behaviour on the Internet (Kauffman and Wang, 2001) to give a few examples.

Against a background of 'hype' about e-Business models, which preceded the dot.com crash of around 2001, it is apparent that very few

---

1.   The eight atomic e-Business models are: direct to customer, full service provider, intermediary, shared infrastructure, value net integrator, virtual community and whole-of-enterprise/government (see Weill and Vitale, 2001, p. 21).

'successful' e-Business models exist. Whilst our interest in Amazon.com, e-Bay, Dell, etc. continues, our emphasis upon the few that are currently successful tends to eclipse the many tens of thousands worldwide that have failed! Indeed, what happened to all the venture capital money, which was used to support the start-up of thousands of e-Business ventures? Clearly, the answer is that most failed, and many investors were left with collapsing share prices.

As the dot.com hype was replaced with the stark reality that many of these new e-Business ventures were unattractive to potential customers, some traditional 'bricks and mortar' firms abandoned their e-Business efforts. For example, in the case of ASPs, many established businesses, such as telecommunications firms and independent software vendors (ISVs), recognized that their 'core business' was far more lucrative than diverting attention to ASP activities. ISVs further saw little value in moving to a remote model of software delivery based upon a subscription, pay-as-you-go pricing model, when they could generate more revenues using a traditional licence fee and maintenance contract model (Currie et al., 2004).

To some authors, the focus on the business model concept was problematic. The inherent problems with business models could be explained by adopting an industry analysis of the markets and hierarchies in which firms compete. According to Porter (2001, p. 73): *the definition of a business model is murky at best. Most often, it seems to refer to a loose conception of how a company does business and generate revenue. Yet simply having a business model is an exceedingly low bar to set for building a company. Generating revenue is a far cry from creating value, and no business model can be evaluated independently of industry structure. The business model approach to management becomes an invitation for faulty thinking and self-delusion.*

Whilst these criticisms are valid (and will be revisited throughout this volume), the success of some e-Business ventures and the failure of many more, we argue, require both an industry-level analysis and a firm (organizational) level analysis. Whilst it is clear that many of the dot.com failures could be analysed in terms of structural problems in the capital markets (Quinn-Mills, 2001), the relative competitive success of other firms can be explained by other factors, notably, entrepreneurial and managerial capability, and the ability to leverage technology for competitive advantage (Weill and Broadbent, 1998). To this end, the fact that technology is largely a commodity (Carr, 2003), accessible to most firms who can afford it, does not adequately explain comparative differences in the use of technology assets, resources and capabilities within and across firms. Nor does it explain comparative success and failure factors with regard to the e-Business models of firms.

Value creation from e-Business models aims to provide a more rigorous intellectual and practical analysis of the e-Business model concept, not forgetting the criticality of an industry-level analysis. But rather than offering a superficial analysis of a few successful e-Business case studies, this edited book draws together theoretical and empirical contributions from leading academic scholars in the field of management information systems (IS). The book is intended as a reader to illustrate the diverse ways in which e-Business models may be researched and analysed.

1.1 Organization of the book

The book is divided into four parts, each of which discusses e-Business in the context of one of the following topics: ontologies and taxonomies, markets and strategies, performance measurement and value creation, and applications and services. In recent years, e-Business models have emerged as a topic of interest within business schools and individual disciplinary areas, such as IS, computer science, sociology, economics and others. This book combines material by scholars mainly from the business school, IS and computer science areas. The first part on ontologies and taxonomies presents contributions, which largely seeks to understand the e-Business model concept and its relationship to other areas, i.e. business strategy and to delineate e-Business models into their component parts. The second part on markets and strategies combines material on both external (market) factors and internal (organizational) strategy making. Here, an important theme has been to examine emerging EMs in the context of user acceptance. Part Three on performance measurement and value creation identifies some of the methods and tools for evaluating success and failure factors from e-Business, which is a perennial theme within the literature. In Part Four, the accent is on software applications and services used in e-Business. This covers the development and implementation of emerging technologies (i.e. ASP) for healthcare, supply-chain e-Management systems and Web services. Whilst this book incorporates a wide range of literature, the omissions are largely due to space limitations rather than a deliberate attempt to exclude other topics. The organization of the book by chapters is as follows:

Chapter 2 is by Seddon, Lewis, Freeman and Shanks, which explores business models and their relationship to strategy. The authors position the business model concept as problematic in the literature. They present two perspectives of the term business model, each of which is distinguished from the term from strategy. The first shows that business models are abstractions of recent conceptualizations of strategy suggested by Porter (2001). The second demonstrates how business models and strategy differ on the degree of competitive focus, with strategy focusing more on competitive positioning, and business models focusing mainly on activity systems designed to create value for their customers. This chapter provides an overview of the business model literature, particularly in terms of its relevance and relationship to strategy.

Following this chapter, Joyce and Winch utilize emerging work on e-Business together with the traditional strategy theory to provide a simple framework for the evaluation of business models for e-Business. These authors use modelling techniques of systems' dynamics to evaluate an e-Business model using the triple pair approach in an effort to capture the casual relationships and rationalize the complexity of organizational resources and the environment in which they compete. The next two chapters discuss ontologies for e-Business models. Osterwalder and Pigneur outline an ontology (rigorous framework) for e-Business models based on their extensive literature review. They demonstrate how the fusion of the ideas in the business model literature and the ideas of enterprise ontologies creates an appropriate basis for the development of a range of new management tools in the e-Business domain. By merging the conceptually rich business model approach with the more rigorous ontological approach and by applying them to e-Business, they provide a foundation for tools, which facilitate the understanding, sharing and communication, change, measuring and simulation of e-Business models. Similarly, Gordjin presents an approach to design an e-Business model, called the e^3-*value* approach. This approach is ontologically founded in business science, marketing and axiology, but exploits rigorous conceptual modelling as a way of working known from computer science. The aim is that an e^3-*value* e-Business model contributes to a better and shared understanding of the idea at stake, specifically with respect to its profit drivers.

In Part Two, the discussion focuses upon e-Business markets and strategies. Three chapters are presented in this section. The first is by Moon, who discusses a causal network analysis of EM business models. Drawing from the research findings on the development of EMs in four UK firms using the constructs: business model, market conditions and user acceptance, a causal network analysis identifies the relationships between antecedent, intervening and outcome variables, which influence business performance from the EMs. An EM paradox model is developed to depict declining revenues and margins due to the failure of EMs to capitalize on differentiated markets or the benefits they bring to buyers. The study shows that EM business performance is influenced by technological and customer turbulence, as well as competitive intensity. Acceptance of technology acts as an important partial moderator to business performance. Next, Newell and Huang offer a chapter broadly concerned with issues of knowledge management and e-Commerce. They argue that knowledge management is useful to examine aspects of e-Commerce and illustrate how such a perspective can help organizations better develop e-Commerce solutions that will add value. This is followed by Grandon and Pearson, who present their survey findings on the perceived strategic value from e-Commerce. The purpose of their chapter is three-fold:

(a) To summarize current research in strategic value and adoption of e-Commerce and suggest future research areas.

(b) To present a theoretical framework that explains the factors associated with the perceptions of strategic value of e-Commerce and e-Commerce adoption as well as the relationship between these two.

(c) To empirically test the validity of the proposed theoretical framework in field studies.

These authors conducted survey research in two different countries involving a total of 183 subjects.

Part Three considers a range of material largely concerned with issues of performance measurement and value creation. Madeja and Schoder present a chapter on value creation from corporate Web sites using results from a broad empirical investigation studying the effectiveness of implementing Web features for corporate performance. The empirical investigation was based on a large-scale survey comprising 469 cases in the German-speaking market, which is a leading international EM. These authors contribute to the growing body of empirical work on e-Business and offer some practical advice for corporate decision makers. Next, Barnes and Vidgen explore the uses of the E-Qual instrument (formerly known as 'WebQual') which was developed as a means of making a quantifiable assessment of subjective customer perceptions of e-Business implementation quality. E-Qual has been refined through many iterations and through application in different domains, both profit and not-for-profit. In this chapter, the authors explicate the E-Qual approach to e-Business evaluation and show how E-Qual has been applied in one particular setting to evaluate a cross-national e-government community, the forum on strategic management knowledge exchange (FSMKE). Following this, Willcocks and Plant examine the business Internet strategies of 78 case study organizations, over a 3-year period (1999–2002). They show that rather than strategy formulation driving corporate success, it was in fact 'strategy execution' that separated leaders from laggards. The leading issues preventing agile behaviour amongst 'bricks and mortar' organizations were largely traditional inhibitors of superior performance, such as cultural and political issues, and others arising from large-scale business process re-engineering projects. Similarly, Beulen and Ribbers look at netsourcing contracts and present findings from a European study which applies incomplete contract theory to outsourcing. It also contains an overview of the relevant theories including the resource-based view, the transaction cost theory, the incomplete contract theory and the relational view.

In Part Four, we consider e-Business applications and services. Three chapters are included. The first is by Guah, who considers the large-scale changes in the UK National Health Service (NHS), which is currently introducing primary service provisioning (PSP). The question here is: to what extent will emerging technologies (applications and services), such as ASP, improve patient experience within the NHS? Like other large-scale organizations, the NHS comprises a complex structure, with decision-making taking place at both the political and organizational levels. This poses problems for vendors who confront numerous difficulties in trying to sell e-Business solutions to the NHS. Following this chapter, Chandra, Kumar and Smirnov offer an integrated model for supply-chain management. These authors' chapter offer a generic development methodology for e-Management of supply chain based on the principles of domain-independent problem solving and modelling, and domain-dependent analysis and implementation. The purpose of such approach is to ascertain characteristics of the problem independent of the specific problem environment. The approach delivers solution(s) or the solution method that are intrinsic to the problem and not its environment. They illustrate this with applications from the automotive industry. Finally, Currie discusses the emerging technology of Web services, which is currently perceived by some sections of the technology sector as the latest *silver bullet* to resolve organizational problems of poor integration of systems and applications. This chapter cautions against an over-optimistic stance for Web services, particularly in the light of the disappointing results from numerous e-Business initiatives, such as ASP. Indeed, all the chapters in this volume point to the need for more rigour and relevance in both developing and implementing e-Business solutions.

References and Further Reading

Amit, R. and C. Zott (2000). Value Creation in E-commerce Business Models. Presentation, *the Wharton Conference of Winners and Losers in the E-commerce Shakeout*, The Wharton School, October 2000.

Amit, R. and C. Zott (2001). 'Value Creation in eBusiness.' *Strategic Management Journal* 22: 493–520.

Bakos, Y. (1998). 'The Emerging Role of Electronic Markets.' *Communications of the ACM* 41(8): 35–42.

Carr, N. G. (2003). 'It Doesn't Matter.' *Harvard Business Review* 81(5 May): 41–51.

Cassidy, J. (2002). *Dot.con: How America Lost Its Mind and Money in the Internet Era*. Perennial, Harper Collins.

Currie, W. (2002). 'Application Outsourcing: A New Business Model for Enabling Competitive Electronic Commerce.' *International Journal of Services and Technology Management* 3(2): 139–153.

Currie, W. (2003). 'A Knowledge-Based Risk Assessment System for Evaluating Web-Enabled Application Outsourcing Projects.' *International Journal of Project Management* 21(3): 207–213.

Currie, W. and P. Seltsikas (2001). 'Exploring the Supply-Side of IT Outsourcing: The Emerging Role of Application Service Providers.' *European Journal of Information Systems* 10(3): 123–134.

Currie, W., B. Desai and N. Khan (2004). 'Customer Evaluation of Application Services Provisioning in Five Vertical Sectors.' *Journal of Information Technology* 19(1): 3–20.

Eisenhardt, K. M. and J. A. Martin (2000). 'Dynamic Capabilities: What Are They?' *Strategic Management Journal* **21**(10/11 October/November): 1105–1121.

Hagel, J. (2002). *Out of the Box: Strategies for Achieving Profits Today and Growth Tomorrow through Web Services*. Harvard Business School Press.

Hagel, J. and J. Seely-Brown (2001). 'Your Next IT Strategy.' *Harvard Business Review* (October): 105–113.

IDC (2000). *International Conference on Managing and Growing a World Class ASP Business*. Hosted by International Data Corporation, 4–6 April, San Francisco, US.

Kauffman, R. and B. Wang (2001). In *5th Annual University of Minnesota Electronic Commerce Conference* (P. B. Lowry, J. O. C., R. R. Watson (eds). *Handbook of Electronic Commerce in Business and Society*, Boca Raton, CRC Press, 2002). CRC Press, Minneapolis, MN.: 27–28.

Kern, T., J. Kreijger and L. Willcocks (2002). 'Exploring Asp as Sourcing Strategy: Theoretical Perspectives, Propositions for Practice.' *Journal of Strategic Information Systems* **11**(2): 153–177.

Lewis, M. (1999). *The New, New Thing*. London, Hodder and Sloughton.

Magretta, J. (2001). 'Why Business Models Matter.' *Harvard Business Review* **10**.

Mahadevan, B. (2000). 'Business Model for Internet-Based E-Commerce: An Anatomy.' *California Management Review* **42**(4).

Nesheim, J. (1997). *High Tech Start-Up*. Saratoga, CA.

Oliva, R., J. Sterman and M. Giese (2003). 'Limits to Growth in the New Economy: Exploring the 'Get Big Fast' Strategy in e-Commerce.' *System Dynamics Review* **19**: 83–118.

Porter, M. (1996). 'What is Strategy?' *Harvard Business Review* (November– December): 61–78.

Porter, M. (2001). 'Strategy and the Internet.' *Harvard Business Review* (March–April): 63–78.

Quinn-Mills, D. (2001). 'Who's to Blame for the Bubble?' *Harvard Business Review* **79**(5): 22–23.

Rappa, M. (2000). *An Evaluation of Business Models*. Millennium Group, http://digitalenterprise.org/models/models.html: 1–9.

Rappa, M. (2004). *Business Models on the Web*. http://digitalenterprise.org/ models/models.html

Ross, J., M. Vitale and P. Weill (2001). *From Place to Space Migrating to Profitable Electronic Commerce Business Models*. Sloan School of Management.

SCN Education B. V., ed. (2000). *ASP – Application Service Providing: The Ultimate Guide to Hiring rather than Buying Applications*. Germany, Vieweg/Gabler.

Soh, C. and L. Markus (2002). 'Business-to-Business Electronic Marketplaces: A Strategic Archetypes Approach.' *International Conference on Information Systems*, Barcelona, Spain.

Timmers, P. (1999). *Business Models for Electronic Commerce*. Chichester, England, John Wiley & Sons Ltd.

Weill, P. and M. Broadbent (1998). *Leveraging the New Infrastructure: How Market Leaders Capitalise on Information Technology*. Harvard Business School Press, Mass.

Weill, P. and M. R. Vitale (2001). *Place to Space – Migrating to e-Business Models*. Harvard Business School Press.

2 Business models and their relationship to strategy[1]

Peter B. Seddon, Geoffrey Lewis, Phil Freeman and Graeme Shanks

Abstract

The term business model is being used increasingly within the domain of e-Business as more and more organizations try to understand how to become more successful by leveraging the Internet. However, there is a great deal of confusion and very little agreement about what the term actually means. In particular, the term business model is frequently confused with strategy. In this chapter we present two perspectives of the term business model that clearly distinguish it from strategy. Under the first perspective, business models are abstractions of Porter's recent conceptualizations of strategy. Under the second, business models and strategy differ on the degree of competitive focus, where strategy focuses more on competitive positioning, and business models focus more on activity systems, that is, on the mechanisms firms use to create value for their customers. We use these perspectives to position the work of other researchers and to clarify the term business model.

2.1 Introduction

The term 'business model' has been used with increasing frequency since the mid-1990s within the domain of e-Business as more and more organizations try to understand how to become more successful by leveraging the Internet. However, the term is poorly defined and there is very little agreement about what it actually means. For example, Michael Porter (2001, p. 73) notes:

> *The definition of a business model is murky at best. Most often, it seems to refer to a loose conception of how a company does business and*

---

1. An earlier version of this chapter was presented as a paper 'Strategy and Business Models: What's the Difference?' by Seddon and Lewis at the Pacific-Asia Conference on Information Systems (PACIS), 2003.

generates revenue. Yet simply having a business model is an exceedingly low bar to set for building a company. Generating revenue is a far cry from creating economic value ... .

Furthermore, the term 'business model' is often confused with the term 'strategy'. Joan Magretta (2002) notes:

Today, 'business model' and 'strategy' are among the most sloppily used terms in business; they are often stretched to mean everything – and end up meaning nothing. But as the experience of companies like Dell and Wal-Mart show, these are concepts of enormous practical value.

A review of the literature, examining leading authors' definitions of both terms, reveals that there is considerable confusion and ambiguity, with a great deal of overlap between these two terms. There are nuances of difference, for example strategy seems more concerned with competition between firms, whereas business models are more concerned with the 'core logic' that enables firms to create value for their customers and owners (Linder and Cantrell, 2000). In addition, it may be that people with an information technology (IT) background tend to use the term 'business model' more often than those from a management background (who use 'strategy'). But across a broad range of papers, a detailed analysis reveals that the concepts used by authors when discussing these two terms are very similar.

Although the terms 'business model' and 'strategy' are very similar in meaning, particularly if one uses Porter's (1996, 2001) definitions of strategy, we present two perspectives of 'business model', consistent with the usage of many of the experts who have used the term, that clearly distinguish it from 'strategy'. One perspective presents business models as abstractions of strategy, capturing aspects of individual-firm strategy that can be applied to many firms. The other perspective classifies business models and strategy on a two-by-two matrix of competitive focus versus firm specificity. Business models are classified as more inward looking, focusing on the activity system side of how an organization creates economic value, whereas strategy is classified as more outward looking, focusing more on competitive positioning.

This chapter is structured as follows. The next three sections, collectively labelled Perspective 1, present the perspective that business models are abstractions of strategy, adopting the Harvard school's definition of strategy, and show that this perspective is consistent with the literature. The three sections after that, collectively labelled Perspective 2, present the competitive focus versus firm specificity matrix, and analyse the literature from this perspective. The chapter concludes with a discussion of the utility of the two perspectives.

2.2 Perspective 1: business models as abstractions of strategy

In this perspective we use Porter's (1996, 2001) conceptualization of strategy as our definition of strategy. If this definition of strategy is used, a business model may be defined as an abstract representation of some aspect of a firm's strategy. This perspective is represented in Figure 2.1 where the vertical axis shows increasing level of abstraction and the horizontal plane shows how strategy and business models are related.

When Figure 2.1 has been presented to our colleagues, they generally ask two questions. The first is 'Why view business models as abstractions of strategy?' Our answer is that the concept-by-concept overlap between the terms 'strategy' and 'business model' – at least as they are defined and used by leading authors in the two fields – is so great that if the abstraction idea is not adopted, there is no point having two terms. However, if business models are defined as abstractions of strategy, which we show below is consistent with the existing literature, then there is a useful reason for having two terms.

The second question that usually flows from first impressions of Figure 2.1 is 'Why is there a one-to-one mapping between a firm and its strategy? Why can't many firms have the same strategy?' Our answer here is that – at least as defined by the latest thinking of the Harvard school of strategy – a firm's strategy is deeply rooted in that particular firm's competitive environment. Strategy is always placed in a highly situated context, with particular competitors, particular customers, particular suppliers, particular ways of assembling, delivering, and charging for products and services, particular ways of responding to market changes, and so on.

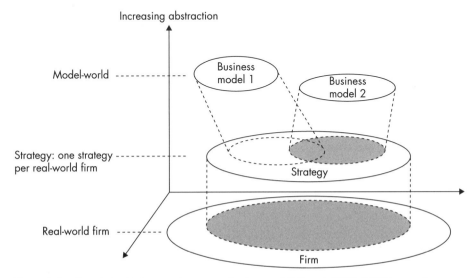

Figure 2.1: The relationship between the concepts 'business model', Porter's (1996, 2001) 'strategy', and a real-world firm.

As Porter (1996) points out, everything has to fit together for the company to make money. By contrast, the goal of business models – at least as we are proposing it here – is to abstract from much of this detail. (The reason for wanting to abstract from the detail is the reason for all abstractions, namely, to draw attention to the things of interest to the modeller, and to suppress extraneous information.) By suppressing irrelevant detail, it is possible to say that many firms have the same business model, or to make high-level comparisons between the business models of different firms. It is in this sense of being abstractions from any particular firm's strategy that the term 'business model' can provide a useful extension to the current bundle of concepts associated with the term 'strategy'.

In Figure 2.1, the real-world firm is represented by the largest ellipse, and strategy by a smaller ellipse, because many things about a firm are ignored in defining its strategy (a firm with a number of strategic business units (SBUs) would have different strategies for each SBU). Business models are represented by even smaller ellipses, because even fewer details are required to specify a business model than to represent a firm's strategy. Figure 2.1 also depicts two business models, representing two different views of the one firm's strategy, because there is literally an unlimited number of different abstractions that one can build based on one particular firm's strategy. Each of the two business models could be applied to other firms.

2.2.1 The Harvard school's latest conceptualization of strategy

It must be emphasized that the relationship between strategy and business model depicted in Figure 2.1 only makes sense if, out of the many definitions of strategy that could be used, one accepts the Harvard school's latest definition of strategy. In this chapter we use Porter's (1996, 2001) conceptualization of strategy because it represents the latest and best of the Harvard school's thinking about strategy. By the 'Harvard school', we mean the work of a series of thought leaders, including academics and consultants, such as Christensen (Learned et al., 1965), Andrews (1971), Porter (1980, 1996, 2001), Porter and Millar (1985), Ghemawat (1991), the Boston Consulting Group, and McKinsey & Company, associated with Harvard. The evolution of Harvard school's thinking on strategy is depicted in Figure 2.2. The pairs of arrows numbered 1a, 1b and 2a, 2b show two 'mutations' in the evolution of the Harvard school's current conceptualization of strategy.

As shown at the bottom of Figure 2.2, the early strengths, weaknesses, opportunities, and threats (SWOT) conceptualization of strategy – which developed at Harvard in the 1960s – was essentially descriptive. SWOT analysis was both inward and outward looking in that it considered both a firm's internal capabilities (its strengths and weaknesses), and external competitive forces (opportunities and threats). As explained by Ghemawat (2002), and indicated by the arrows 1a and 1b in Figure 2.2, in

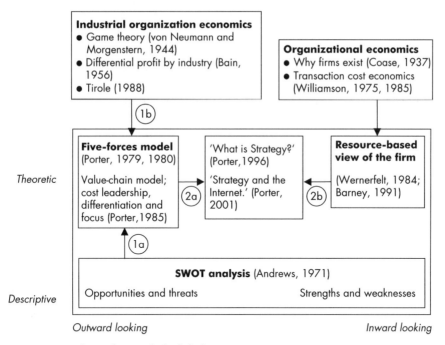

Figure 2.2: Evolution of 'Harvard school' thinking on strategy.

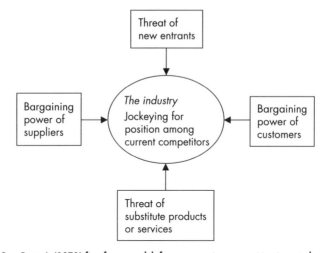

Figure 2.3: Porter's (1979) five-forces model: forces governing competition in an industry.

the late 1970s insights from both SWOT analysis and the industrial organization economics (IOE) literature led Porter to define his five-forces model, and later, his value-chain model. In Figure 2.2, these models are classified as 'theoretic' because they provide explanations of *why* some industries and some firm's strategies are more successful than others.

Porter's (1979) famous five-forces framework, the result of the first 'mutation' in the Harvard school's conceptualization of strategy, is shown as Figure 2.3. It describes the forces governing competition in an *industry*, not the strategy of an individual firm. Its focus is on the factors that enable different industries to have quite different returns on equity (ROE) over long periods, for example ROE of 21% for drugs versus 4% for iron and steel in the US during the 20 years 1971–1990 (McGahan, 1992).

Due to its focus on industries, not firms, the five-forces model does not, however, explain differing returns for different firms in the one industry. For example, although McGahan (1992) found the US iron and steel industry had an *average* 4% return on equity over 20 years, Collis and Ghemawat (1994) found that 20-year returns on assets (ROA) in the steel industry ranged from 13% for Oregon Steel Mills to −2% for Bethlehem Steel.

What explains these large differences in ROA *between* firms in the same industry? Porter and Millar's (1985) paper begins to answer this question. Their value-chain diagram, structured as shown in Figure 2.4 (and based, according to Ghemawat (2002), on earlier work at McKinsey & Company), shows 'nine generic categories' of value-creation activities in a firm's value chain. By this stage in the evolution of conceptualization of strategy, that is 1985, the Harvard school was beginning to show an awareness that the internal workings of individual firms could be an important source of competitive advantage, and therefore an important factor to consider in development of firm-level strategy.

Independently of the above stream of literature, another body of literature, namely that of Organizational Economics (OE) (Coase, 1937; Williamson, 1979) was also developing ideas that were to become important to the Harvard school's current conceptualization of strategy. Ideas from OE

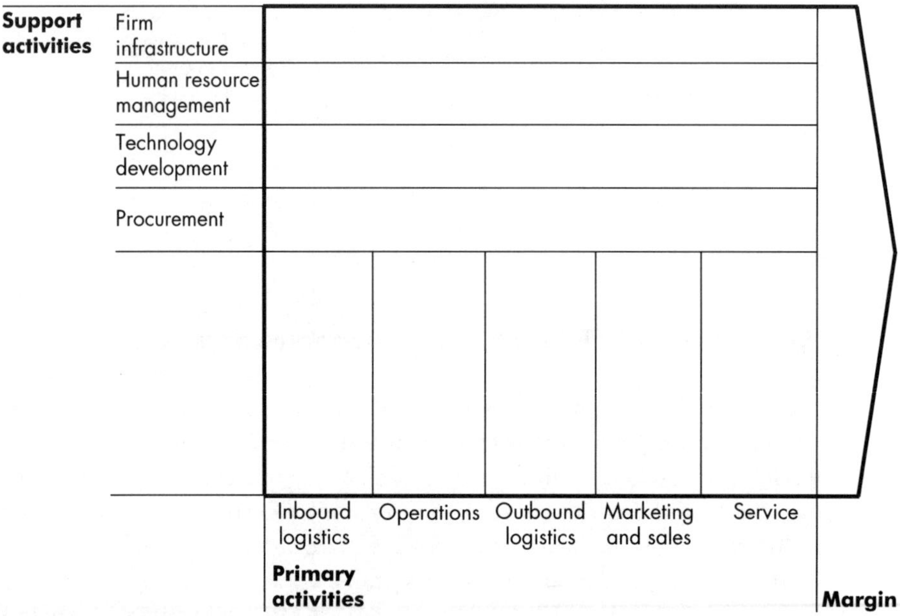

Figure 2.4: Structure of Porter and Millar's (1985) value chain diagram.

led to the development of the resource-based view of the firm (Wernerfelt, 1984; Barney, 1991), which paid far more attention to the inner workings of firms. The resource-based view of the firm suggests that firms compete more on their internal capabilities than the market environment and specific products and services (Grant, 1991). The resource-based view of the firm encompasses the notions of core competency (Prahalad and Hamel, 1990), organizational learning (Teece et al., 1997), and resource commitment (Ghemawat, 1991) as sources of competitive advantage.

Recognizing the strength of OE insights, particularly those of the resource-based view of the firm, led to the second mutation in the Harvard school's conceptualization of strategy. As indicated by arrows 2a and 2b in Figure 2.2, the school's latest conceptualization of strategy is represented by Porter's (1996) paper 'What is Strategy?' and Porter's (2001) 'Strategy and the Internet'. The following quotations from these two papers capture the essence of the Harvard school's latest thinking on the meaning of strategy (and also provide a reference point for the discussion of business models in the next section):

1 The goal of strategy is to achieve a 'superior long-term return on investment.' 'Economic value is created when customers are willing to pay a price for a product or service that exceeds the cost of producing it.' (Porter, 2001, p. 71)

2 'Competitive strategy is about being different.' (Porter, 1996, p. 64)

3 'Strategy is the creation of a unique and valuable position, involving a different set of activities … different from rivals.' (Porter, 1996, p. 68)

4 'Strategy is making trade-offs in competing.' (Porter, 1996, p. 70)

5 'Strategy defines how all the elements of what a company does fit together.' (Porter, 2001, p. 71)

6 'Operational effectiveness and strategy are both essential to superior performance, which, after all, is the primary goal of any enterprise. But they work in different ways.' (Porter, 1996, p. 61)

7 'Operational effectiveness means performing similar activities *better* than rivals perform them.' (Porter, 1996, p. 62)

8 'Strategy involves continuity of direction.' (Porter, 2001, p. 71)

In essence, Porter (1996, 2001) argues that strategy involves defining a company's *long-term position* in the marketplace, making the hard *trade-offs* about what the company will and will not do to provide value to customers, and forging *hard-to-replicate fit* among parts of the '*activity system*' the firm constructs to deliver value to customers, all with a view to making a superior *return on investment*. The five terms in italics are key to this latest Harvard-school conceptualization of strategy. Note that this is a much more operational, capabilities-based, and firm-specific view of strategy than high-level, generic view presented in the earlier five-forces and value-chain conceptualizations of strategy.

Towards the end of his 1996 paper, as part of a five-page discussion of fit (developing point 5 above), Porter presents a diagram that he calls an 'activity system map' (Porter, 1996, p. 73). Figure 2.5 shows an example of one such map, for an imaginary Online Publishing company similar to Reed Elsevier's online division. We have used solid- and dotted-line circles to correspond to the dark- and light-purple circles Porter mentions below. According to Porter (1996, p. 71):

> *Activity system maps, ... show how a company's strategic position is contained in a set of tailored activities designed to deliver it. In companies with a clear strategic position, a number of higher-order strategic themes (in dark purple) can be identified and implemented through clusters of tightly linked activities (in light purple).*

Activity system maps are so close to what many people call business models that it is not clear how Porter's conceptualization of strategy differs from what others have called business models. Given this similarity, it is easy to understand why Porter (2001), quoted in the Introduction, has such a low opinion of the business model literature. However, as discussed below, the 'business models as abstractions of strategy' idea advocated in this chapter may provide a useful new way of approaching the comparison of business models and strategy.

Summarizing, the definitions of strategy in Porter (1996, 2001) represent the current end point of a 50-year evolution of thinking on strategy by people who belong to what we have termed the Harvard school. Key points from the current conceptualization are summarized by the eight points listed above and activity system maps like that in Figure 2.5. We do not argue that the Harvard-school conceptualization of strategy is the only possible interpretation, but we do believe it is a good one. It is therefore this latest Harvard-school conceptualization of strategy that we use as our reference when comparing various authors' conceptualizations of 'business models' with strategy.

2.2.2 Business models as abstractions of Porter's (1996, 2001) conceptualization of 'strategy'

How do business models compare to Porter's (1996, 2001) definition of strategy? The difficulty in answering this question is that so much has already been written about business models, from so many different directions, that as with research on strategy it is impossible to capture the totality of different views on business models in a single paper. To illustrate the diversity of views and interests, Figure 2.6 compares the work of six widely cited business model researchers: Applegate (2000),

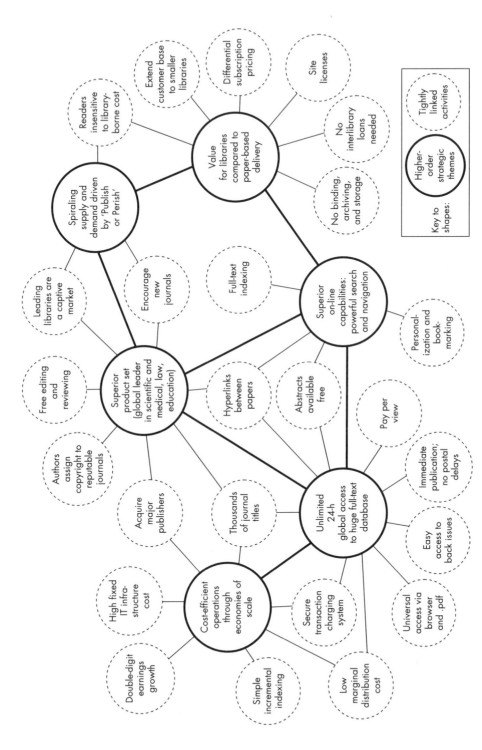

Figure 2.5: An example of a Porter-style (1996, p. 73) activity system map.

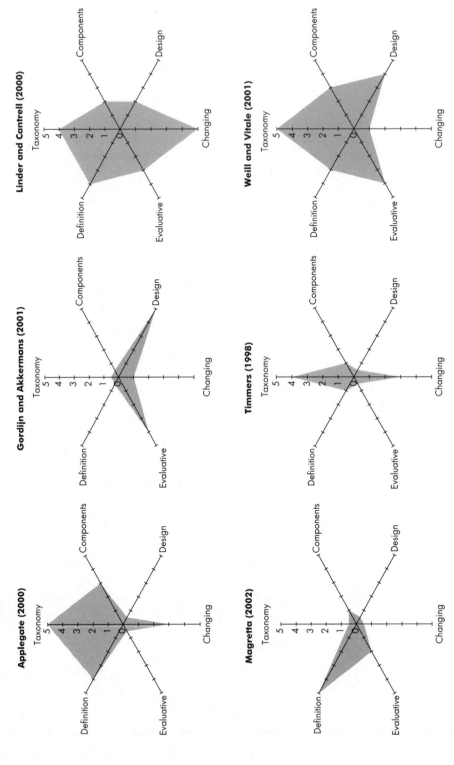

Figure 2.6: Comparing the work of six widely cited researchers using Pateli's (2002) six different themes of business model papers.

Gordijn and Akkermans (2001), Linder and Cantrell (2000), Magretta (2002), Timmers (1998), and Weill and Vitale (2001). The six 'axes' in Figure 2.6 are defined in Table 2.1. The choice of the six themes plotted on the six 'axes' is based on Pateli's (2002, p. 6) Table 2.1, augmented in some cases with material from Linder and Cantrell (2000). Scales for the 'axes' are (1) very minor, (2) minor, (3) covered to some extent, (4) significantly covered, and (5) very significantly covered. Scores for each theme for each document are based on subjective assessment by the present authors.

Given that there is a huge diversity of opinions about various aspects of business models, how is one to decide if business models are different to Porter's (1996, 2001) strategy? Our approach to answering this question is similar to our approach in searching for a definition of strategy. Specifically, we decided to examine in depth a small number of documents that present clear, strongly argued points of view on business

Table 2.1: Six themes of papers on business models

Themes	Definition
Definition	Extent to which the article discusses the definition of what constitutes an business model.
Taxonomy	Extent to which the research effort has been directed towards classifying business models. A huge number of different taxonomies have been published, for example Linder and Cantrell's (2000, Exhibit 6): price models, convenience models, experience models, channel models, intermediary models, trust models, and innovation models, or Timmers' (1998) e-shops, e-procurement, e-mails, e-auctions, etc.
Components	Extent to which the article attempts to break down its business model examples into components. For example, Linder and Cantrell (2000, Exhibit 1) identifies the following business-model components: pricing model, channel model, commerce-process model, Internet-enabled commerce relationship, organizational form, and value proposition. Osterwalder and Pigneur (2002) argue that business models have four main pillars: product innovation, customer relationship, infrastructure management, and financials.
Design tool	Extent to which the article provides graphic tools for representing and designing business models.
Changing	Extent to which the article provides guidelines for developing a business model and for changing from the firm's existing business model to the new one in order to remain profitable. 'Business models wear out. Competition catches up, markets shift, technology changes, and firms must alter their business models to remain viable.' 'A change model is the core logic for how a firm will change over time to remain profitable in a dynamic environment.' (Linder and Cantrell, 2000)
Evaluation	Extent to which the article provides guidelines for evaluating the feasibility of different business models.

Based on Pateli (2002) and Linder and Cantrell (2000).

models. Overall, the selected documents are, we believe, broadly representative of much that has been written on business models. From the many possible documents available, the four documents we selected for this paper are: Magretta (2002), Weill and Vitale (2001), Applegate (2000, 2003), and Linder and Cantrell (2000). In the remainder of this section we examine each document in turn. The questions we ask of each document are:

- How, if at all, is this conceptualization of a business model different to Porter's (1996, 2001) conceptualization of strategy?

- Is this document's view of business models consistent with our suggested approach of treating business models as abstractions of Porter's (1996, 2001) conceptualization of strategy?

The first document we consider is by Magretta (2002). She describes both business models and strategy as being of 'enormous practical value'. Using examples like the traveller's cheque business model (which led to the creation of American Express), the Dell Computer business model, and the Wal-Mart business model, she argues that thinking at these high levels of abstraction enables managers to first, conceive, and second, test out, the viability of possible new ways of doing business. According to Magretta (2002), business models:

> are, at heart, stories – stories that explain how enterprises work. A good business model answers Peter Drucker's age-old questions: Who is the customer? And what does the customer value? It also answers the fundamental questions every manager must ask: How do we make money in this business? What is the underlying economic logic that explains how we can deliver value to customers at an appropriate cost? (p. 92)

Few would disagree that these same questions could be asked of a firm's strategy! In turn, this suggests that, for Magretta, business models and strategy are conceptually very similar. But Magretta goes on to say:

> But a business model isn't the same thing as strategy, even though many people use the terms interchangeably today. Business models describe, as a system, how the pieces of a business fit together. But they don't factor in one critical dimension of performance: competition. Sooner or later – and it is usually sooner – every enterprise runs into competitors. Dealing with that reality is strategy's job … A competitive strategy explains how you will do better than your rivals. (p. 94)

The second statement above still does not help. Saying that 'business models describe, as a system, how the pieces of a business fit together' is so close to point 5 from the above summary of Porter (1996, 2001), that is 'how all the elements of what a company does fit together' as to be indistinguishable. However, Magretta also says that business models do not consider competitive positioning. Combining these two ideas, we arrived at the relationship between business model and strategy depicted in Figure 2.1. In the Figure 2.1 perspective, one deliberately chooses not to model the firm's competitive-positioning information (and possibly many other details as well) in constructing Magretta's interpretation of a business model.

Second, Weill and Vitale's (2001) book on e-Business models presents much more detailed descriptions and examples of business models than most authors. Weill and Vitale explain their eight atomic e-Business models using a specially developed diagramming technique called e-Business model schematics, such as the example in Figure 2.7 (which is a business model for the Online Publisher in Figure 2.5, drawn using Weill and Vitale's notation). In these diagrams, Weill and Vitale (2001) focus on *stakeholders* and *product and information flows*, but make no mention of strategy. Combining atomic models into molecular models, they suggest, provides a convenient shorthand for quickly considering a wide range of possible e-Business opportunities. So how do Weill and

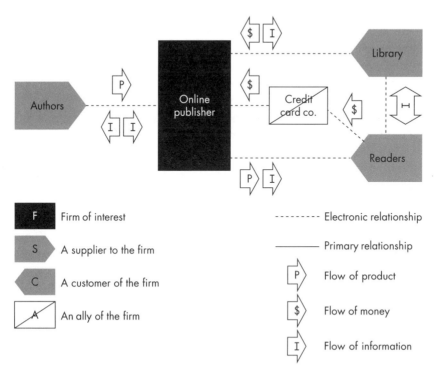

Figure 2.7: Example e-Business model schematic based on Weill and Vitale (2001) (intended to correspond to the activity system map in Figure 2.5).

Vitale (2001) define business models? According to Weill and Vitale (2001), an 'e-Business model' is:

> *A description of the roles and relationships among a firm's consumers, customers, allies, and suppliers that identifies the major flows of product, information, and money, and the major benefits to participants.' (p. 34)*[2]

What is important here is that, consistent with Magretta (2002), neither this definition, nor any of Weill and Vitale's diagrams, makes any mention of either strategy or competition. Weill and Vitale focus on the *who* (consumers, customers, allies, suppliers, and of course, the firm's employees and owners) and the *what* (major flows of product, information, and money). Also important is the observation that their business models are not specific to any firm, and are much more process and stakeholder focused than Porter's (1996, 2001) conception of strategy. Clearly, though, strategy is important to Weill and Vitale's (2001) conceptualization of a business model. Evidence for this is that (a) 'strategic objectives' appears as a column heading in their key Table 12-3 (pp. 265–267), where they summarize and contrast attributes of their eight atomic e-Business models, and (b) they include a three-page section on 'e-Business Strategizing' in the subsequent chapter (pp. 298–300). Thus, for Weill and Vitale (2001) one might well conclude that there is some overlap between the terms 'business model' and 'strategy', but not a lot.

It is apparent that the whole idea of 'atomic business models' is that they can be applied to many different businesses. What Weill and Vitale describe are abstractions, not the strategies of any particular real firm. Therefore, we argue, Figure 2.1 is consistent with Weill and Vitale's conceptualization of the relationship between business model and strategy.

Third, Applegate (2000) provides two different descriptions of the term 'business model'. In her 2000 chapter, she asks 'What is a model?'. She answers by saying that in the world of business a model is:

> *A description of a complex business that enables study of its structure, the relationships among structural elements, and how it will respond in the real world. (2000, p. 53)*

She then goes on to say that one of the properties of models is that they:

> *can be built before the real system to help predict how the system might respond if we change the structure, relationships, and assumptions. (2000, p. 53)*

---

2. Weill and Vitale (2001) explain that their definition is also very similar to Timmers (1998), another frequently cited author on e-Business models.

These two sentences make it clear that for Applegate (2000), a business model is just that, a model. Although she does not discuss how business models compare to strategy, her view is clearly consistent with Figure 2.1.

However, the preceding distinction between model and strategy is not as clear in Applegate et al. (2003). In their 32-page Chapter 2, 'Crafting Business Models', there are six tables containing many detailed examples of different business models – focused distributor business models (for example retailer, marketplace, aggregator, infomediary, and exchange), portal business models (for example horizontal, vertical, and affinity portals), producer business models (for example manufacturers, service providers, educators, advisors, information and news services, and producer portals), etc. – plus examples of actual companies that have used each business model. For example, eBay.com and Freemarkets.com are firms using what Applegate et al. (2003) describe as the 'Exchange' 'focused distributor' business model.

The common characteristics of all these Applegate et al. (2003) models are summarized in Applegate et al.'s Figure 2.1 (p. 47), which describes a business model as having three components:

- the *concept*, which 'describes the opportunity and strategy';

- *capabilities*, which 'define resources necessary to execute strategy';

- the *value* proposition, which explains 'the benefits to investors and other stakeholders'.

Note that the notion of business model as model is absent from the above description. Note also that the word 'strategy' appears in both dot points 1 and 2. In short, there is little to distinguish Applegate et al.'s (2003) 'business model' from Porter's (1996, 2001) 'strategy'.

However, if viewed from a Figure 2.1 perspective, the close correspondence between Applegate's definition of 'business model' and Porter's definition of 'strategy' is not because the two concepts are the same, but rather, because one is just an abstraction of the other. What Applegate et al.'s (2003) tables provide are groups of abstractions of various organizations' core logics for creating value (Linder and Cantrell, 2000). Reinforcing this view, we know from data modelling (Simsion, 2000) that hierarchies of abstractions are always linked by the term 'is-a' relationship (for example, a researcher is-a person, and a person is-a living thing). Similarly, in Applegate's example of eBay, the business model of eBay.com is-a 'Exchange' business model, which in turn, is-a 'Focused Distributor' business model. These is-a relationships are indications of increasing levels of abstraction, which again suggests that our abstraction argument in Figure 2.1 makes sense.

The fourth and final document we consider is by Linder and Cantrell (2000). According to Linder and Cantrell (2000): 'When people say "business model", they're really talking about three different kinds of things: components of business models, real operating business models, and what we call change models.' They go on to say: 'Operating business models are the real thing. An operating business model is the organization's core logic for creating value. The business model of a profit-oriented enterprise explains how it makes money.'

An example of one of Linder and Cantrell's (2000) 'operating business models' is shown in Figure 2.8, where the central oval shape identifies the value proposition, and the solid-line rectangle identifies the revenue source. The similarity between Figure 2.8 and Porter's (1996) activity system maps (Figure 2.5) is striking. It seems that Linder and Cantrell's (2000) business models are little different to Porter's (1996) strategy. But a more thorough reading of Linder and Cantrell (2000) shows that they are looking for common patterns. Their pricing models, experience models, and channel models, etc. are, like Weill and Vitale's (2001) atomic business models, components of various ways of doing business. Again, we argue, it is therefore valid to view Linder and Cantrell's (2000) business models as abstractions of what Porter (1996, 2001) has called strategy. Figure 2.8 is simply drawn at a very similar level of abstraction to one of Porter's activity system maps.

Summarizing, provided one accepts Porter (1996, 2001) as the definition of strategy, it would seem to be in accord with the thinking of all four examples of business models above if a business model were

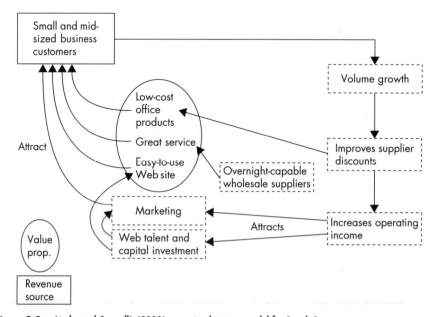

Figure 2.8: Linder and Cantrell's (2000) operating business model for SupplyGenie.com.

defined as an abstract representation of a firm's strategy. Some business models are more abstract than others, but all can be viewed as abstractions from what Porter (1996, 2001) calls a firm's strategy.

2.3 Perspective 2: competitive focus versus firm specificity matrix

In this and the next two sections, we present Perspective 2 on the possible relationship between strategy and business models. Perspective 1 is inconsistent with Perspective 1, but may be more acceptable to those who are uncomfortable about accepting Porter's (1996, 2001) definition of strategy as *the* definition of strategy. In Perspective 1, we sought to identify a single excellent conceptualization of strategy, namely that of Porter (1996, 2001), that could then be used as a reference point for comparing strategy and business models. In Perspective 2, we adopt the less restrictive approach of accepting that there are many alternative definitions of strategy, some more abstract than others. In Perspective 2, it is argued that there are two important dimensions by which one can differentiate *both* strategy and business models:

■ the extent to which different author's definitions of the terms are more or less firm specific;

■ the extent to which different author's definitions of the terms consider competitive positioning.

With respect to firm specificity, the Perspective 2 argument is that all strategies and business models may usefully be placed on a continuum from firm specific to highly generic. This is represented in Figure 2.9 where the vertical axis shows the increasing level of abstraction, and the horizontal plane shows how strategy and business models are related.

As in Figure 2.1, at the base of Figure 2.9, the largest ellipse represents a particular real-world firm. Above the base ellipse, successively higher levels of ellipses depict examples of increasingly more abstract, and therefore more general, representations of both strategies and business models. From the unlimited number of possibilities that could be conceived, Figure 2.9 depicts four representations of strategy and four representations of business models. Strategy 1 and Business Model 1 are at similar firm-specific levels of abstraction. Strategy 2 and Business Model 3 (BM3) are also at similar (generic) levels of abstraction. Many other combinations are possible.

Why is it valuable to classify strategies and business models as shown in Figure 2.9? Our answer is that although identification of common patterns as abstractions is clearly useful (Alexander, 1977; Manns, 2001), comparing strategies and business models of different levels of

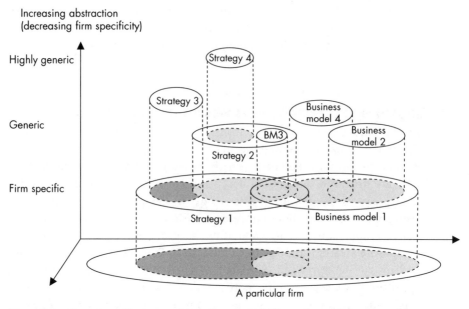

Figure 2.9: Strategies and business models as abstractions of different degree of some parts of a real-world firm.

abstraction is problematic. In the strategy literature, Porter and Millar's (1985) generic strategies – cost leadership, differentiation, and focus – for instance, are so highly generic that they could apply to millions of firms. Each might be represented by Strategy 4 in Figure 2.9. By contrast, Porter's (1996) activity system maps are highly firm specific. For example, the activity system map for the Online Publisher (Figure 2.5) shows how the firm has positioned itself to provide unlimited 24-h global access to a huge full-text database of quality academic research. Strategy 1 in Figure 2.9 could depict this highly firm-specific representation of strategy. Similarly, in the business models literature, Weill and Vitale's (2001) atomic business models are more detailed, more firm specific, than Applegate et al.'s (2003) descriptions of business models. Attempting to compare the business models literature to the strategy literature without recognizing that both strategy and business models are often conceptualized at different levels of abstraction is problematic.

The second important dimension for comparing strategy and business models is competitive focus. For example, most of Porter's work on strategy is more concerned with competition and competitive positioning than the procedural aspects of how value is created. On the other hand, Weill and Vitale's (2001) atomic business models are much more concerned with explaining the flows of goods, services, information, and money in ways that enable different stakeholders to benefit from doing business together, than in competitive positioning.

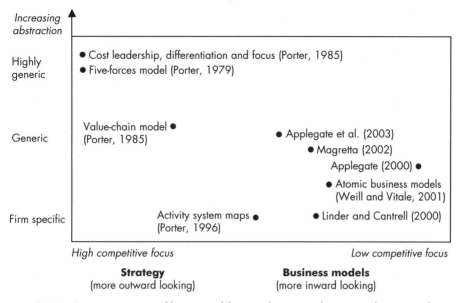

Figure 2.10: Comparing strategy and business models on two dimensions: abstraction and competitive focus (the dots show placement on each dimension).

Using these two insights, that is about firm specificity versus abstraction and competitive focus, we were able to arrange many of the articles discussed in this paper (articles on both strategy and business models) as shown in Figure 2.10. The horizontal dimension in Figure 2.10 is competitive focus; the vertical dimension is firm specificity. The placement of dots in Figure 2.10 is based on the authors' judgment after reading the different documents cited. The next two sections explain why it may be useful to view relationships between different business models and strategies as depicted in Figure 2.10.

2.3.1 Classifying 'Harvard school' conceptualizations of strategy

Although many authors have written about and proposed definitions of strategy, the Harvard school is the thought leader on strategy. Thus, in this section we restrict our attention to four seminal articles from the Harvard school, all authored or co-authored by Michael Porter, and seek to classify them in terms of the two dimensions in Figure 2.10.

First, Porter's (1985) 'generic strategies', described in the following quotation (Porter, 1996, p. 67), are clearly highly abstract:

> In Competitive Strategy (Porter, 1980) I introduced the concept of generic strategies – cost leadership, differentiation, and focus – to represent the alternative strategic positions in an industry. The generic strategies remain useful to characterize strategic positions at the simplest and broadest level.

Further, since these generic strategies are clearly concerned with competitive positioning, we have placed this concept of 'generic strategy' in the top-most band and left-hand side of Figure 2.10.

Second, Porter's (1979) famous five-forces competitive-forces-in-an-industry diagram (Figure 2.3) is generic and also clearly concerned with competitive positioning. So this way of thinking about strategy clearly also belongs in the upper left of Figure 2.10.

Third, Porter and Millar's (1985) paper on ways that IT can be a source of competitive advantage introduced the notion of a value chain (Figure 2.4). The 'nine generic categories' of value-creation activities in a firm's value chain indicate that this way of thinking about strategy belongs quite high up the vertical axis in Figure 2.10. With regard to competitive focus, Porter and Millar (1985) say that their diagram is useful because IT is affecting competition in three vital ways:

■ it changes industry structure and, in doing so, alters the rules of competition;

■ it creates competitive advantage by giving companies new ways to outperform their rivals;

■ it spawns whole new businesses, often from within a company's existing operations.

Since Porter and Millar (1985) are clearly still concerned with competition, though less dramatically than with Figure 2.3, we have placed the value-chain model closer to the middle of the generic band in Figure 2.10.

Finally, Porter's (1996, 2001) view of strategy is much more firm specific than his earlier work. Therefore, we have decided to place activity system maps on the lowest horizontal band in Figure 2.10. In addition, because Porter uses activity system maps to frame thinking about both competitive positioning and the activity systems that enable the firm to produce value for its customers, we have classified these diagrams as being on the middle of the horizontal axis in Figure 2.10.

2.3.2 Classifying conceptualizations of business models

Having classified Porter's various conceptualizations of strategy in terms of the two dimensions shown in Figure 2.10, we now turn to business models. Given the huge diversity of opinions about various aspects of business models (see Table 2.1 and Figure 2.6), how do we position business models in Figure 2.10? Here, we decided to follow the same approach as in Perspective 1, and classify the definitions from four authors, namely, Magretta (2002), Weill and Vitale (2001), Applegate (2000, 2003), and Linder and Cantrell (2000) in terms of the dimensions in Figure 2.10. In the remainder of this section we examine each document in turn, and ask:

■ What do the authors of this document understand by the term 'business model'?

■ Where does the authors' conceptualization fit in terms of the two dimensions in Figure 2.10?

First, according to Magretta (2002), quoted earlier, the key difference between business models and strategy is that the former do not consider competition:

> *But a business model isn't the same thing as strategy, even though many people use the terms interchangeably today. Business models describe, as a system, how the pieces of a business fit together. But they don't factor in one critical dimension of performance: competition. Sooner or later – and it is usually sooner – every enterprise runs into competitors. Dealing with that reality is strategy's job … A competitive strategy explains how you will do better than your rivals. (p. 94)*

Magretta's examples, such as American Express and Dell, are also quite generic. Thus, for Magretta, business models seem to belong in the right-hand side of the generic band in Figure 2.10.

Second, Weill and Vitale's (2001) eight atomic e-Business models, discussed earlier, provide much more detailed descriptions of process than Magretta, but like Magretta are much less concerned with competitive positioning than most of Porter's work. Since Weill and Vitale's (2001) business models are generic, with some (but not a lot) of interest in competitive positioning, we have positioned their work on the right-hand side of the generic band in Figure 2.10.

Third, Applegate's (2000) early work on models that:

> *can be built before the real system to help predict how the system might respond if we change the structure, relationships, and assumptions (2000, p. 53)*

suggests little interest in competitive positioning, though the later work, Applegate et al. (2003), shows much more interest in competitive positioning. Accordingly, we have placed the early work closer to the right-hand boundary in Figure 2.10, and the later work much closer to Porter's work, though both in the generic band in Figure 2.10.

Finally, as discussed previously, Linder and Cantrell's (2000) business models are quite similar to Porter's (1996) activity system maps and to Weill and Vitale's (2001) atomic business models. Since Linder and

Cantrell's (2001) business models are quite specific to one firm, with some interest in competitive positioning, we have classified their work in the firm-specific band, roughly midway along the Competitive Focus dimension of Figure 2.10.

2.4 Conclusion

The terms 'business model' and 'strategy' are both widely used but often quite difficult to distinguish from one another. In this chapter we have presented two alternative perspectives that help highlight differences between the two terms, at least as they have been used by some key authors in the strategy and business-models literatures, and clarify various meanings of the term 'business model'.

The first perspective views business models as abstract representations of some aspects of Porter's (1996, 2001) conceptualization of strategy. Figure 2.1 provides a simple representation of the relationship between a firm's business model(s) and strategy. We demonstrated above that Figure 2.1 is both consistent with much of the literature and helps in drawing a meaningful distinction between the terms 'business model' and 'strategy'.

The second, alternative, perspective views both business models and strategy as being both (a) conceived at different levels of abstraction, and (b) focusing to a greater or lesser extent on competitive positioning. Under this perspective, business models are more focused on *how* businesses create value, whereas strategy is more focused on competitive positioning. Recognizing that (a) and (b) could be viewed as two dimensions for classifying concepts of strategy and business model enabled us to classify the work of various authors in both the strategy and business models literatures as shown in Figure 2.10. Although different from Figure 2.1, the perspective in Figure 2.10 also provides what appears to be a useful way of comparing and classifying business models and strategy that is both consistent with most leading authors' definitions of the terms and also helps in making meaningful distinctions between the terms.

Finally, having noticed that most work on business models tends to fall in a relatively small area of the graph in Figure 2.10, we asked if there was some way to classify the literature on business models that highlighted more effectively the range of topics covered in the literature. That led us to the classification scheme, based on the work of Pateli (2002), depicted in Figure 2.6. Figure 2.6 shows quite dramatically, the range of interests of some leading thinkers on business models.

Clearly, in a world where there are literally millions of articles using the terms 'strategy' and 'business model', there will be a wide range of different definitions of the terms. But since this book contains a number of articles about business models, we believe there is value in considering in some depth what the term 'business model' means, so that readers can be clear about the meaning adopted by the various authors in this book. We hope that both Perspectives 1 and 2 are useful for understanding the range of meanings of the term 'business model' and for distinguishing them from the range of meanings of the term 'strategy'.

References and Further Reading

Alexander, C. (1977). *A Pattern Language*. New York, Oxford University Press.

Andrews, K. R. (1971). *The Concept of Corporate Strategy*. Homewood, Ill, Dow Jones-Irwin.

Applegate, L. M. (2000). eBusiness Models: Making Sense of the Internet Business Landscape. *Information Technology and the Future Enterprise, New Models for Managers*. G. Dickson and G. DeSanctis (eds). NJ, Prentice-Hall: 49–101.

Applegate, L. M., R. D. Austin and F. W. McFarlan (2003). *Corporate Information Strategy and Management: Text and Cases*, 6th edition. New York, McGraw-Hill Irwin.

Bain, J. S. (1956). *Barriers to New Competition*. Cambridge, Mass., Harvard University Press.

Barney, J. B. (1991). 'Firm Resources and Sustained Competitive Advantage.' *Journal of Management* (March): 107–111.

Coase, R. H. (1937). 'The Nature of the Firm.' *Econometrica* 4: 386–405.

Collis, D. and P. Ghemawat (1994). 'Industry Analysis: Understanding Industry Structure and Dynamics.' *The Portable MBA in Strategy*. L. Fahey and R. M. Randall (eds). New York, John Wiley and Sons, 1994.

Ghemawat, P. (1991). *Commitment: The Dynamic of Strategy*. New York, The Free Press.

Ghemawat, P. (2002). 'Competition and Business Strategy in Historical Perspective.' *Business History Review* **76**(Spring): 37–74. http://www.hbs.edu/bhr/PDF/760102.pdf

Gordijn, J. and H. Akkermans (2001). 'Designing and Evaluating eBusiness Models.' *IEEE Intelligent Systems* **16**(4) (July–August): 11–17.

Grant, R. M. (1991). 'The Resource-Based Theory of Competitive Advantage: Implications for Strategy Formulation.' *California Management Review* 33(3): 114–135.

Grant, R. M. (1996). *Contemporary Strategy Analysis: Concepts, Techniques, Applications*, 3rd edition. Blackwell Publishers.

Learned, E. P., C. R. Christensen, K.R. Andrews and W.D. Guth (1965). *Business Policy: Text and Cases*. Homewood, Ill, Irwin.

Linder, J. C. and S. Cantrell (2000). *Changing Business Models: Surveying the Landscape*. Institute for Strategic Change, Accenture. May 24, 2000 http://www.accenture.com/xdoc/en/ideas/isc/pdf/Surveying_the_Landscape_WP.pdf (viewed April 2003).

Magretta, J. (2002). 'Why Business Models Matter.' *Harvard Business Review* (May): 86–92.

Manns, M. L. (2001). Patterns: A Promising Approach to Knowledge Management. *First Annual ABIT Conference*, May 3–5, Pittsburgh, Pennsylvania. http://www.eberly.iup.edu/ABIT/proceedings%5CPatternsAPromising Approach.pdf (viewed April 2003).

McGahan, A. M. (1992). Selected Profitability Data on U.S. Industries and Companies. *Harvard Business School Publishing*, No. 792–066.

Osterwalder, A. and Y. Pigneur (2002). An eBusiness Model Ontology for Modeling eBusiness. *Proceedings of the Bled Electronic Commerce Conference 2002*, Bled.

Pateli, A. (2002). *A Domain Area Report on Business Models*. Athens University of Economics and Business, http://www.eltrun.aueb.gr/whitepapers/ ada_2002.pdf (viewed April 2003).

Porter, M. E. (1979). 'How Competitive Forces Shape Strategy.' *Harvard Business Review* (March–April): 137–145.

Porter, M. E. (1980). *Competitive Strategy, Techniques for Analyzing Industries and Competitors*. New York, Free Press.

Porter, M. E. (1985). *Competitive Advantage: Creating and Sustaining Superior Performance*. New York, Free Press.

Porter, M. E. (1996). 'What is Strategy?' *Harvard Business Review* (November–December): 61–78.

Porter, M. E. (2001). 'Strategy and the Internet.' *Harvard Business Review* (March): 63–78.

Porter, M. E. and V. E. Millar (1985). 'How Information Gives you Competitive Advantage.' *Harvard Business Review* (July–August): 149–160.

Prahalad, C. K. and G. Hamel (1990). 'The Core Competence of the Corporation.' *Harvard Business Review* (May–June): 79–91.

Simsion, G. (2000). *Data Modeling Essentials,* 2nd edition: *A Comprehensive Guide to Data Analysis, Design, and Innovation*. Coriolis Technology Press.

Teece, D. J., G. Pisano and A. Shuen (1997). 'Dynamic Capabilities and Strategic Management.' *Strategic Management Journal* 7: 509–533.

Timmers, P. (1998). 'Business Models for Electronic Markets.' *Journal of Electronic Markets* 8(2): 3–8.

Tirole, J. (1988). *The Theory of Industrial Organization*. Cambridge, MA, MIT Press.

von Neumann, J. and O. Morgenstern (1944). *Theory of Games and Economic Behavior*. Princeton, NJ, Princeton University Press.

Weill, P. and M. R. Vitale (2001). *Place to Space: Migrating to eBusiness Models*. Harvard Business School Press.

Wernerfelt, B. (1984). 'A Resource-Based View of the Firm.' *Strategic Management Journal* 5: 171–180.

Williamson, O. E. (1975). *Markets and Hierarchies*. New York, The Free Press.

Williamson, O. E. (1985). *The Economic Institutions of Capitalism*. New York, Free Press.

3 A framework for codifying business models and process models in e-Business design

Philip Joyce and Graham Winch

Abstract

The development of business models for e-Business has become increasingly popular within both the academic and business arena. We believe that many of the business models for e-Business are static in nature and only provide a historical view. In this chapter we draw upon the emergent knowledge of e-Business together with the traditional strategy theory and provide a simple framework for the evaluation of business models for e-Business. Central to this chapter we use dynamic modelling techniques of systems dynamics to evaluate an e-Business model using the triple pair approach in an effort to capture the casual relationships and rationalize the complexity of organizational resources and the environment in which they compete.

3.1 Introduction

At the heart of any organization is their strategy for doing business. Managers and chief executive officers (CEOs) are faced with the difficult task of successfully steering their organizations through ever changing economic conditions. In this dynamic and often tumultuous environment, managers must take inputs from a wide and varied range of sources, both internal and external to the organization, and process these into actions to best utilize their current resources and their current stream of revenue (or value). Often this is a difficult balancing act to achieve suitable revenues and value for an organization as well as positioning for the possible growth of the organization.

In most organizations the development of a suitable strategy, based on a set of objectives, is used as a means to guide the direction of the organization to obtain a level of value or return while taking into account the threats and opportunities that exist in their current marketplace and environment. Managers can call on a raft of approaches, tools, methodologies and methods to elucidate possible strategies that enable them to gain new insights.

However, these are generally static in nature and do not take into account the dynamic nature of an organization and its relationship with its external environment, and the dynamics within the organization.

The field of strategy and strategy formulation is quite fragmented with no one real archetypal unified theory that is capable of drawing together all the concepts that have been expounded in theory or practice. Instead, theory of the strategic concept, and strategy formulation commonly generated, are often subjectively and mono-dimensionally derived. That is, the strategy is taken from a perspective of industry position, value chain position, geographical market(s) of interest, customers or suppliers perspective, industry culture and/or structure, etc. Hence, managers are often unable to formulate effective strategies in the face of a wide range of influencing forces and different perspectives. Similarly, researchers and practitioners are often unable to draw logical boundaries around the current strategy and the perceived environment that they are attempting to understand. Incorporating these into a strategy capable of being communicated effectively is extremely difficult. However, business systems dynamics provides a method to model complex systems (Sterman, 2000). Importantly, the complexity involved in the diversity of strategy perspectives and subjective nature of strategy formulation needs to be described in a manner that is readily communicated to practitioners and researchers. Indeed, business system dynamics allows for the clear definition of the boundaries of the strategy and the environment it is attempting to depict. To effectively describe the strategy it is imperative that we draw on the current thinking and approaches to strategy and draw out a group of basic concepts formulation. In this case we will draw on:

- industry competition (customers, suppliers and competitors) (Porter, 1980);

- supply chain activities that the organization are involved in both internally and externally (Porter, 1985);

- generic strategy (Mintzberg, 1978);

- resources of the organization taking into account the process inputs and internal capital of human, physical, organizational and cognitive skills of the organization (Barney, 1991);

- organizational norms, values, technical and business skill in managing the business process (Prahalad and Bettis, 1986);

- business processes of the organization and their current business process models (Hammer and Champy, 1993);

■ the form of revenue (tangible and intangible) that will be achieved for the organization in the particular strategy (Kaplan and Norton, 1996).

By drawing on these elements and taking into account the theoretical underpinnings it has been possible to develop business models that can provide an instance of a strategy that is capable of describing, defining and explaining an organization's current approach within a defined area of the market. Curiously, within business research, the concept of a business model is sparsely used. Instead, strategy and strategy formulation research covers many, if not all, of the basic theoretical elements that are included in the business model concept (Hedman and Kalling, 2003).

However, a common challenge in using any form of model-based or supported thinking is in the surfacing and communication of different actors' mental models. In any thinking about the building of an electronically-based business, there are at least three simultaneous views of what it is expected to achieve and how this can made to happen:

■ entrepreneurs have their ideas for successful businesses;

■ technologists envisage ways to implement new complex technological or information systems (IS) to achieve business value;

■ operational managers have their ideas as to how business processes could be enhanced and extended to benefit from new opportunities.

Each of these views could form the basis for a model of the e-Business, extending down from the entrepreneur's vision of how to create value in the business environment, or upwards from the views of operational managers and technologists as to what new opportunities could be exploited from new and alternate applications to the company's assets and processes and/or emerging technical capabilities. However, these originating ideas are typically personal and retained in peoples' minds and not made explicit. Any unifying framework must provide a way by which the entrepreneurial mental models can be surfaced and articulated, and then the models shared with other actors in a way that they can see within them the business processes and technological infrastructures that are the basis of their thinking.

Building from arguments that strategy can be distilled into a business model capable of describing to a manager what an organization is currently attempting to achieve in a particular market, this chapter presents a framework that, it is suggested, can capture such broadly-based strategic models for e-Business design in a way that a chosen model's implications for business process modelling and information infrastructure are also clearly defined. The underlying strategic thinking takes into account the characteristics of the industry being discussed, the resources of the organization, their current business processes and enabling technology. Moreover, the view of strategy and strategy formulation is used to provide a top-down approach in the development of a business model. Similarly, a simultaneous bottom-up approach, utilizing the business process modelling perspective is also presented.

Specifically, the framework applies the stock-flow diagramming convention of System Dynamics to map *business process models* onto *business models*, as originally proposed in Joyce and Winch (2003). The resulting structural models reflect different e-Business model configurations in such a way that the processes by which service to various actors, and most specifically the final customer, will have to be fulfilled. This viewpoint focuses on the two-way flows of three critical system entities – information, goods and/or services, and money. To show the application and practical value of this cognitive framework, the relational structures of Weill and Vitale's 'atomic models' for e-Businesses (e.g. 2001) are used as a starting point and are extended by making more explicit the nature of each of the critical system flows. These business models give a dynamic perspective of the causal links in strategy execution and the organization's competitive environment, and the critical feedback structures that will determine system behaviour and corporate performance, which is often neglected in the current business models.

3.2 Strategy perspective

Strategic theory development by organizations has been one of considerable interest to both academics and practitioners alike and there is a wide diversity of approaches. The process of strategy formulation requires a high level of flexibility and imagination in order to visualize possible strategies that can use the current resources of the organization as leverage in order to develop new revenue streams within their current marketplace. Moreover, this may also provide for the possibility of an organization to enter into alternative marketplaces while utilizing the current resources of the organization.

In order to be successful in the development of a suitable strategy there needs to be careful consideration of the firm's resources (Barney, 1991), the organization's role and the current value chain the organization is involved in (Porter, 1985) and the possible utilization of a well implemented generic strategy (Mintzberg, 1978; Porter, 1980).

3.2.1 Emergent strategy formulation

In the evolution of strategy there is a strong emphasis on how an organization can influence its competitive environment as well as how the competitive environment influences its organization. Mintzberg (1978) outlines strategy formulation in most organizations as the interplay of three basic forces revolving around the:

- dynamic environment that changes continuously but at irregular intervals with frequent discontinuities and wide swings in the rate of change in the environment;

- organizational management or bureaucracy that attempts to stabilize the actions of the organizations while operating in the dynamic environment;

- leadership role of organizations that mediate between the two forces in an attempt to maintain the stability of the organization and their practices while adapting to the many changes of its operating environment.

Mintzberg's (1978) resource base model highlights that strategy is best viewed as a

> *set of consistent behaviours by which the organization establishes for a time its place in its environment, and strategic change can be viewed as the organization's response to the environment change, constrained by the momentum of the bureaucracy (organization) and accelerated or damped by leadership.*

Importantly, Mintzberg outlines that there is interplay between the intended strategy and realized strategy. Moreover, the time delay for an intended strategy to manifest itself can be quite long. In some cases longer than the time it takes an environment to actually change. As a consequence the intended strategy at best could be irrelevant or at worst detrimental to the organization. Similarly, an organization's response to an environment is often in the form of intended strategies that are developed in a prior manner based on the current understanding of the environment. These may be unrealistic, misaligned with the organization itself or not suitable to the current environment. If the environment changes and the organization is unable to capture this, their intended strategies may not be possible.

Mintzberg concludes by outlining that the process of strategy formulation is difficult, requiring managers to make strategy formulation based on vast amounts of information that is often incomplete and soft in nature. Consequently, the process of strategy formulation to strategy implementation is not clear. A major hurdle in this process for many organizations is their understanding of the learning process and the interaction of the environment, organization and the decisions and actions of managers.

3.2.2 Environmental models of competitive advantage

Porter (1980) extends the interrelationship of the three forces defined by Mintzberg by providing and outlining that external forces affect the work of managers in developing strategies. Porter's five forces model provides a framework to identify the external environment in which an organization works. These forces are exemplified as: the threat of new entrants and substitute, the relationship of the suppliers and clients and the present competitors. This approach provides a simplistic method for managers to describe their environment by isolating the threats and opportunities within the described industry and can determine the strategy choice of the organization and the possible outcome in the competitive environment. The generic strategies of 'low cost' and 'differentiation' are often used to develop a level of strategic or sustainable advantage within a market segment. In Porter (1985) an extension to this previous work was the development of the *value-chain model*. This focuses on the activities and functions of the organization and their relationship with their suppliers and customers. This allows an organization to identify the underlying factors that drive cost and possible differentiation potentials. It allows an organization to control and group activities with the possibility of utilizing cost potentials by creating economy of scale advantages or through product differentiation by developing innovative products and services. In this approach there are two underlying simplifications. First, organizations within an industry have access and control of the same strategically relevant resource and compete with a similar strategy. Second, should an industry participant gain specialized resources (resource heterogeneity) capable of providing a competitive advantage, it will be short lived as industry competitors can easily obtain these resources.

3.2.3 Resource-based view

Barney (1991) introduces the concept of the resource-based view (RBV) to address the limitations of environmental models of competitive advantage and attempts to provide a link between heterogeneous resources controlled by an organization, mobility of the resources within the particular industry and the strategic or competitive advantage enjoyed by an organization. A firm's resources are used to enable it to establish strategies to improve the overall efficiency and performance of the organization and these can be quite wide ranging. Barney classifies these resources into three categories:

- *Physical capital resources*: includes the physical resources of the organization such as plant and equipment, technology, location and access to raw materials.

- *Human capital resources*: includes the training, experience, judgment, intelligence, insight from managers and workers within the organization.

■ *Organization capital resources*: includes the formal structure of the organization, planning, controlling and coordinating systems, formal and informal reporting and planning systems, as well as informal relation among groups with the organization and between external organizations in the competitive environment.

Hence, the resources that an organization controls can be examined in terms of its attributes: heterogeneity (i.e. its uniqueness) and immobility (i.e. its obtainability by other competing firms). In terms of these two attributes, if two organizations that have the same resources, and conceive the same strategy, both will improve their efficiency and effectiveness in the same way and importantly to the same extent.

In order for an organization to have the potential of sustainable advantage the resources should have four attributes (Barney, 1991):

■ it must be *valuable* in the sense that it provides opportunities or neutralizes threats to the organization's environment;

■ it must be *rare* among an organization's current and potential competitors;

■ it must be *imperfectly imitable*;

■ *it must be non-substitutable* – there cannot be a strategic equivalent substitute for the resource that is valuable but neither rare nor imperfectly imitable.

Resources that are valuable, rare, imperfectly imitable and non-substitutable can provide sources of sustained competitive advantage to an organization. In this case we find that a resource is *valuable* if it has the ability to reduce cost or increase the price of a product or service. Thereby, a bundle of valuable resources can be used to conceive of and implement strategies. These can be a particular mixture of physical, human and organizational capital resources. If this bundle is not rare then another organization is capable of conceiving and imitating the same strategies. Hence, a key element of RBV is the concept of a *rare* resource. An organization that provides a bundle of valuable resources can be considered a rare resource, as it would be costly or impossible to imitate: imperfectly imitable. Moreover, if substitute resources are possible they must also be expensive to sustain for the competitor, if a competitive advantage is possible and sustainable. The cost of the imitation is often driven by the unique social conditions, casual ambiguity and complexity of the resources (Barney, 1991). Substitutability comes in two forms. First, if an organization is able to use similar valuable–rare resources it could conceivably develop and implement a similar strategy. Second, very different organization resources could provide substitute strategies. Resources that are valuable and rare afford a competitive advantage to the organization provided they are imperfectly imitable and non-substitutable.

3.3 Organizational, economic and technical factors

Strategic management can allow an organization to move into different markets or offer alternatives in their current market. This is often predicated on organizational, economic and technological arrangements and factors.

3.3.1 Organizational arrangement and factors

Organizational strategy becomes a conscious plan to align the firm with opportunities and threats posed by its environment (Ansoff, 1965). This often requires organizations to understand not only the environment the organization is currently operating in but to understand the current resources of the organization, and the possibility of using these as a means to overcome threats and take up any opportunities that may be available to the organization. In any organization their ability to grow within their environment is often predicated on economies of scope in production (goods or service), learning curves and process innovation, and this requires the alignment of the strategy within the organization to be able to achieve this. Indeed, Andrews (1987) was the first to make the distinction between corporate strategy and business strategy. Highlighting that, the corporate strategy is often a super set of business strategies implemented by business units of the organization.

In larger diversified organizations strategy is defined at a corporate (global) level often allowing business units within the organization to develop their own strategies. These strategies are often developed to provide a level of synergy with the corporate strategy to further and support the aims of the organization. In this we find managers of business units have defined strategies that utilize the resources they currently control. Indeed, managers are capable of taking the under-utilized resources of the organization and imperfections in the current market to confer an advantage. One of the main enablers for organizations to achieve this has been through the use of technology. Organizations with strong technological position have been able to not only diversify into adjacent business areas but also allow them to integrate technology into the current business processes. Moreover, due to their experience in the utilization of technology their cost of entry into the adjacent market is greatly reduced (Cameron and Joyce, 2001) or their integration cost of technology into their business processes is greatly reduced (Barrenechea and Ellison, 2000).

Clearly, with the dramatic developments of technology, especially in the area of information technology (IT), not all organizations have been able to achieve these strategies. Prahalad and Bettis (1986) introduce the concept of dominant logic where a set of heuristics rule, norms and beliefs that managers create to guide their actions. A manager's ability to seek new opportunities for the firm and the subsequent strategy is often guided by the dominant logic of the organization. As a consequence new ideas and behaviours are often filtered out as they do not conform to the prevailing dominant logic of the organization. A manager's cognition is often bounded in its scope by the dominant logic of the organization and attempts to maintain the focus of the organization and internal coherence amongst the firm's activities (Chesbrough and Rosenbloom, 2001). This can be seen in the technology developments that have occurred in the computer industry. IBM, during the late 1980s, had a large market share of the mainframe computing industry. IBM were able to capitalize on incremental innovations by providing a unique premium product and excellent customer service. However, their expertise and knowledge became a liability in the face of radically new technology as they failed to anticipate the fundamental change the microprocessor and personal computer revolution would mean to their market share. Clearly, in this case industry technological shift can quickly undermine the strategic direction perused by the organization.

Organizational adoption of new technology can be considered an extension to the concept of architectural innovation whereby an alteration of relationship between processes within an organization will occur. Moreover, this effect is more pronounced in the case of radical business process re-engineering (BPR). This can upset the managerial heuristics of the organization by altering the business process and systems linkages they currently understand, consequently requiring them to change. This is technological shift driven dominant logic change. Christensen (1997) refers to disruptive technology as a form of technology shift and found organizations were capable of adjusting to the change when there was a clear technological opportunity that reinforced the firm's current business, but ineffective when the technology provided access to new markets and customers. Moreover, the allocation of internal resources of an organization can be constrained by managers both within and outside the particular business unit attempting to maintain the dominant logic of the organization.

An alternative strategy often employed in a corporate strategy is the use of discovery-oriented strategy of research and development by the organization's business unit. In this case organizations develop new products, services and technology enabling them to enter into their current markets or new markets. Indeed, the development of entirely new products can be a source of growth, as their demand for the product in the market will increase revenue, which in turn will increase investment in new product development. However, there are a number of examples of organizations following this approach that have not been able to gain this reward after developing new innovations of products and service. In particular, Xerox, a well known technology organization, has developed a wide range of technical innovations that have been exceptionally successful in new markets but have been developed by spin-off organizations (Chesbrough and Rosenbloom, 2001).

3.3.2 Economic arrangement and factors

Utilization of the economic factors for an organization both internally and externally will have a limiting factor on the possible strategic development of new or existing markets as redevelopment of current service or product.

In larger organizations access to a larger set of resources (personal, organization skills and learning, scale of operations, etc.) over and above their own core business allows greater flexibility in developing other streams of revenue. Hence, access to additional possible growth areas. Access to capital for a large organization can provide an environment whereby investments in innovation, quality and differentiation will increase the attractiveness of the product or service within a market and therefore increase the market share. This in turn provides greater sales, revenue and profit providing healthy expected future earnings. Consequently, the organization's share prices increase allowing them to raise even more capital. Indeed, many hi-tech firms have ridden this cycle and have accumulated large investor capital in order to obtain market share. Indeed, Amazon.com have used the 'get big fast approach' to gain market share at the expense of large company losses. Investors believed that the expected market size would be of such a large nature that eventually the profits would cover the initial losses (Oliva et al., 2003).

Many organizations have seen the emergence of IT as a tool capable of providing a level of strategic advantage in a wide range of industries (Porter, 2001). This emergent strategy of technology-enabled strategic advantage has seen organizations review their current set of products and services for their suitability for delivery, utilizing this technology and attempting to extract possible value for the organization. This review is often performed on two distinct fronts:

- *BPR* (Hammer and Champy, 1993): BPR is the analysis and redesign of organization structures and requires the re-evaluation of the current business processes of the organization in an attempt to either extract value within the business processes to reduce costs and to improve product, service, operational quality and speed. Central to

BPR is the gathering, management and dissemination of information that is gained from the business process, especially from the associated value chains. Often this requires the utilization of IT to mediate this process of re-engineering. The cost to the organization at an organizational, human, physical and technological level cannot be under-estimated and must be taken into account. Managers must consider the drain on resources on the organization when undertaking BPR review and implementation and the necessity to consider buying extra resources and expertise from outside the organization.

■ *Extracting value in the strategic investment*: In any strategy there is a need to consider the justification and evaluation of any strategic implementation an organization undertakes. Kaplan and Norton (1996) state that the process of justification and evaluation is central to the process of translating strategy into action. The criterion for strategy justification and evaluation is an extremely difficult area with many techniques grappling with tangible and intangible benefits of such investments. Importantly, the economic value of the strategy must be expounded, and by using a business model it provides a suitable model to examine the justification and evaluation of strategy.

In contrast small to medium enterprises (SMEs) may not have access to additional resources over and above their core business that could enable them to gain additional revenue streams. In this case the development of strategy is often predicated on their ability to utilize current technologies and attempt to diversify into a market that provides an advantage. More often SMEs are not capable of taking this path as they are unable to commit the additional resources (Afuah and Tucci, 2001; Cameron and Joyce, 2001).

One interesting element that has moved strategy into a new direction has been the rise of the entrepreneur in knowledge-based industries as opposed to the traditional manufacturing and physical resource-based economies. In this case we see entrepreneurs attempting to gain a strategic advantage by providing access to capital and being focused on a market-based strategy. Entrepreneurs often follow a market need that is currently not being met within the particular industry. With the rise of the Internet many entrepreneurs considered not only the possibility of establishing new markets and alternative methods of business but an opportunity to challenge existing markets. This can be achieved by offering alternative business processes to customers, suppliers and competitors or other actors in the value chain by utilizing IT, especially Internet technology, to mediate the flow of information between the transacting parties.

A catalyst for this level of change is often achieved from capital from either an internal (budget strategic funding) or external source (external borrowings, bonds, etc.). Indeed, knowledge-based entrepreneurs attempt to develop a new product or service to meet the perceived industry demand through the use of technology. Importantly, the entrepreneur is not bounded by the dominant logic of the organization. Indeed, knowledge-based entrepreneurs attempt to show a direct relationship with the possible revenue streams from the investment taking into account the industry conditions, value of the actors (suppliers, customers, competitors, etc.) and possible enabling technologies. In these cases strategies are developed in an extremely fluid or soft nature and often are communicated utilizing descriptive tools rather than ridged, prescriptive, formalized approach to strategy formulation.

3.3.3 Technology arrangement and factors

The development of new technologies has been one of the great enablers in providing a strategic advantage in terms of economic growth and increasing returns to an organization within a given industry. New technologies, whether they are developed by the particular organization in research development for their specialized industry (or application) or by utilizing technology from alternative industries are capable of providing a specialization or uniqueness of skills or operation that may not be easily matched by their competitors. Consider the idea of the division of labour whereby a process is divided into a large number of routine operations, productivity can be improved by specialization enabling people (and the organization) to learn faster, customize tools and resources to specific tasks and eliminate the wasted effort of moving from one operation to another. In Adam Smith's *Wealth of Nations*, he notes,

> the division of labour is limited to the extent of the market.

This recognizes that economic growth enables greater specialization, which in turn can provide greater productivity and therefore greater economic growth (Sterman, 2000). Indeed, organizations attempt to capture value (and economic growth) from new technology in two different ways (Chesbrough and Rosenbloom, 2001):

- through utilizing existing or newly developed technology from other industries or applications into their current business processes; or

- by developing new or unique technology through the organization's own efforts of discovery-oriented research, R&D, that may enable the development of new business areas.

In the last decade we have seen the proliferation of the Internet as a forum to move information. Indeed, the World Wide Web (WWW) has provided a forum for organizations to dramatically change the way they do business and, combined with the use of IT organizations, are able to review their current business processes. Traditionally, the thinking within organizations has been based around the separate considerations of strategy issues and issues specific to e-Business. However, what is actually needed are ideas and tools that integrate these.

3.4 Business models for e-Business

The term business model is one that is a topic of hot debate and draws considerable comment and differing opinion in both academia and practice (Timmers, 1998; Alt and Zimmermann, 2001; Applegate, 2001; Chesbrough and Rosenbloom, 2001; Weill and Vitale, 2001; Chandra et al., 2002; Hedman and Kalling, 2003; Oliva et al., 2003; Rappa, 2003). The main driving force behind the re-evaluation of the (traditional) business model has been the development of e-Business, e-Commerce and e-Marketing. The focus of the re-evaluation has been on how new technologies, especially the Internet, alter the business model and subsequent strategy. Interestingly, a deep analysis of the business model concept highlights that there is a diversity of views and understanding of the business model for e-Business. This provides a confusing and incomplete picture of the dimensions, and core issues of these business models (Alt and Zimmermann, 2001). The empirical use of the concept has been criticized for being unclear, superficial and not theoretically grounded (Porter, 2001).

3.4.1 Components of the business model for e-Business

A major criticism of the business model can be seen when we examine the strategy theory in the field of business research. In strategy formulation research many, if not all, of the theoretical components of the business model are covered. By focusing on the components of the business model for e-Business we are able to draw on underlying theory of strategy.

Timmers (1998) defines an e-Business model as: *an architecture for the product, service, information flows, including a description of potential benefits for the various actors, and a description of the sources of revenue.* Weill and Vitale (2001) propose a similar definition of: *a business model is a description of the roles and relationships among a firm's consumers, customers, allies and suppliers that identifies the major flows of product, information and money and the major benefits to participants.* Underlying the definition we can break these down into the components of the business model: business strategy, organization form and structure, business process, value chain, core competencies and financial structure. Alt and Zimmerman (2001) presents six components: mission, structure, processes, revenues, legal issues and technology.

Afuah and Tucci (2001) define an e-Business model as *how a firm plans to make money long term using the Internet*. Although simplistic in its nature it builds a framework of components including: customer value (low cost or innovative), scope (products/service), price, revenues sources, connected activities, implementation (required resources), capabilities (organization skills) and sustainability. Interestingly, the proposed list of components is applicable to both e-Business models and the traditional business models. However, the causality between the components, processes and change are not addressed.

Applegate (2001) provides a considered business model framework consisting of three basic components: concept, value and capabilities. It addresses the role of the change process and the relationship between the components of the model. Concept, or business concept, describes the products and services offered, evolutionary business strategy, competitive dynamics, market opportunities and strategy to gain dominant market share. Value of the business model is measured in terms of the revenue to the stakeholders, return to the organization, market share, brand and reputation, and financial performance. Capabilities are delivered by the organization's marketing and sales model, management model, development model and infrastructure model and built by people and partners, organizational structure and culture. Components described in the business model are interdependent and traditional strategic framework tools (e.g. value chain analysis, RBV) can be used to evaluate the suitability of the business model. Importantly, the major difference between the traditional business models and e-Business models are the underlying assumptions and rules of how business will be undertaken in the particular industry.

3.4.2 Description of the business models for e-Business

The wider group of business models for e-Business provide descriptions for particular scenarios and situations. Moreover, e-Business models aim to describe specific business models, which explain how businesses use the Internet to interact and how value is created for the customer and the other stakeholders (Applegate, 2001). There has been an explosion in the number of academic papers that outline a wide range of taxonomies for e-Business models. An early attempt was made by Timmers (1998) who identified eleven e-Business models: e-shop, e-mall, e-procurement, third-party marketplace, e-auction, virtual community, collaborative platform, value-chain service provider, value-chain integration, information brokerage and trust service. Rappa (2003) extended this and classified nine categories for e-Business models: brokerage, advertising, infomediary, merchant, manufacturer, affiliate, community, subscription and utility. Under these, Rappa identifies 36 models that can be classified under his nine categories. Interestingly, both Timmers and Rappa state that there is no single comprehensive taxonomy for classifying e-Business models and yet they do provide taxonomies of e-Business models.

Applegate (2001) outlines a taxonomy of business models for e-Business by using: generic market role (i.e. producers, consumers, distributors and customers), digital business (if dependant of the Internet) and platform (i.e. infrastructure provider for third-party e-Business). Applegate provides some general categories: focused distributor, portals, producers and infrastructure producers in which there are 22 individual instances of e-Business models that fit within the classification of the taxonomy.

Weill and Vitale (2001) define eight finite e-Business models: direct customer, full service (FS) provider, intermediary, whole of enterprise, shared infrastructure, virtual community, value net integrator and content provider. These business models are based on a systematic and practical analysis of several case studies. This work describes eight basic structures as 'atomic' models. These eight structures form the 'atoms', which firms may adopt singly or in more complex arrangements ('molecules') to construct their business model. The models are defined in terms of the actors in the structure of the firm, complementors, customers, and suppliers and the inter-linkages between them. This includes the movement of product, money and information. These atomic models may be described as an 'analysis agenda' for managers attempting to interpret the complexity of an e-Business model in terms of the resources required to implement each or a specific business model.

3.4.3 Business model strategic conceptual framework

In order to provide a framework to evaluate business models for e-Business we must establish a method to highlight the resources involved and the casual relationships with the organization and environment. Figure 3.1 provides a simple business model strategic conceptual framework to highlight the interrelationship with business strategy, business models, business process models and the underlying business processes that are capable of utilizing the enabling technology (i.e. IT and IS). At the centre of the framework is the business model. It provides a method to create an e-Business model by examining the particular context based on the industry – organization environment. The conceptual framework allows managers to bring their thinking together for a common understanding, integrating the strategic formulation within a particular market and the strategic issues specific to e-Business within the organization. It provides a conceptual framework to allow entrepreneurs, managers and technologies to vision their particular strategies.

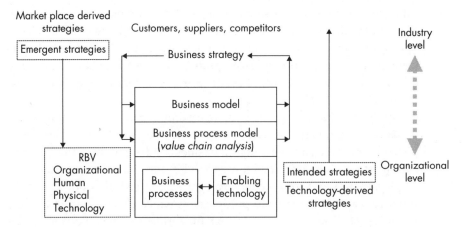

Figure 3.1: Business model strategic conceptual framework.

The framework utilizes the traditional tools of strategic formulation and provides a foundation for identifying the underlying business model or developing a new business model. Value chain analysis provides a method to identify the business process model that is either already in place, highlighting its important business processes, or which could be developed as a new and innovative approach. In the e-Business case we need to consider how enabling technology, especially Internet-based technology, can provide new variants of business process models and business processes. RBV provides a method to identify the resources required by the organization to support the business model under consideration. Importantly, it provides managers with a way to classify them in terms of the strategic importance at an organizational level and industry level. At a business strategy level, Porter's five forces model, for example, could provide the means to identify the external environment that the organization is attempting to compete in, and how the actors (customers, supplier, competitors, etc.) of this environment interact with the business model under consideration (Porter, 1980).

The conceptual framework identifies market-placed and technology-based strategies. From the market-placed strategies perspective these are derived from the market itself and are considered to be the emergent strategies of the market. Knowledge-based entrepreneurs fall into this category. Conversely, technology-delivered strategies are derived from within the organization and often from research and development or a specific resource of the organization.

RBV has been extended in this framework to include technology capital resources as a part of the RBV of business models for e-Business. In this sense, technology cannot only be seen as the rare and valuable resource of competitive advantage, as experienced by the early adopter of Web-based e-Commerce (e.g. Amazon.com), but also as an enabler of business in a new and innovative way that supports an organization within a particular market (e.g. Porter's five force and value chain analysis) or simply provides effective back office processes and information management (e.g. general strategy). Similarly, market-placed strategies often have a strong effect on the emergent strategies of the organization. Conversely, intended strategies bubble up for the organization, and in the e-Business area are often based on the use of technology as a means to communicate with customers, suppliers and competitors. This includes their interaction with their customer and supplier and allows them to revisit their current market and the possibility of moving into new markets. There is a growing realization that the 'economic value from technology can only be derived from the economic and social structure of the situation rather than the inherent characteristics of the technology itself' (Chesbrough and Rosenbloom, 2001).

A major criticism of business models for e-Business has been the lack of evaluation techniques for the models that have been generated. Many of these models are anecdotal or retrospective in nature. Moreover, there has been no evaluation of the taxonomies. Therefore, re-examination of the activities that form the basis for many of these models must be undertaken. This can only be achieved by utilizing innovative modelling approaches to gain a greater insight into the complexity of business models for e-Business.

3.5 A generic framework for e-Business fulfilment modelling

All business transactions are in one way or another a supply chain fulfilment system. Orders for goods or services are fulfilled (i.e. satisfied) by the goods being delivered and a payment being received in exchange. The chain itself could be viewed as a single aggregate-level fulfilment system or a cascade of individual fulfilments, each representing a stage in the chain. There are effectively, therefore, three flow processes comprising all such systems: *information flows*, primarily the orders; *money flows*, payment for goods or service and *delivery of goods or services*.

These are just the primary flows, goods may flow via distributors, and similarly money flows may be via credit cards. These may be seen as refinements, alternatives or extensions of the primary flows above. However, an important consideration is that each of these flows can be two-way: *reverse information flows* might include order acknowledgements, delivery notices, invoices, out-of-stock notifications, etc. It might also include information not directly related to individual order fulfilments (e.g. stock position advisories and so on); *reverse money flows* might be refunds, cash-back, commissions, etc. and *reverse goods flows* might be returns, trade-ins, etc. Leaving aside for a moment the complexity of these flows, it would seem therefore that any supply chain

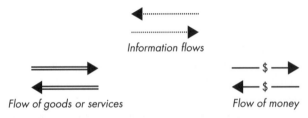

Figure 3.2: The 'triple pair' process flow model of supply chain fulfilment.

or distribution can be reduced to six main flows: two-way information, two-way goods and services, two-way money flows, as shown in Figure 3.2. This is what might be called the *'triple pair'* flow model.

If all the relevant flows relating to a particular supply chain structure could be represented within this *triple pair* model, then the configuration of the six flows can be mapped onto any business model that a company has in place, or wishes to adopt. If the business model is based on e-Commerce processes then this is only a further variant – the information flows are carried out mainly or totally by electronic processes, and the goods and money flows may need some modification to make them coherent with the information processes.

The e-Business may be a new phenomenon and in some cases may create brand new business model opportunities. However, in many situations it is a simple variant of an old theme. Consider e-Business grocery shopping: in the UK supermarkets such as TESCO offer this, in Australia Coles Myers do. Customers can access the 'virtual' super-market electronically and order a personalized list of groceries (with or without modification) or make a complete order from scratch. The order is put together and delivered by van a day or two later – either as part of a scheduled delivery process or on an ad hoc basis. The systems often offer further features like an optional nearest substitute for out-of-stock items. Is this a new retail grocery model? For a hundred years better grocery stores have offered home deliveries. Customers would phone in (or send a maid) and the store would deliver the order by horse-drawn cart, delivery bicycle or motor van, as part of a scheduled route or ad hoc. The order might be a standard order held in a ledger or the storekeeper's head, or might be compiled from scratch. The storekeeper would include a suitable substitute for any out-of-stock item. The electronic processes may facilitate certain aspects of this model and may make minor improvements – e.g. 24 × 7 ordering via the Web site – but it is hardly a completely new way of retailing.

By using the stock-flow diagramming convention of system dynamics we will investigate how *business process models* can be mapped onto *business models*. System dynamics is well suited to this application. There are many excellent texts that describe the principles and processes in system dynamics modelling and Sterman (2000) is a leading example text.

From its earliest days of development (Forrester, 1961), system dynamics has always explicitly reflected industrial and business structures as a complex inter-related set of flows of money, materials and information (though in some contexts the list may be expanded to included people, and 'materials' could include, e.g. livestock and services). In this sense it was always concerned with the structural relationships that make up business processes as well as the softer processes and has been used explicitly to study business processes (see e.g. Powell et al. (2001)). It has also been used to study supply chain systems within the business process concept; Sterman (2000) discusses the role of system dynamics in manufacturing supply chain management, and presents two actual case study applications – the situation of a semiconductor/component manufacturer Symbios and its downstream distribution through original equipment manufacturers (OEMs) (Sterman, 2000, pp. 449–462) and *Fast Growth Electronics'* (a pseudonym) up- and down-stream channels (Sterman, 2000, pp. 449–462).

One of the most popular activities undertaken by students of the approach is to play the 'malt beverage game' – or its less politically correct version – the *Beer Game* (Figure 3.3). This is a manual simulation of the distribution chain for beer and is played on a large board (around 4 m by 1 m or 12 ft by 3 ft) where the stages of the chain are represented. Teams must manage their inventories and supply crates of beer to their customers, by ordering from their upstream suppliers (see also the descriptions in Senge (1990) and Sterman (2000)). There are delays in both the ordering and delivery processes, and communications between teams is limited to order slips only. Minor perturbations in final demand can cause major fluctuations which are usually alarming and

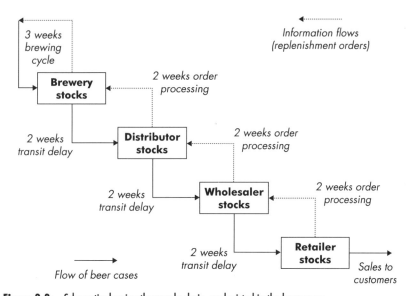

Figure 3.3: Schematic showing the supply chain, as depicted in the beer game.

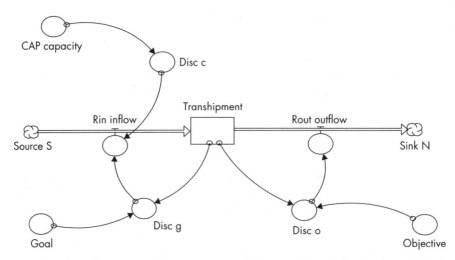

Figure 3.4: A 'supply chain network dynamic process model' drawn with *iThink* (after Chandra et al., 2002).

unexpected to the players – but wholly predictable to the facilitators. Diagrams similar to this typically appear in articles concerning extended supply chains. For example, Chandra et al. (2002, p. 106) present a very similar diagram in their description of the automobile supply chain (Figure 3.4).

System dynamics has also been used effectively to study issues relating to IS system management (Abdel-Hamid and Madnick, 1989; Abdel-Hamid and Madnick, 1991), IS outsourcing (McCray and Clark, 1999) and e-Commerce company strategy (Oliva et al., 2003). Chandra and his co-authors also include reference to the potential of system dynamics in their discussion of a generic development methodology for e-management and conceptual modelling of supply chains (Chandra et al., 2002). They include what they describe as an illustration of a supply chain network dynamic process flow model. Using the system dynamics modelling software *iThink* to re-draft their diagram, their process flow model appears as Figure 3.5.

This model reflects explicitly the stock-flow structure of the process, with goods being despatched, laying as a level (stock) while they are in transhipment, and then being delivered. This structure can be re-drafted using more usual system dynamics nomenclature and the range of icons available in *iThink*. This is presented as Figure 3.5.

Once again, this dynamic process model represents only a very simple process. However, the chain could be readily extended if further stocks or stages are observed or required, and parallel processes could be added to reflect more complex business processes. Using this micro representation of the supply chain network process model leads to the presentation of the *triple pair* model as in Figure 3.6. This now reflects that there is structure and complexity in each of the six flows.

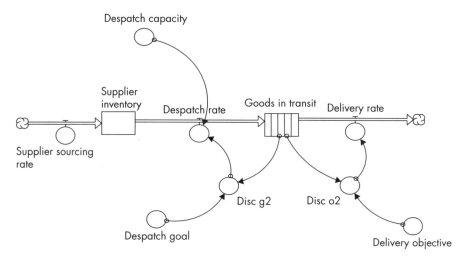

Figure 3.5: A re-drafted depiction of Chandra et al.'s model.

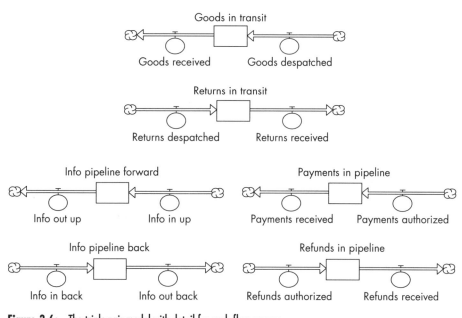

Figure 3.6: The triple pair model with detail for each flow process.

3.6 A triple pair interpretation of Weill and Vitale's business models

In Weill and Vitale's model (2002), the authors consider the range of IT infrastructure capabilities that are needed in the implementation of these business models, and in the more detailed discussion of four of the eight, remark that they 'require surprisingly different IT infrastructure services.' Their detailed analysis raises a number of critical issues in terms of four internal elements or levels – IT components, human IT infrastructure, shared IT services, and shared and standard applications – which are in turn linked with public infrastructures, such as the Internet and communications networks, and to external industry-based infrastructures like bank payment systems, reservation systems and supply chain networks. This approach can enable managers to focus their critical attention on the IT infrastructures needed, can guide them in IT investments and, Weill and Vitale (2001) assert, point to situations where the infrastructure gap might be so large as to require major rethinking on their e-Business plans. It is suggested here that the 'triple pair' flow model approach offers a practical way by which various e-Business models, including those put forward by Weill and Vitale, can be visualized in business process terms. This will then provide a way for specifying the model structure in sufficient detail for information flow models to be envisaged to provide the necessary IT services.

To demonstrate this process two of the Weill and Vitale models are represented in terms of the 'triple double' flows. The expansion is indicative only, as there is likely to be a wide range of detailed processes possible within this and each of the business models.

3.6.1 A triple pair representation of the *direct-to-customer* model

The *direct-to-customer* model is arguably the simplest of the business models, and is characterized by the originators as providing 'goods or services directly to customers, often surpassing traditional channel players.' In this model the primary relationship is directly between the customer and the direct-to-consumer provider (examples given are Dell and Home Depot), with money flowing to the provider and products and information flowing to the customer. In the Weill and Vitale format this business model is represented visually as in Figure 3.7.

This characterization emphasizes the major relationship as being directly between the customer and provider and indicates the basic flows between them. This is sufficient to serve the managerial needs identified earlier. However, this model says very little about the actual business processes that would have to be created to enable transaction fulfilment, and is a significant simplification in the sense that there is no representation reflecting returns. These would require a flow of products in the reverse direction, possibly, if a refund is given, a reverse money flow, and of course information flows in the reverse direction also.

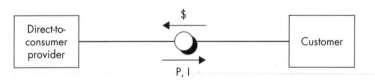

Figure 3.7:   Weill and Vitale's direct-to-customer business model. (Weill and Vitale, 2001, p. 246)

The triple flow model would represents this model in a supply chain perspective and highlight all the necessary flows. Focusing at this point on a good, as opposed to service, type product, the representation of basic flows and some inter-linkages would appear as Figure 3.8. This captures the primary flows and indicates the action links between the flows. In this version the money flow is represented generically, but would be modified to include further or fewer stages dependent upon the forms of payment the provider chooses to accept – cheques, electronic payment authorization via debit card, or payment via an intermediary by credit card. The model is also simplified in terms of the product fulfilment process, where the exact representation would depend on whether the product is made-to-order or delivered from stock, and so on.

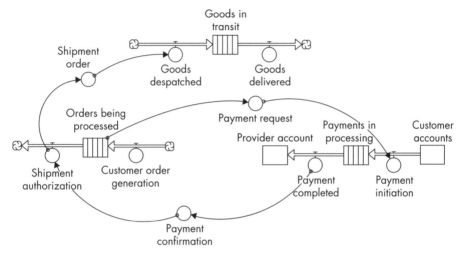

Figure 3.8: Basic 'triple pair' flow structure of direct-to-customer model.

For a fuller representation with two-way flows, the model could incorporate further mechanisms to reflect a possible need for customers to be requested to provide a detailed specification, which might be the case for products such as Dell computers, though this might also be accomplished interactively for Web orders. The model could also accommodate goods returned. The expanded model is shown in Figure 3.9, where earlier inter-linkages are muted to grey to highlight new additions. This could be further expanded to model the detail of the actual business processes that a company would wish to adopt and implement, including the evaluation of alternatives and the creation of more complex multiple business model structures. The model could also link to further business processes not related to the original supply mechanisms; these might include maintenance/service and product guarantee or warranty procedures, customer satisfaction and/or product enhancement suggestion surveys, and marketing for up-grade and/or

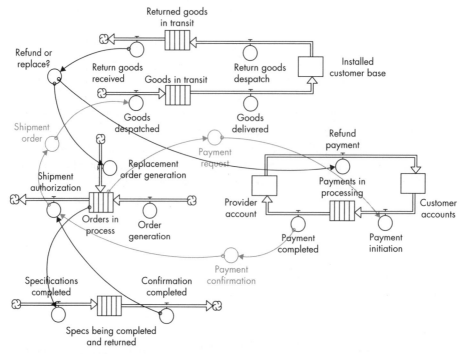

Figure 3.9: Fuller direct-to-customer model with specification confirmation and goods returns.

repeat sales generation, all of which would relate to the installed customer base.

3.6.2 A triple pair representation of the full-service-provider model

A second of Weill and Vitale's atomic models is the FS provider. This business model reflects the situation where access to a range of products or services is provided through a primary provider who might not only supply its own products or services, but also promote and facilitate the purchase of related products and services from partner firms. Examples might include a direct-to-customer product supplier, which offers related insurance, training, accessories and so on. Weill and Vitale characterize this model as Figure 3.10.

Again the primary relationship in this system is between the provider and the customer, but there are additional relationships involving flows of money, product/services, and/or information between the provider and its second-level supply network partners – which Weill and Vitale consider could be suppliers or complementors (resellers) – and between the second-level suppliers and customers.

As this model is essentially an extension of the direct-to-customer model, structures similar to those developed for that model will also exist at the core of this model. For this reason, those common structures will not be included in this model. This model involves the primary

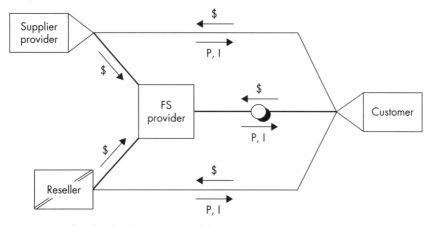

Figure 3.10: Weill and Vitale's characterization of their FS provider model.

purchase with the FS provider triggering additional supply fulfilment, money transactions, and information flow processes. Figure 3.11 suggests that this might typically involve the sending to the customer of information concerning services or products related to their purchase and provided by the FS provider's partner companies. In this version, it is assumed that communication with the customer is triggered as the initial product despatch is authorized, but this could equally be triggered by the initial order or during the order processing. The main net impact of the trigger point would be timing, though if a despatch were not authorized and the initial sale lost, then with the latter versions the customer might still be contacted concerning the secondary products/services.

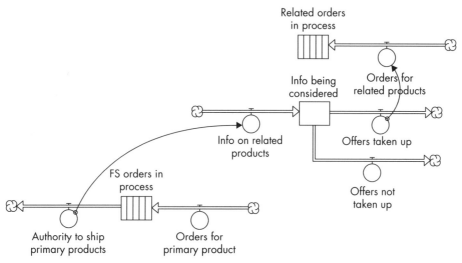

Figure 3.11: Extension to the direct-to-customer model to represent offer of secondary products/services from the FS provider.

The trigger impacts upon an information flow pair. Initially information in the form of the offer for secondary products is communicated to the customer who may or may not accept the offer after consideration (e.g. there might be a 14-day window after initial sale for the purchase of a linked insurance from a partner firm). If an offer is accepted, then information in the form of an order or confirmation is returned to the partner.

Customers must also pay for the related secondary product, and so a money flow is also initiated transferring money from the customer's funds to the secondary supplier's. Once the order process for the related secondary products is complete, then a delivery process for those products or services is also initiated and, after the delivery process delay, they are delivered to the customer. At some point, typically when the order process is complete, a transfer of funds from the secondary supplier to the full cost provider, by way of commission or introduction fee, is also transacted. These further flows are shown in Figure 3.12. Similar structures would have to be completed for all secondary suppliers or other complementary resellers, along with reverse processes for returns, refunds and so on.

As before, these are only typical or possible structures, and other configurations are feasible. For example, orders for the secondary

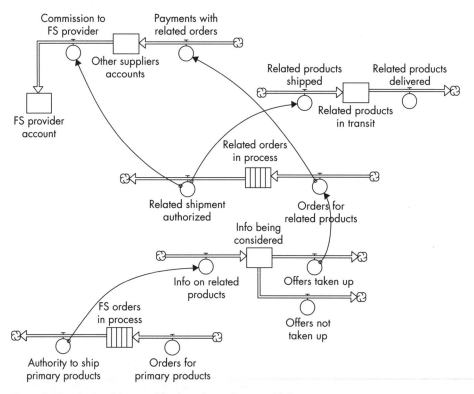

Figure 3.12: Product delivery and fund transfer mechanisms added.

products could be returned to the FS provider with payment. Orders would be passed on to the secondary suppliers for order fulfilment, and payments would also be transferred to the secondary supplier, minus the commission element retained by the FS provider. The process model for this would be slightly different of course, while the net result is similar, and could be considered along with other alternatives. In this way entrepreneurs, process managers and system analysts can review the different alternatives, ensuring that the systems they are each envisaging are consistent and evaluating how well the different alternatives would achieve the business model objectives.

Clearly, in developing these business models this approach provides an integrating vehicle for all managers, entrepreneurs and technologists to surface and share their views and perspectives, and thereby offers an explicit process for assessing and evaluating possible e-Business models. The framework proposed in this paper reinforces to all players in the e-Business development process that sustainable e-Business models should encompass the traditional thinking of business strategy (RBV, Value Chain Analysis, Porter's Five Forces, etc). That is, the business model for e-Business being envisioned and development by the managers and the developed strategy must be undertaken with clear understanding of the organizational, economic and technical resources of the organization and how they are managed, allocated and controlled to provide value to the organization. Moreover, managers must also vision the impact the e-Business model will have on the environment they are attempting to compete in, and the role and status they hold within their value chain and the competing value chains. This must be done alongside a detailed understanding of the necessary underlying business processes and ICT infrastructures to support the model under consideration.

3.7 Conclusion

Criticism of the business models for e-Business has largely been centred around the fact that they tend to be passive snapshot characterizations of the various ways in which information and communication technologies (ICT) can be exploited profitably in the creation of new businesses. As such the new e-Business models may be modifications of existing business models but with the advantages of, e.g. 24×7 access by customers, or may genuinely reflect new and innovative ways of doing creating value. A further criticism is that they have not generally been evaluated in any formal way, in the 'so what ...?' sense. That is, they have not been tested to see if they can produce deeper insights into the notion of an effective e-Business or if they lead to the development of the more detail models or descriptions that would be necessary in the creation of an actual business. If the set of models serves as a form of taxonomy or is intended as a stimulus for further thinking, then this is not necessarily a problem. However, if the models are to be used to support the development of a shared vision for the creation of an actual business and as the basis for designing and implementing the necessary business processes and information infrastructures, then the models must be able to lead to the next phase in business strategy formulation and system operationalization.

This chapter attempts to rectify this by introducing triple pair flow model construct to represent the various business models for e-Business to support the gaining of a greater insight into the complexity of e-Business strategy implementation. This approach captures the casual relationships and rationalizes the complexity of an organization's resources and its environment. The process maps the strategic vision of different e-Business models onto a generic double pair representation of the critical flows of information, products and/or services, and money that would occur in any electronically actuated business. In this way it provides a number of benefits to a team involved in the creation of such a business. Specifically, it:

■ acts as a cognitive framework for surfacing the detail of an e-Business vision, beyond a simple passive characterization;

■ provides a transparent way for the entrepreneurial model to be visualized as the set of business processes that represent the management of the flows essential to the conduct of the business;

■ demonstrates how ICT systems must be configured to make the business work.

Furthermore, by serving as a single representation of these three perspectives, it should enable models to be more easily shared, allow easier evaluations of a company's capability to design and deliver a working system for its own vision, and enable a more seamless move from strategic vision to detailed system design.

This is achieved by a particular use of system dynamics diagramming techniques which are established in the literature as valuable tools in facilitating the surfacing and sharing of mental models, and as a powerful catalyst in the development of consensus within groups. In system dynamics studies, stock-flow diagrams are typically used as the basis for the development of dynamic simulation models (the diagrams can be created by an icon-based graphics interface for a number of specialist commercial simulation software packages). The triple pair models could therefore be converted into simulation models without further structural analysis by the quantification of all relationships. The simulators could then be further used to support strategy formulation and evaluation by playing out, over time, scenarios based on various e-Business model options, and in the refinement of the actual business processes required once the business model is selected.

Importantly though, this approach draws on the foundations of strategy formulation and can provide a good theoretical basis for the formulation and implementation of e-Business strategies that is often lacking in this area.

References and Further Reading

Abdel-Hamid, T. and S. Madnick (1989). 'Lessons Learned from Modeling the Dynamics of Software Project Management.' *Communications of the ACM* **32**: 1426–1438.

Abdel-Hamid, T. and S. Madnick (1991). *Software Project Dynamics: Potential, An Integrated Approach*. Eaglewood Cliffs, NJ, Prentice-Hall.

Afuah, A. and C. L. Tucci (2001). *Internet Business Models and Strategies: Text and Cases*. Boston, MA, McGraw-Hill.

Alt, R. and H. D. Zimmermann (2001). 'Preface Introduction to Special Section – Business Models.' *Electronic Markets* **11**: 3–9.

Andrews, K. (1987). *The Concept of Corporate Strategy*. Homewood, IL, Irwin.

Ansoff, I. (1965). *Corporate Strategy*. New York, McGraw-Hill.

Applegate, L. (2001). 'Emerging eBusiness Models: Lessons Learnt from the Field.' *Harvard Business Review*.

Barney, J. (1991). 'Firm Resources and Sustained Competitive Advantage.' *Journal of Management* **17**: 99–120.

Barrenechea, M. and L. Ellison (2000). *eBusiness or Out of Business: Oracle's Roadmap for Profiting in the New Economy*. McGraw-Hill Trade.

Cameron, D. and P. Joyce (2001). *The Use and Adoption of Electronic Banking by SMEs in Australia*, 6th Annual Collector – Conference on Electronic Commerce," *Coffs Harbour*. Australia.

Chandra, C., S. Kumar and A. Smirnov (2002). 'E-management of Supply Chain: General Models Taxonomy.' *Human Systems Management* **22**: 95–113.

Chesbrough, H. and R. S. Rosenbloom (2001). 'The Role of the Business Model in Capturing Value from Innovation; Evidence from the Xerox Corporation's Technology Spinoff Companies.' *Industrial and Corporate Change* **11**: 529–555.

Christensen, C. (1997). *The Innovator's Delimma*. Boston, MA, Harvard Business Press.

Forrester, J. (1961). *Industrial Dynamics*. Cambridge, MIT Press (Republished by Pegasus Communications, Waltham Mass.).

Hammer, M. and J. Champy (1993). *Reengineering the Corporation: A Manifesto for Business Revolution*. New York, NY, Harper Business.

Hedman, J. and T. Kalling (2003). 'The Business Model Concept: Theoretical Underpinnings and Empirical Illustrations.' *European Journal of Information Systems* **12**: 49–59.

Joyce, P. and G. Winch (2003). *Thoughts on Codifying Business Models and Process Models in eBusiness Design,* 4th International Conference on Web Commerce: Web conference, Perth, Western Australia.

Kaplan, R. S. and D. P. Norton (1996). *The Balanced Scorecard: Translating Strategy into Action.* Boston, MA, Harvard Business School Press.

McCray, G. and T. Clark (1999). 'Using System Dynamics to anticipate the organizational impacts of outsourcing.' *System Dynamics Review* 15: 345–374.

Mintzberg, H. (1978). 'Patterns in Strategy Formulation.' *Management Science* 24: 934–948.

Oliva, R., J. Sterman and M. Giese (2003). 'Limits to Growth in the New Economy: Exploring the 'Get Big Fast' Strategy in e-Commerce.' *System Dynamics Review* 19: 83–118.

Porter, M. (1980). *Competitive Strategy.* New York, Free Press.

Porter, M. (1985). *Competitive Advantage.* New York, Free Press.

Porter, M. (2001). 'Strategy and the Internet.' *Harvard Business Review* 79: 63–78.

Powell, S., M. Schwaninge and C. Trimble (2001). 'Measurement and Control of Business Processes.' *System Dynamics Review* 17: 63–92.

Prahalad, C. and R. Bettis (1986). 'The Dominant Logic: A New Linkage Between Diversity and Performance.' *Strategic Management Journal* 7: 485–501.

Rappa, M. (2003). *Business Models on the Web.*

Senge, P. (1990). *The Fifth Discipline: The Art and Practice of the Learning Organization.* New York, Doubleday.

Sterman, J. D. (2000). *Business Dynamics: Systems Thinking and Modelling for a Complex World.* Irwin/McGraw-Hill.

Timmers, P. (1998). 'Business Models for Electronic Markets.' *Electronic Markets* 8: 2–8.

Weill, P. and M. Vitale (2001). *Place to Space.* Boston, MA, Harvard Business Press.

Weill, P. and M. Vitale (2002). 'What IT Infrastructure Capabilities are Needed to Implement eBusiness Models?' *MIS Quarterly Executive* 1: 17–34.

4 An ontology for e-Business models

Alexander Osterwalder and Yves Pigneur

4.1 Introduction

The terms 'business models' and 'new business models' probably belong to the most misinterpreted terms in e-Business. Nevertheless, innovative business models are constantly emerging in electronic commerce and can become a major stake in the e-Business game (Bloch et al., 1996; Maître and Aladjidi, 1999; Robinson et al., 2000). It is even possible to patent them in some countries. Understanding new business models and helping to design them are important research issues, not so well covered until now.

Business models have become more complex with the emergence of new and affordable information and communication technologies (ICTs). Companies increasingly act in networks and offer complex value propositions through a multitude of distribution channels. For managers it is ever harder to keep track of how their companies really work and how and where profit is generated. Of course every manager and entrepreneur does have an intuitive understanding of how his business works and how value is created. In other words he does have an intuitive understanding of the company's business model, but even though this business model influences all important decisions, in many cases she or he is rarely able to communicate it in a clear and simple way (Linder and Cantrell, 2000). And how can one decide on a particular business issue or change it, if it is not clearly understood by the parties involved?

In this chapter we tackle the business model concept and construct and outline an ontology (rigorous framework) for e-Business models based on an extensive literature review. We aim to show how the fusion of the ideas in the business model literature and the ideas of enterprise ontologies creates an appropriate basis for the development of a range of new management tools in the e-Business domain. By merging the conceptually rich business model approach with the more rigorous ontological approach and by applying them to e-Business, we achieve an appropriate foundation for tools that would allow the understanding, sharing and communication, change, measuring and simulation of e-Business models.

In the next section we give an overview of related work. As shown by Linder and Cantrell (2000), most people speak about business models when they really only mean parts of a business model. We think that the existing business model literature essentially attacks one, two or rarely all of the following three elements, which make up a business model: revenue and product aspects, business actor and network aspects and finally, marketing-specific aspects.

We propose an e-Business model ontology that highlights the relevant e-Business issues and elements that firms have to think of, in order to operate successfully in the Internet era. An ontology is simply a rigorously defined framework that provides a shared and common understanding of a domain that can be communicated between people and heterogeneous and widely spread application systems (Fensel, 2001).

We suggest adopting a framework, which emphasizes the following areas and questions that a business model has to address:

- *Product innovation*: What business the company is in, the product innovation and the value proposition offered to the market?

- *Customer relationship*: Who the company's target customers are, how it delivers them the products and services, and how it builds a strong relationship with them?

- *Infrastructure management*: How the company efficiently performs infrastructure or logistics issues, with whom, and as what kind of virtual enterprise? and finally,

- *Financials*: What is the revenue model (transaction, subscription/ membership, advertising, commission and licensing), the cost model (cost of goods sold, operating expenses for R&D, sales and marketing, general and administrative) and the business model's sustainability?

4.2 Definitions and taxonomies

The term 'business model' is a buzzword with no commonly accepted meaning (see also Chapters 2 and 3). In this chapter we shall try to change this, define the concept and show that business models represent a way of improving doing business under uncertainty. As explained by Petrovic et al. (2001), a business model describes the logic of a 'business system' for creating value, that lies behind the actual processes. In this chapter we use the following working definition for business models, which will serve as a starting point for the more rigorous and detailed e-Business model ontology: a business model is a description of the value a company offers to one or several segments of customers and the architecture of the firm and its network of partners for creating, marketing and delivering this value and relationship capital, in order to generate profitable and sustainable revenue streams.

There exists a growing literature on (e-)Business models by academics and consultants. Some focus upon 'Internet business models' and others, 'business models for the web', but they all embrace aspects of the business logic of a firm with a strong IT-component. The early authors have mainly written about the classification of models in different categories (Timmers, 1998; Tapscott et al., 2000; Rappa, 2001). By contrast, the latest literature has started decomposing business models into their 'atomic' elements (Hamel, 2000; Afuah and Tucci, 2001; Petrovic et al., 2001; Rayport and Jaworski, 2001; Weill and Vitale, 2001). This section gives an overview of the existing literature considering different aspects of business models, which are revenue- and product-specific, business actor- and network-specific and marketing-specific. This review is necessary in order to provide a sound ontology of the e-Business model domain and to understand what should comprise a business model.

Revenue/product aspects.   Rappa (2001) and Tapscott et al. (2000) provide a taxonomy of e-Business models rather than an explanation of what elements such a model contains. Both authors concentrate on revenue- or product-specific aspects.

Business actor and network aspects.   Timmers (1998) provides a taxonomy in which he classifies e-Business models according to their degree of innovation and their functional integration. Gordijn et al. (2001) provide a richer and more rigorous business model framework, which is based on a generic value-oriented ontology specifying what is in an e-Business model. This framework even allows the graphical representation and understanding of value flows between the several actors of a model. Afuah and Tucci (2001) and quite similarly Amit and Zott (2001) outline a value- and actor-centric framework that provides a list of business model components.

Marketing-specific aspects.   Hamel (2000) identifies four main business model components that are related to each other and are decomposed into different sub-elements. The main contribution of this methodology, as well as the one of Rayport and Jaworski (2001) is a view of the overall picture of a firm. Petrovic et al. (2001) divide a business model into sub-models, which describe the logic of a business system for creating value that lies behind the actual processes. Weill and Vitale (2001) also suggest a subdivision in to so-called atomic e-Business models, which are analysed according to a number of basic components.

4.3 e-Business model ontology

As outlined above, business models are constructed around products, customers, infrastructures and financial issues. We understand these business models as the conceptual link between strategy, business organization and information systems (see Figure 4.1). As there is often quite a substantial understanding gap between these 'worlds', the concept of business models could serve as a federator. Strategy people position the company, define and formulate objectives and goals, whereas business process and information system designers have to understand and implement this information. In order to guarantee a smooth strategy execution, firms require a very clear communication of concepts and understandings between the implicated parties. This is where rigorously defined business models come into play. By using an ontological approach to e-Business modelling, one can create a shared and common understanding of the domain and facilitate communication between people and heterogeneous and widely spread application systems (Fensel, 2001). As illustrated in Figure 4.1, we perceive business models as the conceptual implementation (blueprint) of a business strategy that allows to align strategy, business organization and information systems and represents the foundation for the implementation of business processes and information systems. The role of the manager is to adapt a company's business model to external forces, such as competition, legal, social or technological change and changes in customer demand.

We think the understanding and use of conceptual e-Business models is essential in an increasingly dynamic and uncertain business environment for the following reasons:

1   The process of modelling social systems or an ontology – such as an e-Business model – helps to identify and understand the relevant

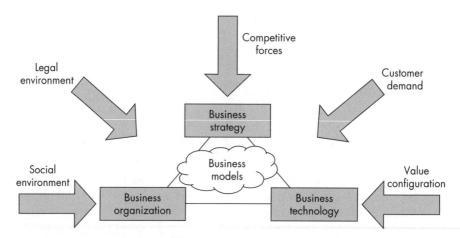

Figure 4.1:   Environment, business models, strategy, process and information systems.

elements in a specific domain and the relationships between them (Morecroft, 1994; Ushold and King, 1995).

2 The use of formalized e-Business models helps managers easily communicate and share their understanding of an e-Business among other stakeholders (Fensel, 2001).

3 Mapping and using e-Business models as a foundation for discussion facilitates change. Business model designers can easily modify certain elements of an existing e-Business model (Petrovic et al., 2001).

4 A formalized e-Business model can help to identify the relevant measures to follow in an e-Business, similarly to the Balanced Scorecard Approach (Kaplan and Norton, 1992).

5 e-Business models can help managers simulate e-Businesses and learn about them. This is a way of doing risk-free experiments, without endangering an organization (Sterman, 2000).

The e-Business model ontology outlined in this chapter is a conceptual tool that contains a set of elements and their relationships and allows expressing the business logic of a specific firm. Our ontology has in some ways been inspired by the different enterprise ontology projects described in academic literature (Toronto Virtual Enterprise, Enterprise Ontology, Core Enterprise Ontology) (Bertolazzi et al., 2001). These ontologies mainly concentrate on processes and organizational representation. The work of the Edinburgh Group (Ushold and King, 1995), e.g. is aimed at proposing an enterprise ontology, i.e. a set of carefully defined concepts that are widely used for describing enterprises in general and that can serve as a stable basis for specifying software requirements. The focus of our work is on the logic and concepts of value creation, at a higher level of abstraction, which is the business model.

At the first level (see Figure 4.2), our ontology is broken down into four simple pillars, which are the 'what', the 'who', the 'how' (Markides,

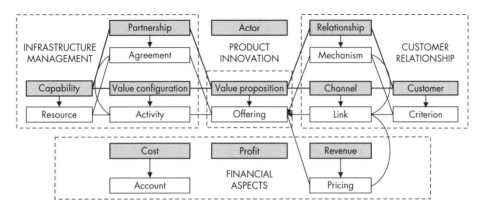

Figure 4.2: Business model ontology.

1999) and the 'how much' of a firm. In other words, these pillars allow to express what a company offers, who it targets with this, how this can be realized and how much can be earned by doing it.

These pillars can be translated into four main business model blocks that are then further decomposed: Firstly, the PRODUCT INNOVATION block, which describes the value proposition of a firm. Secondly, the CUSTOMER RELATIONSHIP block, which describes how a firm gets in touch with its customers and what kind of relationships it wants to establish with them. Thirdly, the INFRASTRUCTURE MANAGEMENT block that describes what activities, resources and partners are necessary to provide the first two blocks. And finally, the FINANCIAL ASPECTS block, which describes the revenue flows and the pricing mechanisms of a firm, or, in other words, how a company makes money through the other three blocks.

4.3.1 Product innovation and value proposition

ICT has had a major impact on product innovation. This comes mainly from the separation of information from its physical carrier and its ease of distribution. Look at this following simple illustration. A book is composed of content and paper. By separating content and carrier the book can be diffused through a variety of electronic or bricks-and-mortar channels. Imagine you were in a local book store and you were looking for something they do not have in stock. If the store had so-called print-on-demand facilities they could download the content and print out the book in a matter of minutes. A similar concept is very common in some music stores. Customers can chose song titles out of a large data base and get them burnt on a CD immediately. In fact, many people already download or buy music over the Internet directly to their homes. In more economic terms these examples mean that one is not limited to the economics of things anymore, but enters the 'new economics of information' (Evans and Wurster, 1997). This simply signifies that a company can easily reach a large number of customers and provide them with very rich information in form of multimedia data, personalized information or customized products. One company that realized this very quickly was Federal Express. In 1994 when they launched their Web site, they were the first to offer online package status tracking that allowed each and every customers to follow their package on its delivery. While this has not profoundly changed the shipping industry, other sectors, such as the music and film industry risk to be completely transformed because their products can be entirely digitized. An example of the trembling fundaments of the music industry was the notorious fight of the major record companies against the file-trading platform called Napster (Rupp and Esthier, 2003). But the majors' traditional business models are increasingly challenged (Durlacher, 2001). In general, companies that are not able to constantly innovate risk to fall into the commoditization trap because successful products are rapidly copied by an ever more global competition. Recent research shows that superior market performers are essentially companies that are able to innovate and constantly transform their value proposition (Kim and Mauborgne, 1997; Chen and Kai-ling Ho, 2002).

Product innovation covers all aspects of what a firm offers its customers. This comprises not only the company's bundles of products and services but the manner in which it differentiates itself from its competitors. We conceptualize this with a formal approach to value propositions (see Table 4.1 and Figure 4.3), which consists of the VALUE PROPOSITION component and its elementary OFFERING(s).

A VALUE PROPOSITION can be understood as the statements of benefits that are delivered by the firm to its external constituencies (Bagchi and Tulskie, 2000). We describe it as the definition of how items of value, such as products and services as well as complementary value-added services, are packaged and offered to fulfill customer needs (Kambil et al., 1997). The VALUE PROPOSITION is an overall view of a firm's bundle of products and services that together represent a value for a specific CUSTOMER SEGMENT. It describes the way a firm

Table 4.1: Value Proposition

A VALUE PROPOSITION is an overall view of a firm's bundle of products and services that together represent a value for a specific CUSTOMER SEGMENT
 – it represents value for *TARGET CUSTOMER(s)*
 – it is based on *CAPABILITY(ies)*

It is composed of a set of one-or-more **OFFERING**(s)

An elementary OFFERING describes a part of a firm's bundle of products and services
 – it has a DESCRIPTION
 – it has a REASONING {USE, RISK REDUCTION, EFFORT REDUCTION}
 – it has a LIFE CYCLE {CREATION, APPROPRIATION, CONSUMPTION, RENEWAL, TRANSFER}
 – it has a VALUE LEVEL {ME-TOO, INNOVATIVE INNOVATION, EXCELLENCE, INNOVATION}
 – it has a PRICE LEVEL {FREE, ECONOMY, MARKET, HIGH-END}

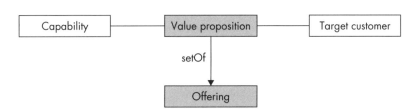

Figure 4.3: Value proposition.

differentiates itself from its competitors and is the reason why customers buy from a certain firm and not from another.

While the VALUE PROPOSITION element gives an aggregated view of the value a company offers its customers, its elementary OFFERING(s), describe the different aspects of a VALUE PROPOSITION. By outlining these different components a firm can better observe how it situates itself compared to its competitors. This will allow a company to innovate, to differentiate and to achieve a competitive position. An OFFERING describes a part of a firm's bundle of products and services. It illustrates a specific product, service, or even product or service feature and outlines its assumed value to the customer. An OFFERING is characterized by the properties DESCRIPTION, REASONING, LIFE CYCLE, VALUE LEVEL and PRICE LEVEL.

The attribute REASONING captures the reasoning on why the firm thinks its VALUE PROPOSITION could be valuable to the customer. Normally value is created either through use (e.g. driving a car), reduction of the customer's risk (e.g. car insurance) or by making his life easier through reduction of his efforts (e.g. home delivery of groceries).

Besides reasoning on its sense a value proposition should also be studied over its entire LIFE CYCLE (Anderson and Narus, 1998). Therefore we create an attribute, which has the goal of capturing at which one of the five stages of the value life cycle (based on (Ives, 1999)) an elementary OFFERING creates value. This can be at the moment of the value creation (e.g. customization), its appropriation (e.g. Amazon's one-click shopping), its consumption (e.g. listening to music), its renewal (e.g. software updates) or its transfer (e.g. disposal of old computers, selling of used books).

Furthermore, we suggest quantifying the value and price of an OFFERING. Measuring the VALUE LEVEL of a company's offer allows a firm to compare itself to its competitors. To do this we have created a qualitative value scale that relates to the value offered by competitors rather than using a quantitative scale that ranges from low to high. Our measure goes from me-too value (e.g. commodities), over innovative imitation (e.g. pocket pc) and excellence (e.g. Swiss watches) to innovation (e.g. Viagra in the 1990s).

This attribute PRICE LEVEL compares the value proposition price to the competition's one. The scale goes from free (e.g. online newspapers) over economy (e.g. Southwest, EasyJet, RyanAir) and market (e.g. stocks) to high-end (e.g. Rolex).

By capturing the two elementary characteristics of an offering, the VALUE LEVEL and the LEVEL (Anderson and Narus, 1998), a company can draw a so-called value map (Kambil et al., 1997). This helps defining its relative position in an industry along the price-value axis. Such a map also contains the value frontier, which defines the maximum value (performance of a value proposition) currently feasible for any given cost (minimum price of a value proposition). Market leaders will either extend and rethink their position in the value map to differentiate themselves from their competitors or radically innovate to shift the value frontier.

Mini case: easyMoney.com

easyMoney.com is a credit card company founded by Haji-Ioannou who has also created easyJet, easyCar, easyInternetCafé, easyValue.com and easyCinema.com. Its value proposition consists of customized credit cards at attractive prices. Through transparent pricing, clear product offerings, the use of ICT and avoiding cross-subsidies between products and customers the credit card client only pays for what he gets.

Customers design their own credit card on easyMoney.com's Web site according to their personal needs. With the so-called Card Builder they can select their own individual combination of interest rate, cashback rewards, annual fee and servicing options. Credit card costs depend directly from these choices and the customer only pays for what he gets. Through customization he can reduce his financial risk of paying for options he does not need nor use. Applications are made electronically via easyMoney.com's Web site. This reduces the customer's effort and lets him apply conveniently from his home or workplace PC. The easyMoney.com credit card is accepted at over 19.1 million locations worldwide displaying the MasterCard logo. By configuring his own credit card the customer benefits from attractive prices and he only pays for what he gets. The customer has the possibility to change the combination of the features of his card up to three times a year without charge. This helps him to avoid the risk of not being able to adopt credit card options to his actual needs.

Table 4.2 gives an overview of the VALUE PROPOSITION of easyMoney.com and its elementary OFFERING(s).

4.3.2 Customer relationship

This business model block refers to the way a firm goes to market, how it actually reaches its customers and how it interacts with them. ICT has traditionally had a very strong influence on the ways companies organize their customer relationships. The use of databases for managing customer-related information, the introduction of scanners in supermarkets, the offering of toll-free numbers connected to call centres or the use of new distribution and communication channels are just some of the numerous applications that have transformed customer relationship.

Especially the dissemination of the Internet has further increased the range of possibilities of interacting with customers. Generally, it can be said that the falling cost and improving performance of ICT has contributed to the facilitation of customer-related information gathering and customer- and product-related information diffusion. Data warehousing, data mining and business intelligence are just some of the technologies that have allowed managers to gain insight on their

Table 4.2: The core VALUE PROPOSITION of easyMoney.com

	Card builder	Personalized credit card	Online account management
Description	With the so-called Card Builder, customers can select their own individual combination of interest rate, cashback rewards, annual fee and servicing options. They build their own personalized credit card.	The easyMoney.com credit card is accepted at over 19.1 million locations worldwide displaying the MasterCard logo and is financially attractive.	Customers can handle their account online and receive their statements electronically. At every moment they have an up to date overview of their account history.
Reasoning	A customized credit card reduces the financial risk of paying for options the customer does not need nor use.	By configuring his own credit card the customer benefits from attractive prices because he pays for what he gets.	Clients can conveniently manage their accounts from their PC and profit from lower handling costs.
Value life cycle	Value creation	Value consumption	Value consumption
Value level	Innovation	Innovation	Innovation/me-too
Price level	Free	Economy	Free

customers buying behaviour and improve customer relationship. Exploiting customer information can allow managers to discover new and profitable business opportunities and to ameliorate customer satisfaction. ICT also helps companies to provide their customers and prospects with ever richer information (Evans and Wurster, 1997) and offer them innovative ways of interaction and thus contribute to the firms value proposition.

Finally, in order to serve customers better or to reach new markets companies introduce new distribution and communication channels, such as the Internet or mobile phones, but also new relationship mechanisms, such as personalization and trust.

The CUSTOMER RELATIONSHIP block covers all customer-related aspects. This comprises the choice of a firm's TARGET CUSTOMERs, the CHANNELs through which it gets in touch with them and the kind of RELATIONSHIPs the company wants to establish with its customers. The CUSTOMER RELATIONSHIP describes how and to whom it delivers its VALUE PROPOSITION, which is the firm's bundle of products and services.

Target customers

Selecting a company's target customers is all about segmentation. Effective segmentation enables a company to allocate investment resources to target

Table 4.3: Target customer

A TARGET CUSTOMER segment defines the type of customers a company wants to address.
– it receives a VALUE PROPOSITION(s)

It is composed of a set of one-or-more **CRITERION**(s)

An elementary CRITERION defines the characteristics of a TARGET CUSTOMER group.

customers that will be most attracted by its value proposition. The most general distinction of target customers exists between business and/or individual customers, commonly referred to as business-to-business (B2B) and business-to-consumer (B2C). The TARGET CUSTOMER definition will also help a firm define through which channels it effectively wants to reach its clients (see Table 4.3 and Figure 4.4).

Segmentation has a long history and goes back to the 1950s (Winter, 1984). But even nowadays, in the one-to-one marketing era, where customers can potentially be addressed one by one, market segmentation keeps its value. In fact, ICT helps companies make the strategic choice to target their market at any level between 'mass' and 'one-to-one' by balancing revenue against cost (Wedel, 2001). Especially post hoc market segmentation techniques like data mining, multidimensional segmentation and data clustering with artificial neural networks can lead to more efficient marketing and enhance profitability (Neal and Wurst, 2001). With the expansion of reach through ICT, such as the Internet, companies increasingly target not only groups that are geographically localizable, but also widely dispersed online communities with common characteristics. Hagel and Armstrong (1997) divide these into communities of transaction, interest, fantasy and relationship.

In order to refine a customer segmentation companies decompose a TARGET CUSTOMER segment into a set of characteristics, which we call CRITERION. These could be of geographical or socio-demographic nature (Kotler, 1999).

Distribution channels

Generally speaking, distribution channels are the connection between a firm's VALUE PROPOSITIONs and its TARGET CUSTOMERs (see Table 4.4 and Figure 4.4).

A CHANNEL allows a company to deliver value to its customers, either directly, e.g. through a sales force or over a Web site, or indirectly through intermediaries, such as resellers, brokers or cybermediaries. The topic of channels has become exciting in recent years with the proliferation of new successful channels and the promise of a stream of more new ones resulting from advances in ICT (Wyner, 1995). But this magnitude of change demands a strategic perspective that views channel

Table 4.4: Distribution channel

A CHANNEL describes how a company gets in touch with its customers. Its purpose is to make the right quantities of the right products or services available at the right place, at the right time to the right people (Pitt et al., 1999) – subject of course, to the constraints of cost, investment and flexibility (Anderson et al., 1997).
 – it delivers a VALUE PROPOSITION(s)
 – it delivers to a TARGET CUSTOMER(s)

It is composed of a set of one-or-more **LINK(s)**

A channel LINK describes a part of a firm's CHANNEL and illustrates specific marketing roles. The channel LINK(s) of the different channels may sometimes be interrelated, in order to exploit cross-channel synergies. In addition to the traditional role of simply delivering value, modern channels and their channel links increasingly have a potential for value creation and thus contribute to a firm's VALUE PROPOSITION (Wyner, 1995).
 – it has attributes inherited from VALUE PROPOSITION OFFERING
 – it is delivered by an ACTOR(s)

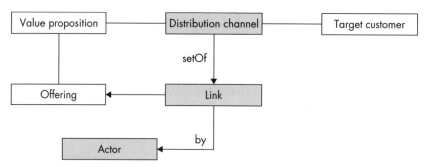

Figure 4.4: Distribution channel.

decisions as choices from a continually changing array of alternatives for achieving market converge and competitive advantage (Anderson et al., 1997). ICT-based channels, and particularly the Internet, have a great potential to complement rather than to cannibalize a business's existing channels (Porter, 2001; Steinfield et al., 2002). However, selling through several channels simultaneously eventually causes channel conflict when they compete to reach the same set of customers (Bucklin et al., 1997). Therefore, understanding channels through a conceptual approach becomes ever more important.

While the CHANNEL element gives an aggregated view of how a company reaches its customers it can be further decomposed into its channel LINK(s). We do this because channels are not the basic building blocks of a marketing systems; the channel tasks or roles, which we call LINKs are (Moriarty and Moran, 1990). Since a channel LINK can be considered as a part of the VALUE PROPOSITION or as an OFFERING, it

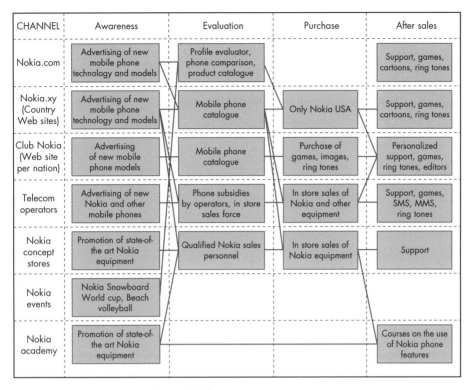

CHANNEL	Awareness	Evaluation	Purchase	After sales
Nokia.com	Advertising of new mobile phone technology and models	Profile evaluator, phone comparison, product catalogue		Support, games, cartoons, ring tones
Nokia.xy (Country Web sites)	Advertising of new mobile phone technology and models	Mobile phone catalogue	Only Nokia USA	Support, games, cartoons, ring tones
Club Nokia (Web site per nation)	Advertising of new mobile phone models	Mobile phone catalogue	Purchase of games, images, ring tones	Personalized support, games, ring tones, editors
Telecom operators	Advertising of new Nokia and other mobile phones	Phone subsidies by operators, in store sales force	In store sales of Nokia and other equipment	Support, games, SMS, MMS, ring tones
Nokia concept stores	Promotion of state-of-the art Nokia equipment	Qualified Nokia sales personnel	In store sales of Nokia equipment	Support
Nokia events	Nokia Snowboard World cup, Beach volleyball			
Nokia academy	Promotion of state-of-the art Nokia equipment			Courses on the use of Nokia phone features

Figure 4.5: Channel matrix at Nokia mobile phone.

has the same kind of properties: REASONING, VALUE LEVEL AND PRICE LEVEL with the same meaning.

The channel concept covers the customer's entire CUSTOMER BUYING CYCLE (based on (Ives and Learmonth, 1984; Ives, 1999; Muther, 2002)). This reflects all possible contact points between a supplier and a customer (Muther, 2002). The customer buying cycle is divided into four phases, namely the customer's awareness, his evaluation of the company's VALUE PROPOSTION, the moment of purchase and after sales.

In Figure 4.5 we propose a tool for channel design and management that is based on the customer buying cycle (Ives and Learmonth, 1984; Ives, 1999; Muther, 2002) and the so-called Hybrid Grid (Moriarty and Moran, 1990; Dolan, 2000).

This tool consists of a matrix with the different phases of the customer buying cycle on the one axis and a company's range of CHANNELs on the other axis. We illustrate this in Figure 4.5 with a simplified example of the mobile phone manufacturer Nokia, who has a wide range of virtual, physical, owned and partner CHANNELs. The boxes in Figure 4.5 which you find at the intersection of the CHANNELs and the four phases of the customer buying cycle represent the aggregated channel LINKs of the company. These channel LINKs are connected to each other inside and/or across different CHANNELs. Nokia's most important sales channels are the national mobile phone network operators, which sell the bulk of its phones, and, the various electronics or other retailers. But the other channels, such as Nokia.com, Club Nokia or Nokia Academy (a place to learn about Nokia phone features) also have a very important role to play. Club Nokia, for instance, re-establishes a direct communication link between Nokia and the final customer, which has traditionally been the operators' sphere of influence. This link has an enormous value in loyalizing customers, selling them additional products and collecting information on their behaviour.

Customer equity

Besides the customer interaction points (i.e. channels), companies must also analyse the nature of the interactions, because they affect the strength of the relationship a company builds with its customers. But as interactions come at a given cost, firms must carefully define what kind of relationship they want to establish with what kind of customer. Profits from CUSTOMER RELATIONSHIPs (see Table 4.5 and Figure 4.6)

Table 4.5: Customer equity and relationship

The CUSTOMER RELATIONSHIP component describes the relationship a company establishes with a target CUSTOMER SEGMENT for contributing to the customer equity of the company by improving acquisition, retention and add-on selling.
– it concerns a VALUE PROPOSITION(s)
– it is established with TARGET CUSTOMER(s)
– it contributes to CUSTOMER EQUITY {ACQUISITION, RETENTION, ADD-ON SELLING}

Set of one-or-more **MECHANISM**(s)

A relationship MECHANISM describes the function it accomplishes between the company and its customers. It may also be a channel LINK or a part of the VALUE PROPOSITION
– it has a FUNCTION {PERSONALIZATION, TRUST, BRAND}
– it inherits from the channel LINK component

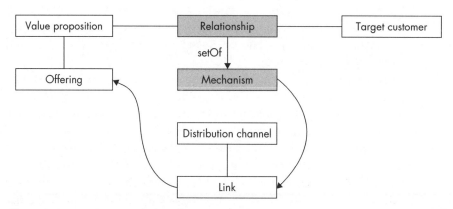

Figure 4.6: Customer equity and relationship.

are the lifeblood of all businesses. These profits can be achieved through the acquisition of new customers, the enhancement of profitability of existing customers and the extension of the duration of existing customer relationships (Grant and Schlesinger, 1995). Companies must analyse customer data in order to evaluate the type of customer they want to seduce and acquire, is profitable and worth spending retention efforts and is likely to be subject to add-on selling (Blattberg et al., 2001). The trend to move from simple transactions to more complex customer relations makes sense, since an arsenal of new ICT tools has made this possible at reasonable costs.

Maximizing CUSTOMER EQUITY must be one of the main goals of a company. In other words a firm must understand how it can get most out of its customers by optimizing its strategy in acquiring and retaining customers and selling them additional value propositions.

Acquisition.   It is very straightforward to say that companies must acquire customers to do business. Even firms with high retention rates lose customers and thus must continuously acquire new customers to stay in business. As customer acquisition is a very expensive affair and because the relationship developed during the acquisition phase strongly influences retention and add-on selling it must be carefully managed and evaluated. Hewlett Packard, for instance, sells very cheap inkjet printers and makes money from ink cartridges. Many mobile phone operators subsidize new and expensive mobile phone models to make them affordable to customers and cash in on the new services they can sell them (e.g. data and multimedia services).

Retention.   The goal of customer retention is to leverage customer acquisition investments. As customer acquisition is normally more expensive than retention it makes sense to find ways and mechanisms to extend the duration of the relationship between firm and customer. Of course the focus must be set mainly on the most profitable customers. Blattberg et al. (2001) mention the following drivers that affect customer retention: customer expectation versus delivered quality, the value of the good or service, product uniqueness and suitability, loyalty mechanisms, ease of purchase, customer service and ease of exit. In our model we consider only the mechanisms that can be directly assigned to retaining customers, such as loyalty programs, customer defection programs or installing switching cost. For example, a customer changing airlines will lose his loyalty 'miles', while a customer leaving Amazon.com will have to re-enter his personal data, re-create his wish lists, and re-create a profile for personalized book recommendations based on purchase history.

Add-on selling.   Add-on selling is the activity associated with selling any additional products and services to current customers (Blattberg et al., 2001). These products can, but do not necessarily have to be related to each other. getAbstracts.com, a start-up that sells abstracts of business books online also allows its customers to purchase these books directly over their Web site. Telecommunication companies and recently also mobile phone operators try to increase their revenues by selling their existing customers additional data services.

A set of MECHANISMS characterizes the nature of the relationship. Each MECHANISM has a FUNCTION in the relationship building with a company's customers. It can personalize a relationship, contribute to customer trust, or contribute to brand building.

Personalization. Historically, vendors had a personal relationship with their customers (e.g. the Mom and Pop grocery store where the shopkeeper knows every client personally and is familiar with his needs and habits). But the size of today's companies, their lower employee-to-customer ratios and the high turnover among employees has made personal one-to-one human relationships between customer and supplier rare. ICT now allows companies to re-introduce a more personalized relationship with their customers at a reasonable cost. Customer profiles with historical buying behaviour, tastes and needs and their contact history with the firm are stored in large databases. Afterwards, this data can be used to simulate a kind of Mom and Pop store relationship.

An important field of personalized mechanisms is one-to-one marketing. This is nothing else than tailoring marketing activities to specific customers, their needs, behaviour and their particular transaction history. Imagine the impact on customer loyalty of an airline customer that by accident has taken two delayed flights the same week. Would not he be pleased if his airline were able to detect this incidence and address him personally with an excuse letter or maybe even a goodie? Another field of one-to-one marketing are so-called personalized product recommending systems, which are based on attributes, item-to-item correlation or user-to-user correlation (Schafer et al., 2000). The first technique is based on a set of rules that makes recommendations derived from a customer's profile of attributes. The second technique identifies items frequently found in association with items in which a customer has expressed interest. The third technique, also known as collaborative filtering and to date the most powerful method (Sarwar et al., 2000), recommends products to a customer based on the correlation between that customer and other customers who have a similar purchase behaviour.

Trust. 'Trust of a party A in a party B for a service X is the measurable belief of A in that B will behave dependably for a specified period within a specified context' (Dimitrakos, 2001). This shows that the notion of expectation is central to the concept of trust (Jones, 2002). In a business environment that has become increasingly global, transactions more and more virtual and where the implicated parties do not necessarily know each other anymore before conducting business, new trust mechanism have gained importance. ICT offers a large range of innovative or improved mechanisms to build trust in e-Business environments (Friedman et al., 2000) by improving the expected output of a transaction.

Especially the role of reputation in contributing to trust has received a boost through ICT. The large body of literature on this subject shows how reputation is based on independent user communities (Hagel III and Armstrong, 1997; McWilliam, 2000), dedicated reputation systems or third parties. Labelling services, such as TRUSTe's Privacy Seal (McKnight et al., 2000), certification services as provided by VeriSign, or authorization and verification services are just some of the trust mechanisms offered by third parties. Further, rating companies also receive much attention by customers. SmartMoney.com, the online branch of the well-known investor's magazine provides annual ratings of online and offline brokers and a fancy little tool called 'broker meter' that will show you how fast your broker's site is compared to other brokers.

More traditional trust instruments, but often enhanced through ICT enhanced, are mediation services in case of disputes or insurance guaranties to prevent financial loss. Technology and its perception can also play a role in establishing trust. Credit card transactions on the Internet, e.g. are often perceived as particularly insecure, even though it might be more dangerous to hand over your credit card to a malicious waitress in a restaurant.

Brand. Brands constitute a pivotal resource for generating and sustaining competitive advantage (Aaker, 1989). They help creating a distinction among entities that may satisfy similar costumer needs (Berthon et al., 1999) and they help the communications programs to not inadvertently send conflicting or confusing messages to customers (Joachimsthaler and Aaker, 1997). Nokia, the Finnish mobile phone manufacturer, established an incredibly strong brand in the mobile phone market by creating an image of a young and dynamic innovator. It achieved this through sponsoring such events as the Nokia Snowboard World Cup tour and a number of top-ranked beach volleyball professionals. Further, Nokia also uses ICT for branding proposes. Owners of a Nokia phone can join the Club Nokia online by entering the serial number of their phone and then benefit from games, cartoons, movies, images and ring tones. This branding strategy proved to be very successful resulting in a No. 6 ranking in Interbrand's year 2002 list of the world's top 100 brands (Bensinger, 2003).

Mini case: Customer relationships at Orange Switzerland

Orange is one of the three mobile telecommunication operators in Switzerland and is a 100% subsidiary of France Télécom. With about

1600 employees, 78 points of sale and its Network that covers 98% of the Swiss population it makes a turnover of CHF475 million and an EBIDTA of CHF33 million. Besides building and maintaining its networks, managing customer contracts belongs to Orange's main business tasks. In the following lines we outline a part of the company's relationship strategy in acquisition, retention and add-on selling by using the framework described in this chapter. The columns represent the RELATIONSHIP elements and the relationship MECHANISM elements of Orange and the lines represent the elements' attributes. It remains to be said that besides the elements outlined below, Orange maintains a number of sponsorships, such as OrangeCinema, OrangeOpera and HandyHero in order to contribute to brand building (see Figure 4.7).

4.3.3 Infrastructure management

The Infrastructure Management block is about the how a company creates value and maintains customer relationships. It describes what abilities are necessary to provide its VALUE PROPOSITION. Infrastructure Management outlines the value network that generates economic value through complex dynamic exchanges between one or more enterprises, its customers, suppliers, strategic partners and the community (Allee, 2000). In other words, this block specifies the business model's capabilities and resources, their owners and providers, as well as who executes which activity and how they relate to each other. As linkages are more and more electronic, the members of a network are flexible in coordinating schedules, sharing assets, utilizing each other's competencies and resources, and they develop, pursue and close business together (Andrews and Hahn, 1998).

In order to understand this value network the Infrastructure Management block describes the value system configuration (Gordijn et al., 2001) that is necessary to deliver the value proposition. This comprises the activity configuration of the firm, in other words the activities to create and deliver value, and, the relationship between them, the in-house capabilities and resources and those acquired through the firm's partner network.

Capabilities and resources

In order to provide its VALUE PROPOSITION a firm has to dispose of a set of CAPABALITY(ies). Wallin (2000) describes capabilities as repeatable patterns of action in the use of assets to create, produce, and/or offer products and services to the market. These capabilities depend on the assets or resources of the firm (Bagchi and Tulskie, 2000). And, increasingly, they are outsourced to partners, while using e-Business technologies to maintain the tight integration that is necessary for a firm to function efficiently. In other words, ICT has made it easier and economically reasonable for companies to 'unbundle' and outsource

Goal	Acquisition			Retention	Add-on selling		
Relationship description	Orange tries to make new phone models affordable and tries to be present in the market as a young brand for communicating human emotions			Orange rewards loyalty and communications of its customers with points, which can be used to buy a new mobile phone or pay bills	Orange tries to make customers use data services, such as WAP, SMS and MMS as much as possible (especially teenagers)		
Name of the relationship mechanism	Phone subsidies	Orange world portal	Habbo hotel	Loyalty points	Location based services	SMS Publisher	Orange heartbreak
Relationship mechanism description	Orange pays a part of or the whole price of a new phone a customer wants to buy in exchange for a 12-month contract with Orange	A portal that provides a mixture of news, sports, entertainment and mobile phone features, such as games. Customer login for Orange phone account management	A virtual meeting place with public and private rooms where people can gather and chat, handle e-mail, instant messages and SMS	–	Location based services for places of interest, route planning, traffic and cinema guides	A tool that allows customers to create their own SMS-channel to send information to channel-subscribers	SMS-based services that allow (teen) customers to flirt anonymously by using their mobile phone
Reasoning	Risk: Minimizes the risk to be stuck with an expensive phone that is soon outdated. Use: Customers can afford the newest mobile phones with the newest phone features (e.g. MMS)	Use: Provides customers and prospects with an information portal and mobile entertainment services. Allows customers to manage their phone account	Use: Provides potential (teen) customers with a place to hang out and manage their e-mail, instant messages and SMS	Risk: Minimizes the risk to be stuck with an expensive phone that is soon outdated. Use: Customers can afford the newest mobile phones with the newest phone features (e.g. MMS)	Efforts: minimizes the efforts for finding useful and location-based information	Use: Allows customers to send information to a list of people that are interested in the same topics (e.g. info for the members of a hobby soccer team)	Use: Allows teenagers to resolve the most pressing problems of their age – love issues – without losing their face
Customer buying cycle	Evaluation	Awareness	Awareness	After sales	After sales	After sales	After sales
Value level/ price level	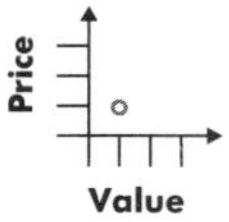 [Price/Value chart]	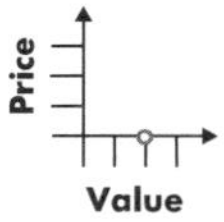 [Price/Value chart]	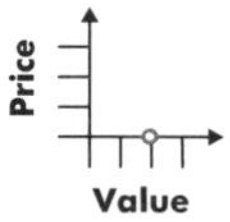 [Price/Value chart]	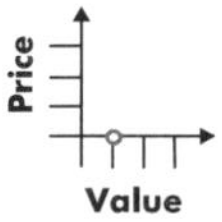 [Price/Value chart]	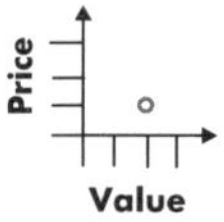 [Price/Value chart]	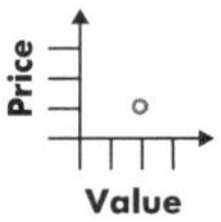 [Price/Value chart]	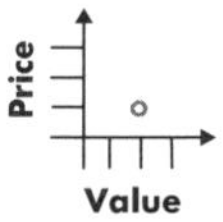 [Price/Value chart]
Function	–	Brand	Brand	–	Personalization	Personalization	–
Channel	Orange shops Retailers	Internet	Internet	–	Mobile phone	Mobile phone Internet	–
By	Self	Self	Self	Self	Self (and with partners)	Self	Self
Target customer	All prospects	Customers and prospects	Teen customers and prospects	All current customers	Nomad customers	Active teen customers	Teen customers

Figure 4.7: Customer relationship of Orange.

capabilities and resources that do not belong to their core competencies (Hagel III and Singer, 2000).

The IT retailer Dell illustrates the concept of core capabilities. The company essentially masters two domains, which are supply chain excellence and 360° mastery of the customer relationship over the Internet or through call centres. The former allows the company just-in-time delivery of required components, build-to-order production and thus low stocks and consequently competitive prices. The latter is crucial because Dell does not dispose of a dealer network and for cost reasons only makes use of direct channels to sell its product. If it does not excel in customer relationships it has no possibility to reach, gain or retain customers. An other impressive example of concentrating and core competencies is EasyJet.com, which focuses on the maintenance of a cheap fleet of airplanes with high air time and the ability to fill airplanes. Both allow EasyJet.com to provide its main offering of relatively low airfares (Table 4.6).

In order to create value, a firm needs resources (Wernefelt, 1984). Grant (1991) distinguishes tangible and intangible assets and people-based skills. Tangible resources include plants, equipment and cash reserves. Intangible resources include patents, copyrights, reputation, brands and trade secrets. Human resources are the people a firm needs in order to create value with tangible and intangible resources.

Activities

As outlined above, the main purpose of a company is the creation of value that customers are willing to pay for. This value is the outcome of a configuration of inside and outside activities and processes. The VALUE CONFIGURATION shows all activities necessary and the links among them, in order to create value for the customer. To define the value creation process in a business model, we use the value chain framework (Porter, 2001) and its extension, such as defined by Stabell and Fjeldstad (1998). These two authors extend the idea of the value chain with the

Table 4.6: Capabilities and resources

A CAPABILITY describes the ability to execute a repeatable pattern of actions. A firm has to dispose of a number of capabilities to be able to offer its VALUE PROPOSITION. CAPABILITIES are based on a set of resources from the firm or its PARTNER(s).
– it allows to provide the VALUE PROPOSITION(s)

It is composed of a set of one-or-more **RESOURCE**(s)

RESOURCES are inputs into the value-creation process. They are the source of the CAPABILITIES a firm needs in order to provide its VALUE PROPOSITION.
– it has TYPE {TANGIBLE, INTANGIBLE, HUMAN}
– it is delivered by an ACTOR(s)

value shop and the value network. Former describes the value creation process of service providers (e.g. consultancies), whereas latter describes brokering and intermediary activities (e.g. banks and telecommunication companies). It is in this component of the e-Business framework that we describe such activities as Supply Chain Management (SCM), Efficient Customer Response (ECR), or e-Procurement.

We distinguish between three basic value configuration types, which are the value chain (Porter, 2001), the value shop and the value network (Stabell and Fjeldstad, 1998).

The VALUE CHAIN contains the different activities a firm performs to deliver low-cost or differentiated products. The activities of the value chain framework (Porter, 2001) include inbound logistics, operations, outbound logistics, marketing and sales, and service. The value creation logic of a value chain is the transformation of inputs into products. The main interactivity relationship logic is sequential (Stabell and Fjeldstad, 1998).

The VALUE SHOP represents an extension to the value chain framework provided by Porter (2001). Stabell and Fjeldstad on (Ives and Learmonth, 1984; Ives, 1999; Muther, 2002) argue that service provisioning has a different value creation logic than manufacturing. Service providers tend to come up with new solutions, rather than fixing on one solution and reproducing it time and again such as in the value chain. In this value configuration a firm concentrates on discovering what the client wants, figures out a way to deliver value, determines whether the customer's needs were fulfilled and repeats the process in an iterative way if necessary. The proposed activities of the value shop contain problem finding and acquisition, problem solving, choice, execution and control and evaluation. The value creation logic of a value shop is resolving customer problems. The main interactivity relationship logic is cyclical, spiraling (Stabell and Fjeldstad, 1998).

In the VALUE NETWORK value is created by linking clients or customers who are or wish to be interdependent. The firm itself is not the network, but it provides a networking service (Stabell and Fjeldstad, 1998). Afuah and Tucci (2001) see the value network as a direct outgrowth of brokering. According to these authors this is the value configuration that exists when a firm is an intermediary, such as a broker or a market maker. Rather than focusing on logistics such as the importation and delivery of raw materials and how they are transformed into finished goods (i.e. the value chain), the intermediary must focus on network promotion and contract management, service provisioning and infrastructure operations. The value creation logic of a value network is linking customers. The main interactivity relationship logic is mediating (Stabell and Fjeldstad, 1998).

Activities are at the heart of what a business does. They are actions a company performs in order to create and market value and generate profits. An ACTIVITY is executed by an ACTOR, which can be the firm or one of its partners. Activities relate to owned or partner RESOURCES and they are linked in a VALUE CONFIGURATION (see Table 4.7 and Figure 4.8).

The activity LEVEL distinguishes between the firm's primary and support activities (Porter, 1985). Primary activities are those that are involved in the creation of the value proposition and its marketing and delivery. Support activities are the underlying fundament that allow the primary activities to take place. This includes activities such as firm infrastructure, human resource management, technology development and procurement (Porter, 1985).

The activity NATURE depends on the CONFIGURATION TYPE attribute in the VALUE CONFIGURATION element. The three types of configurations have different kinds of activities:

- *Value chain*: inbound logistics, operations, outbound logistics, marketing and sales, and services;

Table 4.7: Value configuration and activities

The VALUE CONFIGURATION of a firm describes the arrangement of one-or-several ACTIVITY(ies) in order to provide a VALUE PROPOSITION.
– it provides VALUE PROPOSITION(s)
– it relies on CAPABILITY(ies)
– it has a type {VALUE CHAIN, SHOP, OR NETWORK}

The VC is composed of a set of one-or-more **ACTIVITY**(ies)

An ACTIVITY is an action a company performs to do business and achieve its goals.
– it has a LEVEL
– it has a NATURE
– it requires {Fits, Flows to, or Shares} a RESOURCEs
– it is performed by ACTORs

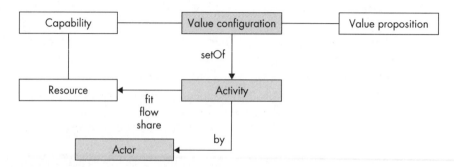

Figure 4.8:   Value configuration and activities.

■ *Value shop*: problem finding and acquisition, problem solving, choice, execution, and control and evaluation;

■ *Value network*: network promotion and contract management, service provisioning, and network infrastructure operation.

An *activity* relates to one or several RESOURCES. Their linkages have a specific nature. We distinguish between fit, flow and share (based on Malone et al. (1999)). An ACTIVITY fits a RESOURCE when more than one ACTIVITY is required by a RESOURCE. An ACTIVITY flows to a RESOURCE when the outcome of an ACTIVITY is required by a RESOURCE. An ACTIVITY shares a RESOURCE when more than one ACTIVITY uses the same RESOURCE.

Mini case: Value configuration at ColorPlaza

We illustrate the VALUE CONFIGURATION, ACTIVITIES, RESOURCES and PARTNERSHIPS through ColorPlaza, a Swiss company in the photography industry (see Figure 4.9). The columns in Figure 4.9 represent a specific ACTIVITY and the lines represent the activities' attributes and relationship to RESOURCE(s) and ACTOR(s).

ColorPlaza let us their customers upload their digital photos over the Internet and get them printed on photo paper, t-shirts and other gadgets, which are then delivered directly to their homes. In fact, ColorPlaza was so successful with this service that it is now sold under the name of big partners, such as Sony Europe, Nokia or Microsoft (through the Windows XP operating system). These tight co-operations are based on a close integration of the IS of the different partners involved.

Partnerships

A company's partner network outlines, which elements of the activity configuration and which resources are distributed among the firm's partners. In e-Business literature there are several terms arising for these new forms of strategic networks in the value creation process, some call them b-webs (Tapscott et al., 2000), or fluid and flexible organizations (Selz, 1999), others call them value networks (Nalebuff and Brandenburger, 1997). The appearance of such networks of firms in which market and hierarchical governance mechanisms coexist has significantly enhanced the range of possible organizational arrangements for value creation (Gulati and Singh, 1998). In general, partnerships and alliances have become an essential component in the strategies implemented by most companies. Although they have been used by some firms for decades already, today's partnerships and alliances have changed in nature. The more traditional concepts of joint ventures (e.g. for penetration of new geographic markets) have made place to strategic alliances that aim at creating and enhancing the competitive positions of the firms involved,

ACTIVITY name	ACTIVITY description	Level	Nature	Related to RESOURCE	By ACTOR
Upload of digital images and order	The digital images have to be uploaded from the customer's camera or PC	Primary activity	Inbound logistics	Shares image network	Customer
Transfer of digital images to the printing facilities	The digital images have to be transferred from the customer to the printing facilities	Primary activity	Inbound logistics	Fits print infrastructure	FotoWire
Buy, receive and store material to print on	The primary material to print on has to be received and eventually stored	Primary activity	Inbound logistics	Fits print infrastructure	ColorPlaza
Print digital images on photo paper or goods	The digital images have to be printed on either photo paper or goods, such as t-shirts, cups etc.	Primary activity	Operations	Flows to packaging staff	ColorPlaza
Pack goods for delivery	The order has to be packaged for home delivery	Primary activity	Outbound logistics	Shares delivery network	ColorPlaza
Deliver packages	The orders have to be delivered to the customer's home	Primary activity	Outbound logistics	Flows to customer	Postal service
Answer complaints	Possible complaints have to be answered to the customer's satisfaction	Primary activity	Services	Shares call centre	ColorMailer
Sell ColorMailer services	ColorMailer's services have to be marketed to potential customers	Primary activity	marketing	Flows to channels	ColorPlaza / SONY / NOKIA / Microsoft / Agfa

Figure 4.9: ColorPlaza value configuration, activities, resources and partnerships.

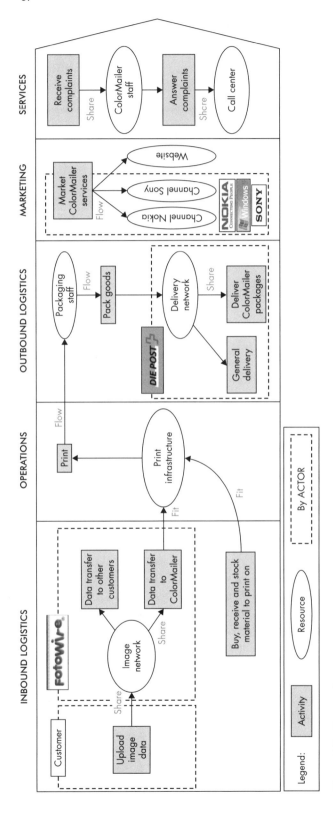

Figure 4.9: (*Continued*)

Table 4.8: Partnership

A PARTNERSHIP is a voluntarily initiated co-operative agreement formed between two or more independent companies in order to carry out a project or specific activity jointly by coordinating the necessary CAPABILITIES, RESOURCES and ACTIVITIES.
- it supports the VALUE PROPOSITION(s)
- it relies on CAPABILITY(ies)

It is composed of a set of one-or-more **AGREEMENT**(s)

An AGREEMENT specifies the function and the terms and conditions of a partnership with an ACTOR
- it has a REASONING
- it has a DEGREE OF INTEGRATION
- it has a DEGREE OF DEPENDENCY
- it is made with ACTOR(s)

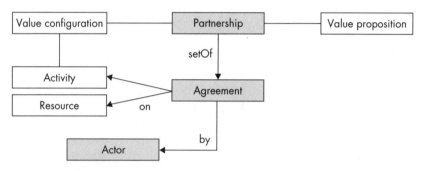

Figure 4.10: Partnership.

in a highly competitive environment (Dussauge and Garrette, 1999) (Table 4.8 and Figure 4.10).

One of the goals behind many partner agreements is the optimization of a company's operations. This can take the form of outsourcing (i.e. make or buy), but also shared infrastructure (Lu, 2001). By entering these agreements a firm can profit of its partner's or supplier's economies of scale or of it is specialized knowledge, which it could not achieve on its own. In the apparel industry, the big player is like Benetton, The Gap or Hennes and Mauritz rely heavily on partners for their supply and production network (Camuffo et al., 2001). However, they apply different models. Benetton builds on a strong upstream vertical integration through its 32 production centres for strategic and capital intensive activities (weaving, cutting and dyeing) and out sources production of clothes (sewing) to a network of small and midsize enterprises that are directly controlled by the production centres. Benetton's competitors on the other hand rely on complete outsourcing. An example of shared infrastructure is the alliance between the Swedish car manufacturer Volvo and Renault of France in 1990. To stay competitive they initiated joint co-operation in R&D, design and procurement, as well as in manufacturing components for cars, trucks and buses (Mason, 1993).

A second motivation for partnering in today's uncertain competitive environment is the goal of increasing anticipation and thus reducing the risk premium (Mariti and Smiley, 1983). Companies are unable to afford launching costly experiments in the field anymore, because they have become too expensive and prefer engaging in temporary alliances with competitors (i.e. *Co-opetition*) (Brandenburger and Nalebuff, 1996). The co-operation by the wireless industry leaders in 1998 to create an open standard OS for data-enabled mobile phones illustrates this nicely. Jointly, Ericsson, Nokia, Panasonic, Motorola, Psion, Samsung Electronics and Siemens set up a collectively owned software licensing company called Symbian. By doing this they avoided risking a balkanized mobile telephony market with incompatible operating systems, decreased R&D costs and reduced uncertainty. The players had a strong incentive to cooperate on the OS in order to profit from increasing returns of network externalities and compete on other grounds.

A third motivation for partnering is the goal of leveraging a business model and a company's competencies through partnerships in order to acquire specific resources. A frequent form of resource acquisition is partnerships to conquer foreign markets. In 1992, Playboy, a famous magazine for men decided to set up a joint-venture with VIPress, a Polish press group, to launch its Polish edition (Dussauge and Garrette, 1999). RiverOne, an online market for electronics parts sells knowledge to support buying decisions. Using the firm's online research centre, electrical engineers can view product specification, learn how to use components, and compare alternatives across an aggregate catalogue of some 7 million parts (Dai and Kauffman, 2002). Instill Corporation, an electronic market for the food services industry not only helps restaurant chain operators improve procurement, but also standardize and integrate purchase data, which enables buyers to understand how their expenses were allocated across different purchase areas (Dai and Kauffman, 2002).

As PARTNERSHIPs are voluntarily initiated co-operative AGREEMENT(s) between two or more independent companies to carry out an activity jointly they are based on a commonly negotiated terms and conditions. Companies engage in partnerships for specific reasons. The attribute REASONING describes the firm's motivation to conclude a partner agreement and outlines its analysis. We distinguish between three rough categories of motivation; these are optimization and economies of scale, reduction of risk and uncertainty and finally acquisition of resources.

The DEGREE OF INTEGRATION measures how closely two ACTORS are linked together. This can differ from one type of partnership and agreement to another. The loosest link between two ACTORS is through independent third-party marketplaces (e.g. stock markets) and the closest link are tightly integrated supply chains (e.g. traditional EDI). Of course the frontier is unclear and there are plenty of cases situated between these two extremes. MarketSite, Commerce One's online marketplace has customized catalogues for Schlumberger, an American oil exploration company with the prices and product offering the company prenegotiated with vendors (Ovans, 2000). Private cataloguing is favoured in transactional purchasing, where the reason for joining online markets is to reduce operating costs (Dai and Kauffman, 2002). An interesting example of a closely integrated relationship between two companies can be found in the retailing business. As ICT has lowered coordination and transaction costs and facilitated the flows of information, many retailers have introduced a concept called Vendor Managed Inventory (VMI). This is a process where the supplier generates orders for his customer based on demand information sent electronically by the customer. This means that the buyer completely transfers supply management to his supplier, who controls the stock of the buyer and refurnishes automatically, when necessary. Benefits comprise lower inventory for supplier and customer, lower administrative costs and increased sales.

Assessing dependency in partnerships is of crucial importance for the future development of a business model. Of course the DEGREE OF DEPENDENCY is somewhat related to the degree of integration. A closely integrated relationship between two ACTORS is naturally much harder to cancel than a transactional relationship. As outlined above, VMI makes sense for economical reasons, but it also means that a firm shifts responsibility, authority and hence knowledge about replenishment to its supplier and therefore enters a dependent relationship (Tanskanen et al., 2002). When the American no-frills Airline, Southwest, signed a 10-year engine maintenance contract with General Electric, paying GE on a rate per flight hour basis for practically all engine maintenance it entered an even bigger dependency. But through this agreement Southwest was able to reinforce its low-cost airline strategy by reducing its capital investments and cutting maintenance costs substantially (Corbett, 2001).

4.4 Conclusion

There are several reasons why business models and e-Business models are relevant for managers. First of all, even though many people talk about them, business model concepts and a common understanding of what is meant by business models are still in their infancy. Executives, reporters and analysts who use the term do not have a clear idea of what it means. They use it to describe everything from how a company earns revenue to how it structures its organization (Linder and Cantrell, 2000).

The second reason why the e-Business model concept is interesting to be studied is that it can be an adequate methodology and foundation for managerial tools and IS Requirements Engineering to react to the increasingly dynamic business environment. As product life cycles become shorter, competition global and the use of ICT an imperative, managers have to find new ways to act and decide in this complex environment. Managers have to understand the new opportunities offered by ICT, integrate them into their existing business models and share them with other stakeholders. The e-Business model ontology we propose in this paper and the tools that build on it are a first step to facilitating management under uncertainty.

The Business Model Ontology has the goal of providing a framework to better formulate, understand, analyse and share a company's business model. We believe that the concept of business models can serve as a federator between business strategy, business organization and information systems and improve the alignment between them.

Further research includes computerizing the business model ontology to fully exploit the conceptual foundation outlined in this paper. For instance, one could imagine a visualization tool to display channel strategies and partner networks or analyse and compare value propositions, similar to the examples sketched above. Business models could also be used as a scenario-based forecasting approach (Van der Heijden, 1996) that would be helpful before defining a strategy of adoption, deployment, and management of a business logic. Further, business models seem interesting for improving change management (Linder and Cantrell, 2000). Finally, one could even imagine a business model simulator (Sterman, 2000; Richards and Morrison, 2001) where stakeholders would gain important insights on their actions and would learn about their business models by simulating and experimenting with them in a risk-free environment.

References and Further Reading

Aaker, D. A. (1989). 'Managing Assets and Skills: The Key to Sustainable Competitive Advantage.' *California Management Review* 31(2): 91–106.

Afuah, A. and C. Tucci (2001). *Internet Business Models and Strategies*. Boston, McGraw-Hill.

Allee, V. (2000). 'Reconfiguring the Value Network.' *Journal of Business Strategy*, July/August, 21(4): 36–39.

Amit, R. and C. Zott (2001). 'Value Creation in eBusiness.' *Strategic Management Journal*, 22(6/7): 493–520.

Anderson, E., G. Day and K. Rangan (1997). 'Strategic Channel Design.' *Sloan Management Review*, Summer.

Anderson, J. and J. Narus (1998). 'Business Marketing: Understand What Customers Value.' *Harvard Business Review*.

Andrews, P. P. and J. Hahn (1998). 'Transforming Supply Chains into Value Webs.' *Strategy & Leadership*, July/August, **26**(3): 6–11.

Bagchi, S. and B. Tulskie (2000). eBusiness Models: Integrating Learning from Strategy Development Experiences and Empirical Research. *20th Annual International Conference of the Strategic Management Society*, Vancouver.

Bensinger, A. (2003). 'The Call on Nokia: Buy.' *Business Week Online* [accessed: January, 2003] http://www.businessweek.com/investor/content/jan2003/pi2003017_1173.htm.

Berthon, J.-P., J. Hulbert and L. Pitt (1999). 'Brand Management Prognostications.' *Sloan Management Review* **40**(2): 53–55.

Bertolazzi, P., C. Krusich and M. Missikoff (2001). 'An Approach to the Definition of a Core Enterprise Ontology: CEO.' *International Workshop on Open Enterprise Solutions: Systems, Experiences, and Organizations, Rome.*

Blattberg, R., G. Getz and J. Thomas (2001). *Customer Equity*. Boston, Harvard Business School Press.

Bloch, M., Y. Pigneur and A. Segev (1996). Leveraging Electronic Commerce for Competitive Advantage: a Business Value Framework. *9th International EDI-IOS Conference*, Bled, Slovenia.

Brandenburger, A. and B. Nalebuff (1996). *Co-opetition*. New York, Doubleday.

Bucklin, C., P. Thomas-Graham and E. Webster (1997). Channel Conflict: When is it Dangerous? *McKinsey Quarterly* (3).

Camuffo, A., P. Romano and A. Vinelli (2001). 'Back to the Future: Benetton Transforms its Global Network.' *Sloan Management Review* **43**(1): 46–52.

Chen, E. and K. Kai-ling Ho (2002). 'Demystifying Innovation.' *Perspectives on Business Innovation* (8).

Child, J. and D. Faulkner (1998). *Strategies of Co-operation—Managing Alliances, Networks, and Joint Ventures*. New York, Oxford University Press.

Corbett, M. F. (2001). Outsourcing at Southwest Airlines: How America's Leading Firms Use Outsourcing. Firmbuilder.com. [accessed: February, 2003] http://www.firmbuilder.com/articles/19/42/597/

Dai, Q. and R. J. Kauffman (2002). 'Business Models for Internet-Based B2B Electronic Markets.' *International Journal of Electronic Commerce*, **6**(4): 41–72.

Dimitrakos, T. (2001). *System Models, e-Risks and e-Trust*. IFIP I3E, Zurich, Kluwer Academic Publishers.

Dolan, R. (2000). *Going to Market*. Teaching Note, Harvard Business School.

Durlacher (2001). Impacts of Digital Distribution on the Music Industry. Research Report, Durlacher Ltd.

Dussauge, P. and B. Garrette (1999). *Cooperative Strategy – Competing Successfully through Strategic Alliances*. Chichester, Wiley.

Evans, P. and T. Wurster (1997). 'Strategy and the New Economics of Information.' *Harvard Business Review*.

Fensel, D. (2001). *Ontologies: Silver Bullet for Knowledge Management and Electronic Commerce*. Heidelberg, Springer-Verlag.

Friedman, B., P. Kahn and D. Howe (2000). Trust Online. *Communications of the ACM* December, **43**(12).

Gordijn, J., J. Akkermans and J. van Vliet (2001). 'Designing and Evaluating eBusiness Models.' *IEEE Intelligent Systems* July/August, **16**(4): 11–17.

Grant, A. and L. Schlesinger (1995). Realize Your Customers' Full Profit Potential. *Harvard Business Review* September–October 1995: 59–72.

Grant, R. M. (1991). 'The Resource-Based Theory of Competitive Advantage: Implications for Strategy Formulation.' *California Management Review* Spring, 33(3): 114–135.

Gulati, R. and H. Singh (1998). 'The Architecture of Cooperation: Managing Coordination Costs and Appropriation Concerns in Strategic Alliances.' *Administrative Quarterly*, December, 43(4): 781–814.

Hagel III, J. and A. Armstrong (1997). *Net Gain: Expanding Markets through Virtual Communities*. Boston, Harvard Business School Press.

Hagel III, J. and M. Singer (2000). 'Unbundling the Corporation.' *McKinsey Quarterly* (3): 148–161.

Hamel, G. (2000). *Leading the Revolution*. Boston, Harvard Business School Press.

Herman, J. (2002). 'Global Value Webs.' *Supply Chain Management Review* 6(4): 30–37.

Ives, B. (1999). Customer Service Life Cycle. Center for Virtual Organization and Commerce, Louisiana State University. [accessed: November, 2002] http://isds.bus.lsu.edu/cvoc/projects/cslc/html/

Ives, B. and G. Learmonth (1984). 'The Information System as a Competitive Weapon.' *Communications of the ACM* 27(12): 1193–1201.

Joachimsthaler, E. and D. A. Aaker (1997). *Building Brands without Mass Media*. *Harvard Business Review* January/February 97, 75(1): 39–37.

Jones, A. (2002). 'On the Concept of Trust.' *Decision Support Systems* 33(3): 225–232.

Kambil, A., A. Ginsberg and M. Bloch (1997). Rethinking Value Propositions. Working Paper, NYU Center for Research on Information Systems.

Kaplan, R. S. and D. P. Norton (1992). 'The Balanced Scorecard–Measures that Drive Performance.' *Harvard Business Review*, January/February 92, 70(1).

Kim, W. C. and R. Mauborgne (1997). 'Value Innovation: The Strategic Lobic of High Growth.' *Harvard Business Review* January–February.

Kotler, P. (1999). *Marketing Management*. New Jersey, Prentice Hall.

Linder, J. and S. Cantrell (2000). Changing Business Models: Surveying the Landscape. Accenture Institute for Strategic Change.

Lu, D. (2001). 'Shared Network Investment.' *Journal of Economics* 73(3): 299–312.

Maître, B. and G. Aladjidi (1999). *Les Business Models de la Nouvelle Economie*. Paris, Dunod.

Malone, T. W., K. Crowston, J. Lee, B. Pentland, C. Dellarocas, G. Wyner, J. Quimby, C. Osborne, A. Bernstein, G. Herman, M. Klein and E. O'Donnell (1999). 'Tools for Inventing Organizations: Toward a Handbook of Organizational Processes.' *Management Science* 43(3): 425–443.

Mariti, P. and R. H. Smiley (1983). 'Co-Operative Agreements and the Organization of Industry.' *Journal of Industrial Economics*, June, 31(4): 437–451.

Markides, C. (1999). *All the Right Moves*. Boston, Harvard Business School Press.

Mason, J. C. (1993). 'Strategic Alliances: Partnering for Success.' *Management Review*, May, 82(5): 10–15.

McKnight, D. H., V. Choudhury and C. Kacmar (2000). Trust in e-Commerce Vendors: A Two-Stage Model. *International Conference on Information Systems (ICIS)*, Brisbane, Association for Information Systems.

McWilliam, G. (2000). 'Building Stronger Brands through Online Communities.' *Sloan Management Review*, Spring: 43–54.

Morecroft, J. D. (1994). Executive Knowledge, Models, and Learning. *Morecroft. Modeling for Learning Organizations*. J. D. Morecroft and J. D. Sterman (eds). Portland, Productivity Press: 3–28.

Moriarty, R. and U. Moran (1990). 'Managing Hybrid Marketing Systems.' *Harvard Business Review*, November–December.

Muther, A. (2002). *Customer Relationship Management – Electronic Customer Care in the New Economy*. Heidelberg, Springer.

Nalebuff, B. and A. Brandenburger (1997). 'Co-opetition: Competitive and Cooperative Business Strategies for the Digital Economy.' *Strategy & Leadership*, November/December 97, **25**(6): 28–23.

Neal, W. and J. Wurst (2001). 'Advances in Market Segmentation.' *Marketing Research* Spring, 13(1): 14–18.

Ovans, A. (2000). 'e-Procurement at Schlumberger.' *Harvard Business Review* **78**(3): 21–23.

Petrovic, O., C. Kittl and R. D. Teksten (2001). Developing Business Models for eBusiness. *International Conference on Electronic Commerce* 2001, Vienna.

Pitt, L., P. Berthon and J.-P. Berthon (1999). 'Changing Channels: The Impact of the Internet on Distribution Strategy.' *Business Horizons*, March–April.

Porter, M. E. (1985). 'How Information Gives you Competitive Advantage.' *Harvard Business Review*, July/August, **63**(4): 149–160.

Porter, M. E. (2001). 'Strategy and the Internet.' *Harvard Business Review*, March.

Rappa, M. (2001). Managing the Digital Enterprise – Business Models on the Web. North Carolina State University [accessed: November, 2002].

Rayport, J. F. and B. J. Jaworski (2001). *Cases in E-Commerce*. Boston, McGraw-Hill/Irwin.

Richards, I. and J. Morrison (2001). Using flight simulators to build robust dot-com strategies. Accenture.

Robinson, M., D. Tapscott and R. Kalakota (2000). *eBusiness 2.0: Roadmap for Success*. Addison-Wesley.

Rupp, P. and T. Esthier (2003). A Model for a Better Understanding of the Digital Distribution of Music in a Peer-to-Peer Environment. HICSS 36, Hawaii.

Sarwar, B., G. Karypis, J. Konstan and J. Riedl (2000). Analysis of Recommendation Algorithms for E-Commerce. *ACM Conference on Electronic Commerce*.

Schafer, B., J. Konstan and J. Riedl (2000). 'E-Commerce Recommendation Applications.' *Journal of Data Mining and Knowledge Discovery* 5(1/2): 115–152.

Selz, D. (1999). Value Webs – Emerging forms of fluid and flexible organizations. MCM Institute. St.Gallen, University of St.Gallen.

Stabell, C. B. and O. D. Fjeldstad (1998). 'Configuring Value for Competitive Advantage: On Chains, Shops, and Networks.' *Strategic Management Journal* **19**: 413–437.

Steinfield, C., H. Bouwman and T. Adelaar (2002). 'The dynamics of Click-and-Mortar Electronic Commerce: Opportunities and Management Strategies.' *International Journal of Electronic Commerce*, Fall, 7(1): 93-119.

Sterman, J. D. (2000). *Business Dynamics: Systems Thinking and Modeling for a Complex World*. Boston, McGraw-Hill.

Tanskanen, K., J. Holström and R. Kaipi (2002). 'VMI: What are you losing if you let your customer place orders?' *Production Planning & Control* 13(1): 17–25.

Tapscott, D., D. Ticoll and A. Lowy (2000). Digital Capital – Harnessing the Power of Business Webs. Boston, Harvard Business School Press.

Timmers, P. (1998). 'Business Models for Electronic Markets.' *Journal on Electronic Markets* 8(2): 3–8.

Ushold, M. and M. King (1995). Towards a Methodology for Building Ontologies. *Workshop on Basic Ontological Issues in Knowledge Sharing Held in Conjunction with IJCAI-95*, Montreal.

Van der Heijden, K. (1996). *Scenarios: The Art of Strategic Conversation*, New York, John Wiley & Sons.

Wallin, J. (2000). Operationalizing Competences. *International Conference on Competence-Based Management*, Helsinki, Finland.

Wedel, M. (2001). 'Is Segmentation History?' *Marketing Research*, Winter, 13(4): 26–29.

Weill, P. and M. R. Vitale (2001). *Place to space: Migrating to eBusiness Models*. Boston, Harvard Business School Press.

Wernefelt, B. (1984). 'A Resource-based View of the Firm.' *Strategic Management Journal*, April–June 84, 5(2): 171–181.

Winter, F. (1984). 'Market Segmentation: A Tactical Approach.' *Business Horizons*, January/February 84, 27(1): 57–63.

Wyner, G. (1995). 'Researching Channels.' *Marketing Research*, Summer, 7(3): 42–44.

5 e-Business value modelling using the *e³-value* ontology

Jaap Gordijn

Abstract

A first step in developing e-Business ideas is to understand such an idea thoroughly. In the recent past, industry has clearly demonstrated that such an understanding lacks or at least is insufficient, resulting in failures and sometimes bankruptcies. In this chapter we present an approach to design an e-Business model, called the *e³-value* approach. This approach is ontologically founded in business science, marketing and axiology, but exploits rigorous conceptual modelling as a way of working known from computer science. The aim is that an *e³*-value e-Business model contributes to a better and shared understanding of the idea at stake, specifically with respect to its profit drivers. If the model is attributed with various assumptions, such as economic valuation of objects produced, distributed, and consumed, we can derive profitability sheets using the business model. These can be used to assess whether the idea seems to be profitable for all actors involved in the idea. We illustrate the *e³-value* approach by a project we carried out for an Internet service provider.

5.1 Introduction

Over the past few years, many innovative e-Business ideas have been considered. Such ideas reveal new value propositions, which are enabled by new technological possibilities, such as the widespread use of the Internet and associated technologies. The late 1990s was characterized by much hype about e-Business. More recently, it became clear that numerous e-Business initiatives were unsuccessful (Shama, 2001). Many firms were able to create new revenue streams from e-Business. Those which relied upon these revenue streams have largely gone out of business. An important reason for the failure of most e-Business ventures was the lack of a sound value proposition for customers. Moreover, many ventures did not contribute sufficiently to the profitability of firms, especially where their efforts focused more upon maximizing market share and establishing a trusted brand name rather than revenue generation. Notwithstanding this point, many believe that e-Business has the potential for offering firms the opportunity to utilize the Internet and related technical innovations in a profitable way. Indeed, some industries need to develop new value propositions if they are to survive. For instance, the digital content industry is facing challenges with respect to new value propositions utilizing Internet technology, e.g. how to earn money by streaming music to an end-consumer's device.

One of the key problems with innovative e-Business ideas is that, initially, they tend to be formulated vaguely, and often lack a precise description. As a result, many innovative e-Business ideas are somewhat unfocused and inaccurate. This makes it different to put the idea into operation, and to develop a supporting information system. What is needed is an in-depth exploration process of an e-Business idea, to understand the idea better as well as to formulate it more precisely, and to focus the idea into a direction that is feasible from an economical and technical perspective.

This chapter provides an ontological perspective on the exploration of such innovative e-Business ideas. Our e^3-value ontology (see also Gordijn, 2002) to do so is on the one hand based on the analysis of *economic value* creation, distribution, and consumption in a multi-actor network. On the other hand, the e^3-value ontology is founded on *requirements engineering* and underlying *conceptual modelling* techniques, borrowed from the information systems community. Requirements engineering is the process of developing requirements through an iterative co-operative process of analysing the problem, documenting the resulting observations in a variety of representation formats, and checking the accuracy of the understanding gained (Loucopoulos and Karakostas, 1995).

This chapter is structured as follows. Firstly, we begin with an explanation of why we need an e-Business ontology. Hereafter, the next section introduces the e^3-value ontology in detail, and explains the use of the ontology by discussing a real-life project on Internet service provisioning that successfully applied the ontology. The next section extends the baseline ontology with facilities for operational scenarios, which are used to do profitability sensitivity analysis (see Section 5.5 below). The Section 5.5 discusses related ontologies, such as the Artificial Intelligence applications institute (AIAI) enterprise ontology, the TOronto Virtual Enterprise (TOVE) ontology and the resource event agent (REA) ontology. Finally, we discuss our conclusions and suggestions for further research.

5.2 Why an e-Business model ontology?

Before presenting the e^3-value ontology in detail, we will first discuss the rationale for the ontology. In short, the ontology is intended to design and analyse innovative e-Business models. We restrict ourselves to *innovative* e-Business models, meaning that we focus on e-Business models with value propositions that are not understood by the large audience. Furthermore, we look at e-Business models that are about doing business transactions between enterprises and/or end-consumers, often referred to as *e-Commerce*.

As we will demonstrate later in the chapter, the main purpose of our *e³-value* ontology is to articulate e-Business models for networked enterprises for the following reasons:

■ to reach a better understanding of the e-Business model by the stakeholders involved;

■ to be able to do an analysis and profitability assessment of the e-Business model for all parties involved.

5.2.1 Reaching a better understanding

e-Business models often suppose that a *consortium* of enterprises *jointly* deliver a service to end-customers, in contrast to traditional business models where a *single* supplier offers a product to a *single* customer. Such multi-enterprise offerings require that all participating parties have a common understanding of the offering to be supplied. We have been involved in a series of business development tracks, and many of such multi-enterprise offerings result in unclear, and sometimes even inconsistent offerings. A main cause is misinterpretation of the e-Business idea underlying the offering.

In addition, even in a single enterprise, misinterpretations of an e-Business idea occur because different stakeholders are involved while formulating such an idea. We encountered stakeholders on the CxO level, but also parties responsible for design and execution of business processes (many e-Business projects still fail because a good idea is not translated into consequences for operations), and Information and communication technology (ICT) stakeholders (e-Business relies on the enabling role of ICT). So, development of an e-Business idea often leads to misinterpretation of such an idea due to involvement of many enterprises, and a broad range of stakeholders representing these enterprises.

How can we contribute to avoid this misunderstanding? For this purpose, our *e³-value* methodology (Gordijn, 2002) provides an *ontology* to conceptualize and to visualize an e-Business idea. An ontology provides concepts, relations between these, and rules which are supposed to be interpreted the *same way* by stakeholders, to conceptualize a specific domain. 'Conceptualization' means describing rather formally a universe of discourse (UoD) (e.g. a business idea) to allow for understanding of, and reasoning about such an UoD. To create the required common understanding, our ontology borrows accepted terminology from the realm of business sciences, more specifically terminology on dynamic value constellations (Normann and Ramírez, 1993, 1994; Porter, 2001), marketing (Kotler, 1998), and axiology (Holbrook, 1999). For instance, e^3-value concepts are: *actor*, *value exchange*, *value activity*, and *value object*. Using these notions, we model networked constellations of enterprises and end-consumers, who create, distribute and consume things of economic value.

For conceptualization many description languages can be used. These languages differ in the statements they make about a UoD, in their level of formality, and also in their intended users. Since our audience consists of CxOs and business analysts, we have chosen for a *graphical* language. Most of these people do not have the time or the skills to read textually represented formal documents. To put it differently: a picture says more than 1000 words. The realm of computer science has invented many (semi) formal graphical languages to be able to easily communicate complicated aspects of computer software. As such our e^3-value approach utilizes terminology from business science, but borrows representation and visualization methodology from computer science.

5.2.2 Analysing an e-Business model

In the recent past, industry has shown that many prospective e-Business models have not been thoroughly analysed before put into practice. There were many examples of poor e-Business models, leading to the failure of tens of thousands of dot.coms. This was largely because new ventures, having received first-round venture capital, failed to generate revenues, and therefore the ability to secure second-round funding becomes critical to their survival (Cassidy, 2002).

The e^3-value approach provides constructs to represent a networked business model, consisting of actors (enterprises and end-consumers) and what they exchange of economic value with each other. If we ask parties to assign economic value to objects they provide and obtain, we can reason about potential profitability of the e-Business models. Moreover, we may use strategic scenario decision taking techniques to do sensitivity analysis on the e-Business model under consideration. Since e-Business models often suppose offerings provisioned by multiple enterprises rather than by one, it is important that all these enterprises have a reasonable chance to make profit. Otherwise, the multi-party offering falls apart.

5.3 The e^3-value ontology

This section presents our e-Business *ontology*, called e^3-value, which offers constructs for modelling e-Business cases from an economical perspective. Cornerstone of this ontology is the notion of economic value, and how actors create, exchange and consume objects of economic value.

The *e³-value* is divided into three viewpoints, which each represent related statements on an e-Business model:

■ The *global actor* viewpoint shows:

   1 the *actors* involved in an e-Business idea;

   2 the *objects of economic value* created, exchanged and consumed by these actors;

   3 objects of value, which actors expect in return for an object of value delivered, also called the mechanism of *economic reciprocity*;

   4 objects which are offered or requested *in combination*;

   5 *phenomena*, such as consumer needs, that cause *exchanges* of objects between actors.

■ The *detailed actor* viewpoint(s) shows:

   1 *partnerships* between actors, which show that actors request or offer objects of value jointly;

   2 *constellations* of actors, which need not be seen on the global actor viewpoint, e.g. to avoid unnecessary complexity;

   3 plus: *expressions* as on the global actor viewpoint, but then only for actors expressed on the detailed viewpoint.

■ The *value activity* viewpoint(s) shows:

   1 the value-creating or adding activities and their assignment to actors.

The main purpose of the *global actor* viewpoint is to explain the overall value model to all stakeholders, including CxO type of stakeholders, involved. It hides complexity, which can be shown on detailed actor viewpoints. The reason to introduce a *detailed actor* viewpoint can be twofold: (1) representation of constellations: a decomposition of a part of the global actor viewpoint to reduce complexity, and, (2) representation of partnerships: actors who decide to offer and/or request products or services as one virtual actor to/from other actors. The *value activity* viewpoint(s) shows what actors do to create profit or to increase value for themselves. Its main motivation is to separate discussions of who is participating in the e-Business idea from who is doing what.

We illustrate the ontology by means of a project we have carried out in the free Internet service provisioning arena. The e-Business idea underpinning this project is that users, in order to access the Internet, only have to pay a fee for a telephone connection, what they are used to do for other, paid, Internet access services also. In short, these telephone connection revenues are used to finance the entire operation.

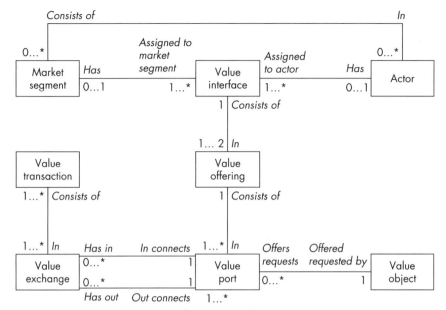

Figure 5.1: Concepts and relations of the e^3-value ontology[1] (global actor viewpoint).

This e-Business value model is shown in Figure 5.2 (global actor viewpoint), Figure 5.6 (detailed actor viewpoint), and Figure 5.8 (value activity viewpoint).

5.3.1 The global actor viewpoint

The explanation of our ontology is structured by presenting a description for each concept, properties of the concept, relations with other concepts, and the way of visualization in a value model such as depicted in Figure 5.2. A concept and relation is illustrated by one or more examples. Figure 5.1 presents the ontology graphically using UML class diagrams (Rumbaugh et al., 1991; OMG, 1999).

Actor

An actor is perceived by his/her environment as an economically independent (and often also legal) entity. Enterprises and end-consumers are examples of actors. A profit and loss responsible business unit, which can be seen as economically independent is an actor, although such a unit need not be a legal entity.

Economically independent: Refers to the ability of an actor to be profitable after a reasonable period of time (in case of an enterprise), or

---

1.   The notation is based on UML class diagrams. Rectangles are concepts, related by associations (lines). Concepts play a role in an association. Also, cardinality constraints are expressed; * represents 'many', for instance, a market segment has 1 or more value interfaces.

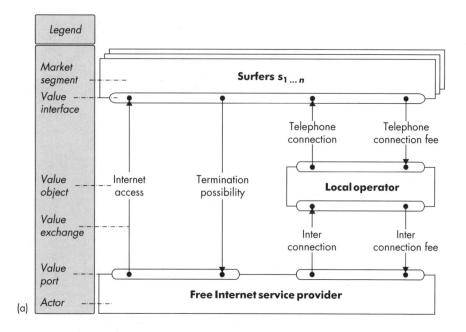

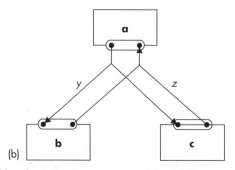

Figure 5.2: Value model for a free Internet access service. (a) The global actor viewpoint; (b) Actor **a** can decide to exchange value objects with actor **b** or actor **c**.

to increase value for him/herself (in case of an end-consumer). For a sound and viable e-Business idea, we require that each actor can be profitable or can increase his/her value. Nevertheless, we acknowledge that in the recent past, many e-Business ideas were put in operation for which this was not the case. Such ideas are not sustainable and are consequently not in the scope of our research.

Properties: An actor has a name, e.g. a company name, or a name that represents the role such an actor plays.

Visualization: An actor is depicted by a rectangle, with his/her enterprise or role name.

Example: The global actor viewpoint (see Figure 5.2) shows a *free Internet service provider* and a *local operator*. Also, *surfers* are presented as a market segment (to be discussed), which essentially is a set of actors valuing objects equally. The free Internet service provider is an actor who offers a service that the surfer is interested in: Internet access for free. The local operator exploits the local loop: the last mile of copper wire between a telephone switch and the home of a surfer. This loop is needed to set up a telephone connection between a surfer and the free Internet service provider. This telephone connection is used by the surfer's and provider's telecommunication equipment to access the Internet.

Value object

Actors exchange value objects. A value object is a service, a good, money, or even an experience, which is of economic value for at least one of the actors involved in a value model. Actors may value an object differently and subjectively, according to their own valuation preferences (Holbrook, 1999).

From a modelling point of view, we are interested in the *kind of* value objects which actors exchange, and not so much in the actual instances themselves. Therefore, when we speak about *value object*, we mean the kind of value object, or the prototype for all instances of a particular value object. In some cases, it is necessary to refer to the actual instances of objects of value exchanged by actors. We then call these objects *value object instances*.

Properties: A value object has a name. While choosing a name, one should keep in mind that it expresses the object from an economic value point of view.

Visualization: A value object is presented by showing the name of the object nearby a value exchange (to be discussed below), representing a potential trade of such an object, or by showing the name nearby value ports offering or requesting objects (see below).

Example: Many value objects in Figure 5.2 speak for themselves. The value object *termination possibility* is however non-trivial. *Termination* in the world of telecommunication operators means that if someone tries to set up a telephone connection by dialling a telephone number, someone else must pick up the phone, i.e. *terminate* the connection. If someone is willing to cause termination of a large quantity of telephone calls, most telecommunication operators are willing to pay such an actor for that. This is exactly what the free Internet service provider does: she/he aggregates a large number of *termination possibilities* from surfers and gets paid for that.

Also, the value object *interconnection* needs explanation. At the time the project was carried out there was in The Netherlands only one actor who operated the local loop, the last mile of copper wire between a telephone switch and the home of a surfer. From a surfer point of view, this local operator delivers an end-to-end telephone connection, in this case between the surfer and the free Internet service provider. However, the local operator does not operate a network that connects the surfer with the free Internet service provider directly. She/he only owns a part of that network. In such a case, the local operator must use an additional network, connected to the free Internet provider, which is owned by another operator to provide the surfer an end-to-end connection. In other words, the local operator must obtain *interconnection* from another Telco. In return for this, the local operator pays an interconnection fee.

Value port

An actor uses a value port to provide or request value objects to or from his/her environment, consisting of other actors. Thus, a value port is used to interconnect actors so that they are able to exchange value objects. A value object flowing in or out allows an actor to denotes a change of ownership, or a change in rights. The concept of port is important, because it enables an abstraction away from the internal business processes, and to focus only on how external actors and other components of the e-Business value model can be 'plugged in'. This is the value analogue of the separate external interfaces familiar from technical systems theory (Borst and Akkermans, 1997). Take, e.g. a bipolar in–out value multi-port, which is a characteristic combination occurring in e-Business value models: an e-service port out and a money port in, or the other way around. Such a bipolar value port combination can be very well compared to an electrical wall outlet. As an external user, you do not want to be involved in what happens behind the wall outlet as long as it gives the right quality of service. The same approach holds for how external parties in an e-Business value model view the value ports of a service-offering actor: the ports only define how the external connections to other actors should be made.

Properties: A value port has a *direction*, which can have the values *in* (shortly called an in-port) or *out* (called an out-port) indicating whether a value object flows in or out of an actor (seen from that actor).

Relations: A value port *offers* or *requests* one value object. This cardinality constraint again emphasizes that we are not so much interested in value object instances themselves, but rather in the prototype for such instances. A value object can be *requested by* or *offered by* zero or more value ports.

Visualization: The value port is depicted by a small black filled circle (see Figure 5.2). Value *in*-ports have an incoming arrow. The name of the value object offered/requested by the port can be depicted.

Value offering

A value offering models what an actor offers to (an out-going offering) or requests from (an in-going offering) his/her environment, and closely relates to the *value interface concept* (see below). A value interface models an offering of an actor to his/her environment, *and* the offering such an actor requests in return from his/her environment. In contrast, an offering is a set of equally directed value ports exchanging value objects, and implies that all ports in that offering should exchange value objects, or none at all.

A value offering is of use for representing a number of situations. First, some objects may only be of value for an actor if they are obtained in combination. In-ports exchanging such objects then form an in-going offering. Second, actors may decide to offer objects only in combination to their environment. In-ports offering such objects then form an out-going offering. An example of an out-going offering is the case of *mixed bundling*. Mixed bundling refers to the mechanism that an actor wants to offer value objects in combination rather than separately, because that actor supposes that different products sold in combination yield more profit than that if they were sold separately (Choi et al., 1997).

Relation: A value offering *consists of* one or more equally directed value ports. A value port is *in* exactly one offering.

Value interface

Actors have one or more value interfaces. In its simplest form, a value interface consists of one offering, but in most cases, a value interface group has one in-going and one out-going value offering. It shows then the mechanism of economic reciprocity. *Economic reciprocity* refers to rational acting actors. We suppose that actors are only willing to offer objects to someone else, if they receive adequate compensation (i.e. other value object(s) in an in-going offering) in return. So, with the value interface, we can model what an actor is willing to offer, something of value to his/her environment but requests something in return, whereas a value offering, models that objects which can only be requested or delivered in combination.

The exchange of value objects is atomic at the level of the value interface. Either all ports in a value interface (via value offerings) each precisely exchange one value object instance, or none at all. This ensures that if an actor offers something of value to someone else, she/he always gets in return what she/he wants. How this is ensured is a matter of a robust business process design, trust and associated control mechanisms (see e.g. Tan, 2002), legal agreements, or sometimes use of technology, but this is not expressed by the value model.

Relations: A value interface is *assigned to* zero or one actor and *consists of* one or two value offerings, in the latter case being an out-going and an in-going offering. Each actor has its own value interface. Multiple value interfaces can be assigned to an actor and a value offering belongs to exactly one value interface.

Visualization: The value interface is visualized by a rounded box at the edge of an actor. Value ports are drawn in the interior of the rounded box. Note that a value offering is not visualized explicitly. However, value offerings can be easily seen by grouping all out-going value ports in a value interface (the out-going offering), or by grouping all in-going value ports in a value interfaces (the in-going offering).

Example: Consider in Figure 5.2 the surfer. The in-going offering consists of telephone connection and Internet access. These objects are seen as one offering because they are only of value in combination for the surfer. An Internet connection is worthless without the telephone connection that is used for data transport. Also, for a surfer, the telephone connection is not of value without Internet access. The out-going offering contains the compensations for the obtained telephone connection and Internet access. These two offerings are grouped into a value interface to show that a surfer compensates its environment for obtaining a telephone connection and Internet access, with a fee and a termination possibility.

Value exchange

A value exchange is used to connect two value ports with each other. It represents one or more potential trades of value objects between value ports. As such, it is a prototype for actual trades between actors. It shows which actors are willing to exchange value objects with each other.

Relations: The value ports involved in a value exchange are represented by the *has in* and *has out* relations, which relate to exactly one in-port and to exactly one out-port. A value port may *connect* to zero or more value exchanges.

Figure 5.2(a) exemplifies a situation with a port connected to more than one value exchange. Value ports of actor **a**, offering/requesting value objects *y* and *z*, connect via value exchanges to ports of actor **b**, but also connect to ports of actor **c**. This situation models that an actor **a** and actor **b** are willing to exchange objects of value, and so do actor **a** and actor **c**. Note that the model does not represent the number of value exchanges over time, nor their ordering in time.

Visualization: A value exchange is shown as line between value ports. The name of the value object which is exchanged, is presented nearby the value exchange.

Value transaction

A value interface prescribes the value exchanges that should occur, seen from the perspective of an actor the value interface is connected to, because all ports in a value interface should exchange objects, or none at all. Sometimes, it is convenient to have a concept that aggregates all value exchanges, which define the value exchanges that must occur as consequence of how value exchanges are connected, via value interfaces to actors. We call this concept a value transaction. In its simplest form, a transaction is between two actors. However, a transaction can also be between more than two actors. We call such a transaction a *multi-party* transaction. Figure 5.2(b) shows a multi-party transaction between a surfer, a local operator, and a free Internet service provider.

Relation: A value transaction *consists of* one or more value exchanges. Note that the exchanges in a transaction should be consistent with the way these exchanges are connected to value interfaces. A value interface requires that if a value object is exchanged via a port, also exchanges must occur via all its other ports. These exchanges must be also part of the transaction.

Figure 5.3 exemplifies why a value exchange can be in multiple transactions. In this example, actor *a* offers two value objects, and wants to have two value objects in return. There are two sets of actors who are a capable of participating in the exchange of values with actor **a**: actors (**b$_1$**, c), and actors (**b$_2$**, c). Clearly, actor **a** must exchange values with actor **c** (there is no alternative), but there is a choice between actor **b$_1$** and actor **b$_2$** for the other exchanges. Consequently, we can distinguish two transactions with overlapping value exchanges. Transaction 1 consists of the value exchanges e_1, e_2, e_3, and e_4 and transaction 2 consist of the value exchanges e_1, e_2, e_5, and e_6. Value exchanges, which are in more than one transaction, occur in multi-party transactions, of which Figure 5.3 is an example.

Visualization: A value offering is shown by a line intersecting the value exchanges it contains. The intersection points are shown by small filled circles.

Example: Figure 5.3 shows a three-party offering between the free Internet service provider, a surfer, and a local operator. A surfer needs both to obtain Internet access, and to obtain a telephone connection, to be able to browse the Internet. From the surfer's value interface can be concluded that all four value exchanges connected to it are part of one transaction: either all ports of surfer's interface each exchange a value object or none at all.

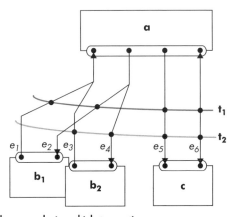

Figure 5.3: A value exchange can be in multiple transactions.

Market segment

In the marketing literature (Kotler, 1998), a market segment is defined as a concept that breaks a market (consisting of actors) into segments that share common properties. We employ the notion of market segment to show that a number of actors assign economic value to objects equally. This construct is often used to model that there is a large group of end-consumers who value objects equally. We realize that in practice no actor will value objects exactly the same, but supposing an equal valuation for some actor groups is a simplification needed to arrive at, comprehensible yet understandable, value models.

In most cases, the individual actors of a market segment are left implicit. With *implicit* we mean that we do not model these actors individually. This is also the modelling purpose of the market segment construct: to have a shorthand for a large number of actors. However, actors are independent companies or individuals. As such, a specific actor, being part of a market segment, may exchange also other value objects than those mentioned in that market segment. Consequently, a market segment groups *value interfaces* of actors, exchanging objects that are valued equally, rather than that it groups actors themselves. If an actor, who is part of a market segment, has additional value interfaces, which other actors in that segment do not have, we model such an actor also *explicitly*.

Finally, value exchanges drawn to a segment can be seen as a shorthand notation for value exchanges to all actors in that segment. If we assume that market segment **b** (implicitly) consists of actors b_1, b_2, and b_3, and these actors value objects the same way, Figure 5.4(b) is a shorthand notation for Figure 5.4(a).

Properties: A market segment is given a name, in must cases in plural form, such as customers, surfers, or alike. A market segment has a *count*, which indicates the number of actors in the segment. The count can be a number, unbound, or unknown.

Relations: As a market segment is a set of actors, a value interface can be *assigned to* zero or one market segment, just as an interface can be assigned to an actor. Objects exchanged via this value interface are valued equally by actors in the segment.

An actor can be *in* a market segment. This relationship is needed to represent actors who have, besides value interfaces of a market segment, additional value interfaces of themselves. The additional interfaces are then related to the actor him/her, while the relationship between actor and market segment is used to represent an actor's interfaces she/he has as a result of his/her membership in a market segment.

Visualization: A market segment is shown as three stacked actors. A value interface of a market segment is presented on one of the edges of the topmost actor. An explicitly modelled actor who is also part of a market segment is mentioned in the name of the market segment.

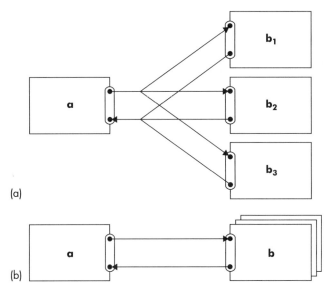

(a)

(b)

Figure 5.4: A value model without and with market segment. (a) Actor **a** exchanges value objects with actors **b₁**, **b₂** or **b₃**, who may value these objects differently; (b) Actor **a** exchanges value objects with actors **b₁**, **b₂** or **bₙ**, who value these objects equally.

Example: The *surfers* segment (Figure 5.5) consists of implicit actors who want to access the Internet.

Summary
In conclusion, the global actor viewpoint shows the top-level actors in a value model, without discussing constellations and partnerships yet. Also, the assignment of value activities to actors is not shown by this viewpoint. The global actor viewpoint shows the objects of value exchanged between actors. The market segment notion is useful if a large number of actors exists, who are supposed to assign economic value to value objects the same way.

The global actor viewpoint can be constructed in brainstorm sessions and workshops with all key actors. Also, this viewpoint can be used to present and explain the overall value model to stakeholders.

For the free Internet access service, the global actor viewpoint illustrates that the so-called free service is offered to surfers, but is not for free at all, since the surfer has to pay for a telephone connection. Also, this viewpoint shows that a local operator is needed to offer an Internet access service to surfers (Figure 5.6).

5.3.2 The detailed actor viewpoint
The purpose of a *detailed actor viewpoint* (see Figure 5.7) is twofold. First, a detailed actor viewpoint can be used to *detail* an actor identified on

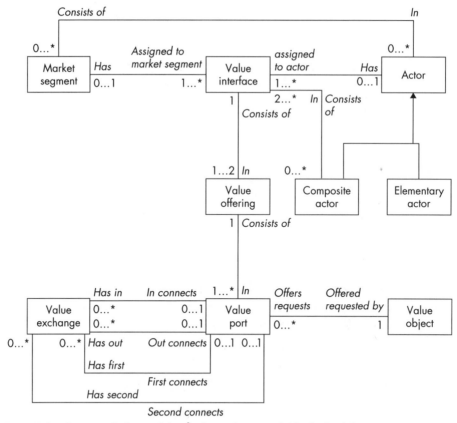

Figure 5.5: Concepts and relations of the e^3-value ontology extended for the detailed actor viewpoint. A composite actor and an elementary actor are generalized into an actor.

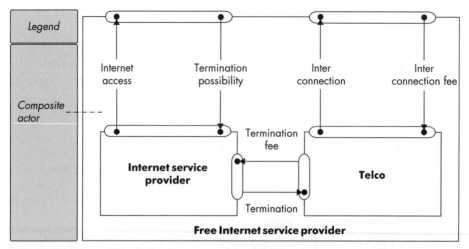

Figure 5.6: Value model for the free Internet case: the detailed free Internet service provider actor view.

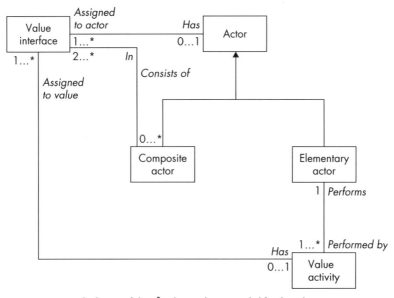

Figure 5.7: Concepts and relations of the e^3-value ontology extended for the value activity viewpoint.

the global actor viewpoint into more actors. We call such an actor a *value constellation*. A value constellation can be used to isolate parts of the value model to a limited number of actors, who can decide on that specific part without consulting other actors participating in the e-Business idea too much. A value constellation is also a way to reduce complexity on the global actor viewpoint, such that all actors can understand this viewpoint. A second reason to introduce a detailed viewpoint is the representation of *partnerships* between actors. As such, a number of actors may decide to present themselves, as a virtual enterprise actor, to their environment (see e.g. Davidow and Malone, 1992). These actors then decide on one common value interface to their environment.

Composite actor and elementary actor

For both earlier mentioned modelling purposes, we specialize the actor concept into a composite actor and an elementary actor (see Figure 5.5).

A *composite actor* groups value interfaces of other actors. Also, a composite actor has its own value interfaces to its environment. These composite actor's value interfaces allow us to (1) abstract away from the composite's internals or (2) to show a common value interface from actors who decide to present themselves as a virtual enterprise.

An *elementary actor* does not contain value interfaces of other actors. Such an actor is the lowest decomposition level that can be reached from an actor perspective.

Note we group *value interfaces* and not *actors* into a composite actor. The reason for this is that in case of partnerships, an actor may decide to offer objects jointly with objects of other actors, but also may decide to offer other objects on its own. Consequently, it is not the actor that is grouped, but what she/he is offering for a specific case. The same holds for introducing a composite actor in case of value constellations. Such an actor can group a number of value interfaces of the actors it contains, while interfaces of these actors may also appear somewhere else in the value model.

Relations: A composite actor *is an* actor. An elementary actor *is* also *an* actor. This means that all properties and relations identified for actors, will also hold for composite and elementary actors. A composite actor *consists of* minimal two value interfaces of other actors. We need at least two interfaces to be able to group meaningfully.

Visualization: A composite actor is visualized by drawing a rectangle around the actors whose value interfaces are grouped. Inside this rectangle, the value interfaces of the actors must be shown, which are grouped by the composite actor.

Example: The free Internet service provider appears to be a value constellation, which consists of two other actors: (1) an *Internet service provider* offering Internet access (e.g. by exploiting access servers) and (2) a specific *Telco* handling interconnection of telephone calls between the Internet service provider and the local operator.

The detailed actor viewpoint shows also exchanges of value objects between the Internet service provider and *Telco*. The provider terminates connections by exploiting an Internet access server (effectively a large modem-bank), which answers telephone calls made by the modems of surfers. Termination of large quantities of telephone calls is of value for *Telco*. Consequently, *Telco* pays the Internet service provider a termination fee.

Value exchange revisited

We have introduced the value exchange concept earlier to relate ports of actors exchanging objects. These connected ports have *opposite* directions. The value exchange construct is also used to relate value ports of a composite actor to value ports of actors being part of the composite. In this case, connected ports have *equal* directions. An object offered via an out-port of a composite actor still has to be offered via an out-port of one of the actors in the composite. Also an object requested via a composite actor's in-port must be requested by an in-port of one of the actors it contains.

Properties: To represent the various applications of value exchanges, we distinguish four types (see Table 5.1). A type 1 exchange relates ports of actors trading objects, while a type 2 exchange relates ports of a composite actor with ports of the actors it contains. Other types are discussed in the remainder of this chapter.

Relations: To stress that a type 2 value exchange, which connects ports with equal directions is different from a type 1 value interface

Table 5.1: Various value exchange types

Value exchange type	Relates port 1 of an	With port 2 of an	Ports have direction
1	Actor	Actor	Opposite
2	Composite actor	Actor	Equal
3	Elementary actor	Value activity	Equal
4	Value activity	Value activity	Opposite

which connects ports with opposite directions, other associations are shown in the ontology. A value exchange *has a first* value port of the composite actor, and *has a second* value port of one the actors contained by the composite actor.

Example: Figure 5.7 exemplifies a type 2 value exchange. The ports of the composite actor free Internet service provider are mapped on ports of value interfaces of the Internet service provider and *Telco*.

Summary

The detailed actor viewpoint intends to represent actors jointly offering or requesting a product or service to their environment, also called a partnership. Moreover, the viewpoint is used to detail specific parts of an e-Business value model, which are abstracted away on the global actor viewpoint (the value constellation). Strictly spoken, a composite actor groups value interfaces of other actors, not the actors themselves.

5.3.3 The value activity viewpoint

The main purpose of the *value activity* viewpoint is to illustrate the assignment of value activities to actors. Figure 5.8 shows this viewpoint for parts of the free Internet service provider. How value activities are assigned to the various possible actors is a free variable that, as a result of the extended enterprise network setting, leads to many design options and choices in e-Business value models. Hence, this assignment is a key consideration in strategic e-Business decision making.

Value activity

An important issue in value model design is the *assignment* of value activities to actors. Therefore, we are interested in the collection of operational activities which can be assigned as a whole to actors. Such a collection we call a value activity. Actors perform value activities, and to do so, a value activity must yield profit or should increase economic value for the performing actor. Consequently, we only distinguish value activities if at least one actor, but hopefully more, believes that she/he can execute the activity profitable. Value activities can be decomposed

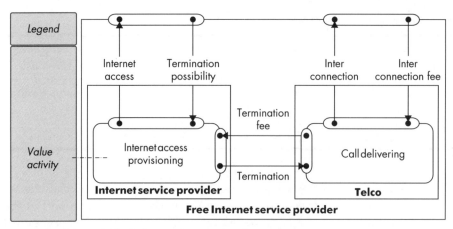

Figure 5.8: Value model for the free Internet case: the value activity view.

into smaller activities, but the same requirement stays: the activity should yield profit. This also gives a decomposition stop rule.

Relations: A value activity *has* one or more value interfaces, just like actors and market segments. A value interface belongs to exactly zero or one value activity. A value activity is *performed by* precisely one elementary actor. Finally, multiple value activities can be *performed by* an actor.

Visualization: A value activity is graphically presented by a rounded box, which is drawn inside the actor who performs the activity.

To draw readable diagrams, we sometimes omit value interfaces, ports and exchanges. In Figure 5.8, the Internet service provider shows no value interfaces anymore, while Figure 5.6 shows for the same actor two value interfaces. If a value interface of an actor has the same structure as a value interface of a value activity she/he performs, we may decide not to present the value interface of the actor. Two value interfaces have the same structure if each port of the first value interface can be matched with precisely one port of the second value interface, and vica versa. Matching of two ports is possible if both ports have the same direction and if they exchange the same value object. However, an omitted value interface conceptually exists, also value exchanges to connect an actor's value interface to a value interface of his/her value activity conceptually exist. The same holds true for composite actors: we may decide to omit value interfaces of a composite actor if they have the same structure as the value interfaces of actors with the same composite as theirs.

Example: The Internet service provider performs an Internet access provisioning activity. This activity comprises investment in and maintenance of Internet access servers. Another activity, which might be thought of is, e.g. a web hosting service. *Telco* executes an activity named call delivering. This activity is the exploitation of a physical network between the local operator and the Internet service provider for data transport. For all these activities, we assume that they are, after some period, profitable for the actors performing these activities.

Value exchange revisited

We also use the value exchange to connect ports of value activities with ports of the actor performing these activities. These are called type 3 value exchanges. Such ports must have the same direction. Also, ports of value activities, which are performed by the same actor can be connected by using type 4 value exchanges. These exchanges represent 'internal' trades of an actor. Such exchanges connect ports with an opposite direction.

Summary

The value activity viewpoint represents the assignment of value activities to actors. By assuming that a value activity is commercially interesting to be performed by at least one actor, but preferably more actors, we can shift activities from one actor to another actor, thereby discussing who is doing what. Especially if roles of actors are not clear, which is often the case for innovative e-Business projects, negotiating the assignment of activities to actors is an important part of the exploration track.

5.4 The e^3-value ontology and operational scenarios

Operational scenarios are used to capture parts of the e-Business idea and to contribute to a common understanding between stakeholders. Moreover, we use operational scenarios to evaluate an e-Business model. In this section, we focus on a scenarios role to capture parts of an e-Business value model, and more specifically we show how scenarios are used to specify by what phenomena exchanges of objects are caused. To represent operational scenarios, we utilize use case maps (UCMs), a generic lightweight scenario representation mechanism. The following sections discuss UCMs, and bind UCMs to our e^3-value ontology.

5.4.1 UCMs

A UCM is a visual notation to be used by humans to understand the behaviour of a system at a high level of abstraction (Buhr, 1998). It is a scenario-based approach intended to explicate cause–effect relationships by travelling over paths through a system.

The basic UCM notation is very simple, and consists of three basic elements: responsibilities, paths and components. The term component should be interpreted in a broad sense: it may be a software component,

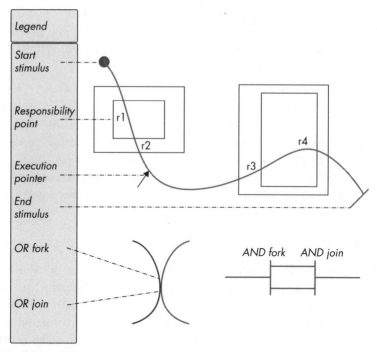

Figure 5.9: UCM constructs.

but it can also represent a human actor or a hardware system. A simple UCM exemplifying the basic elements is shown in Figure 5.9. A path is executed as a result of the receipt of an external stimulus. Imagine that an execution pointer is now placed on the start position (bullet at the top). Next, the pointer moves along the indicated scenario path, thereby entering and leaving components, and touching responsibility points. A responsibility point represents a place where the state of a system is affected or interrogated. The effect of touching a responsibility point is not defined in the UCM itself since the concept of state is not part of a UCM; typically, this effect is described in natural language. Finally, the end position is reached (stroke perpendicular to the scenario path) and the pointer is removed from the diagram.

In Figure 5.9 two frequently used UCM constructs are shown. The AND construct is used to spawn (AND fork) and synchronize (AND join) multiple parallel scenario paths. The OR construct is a means to express that a scenario path continuous in alternative directions.

To be meaningful, the UCM notation must be bound to some other notation, in our case the *e³-value* ontology. More specifically, we have to articulate the components UCM scenario paths can touch using responsibility points. Therefore, we present UCM's the same way as we did for our *e³-value* ontology, and relate scenario paths to *e³-value* ontology constructs.

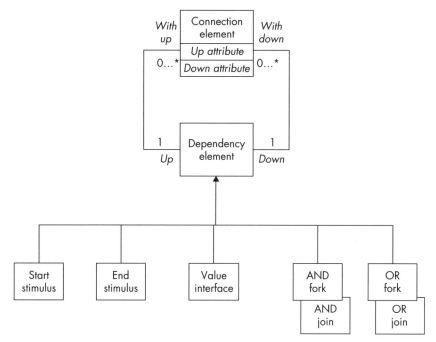

Figure 5.10: An ontology of UCMs based on Amyot and Mussbacher (2000).

5.4.2 An ontology for UCMs

A UML model for the representation of UCMs is shown in Figure 5.10. It is based on a UCM UML model by (Amyot and Mussbacher, 2000). Below we discuss the various UCM constructs, and exemplify their use in the free Internet access project. Value viewpoints enriched with UCMs are shown in Figure 5.11 (the global actor viewpoint) and Figure 5.12 (a detailed actor viewpoint).

We utilize a simple form of Buhr's UCMs. The two constructs used are *dependency elements* and *connection elements*.

Dependency element

A scenario is expressed by dependency elements, interconnected by connection elements (see below). Essentially, a scenario gives dependencies between value interfaces (a kind of connection element) so that we can reason for an entire model what happens with other value interfaces if we exchange values via one particular value interface.

Properties: Each dependency element can have a textual label for naming purposes.

Relations: A dependency element has one upper connection element and one lower connection element.

Visualization: Dependency elements are drawn using normal lines.

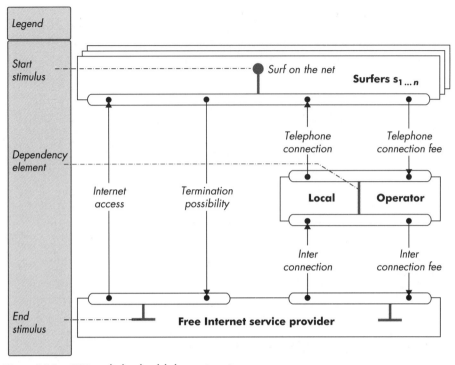

Figure 5.11: UCMs applied to the global actor viewpoint.

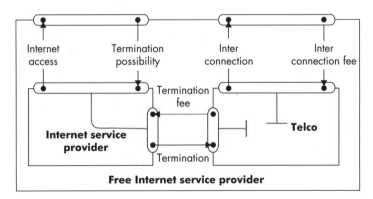

Figure 5.12: UCMs applied to the detailed actor viewpoint.

Connection element

A connection element connect various dependency elements. Dependency elements can be start and stop stimuli, AND/OR forks or joins and value interfaces (see below).

Properties: Each connection element can have a textual label for naming purposes.

Relations: A connection element has zero or more up-dependency elements. The same holds for down-dependency element.

Visualization: Connections elements are visualized, depending on their specific kind (see below).

Stimulus element

Scenarios start with one or more *start stimuli*. A start stimulus represents an event, possibly caused by an actor. If an actor causes an event, the start stimulus is drawn within the box representing the actor. A scenario also has one or more *end stimuli*. They have no successors.

Visualization: A start stimulus is visualized by a filled circle; an end-stimulus is presented by a line, placed in an angle of 90° on the line visualizing a dependency element. If an actor causes a stimulus, it is drawn in the interior of such an actor.

Example: The need for an actor to surf on the Internet is an example of a start stimulus. Such a stimulus results in a number of value exchanges between the actors participating in the value model.

AND and OR continuation elements

An *AND fork* connects a dependency element to one or more dependency elements, while the *AND join* connects one or more dependency elements to one other dependency element. It splits a scenario into more sub scenarios or merges sub scenarios into one scenario (see for a path the discussion below). An *OR fork* models a continuation of the scenario into one direction, to be chosen from a number of alternatives. The *OR join* merges two or sub scenarios into one scenario.

Visualization: An *AND* fork/join is shown as a line, placed in an angle of 90° between lines visualizing dependency elements. An *OR* fork/join is presented by a number of lines joining into one (a join), or by a line splitting into more lines (a fork).

Value interface

Another way to connect dependency elements is to use a value interface. We use value interfaces (connected by dependency elements) to create profitability sheets on a per actor basis to assess profitability (see the following section). Such a sheet shows when objects of value are leaving or entering an actor as a result of scenario path execution.

5.5 Profitability sheets

If we ask enterprises and end-consumers to assign economic value to the value objects they obtain and offer, and we know the number of start stimuli per time frame (say a month), we can assess potential profitability for each actor involved. We capture profitability numbers

Table 5.2: Structure of a profitability sheet

Actor	Actor name	
Scenario path	Path name	
Number of occurrences/ timeframe	Number of occurrences	
	Value object-in	Value object-out
	Euro x_1	Euro y_1

in profitability sheets on a per actor bases. Table 5.2 shows the structure of such a sheet.

To create profitability sheets for actors, we utilize our UCM scenario paths. These paths put into operation a scenario, and show which value objects are exchanged by actors via their value interfaces, as a result of the occurrence of one or more start stimuli. Profitability sheets are constructed by following each scenario path. By doing so, we find the objects of value each actor exchanges as a result of executing the path. Each time we cross a value interface, we add the object(s) flowing out the interface of that actor to the actor's profitability sheet in the column *value object-out*, while the objects flowing into an actor are added to the actor's profitability sheet in the column *value object-in*.

For enterprises, profitability analysis boils down to a net cash flow analysis: for enterprises we only take into account value objects denoting money. This is confirm traditional investment analysis (Horngren and Foster, 1987), that takes the net present value of all in-going and out-going money streams (including an initial investment). Given a certain discount rate, this net present value should be at least a positive number for each enterprise involved.

On the other hand, for end-consumers, profitability analysis is far more difficult. End consumers are interested to increase their economic utility, or to do a best-for-money deal. The problem here is that we have to assign economic value (in terms of a monetary unit) to non-money objects such as Internet access. According to axiology literature (Holbrook, 1999) valuation by end-consumers is subjective and may include many factors. Nevertheless, we have found it very useful to discuss with stakeholders at least factors which might influence valuation of objects by end-consumers. This leads to a better understanding of enterprises why an end-consumer wants to buy a value object in the first place.

Finally, focusing on profitability numbers themselves is not of particular interest since there are so many assumptions they are based upon. We have learned that doing sensitivity analysis is far more important. With sensitivity analysis, we vary factors in the model we are uncertain about, for instance the number of start stimuli, the way actors assign economic value to objects, or the structure of the model itself. More information on doing sensitivity analysis on e^3-value models can be found in (Gordijn and Akkermans, 2003).

5.6 Related enterprise ontologies

A number of other enterprise ontologies exist. Here we discuss the AIAI enterprise ontology, the TOVE ontology, the REA ontology and Osterwalder's ontology.

5.6.1 AIAI enterprise ontology

The AIAI enterprise ontology (Uschold, 1998) defines a collection of terms and definitions relevant to business enterprises. Two enterprise ontology concepts relate to our ontology but have a different interpretation: (1) *activity* and (2) *sale*. In the enterprise ontology, *activity* is the notion of actually doing something, the how. Our related definition, *value activity*, abstracts from the internal process and in contrast stresses the externally visible outcome in terms of created value, independent from the nature of the operational process. Thus, the defining boundary of what an activity differs: in the e^3-value ontology the decomposition stop rule is to look at economically independent activities; business process or workflow activities have different decomposition rules, as such activities need not be economically independent. The enterprise ontology further defines a *sale* as an agreement between two legal entities to exchange one good for another good. In our ontology, the concept of sale roughly corresponds to the concept of *transaction*, with the important difference that a sale is an actual agreement, while a transaction is only a potential one. A transaction contains *value exchanges*. In the enterprise ontology, only two goods are exchanged in a sale. In contrast, in our ontology a transaction contains an arbitrary number of value exchanges. This is needed to model a *bundle* of goods that is offered or requested as a whole. Furthermore, our ontology is capable of multi-party transactions. The project in this chapter illustrates the need for such a concept.

5.6.2 TOVE

The TOVE ontology (Fox, 1998) identifies concepts for the design of an agile enterprise. An agile company integrates his/her structure, behaviour and information. The TOVE ontology currently spans knowledge of activity, time and causality, resources, cost, quality, organization structure, product and agility. However, the interfaces an enterprise has to its environment are lacking in TOVE. Generally, the notion of the creation, distribution, and consumption of value in a stakeholder network is not present in the TOVE ontology. Hence, the

TOVE ontology concentrates on the internal workflow of a company, whereas our ontology captures the outside value exchange network.

5.6.3 REA

The REA ontology (Geerts, 1999) shows from an ontological perspective many similarities with the *e³-value* ontology. REA calls *actors agents*. Agents are offering or requesting *resources* (in *e³-value* called *value objects*) by economic *events*. The latter can be compared to *value ports* in *e³-value*. REA relates economic events of different actors by *exchanges* which correspond to *e³-value* value exchanges. Finally, economic events of an agent are related by a *duality* relation. This models economic reciprocity which is handled by *e³-value* by the notion of *value interface*.

From an ontological perspective, *e³-value* and REA differ with respect to the notion of *value activity*. This concept lacks in REA, but is important for e-Business idea exploration. A value activity is a potential profitable activity for one or more actors. Due to e-Business development tracks are characterized by shifts in actors performing these activities, it is important to model value activities explicitly.

From a methodological point of view, REA is not an approach for business development, whereas *e³-value* provides a methodology for doing so, e.g. by value model construction and reconstruction, and by profitability-based sensitivity analysis.

5.6.4 Osterwalder and Pigneur ontology

Osterwalder and Pigneur (2003) propose an ontology for business models consisting of four pillars: (1) product innovation, (2) customer relationship, (3) infrastructure management and (4) financial aspects (see also Chapter 4). The product innovation pillar covers aspects of value that the firm offers to its customers. The customer relationship aspect is about the definition of target customers, the channels used to reach and communicate with customers, and the kind of relationship a firm wants to establish with a customer. Infrastructure management focuses on the capabilities, value configurations, and partnerships necessary in order to create value and reach the customer. Finally, their ontology includes facilities for representing financial aspects of a business model. Ontologically, this ontology is rather comprehensive, but not sufficiently lightweight. The latter is for instance important for having a tractable instrument in workshops.

From a methodological viewpoint, the ontology currently lacks a convenient way for visualizing business models, which is important for using the ontology in a practical way. Additionally, the ontology seems not so much intended for designing business models themselves, but is more biased towards ontologically stating what a business model actually is.

5.7 Conclusion and further research

In this chapter, we have presented the e^3-value ontology for e-Business models. Our ontology provides a rigorous approach for specifying and analysing e-Business models. The intent of our modelling methodology is twofold.

First, the methodology should contribute to a better understanding of a particular e-Business model. Since most e-Business models involve many enterprises, the risk of not having a shared understanding is high. Moreover, even for a single enterprise, participation of a wide range of stakeholders is required, who may not speak the language of another participant. We address this issue by providing a rigorous framework of concepts and relations between these, which together can be used to conceptualize an e-Business idea. In addition, we have for most concepts in the ontology a visual presentation. By using this visualization, we can present the heartbeat of an e-Business model graphically.

In addition to the creation of a shared understanding of the e-Business idea there is a second reason to use the e^3-value ontology. Once an e-Business model has been conceptualized and visualized, it can be analysed (e.g. using ontological rules that state what a value e-Business model is), and it can be assessed for potential profitability. This makes the ontology more than a conceptualizing instrument.

There are plenty of opportunities to do more research along the lines of the e^3-value ontology. Below, we mention a few of such lines. For example, models made by using the e^3-value ontology focus on economic value only, whereas most e-Business idea require a (re)implementation of inter-organizational business processes and cooperating information systems. How can we use business models to construct such processes and information systems? Another research track is in the field of trust. Business models assume that value exchanges via interfaces are always atomic. In other words: if A pays B for a good, B will deliver the good to A. Needless to say that this is not always the case in practice. So, how can we extend the ontology with constructs to guarantee this atomicity of value exchanges, for instance by trust means? Finally, e^3-value ontological concepts themselves need to be worked out. For instance, what kinds of value objects exist? Is there a principal difference between services and goods in the context of business models? What different forms of actor (de) compositions are convenient for modelling? We now have partnerships and value constellations, but perhaps other ones are applicable?

In sum, ontologically founded business value modelling is a starting, yet promising field of research. A particular strength of business value modelling is the capability to overcome the bridge between verbally articulated strategic intents of networked enterprises, and the way of putting these intents into operation by means of inter-organizational business processes and information systems, in a concise yet thorough way.

References and Further Reading

Amyot, D. and G. Mussbacher (2000). On the Extension of UML with Use Case Maps Concepts. *UML 2000 – The Unified Modeling Language. Advancing the Standard*, Vol. **1939** of LNCS. A. Evans, S. Kent, and B. Selic (eds). Berlin D, Springer Verlag: 16–31.

Borst, W. N. and J. M. Akkermans (1997). 'Top.Engineering Ontologies.' *International Journal of Human–Computer Studies* **46**: 365–406.

Buhr, R. A. J. (1998). 'Use Case Maps as Architectural Entities for Complex Systems.' *IEEE Transactions on Software Engineering* **24**(12): 1131–1155.

Cassidy, J. (2002). *Dot.con*. Perennial, Harper Collins.

Choi, S. J., D. O. Stahl and A. B. Whinston (1997). *The Economics of Doing Business in the Electronic Marketplace*. Indianapolis, IN, MacMillan Technical Publishing.

Davidow, W. H. and M. S. Malone (1992). *The Virtual Corporation – Structuring and Revitalizing the Corporation for the 21st Century*. New York, NY, HarperCollings.

Fox, M. S. and M. Gruninger (1998). 'Enterprise Modelling.' AI Magazine, *Fall* **19**(3): 109–121.

Geerts, G. and W. E. McCarthy (1999). 'An Accounting Object Infrastructure For Knowledge-Based Enterprise Models.' *IEEE Intelligent Systems and their Applications* (July–August): 89–94.

Gordijn, J. (2002). *Value-based Requirements Engineering: Exploring Innovative e-Commerce Ideas*. PhD thesis, Free University Amsterdam, NL. Also available via http://www.cs.vu.nl/~gordijn/thesis.htm.

Gordijn, J. and J. M. Akkermans (2003). 'Value Based Requirements Engineering: Exploring Innovative e-Commerce Idea.' *Requirements Engineering Journal*, in print, Web version: http://link.springer.de/link/service/journals/00766/contents/03/00169.

Holbrook, M. B. (1999). *Consumer Value: A Framework for Analysis and Research*. New York, NY, Routledge.

Horngren, C. T. and G. Foster (1987). *Cost Accounting: A Managerial Emphasis*, 6th edition. Englewood Cliffs, NJ, Prentice-Hall.

Kotler, P. (1988). *Marketing Management: Analysis, Planning, Implementation and Control*. Englewood Cliffs, NJ, Prentice Hall.

Loucopoulos, P. and V. Karakostas (1995). *System Requirements Engineering*. Berkshire, UK, McGraw-Hill.

Normann, R. and R. Ramírez (1993). 'From Value Chain to Value Constellation: Designing Interactive Strategy.' *Harvard Business Review* (July–August): 65–77.

Normann, R. and R. Ramírez (1994). *Designing Interactive Strategy – From Value Chain to Value Constellation*. Chichester, UK, John Wiley & Sons Inc.

OMG Unified Modeling Language Specification, Version 1.3. 1999.

Osterwalder, A. and Y. Pigneur (2003). Towards Strategy and Information Systems Alignment through a Business Model Ontology, to appear in the *Proceedings of the 23rd Annual International Conference of the Strategic Management Society (SMS) Baltimore*.

Porter, M. E. (2001). 'Strategy and the Internet.' *Harvard Business Review* (March): 63–78.

Porter, M. E. and V. E. Millar (1985). 'How Information Gives you Competitive Advantage.' *Harvard Business Review* (July–August): 149–160.

Rumbaugh, J., I. Jacobson, and G. Booch (1999). *The Unified Modelling Language Reference Manual*. Reading, MA, Addison Wesley Longmann, Inc.

Shama, A. (2001). 'Dot-coms Coma.' *The Journal of Systems and Software* 56(1): 101–104.

Tapscott, D., D. Ticoll and A. Lowy (2000). *Digital Capital – Harnessing the Power of Business*. London, UK, Nicholas Brealy Publishing:.

Tan, Y. H. (2002). 'Formal Aspects of a Generic Model of Trust for Electronic Commerce.' *Decision Support Systems* 33(3): 233–246.

Uschold, M., M. King, S. Moralee and Y. Zorgios (1998). 'The Enterprise Ontology.' *The Knowledge Engineering Review* 13(1): 31–89.

Part Two

---

e-Business Markets and Strategies

6 A causal network analysis of e-market business models

Jon Moon

Abstract

The proliferation of e-market (EM) business models has been a major interest to academics and practitioners alike. Yet gaining profits from EMs has been a challenge, with many business models proving to be flawed and unsustainable. The failure of EMs has focused attention on the business models that generate revenues for the firm and add value to the customer. Defining and delineating the key constructs and variables pertaining to EM business models is difficult, yet important for understanding causal relationships leading to successful business performance. This research study focuses upon the development of EMs in four UK firms using the constructs: business model, market conditions, and user acceptance. From structured interviews with executives, data is collected on the EM business models, which is analysed using process decomposition diagrams. A causal network analysis identifies the relationships between antecedent, intervening and outcome variables, which influence business performance from the EMs. An EM paradox model is developed to depict declining revenues and margins due to the failure of EMs to capitalize on differentiated markets or the benefits they bring to buyers. EM business performance is influenced by technological and customer turbulence, as well as competitive intensity. Acceptance of technology acts as an important partial moderator to business performance.

6.1 Introduction

Internet services that bring many buyers and sellers together to transact are termed EMs. EMs aim to reduce the cost of a buyer seeking a suitable supplier of a product or service and reduce the cost for a seller to find buyers (Grover and Teng, 2001). The failure of many EMs has focused attention on the business models that generate revenues for the firm and add value to the customer. Defining and delineating *EM business models* is challenging (Timmers, 1999). One method is a taxonomy that examines sources of revenue generation (Rappa, 2000). Another is to deconstruct e-Business models into atomic models that represent the core building blocks of all e-Business ventures (Weill and Vitale, 2001). Porter (2001) and Amit and Zott (2001) argue that a business model should be defined by how it creates value, not just revenue.

The theory of EMs is rooted in the EM hypothesis (EMH) (Malone et al., 1989). EMH describes the principles, nature and evolution of EMs. In their description of EMH, Malone et al. (1989) observe: 'By reducing the costs of coordination, IT will lead to an overall shift toward proportionately more use of markets – rather than hierarchies – to coordinate economic activity.' Garbade (1982) delineated EMs into four categories: direct search markets, brokered markets, dealer market, and auction markets. A four-layer framework for measuring the size of the Internet economy was developed by Barua et al. (1999). Two of the layers of the framework (the intermediary layer and the *commerce layer*) were used to describe general Internet commerce business models (Mahadevan, 2000). Mahadevan divided the models into three *market structures*: portal, market makers, and product/service providers.

Other studies (Davis, 1989) have developed the concept of user acceptance of e-Business models. By developing attributes of user acceptance, it is possible to determine the significant barriers to business performance and success of Web sites. Dai and Kauffman (2002) examined EM business models in terms of their roles and functions. They found that business-to-business (B2B) EMs offer basic market functions, satisfy management needs, and serve as technology adapters. They identified a number of business models and concluded that, although B2B EMs may be in their formative stages, value is embedded in these virtual markets.

The concept of reduced transaction costs is paramount in studies on EMs. Bakos (1997) examined two areas: *search costs* in differentiated and commodity markets and *strategic conduct* in e-marketplaces. Through the application of economic models, an understanding of both the conduct of participants in EMs and the consequences of changes in search costs emerged. For commodity markets, the concept of *reservation price* (Bakos, 1991) was used. This concept works on the principle that the expected gain from using an EM would equate to the previous cost of searching. Bakos argued that the resulting impact of search costs on commodity markets would be fourfold:

▪ seller prices would decrease as search costs decreased;

▪ the amount of searching would increase as search costs decrease;

▪ the amount of searching would increase as seller prices become more dispersed;

▪ as sellers' prices become more dispersed, buyers' costs decrease.

For differentiated markets, Bakos utilized the *unit circle model* (Salop, 1979) that works on the basis of a buyer searching until they locate a product or service close enough to their preference. As search costs decrease, buyers become more demanding and are prepared to search for a product or service that more closely meets their ideal requirements. On this principle, as search costs decrease, price premiums and seller margins increase. A later study on the effect of reducing search costs on the emergence of new markets or the maintenance of existing markets, Bakos (1997) suggests that a seller's best strategy for EMs may be to control the type of system introduced. A system that emphasized product rather than price may enable some retention of margin and even command a fee for its use. He used the example of ticketing in the airline industry. Lower search costs (for the consumer) are compensated for by making it difficult to compare prices due to complex fare structures and availability (Dahl and Miller, 1990). A move by American Airlines to simplify fare structures was resisted by other airlines. Bakos argues that airline reservation systems fit the model of an EM in a differentiated market. Some early research indicates that EMs are more efficient than conventional markets as far as price levels and price elasticity. Where significant price dispersion has been found, it can be explained by retailer-specific factors, such as branding and trust (or fear of transaction risks) or price discrimination strategies (Smith et al., 1999).

In a study of computerized loan systems in the home mortgage market, Hess and Kemerer (1994) concluded that either the full results predicted by EMH require a longer gestation period or that it needs some modification to fully explain the observed results. The work looked at five case studies and observed that the best of those cases could be described as an electronic hierarchy. Hess and Kemerer proposed some alternative views that provide some insight into why the take up of EMs may not be as easy or as rapid as the EMH may indicate. For example, transaction risk depicts the risk of opportunistic behaviour by the other party to a transaction in an EM. This may indicate that buyers prefer to form more tightly coupled, cooperative relationships with suppliers. This equates to an amended form of EMH termed the 'move to the middle' hypothesis (Clemons and Row, 1992). Suppliers may refuse to participate in EMs because they perceive that most benefits would be captured by buyers and that there are declining marginal returns (Clemons et al., 1993). There are 'non-contractible investments' in any transaction that may lead buyers to limit the number of suppliers they engage (Bakos and Brynjolfsson, 1993).

If transactions via an EM are like any other contract, difficulties arise in writing complete contracts that adequately specify the tangible and intangible elements required to satisfy the buyer that a transaction has been successful. Some contractual requirements may be difficult to specify. In an EM, face-to-face communication between the parties is unlikely, so issues of trust are likely to be more pronounced than in traditional buyer–seller relationships (Silver, 1984; Pisano et al., 1988, 1989; Mowery and Rosenberg, 1989).

Since transaction cost economics (TCE) only partially explains the drivers for EMs, it is important to examine other tangible and intangible elements of buyer–seller behaviour, such as the quality of the goods and supplier. In a study on Inventory Locator System (ILS), Choudhury et al. (1998) found that current models did not reflect the true complexity of EMs. They provide examples of the system helping buyers find better prices and of sellers obtaining a price premium through providing more detailed or accurate information about parts and their availability. The study also concludes that ILS has had little effect on the use of brokers in the industry, or on inventory levels. A study of AUCNET, the Japanese electronic car auction market, provided evidence that use of an EM actually resulted in higher prices for the seller (Lee, 1998). This was the result of both the application of rigorous quality control concerning the vehicles reaching the market and the lack of seller transport costs through not having to physically take unsold cars back to their home location.

The evidence from the various studies suggests that the general proposition of EMH is useful, but partial evidence fails to provide a complete picture of EMH. This view is supported by a study of retail financial services and the music industries. Daniel and Klimis (1999) compared the EMH to the observed status of EMs in those markets. The study found that EMH is generally accepted as valid and that it can be expected that both industries will evolve toward personalized markets and that there might be two variants of these markets. Regionalized personal markets (buyers prefer suppliers that are not very remote or who do have established credibility – financial services). Reverse markets (suppliers bid to win business from published buyer requirements). This is a concept that had previously been proposed by Hagel and Armstrong (1997). There was a lack of evidence of unbiased marketplaces and that this might be due to factors, such as a lack of numbers of retailers that have transitioned to EMs, the persistence of customer preferences to shop in the physical world or customers remaining loyal to suppliers instead of searching EMs.

From the discussion above, it is possible to conclude that studies of a variety of industries indicate that EMH does not fully describe the observed facts although it does appear to have a reasonable degree of validity. Perhaps the dichotomy of EMs and EMH can best be summarized by Grover and Ramanlal (1999) who discussed ways in which sellers can survive the intensely competitive environment foreseen by EMH. Discussing six myths and counter-myths of IT and markets, they concluded that if EMs are effective markets facilitated by IT, there are four drivers towards price competition: reduction in transaction costs, reduction of perceived product complexity, reduction in asset specificity, and increase of free information flow.

It may be possible for suppliers to utilize IT for their own benefit and that EMs may not always work in the customer's favour. Examples might include making price comparison difficult or exploitation of small niches, or the AUCNET example where careful control of the quality of goods brought to the EM combined with lower seller costs actually keeps prices higher than in traditional markets. Quantitative aspects relating to EMs do not show the whole picture. Qualitative aspects concerning the buyer–seller relationship, trust and tacit contractual terms are all important in understanding how EMs work.

This study extends the work on EMs by examining four business models using the constructs of business model, market conditions, and user acceptance, all of which influence business performance from EMs. Two research questions are developed from the literature:

Q1: How is the business performance of an EM influenced by the nature of the EM business model?

Q2: Does acceptance of EM technology by potential customers of the EM moderate an EMs business performance?

6.2 Research methodology

To answer the research questions, a research methodology was needed to elicit data to describe the relationships between the variables. An exploratory–descriptive case study approach was adopted (Lynd and Lynd, 1929; Whyte, 1955; Bickman and Rog, 1998) with the unit of analysis the EM of the firm. A sample of four firms was chosen, reflecting a variety of B2B EMs. A small sample size is appropriate when the objective of the research is theory building rather than testing (Eisenhardt, 1989) and when the data collected is used for descriptive and analytical purposes rather than the basis of comparison. This research seeks to identify some of the key business performance issues resulting from a particular type of EM business model.

6.2.1 Data collection and analysis

The technique used for collecting qualitative data for the business model, market conditions, and user acceptance constructs was structured interviews (Bickman and Rog, 1998). Interviews were conducted at each of the firms studied. The interviews were conducted at the offices of the firms and were carried out with the participation of senior executives of the firm:

1 Firm A: CEO and Financial Director.

2 Firm B: Managing Director, Head of Strategy and Marketing Director.

3   Firm C: Financial Director and CEO.

4   Firm D: Managing Director and Sales Director.

The interviews were held over a period of 3 months using the interview structure attached as Appendix 6A. The short period of time for the initial interviews was an advantage, which enabled repeat visits to the firms after only 1 month to collect additional data. This provided the opportunity to capture any changes to EM business models. Interviews were conducted both as individual sessions and then as joint sessions between the interviewer and the personnel employed by the participating firm. All interviews were recorded and transcribed onto Word 2000 software. The interviewees signed off transcribed interviews as a fair reflection of the discussions that took place.

The EM business models are analysed by way of process decomposition diagrams (Bickman and Rog, 1998; Malone et al., 1999) together with descriptive rich text (Yin, 1994). This qualitative method of representing the business model allowed common features as well as differences between models to be clearly identified and documented. Researching the firms' Web sites and documenting the services the firms offered initially the constructed models. The models were then validated during the course of the structured interviews and modified to reflect the views of the research partner firms' people. Causal network analysis is used to identify key variables, which influence business performance from EM business models.

6.3 Case studies

A brief description of the firms, a pseudonym and the reason for their inclusion is outlined in Table 6.1.

Table 6.1: Case study sample

Firm	A	B	C	D
Pseudonym	Integrated Solution.com	Purchasing.com	Industry.com	Evolve.com
Reason for inclusion	Broad range of services offered that provide for a complex and interesting business model	A straight forward EM concept, but with additional functionalities. Horizontal market model	A vertical industry EM, operating a simple business model	An example of a firm that is evolving its business model quickly in response to market conditions

6.3.1 Process description of business models

For each of the four sample firms, a process model was developed to represent their business model using a process summary display. The process models were constructed initially using data provided by the firms (sales literature, Internet, Web sites, and verbal descriptions). The process models provide insight into the operations undertaken by the firms. These models are illustrated in Appendix 6B.

Although all of the models examined are EMs, Firm A is highly specialized and offers a very broad range of services other than the EM. Firm B is a generic purchasing portal, which is the main focus of its activity. Firm C focuses on EM activities, but is highly specialized, operating in one market only. It may therefore share some characteristics with Firm B. Firm D has a much broader range of activities than any of the other firms and is evolving towards an application service provider (ASP) business model.

6.3.2 Themes emerging from the interviews

During the interviews, a number of themes emerged that related to the research model constructs. A cross-case analysis was conducted. This method enables a deeper understanding of causes and effects observed during the case studies. Although, it has been argued that cross-case comparisons are inappropriate in qualitative studies (Denzin, 1983; Guba and Lincoln, 1994), it is important to assess the applicability of the research results across similar cases (Firestone and Herriott, 1983). This is supported by Yin (1994) who advocates a *replication strategy* in case research. The approach adopted in the presentation of the results that follow is one of *variable oriented strategies* (Miles and Huberman, 1994). Specifically, the examination of recurring themes is a technique that can identify variables that would not be wholly clear without cross-case analysis (Eisenhardt, 1989).

6.3.3 Business model, market conditions and user acceptance

Table 6.2 is a clustered summary of the themes identified from the interviews conducted in the four firms using the constructs: business model, market conditions, and user acceptance. The table is constructed to cross reference the theme to the firms (A, B, C, or D) that identified the theme. In this way, a degree of commonality can be observed.

Whilst quantitative studies may yield strong causal attributes, qualitative analysis is also a very powerful methodology for assessing causality since it is able to include the connections between underlying variables and processes (Miles and Huberman, 1994). A technique that is very useful for qualitative analysis is that of analytic induction (Manning, 1982). After identifying an initial explanation of a phenomenon identified in a single case, other cases are examined to determine whether or not the

Table 6.2: Clustered summary table of themes

Construct	Theme	Firm	Illustration
Business Model	Retention of technical staff is critical to continued success	A	I ... technical staff once qualified as programmers can move on quickly.
	Sales is a key process	A B	II ... Return on IT Investments (ROI) service is a foot in the door and is the evidence people need to make a decision. This process is seen as a key differentiator.
	Credibility is key	A	Product must work from day one ...
	Target first adopter firms to maximize success	A	... they are most likely to buy.
	Future is more complex software that can automate more	A	
	Future focus will be on becoming an ASP business model	A C D	... that might involve the development of specialist software applications that could be downloaded and licensed via the Web in an ASP type business model.
	Supplier Management through the use of service level agreements (SLAs) is key	B	... a key part of the management of suppliers involves the setting up and monitoring of SLAs.
	Margin is a challenge	B C D	Exchanges put pressure on margins because of the increased transparency, and we are experiencing margin reductions
	Evolving service lines (e.g. professional services, changing from EM to managed Service Providers (MSP))	C D	... takes the firm away from reliance on a transaction fee in what is essentially a commodity market, subject to eroding margins.
	Risk of market bias	C D	It might be possible for a few large players to manipulate the market price ...
	Industry knowledge a key differentiator	D	
Market conditions	Market is difficult, but growth will still occur	A B	Growth will still occur, but at a slower rate.

(continued)

Table 6.2: (*continued*)

Construct	Theme	Firm				Illustration
						… we are moving into a recessionary phase in the UK and that will make customers focus on propositions centred on cost reduction rather than expansion.
	Market is buoyant			C		… market is reasonably buoyant at present.
	Market is tough				D	Market conditions are very volatile and very tough … markets are going out of business as cash runs out Through excessive burn rates of working capital and adoption by users remains slow.
User acceptance	Technology acceptance is a significant barrier to success: it limits the market's liquidity	A	B	C	D	Technology acceptance is an issue, but possibly less so with early adopter firms. … the service is not difficult to sell, but getting people to use it is a major challenge. … in a very traditional industry sector, getting the new technology accepted by users is not easy.
	Quality of customer data is poor	A			D	If clients have not cleaned the data used to populate (the EM) then users tend not to be confident and are slow to adopt it.
	Training users has to be included in the service	A			D	
	Cost of implementing for customers higher than expected				D	… this was complex, time consuming and expensive.
	Design of the Web pages helps increase adoption	A			D	This ensures intuitive navigation for users and that the product is easy to use.
	Customers do not expect to have anything to do with their processes once they are outsourced	A				This is a governance issue.
	Buyers to not want to damage the existing relationships with suppliers		B	C		Buyers have already invested in relationships with their suppliers and therefore do not want to take the risk of conducting transactions with sellers who are unknown to them.

phenomenon (a causal linkage) is supported in a more generalizable sense. From the results recorded in Table 6.2 a number of themes emerged. These themes are observed phenomena to which a cause can be attributed. Interviewee responses concerning business models revealed a number of insights, such as, the importance of a robust sales process. The majority of the firms also stressed that business models were likely to evolve over time. For example, the move to an ASP from an EM model.

All the firms felt that margins were inevitably going to fail because the EM model increased transparency of prices in the marketplace (Bakos, 1997). They reasoned that an increase in sellers in the market would result in buyers demanding lower prices. This would reduce sellers' margins. Buyers and sellers did not want to pay the commissions or transaction fees being demanded by the market operator. This despite the observation that some of the EMs had spent very significant sums in cleaning and formatting product data supplied by sellers so that it would be compatible with the Web site structure. On the other hand, buyers argued that because they brought large buying power to the market (and therefore attracted sellers to the marketplace) they did not want to pay standard fees or commissions either. The effect of this was a substantial reduction (up to 90%) in the fees the EM was able to charge users. This finding pointed to the need for a revision in the EM business model. The exception to this was Firm C, who specialized in an industry specific market in which the number of transactions was low, but of high value. This also fits with Bakos' finding on commodity and differentiated markets (1997).

The interviews provided some interesting insights into the area of technology acceptance. All firms experienced issues in getting people to readily adopt the EM technology. In one case (Firm A) it was felt that it was not such an issue where customers were generally early adopters of technology. In order to get customers to use the EM frequently, the EMs had to invest substantially in training the customers' staff. For the most part, this was carried out free of charge, thus putting further pressure on margins. Some of the causes of non-adoption included:

- Web site design.

- Ownership of the buying process (e.g. customer has to take some responsibility to ensure implementation).

- Fear of damaging relationships with existing suppliers.

6.4. Causal network analysis

The causal network diagram (see Figure 6.6, page 154) identifies a number of variables that influence business model success based on the output of the interviews conducted and the themes identified in Table 6.2:

- EM concept (business model).

- Acceptance of technology.

- Buyer–seller relationship.

- Business model success.

- Market transparency.

- Web page design.

- Data (information) quality.

- Liquidity.

- Competitive intensity.

- Customer turbulence.

- Technological turbulence.

It relates the antecedent, intervening and outcome variables, which provide insight into causation. The arrows signify the directional relationship and strength of the relationship between the variables. The strength was determined by whether or not the relationship occurred in one or more of the cases analysed. The causal network analysis was constructed using the method described by Miles and Huberman (1994).

There are several key insights that can be extracted from examination of the causal streams associated with the business model variable. The first insight relates to what is not present in the causal network diagram. None of the four cases mentioned the measurement of performance as an important determinant of success. This might account for why the business performance measures did not reflect a balanced scorecard approach.

The causal streams that appear key are as follows:

1 EM concept → Buyer–seller relationship → Acceptance of technology → Business model success.

2 EM concept and type of EM → Market transparency → Reduced margins.

3 Web page design and data quality → Acceptance of technology →
   Business model success.

4 Web page design → Acceptance of technology and use of market
   (Liquidity) → Business model success. > Technical staff retention →
   Product quality and business model success.

The first point of importance is that causal streams 1 and 2 infer that the
very concept of EMs causes a transparency in the marketplace that, in
turn, causes reduced margins. Second, that acceptance of technology is
influenced by Web page design and data quality (causal stream 3) and
third is the relationship between product quality and technical staff
retention (causal stream 4).

6.4.1 Limitations and further research

The research carried out for this paper has a number of limitations.
Since the research was conducted at the height of the dot.com boom, the
EM business models were generally unstable due to the high volatile
market. The comment by respondents that EM business models
may evolve into an ASP business model was, in hindsight, somewhat
naive in the light of recent research which points to low customer
satisfaction from adopting an ASP solution. The sample of EM business
models was limited to only four in this study, which suggests that
generalization across industry sectors is inappropriate. The interviews
were carried out with a limited number of personnel, all from within
the firms, so it was not possible to compare supply-side views with
customer responses. The structured interview format may also be a
limitation, as the questions only related to the constructs being tested.
The qualitative methodology utilized in this work has limitations, as no
financial performance measures were collected. Further research could
be carried out to verify the model presented in Figure 6.1 using a
quantitative methodology. Further work could examine a broader range
of EMs, including a cross-national comparison. The construct of
technology acceptance could be applied more precisely to EM business
models.

6.5 Discussion and conclusion

The results of the four case studies have revealed a number of key
concepts and variables, which contribute to the existing literature on
buyer–seller relationships (Imrie and Morris, 1992). Analysis of the
specific processes identified as defining the firms' characteristics

revealed significant similarity only between Firms B and C. Analysis of the case study data identified a number of common themes, including inferences that most of the firms saw the future to be adoption of an ASP business model, that the EM concept lead to downward pressures on margins and that technology acceptance by potential users was crucial to success.

Causal network analysis identified a number of variables that influenced business model success. This analysis pointed to several influential variables not previously identified in the research model posited in Figure 6.1 (page 146). The variables identified by others in prior research were: Web page design (Zhang and Von Dran, 2002), data (information) quality (Lederer et al., 2000), market transparency (Bakos, 1997), customer and technological turbulence and competitive intensity (Slater and Narver, 1994), and buyer–seller relationship (Bakos and Brynjolfsson, 1993; Timmer, 1999). These were observed through the interviews as being influencers of business model success. The causal network analysis infers that EMs increase market transparency and that this impacts business performance by reducing margins. Therefore, the inference must be that profitability from EM business models is difficult to achieve. Further, several other variables impact business performance: acceptance of technology by potential users, the liquidity of the market, Web page design, technical staff retention, and data quality as described in above. The results suggest that EMH (Malone et al., 1999) does not provide a true description of EM evolution. Rather, that because the profitability of EMs is likely to be limited by their very nature, firms see profitable evolution of the EM business model and the provision of professional services (consultancy and training) rather than the personalized markets posited by Malone et al. (1989) in EMH.

The fact that EMs do not seem profitable or that they are not seen as being a sound basis for a business model is not totally surprising. Bakos (1997) studied the effects of search costs on EMs and concluded that the best way to maintain margins would be for the EM to control market transactions and access to customers. For independent EMs, this presents a dilemma because they need the buyers and sellers to establish liquidity in the market and thus generate revenue. But because of this, the major buyers and sellers have a high degree of leverage over what the EM charges (a case of the EM needing the buyers and sellers more than the buyers and sellers needing the EM). Therefore, the power lies with the buyers and sellers. The case data indicated that pressures from both buyers and sellers tended to drive down the fees (and the margin) that EMs could command. To explain the findings, it is best to revisit the research questions and answer them based on the data and analysis presented above.

6.5.1 Q1: How is the business performance of an EM influenced by the nature of the EM business model?

Looking at the four business models studied and seeking to fit them into the evolutionary steps of EMH (Table 6.1) is difficult. For example, what is the real difference between a biased and an unbiased market? Malone et al. (1989) sought to differentiate on the basis that the technology would allow buyers' access to all possible sellers. Technologically, all of the business models studied here allow buyers' access to all the sellers registered within the EM. However, the number of sellers registered is only a small proportion of the total number of sellers available via other (i.e. non-electronic) channels. Therefore, one might argue that these EMs are biased compared to the total market for the goods and services being offered. This is true for all of the four models studied.

None of the four firms intends evolving towards a *personalized market*, as predicted in EMH. Instead, they see the future in an ASP business model and in the provision of training and consultancy services. Two intend to retain an EM business model on the basis that they believe they have a degree of competitive advantage either through easy access to customers or through strength of industry backing. Indeed, since embarking on this research, Firm C has ceased trading.

All firms operate either a transaction-based fee structure or a commission-based fee structure. Bakos (1997) split the effects of EMs on pricing into commodity and differentiated products. For the firms studied in this research (two commodity and two differentiated, by their view) the effect on pricing was always downward and thus their revenue and margins were squeezed to unsustainable levels; the arguments of the customers of EMs were simple.

For sellers, unless they had access to new markets or a much larger potential customer base, the market would only succeed in squeezing their margins. Therefore, the sellers wanted a lower pricing or commission tariff because in reality they were simply selling to their old customers via a different (lower priced) channel. For buyers, the only benefit of an EM would be if they got lower prices and that would only happen if there were lots of sellers in the marketplace. Sellers would, in turn, be attracted by large buyers in the market and therefore, the buyers should not have to pay at all to use the market. The arguments proposed by the EM customers do fit with the ideas posited by Bakos (1997), and could also fit with the ideas of proposed in TCE (Williamson, 1981) and identified as relevant to EMs (Lee et al., 1996; Timmers, 1999).

With respect to the business models of the four firms studied in this research, in accordance with the classifications posited by Timmers (1999) they are:

1   Firm A: Value-chain service provider.

2   Firm B: e-Procurement.

3   Firm C: e-Auction.

4   Firm D: Third party marketplace.

Research question 1 can be answered by observing that the exact nature of the EM business model is not as important as the fact that the business model is *any* form of EM. The evidence collected during the course of this research suggests that if the business model is an EM seems to infer that sustainability will be an issue because revenues and margins will decrease over time. We label this observation as the *'Electronic Market Paradox.'*

6.5.2 Q2: Does acceptance of EM technology by potential customers of the EM moderate an EMs business performance?

In all cases, acceptance of technology was perceived to be a key influence in the success of EM business models. Causal network analysis identified technology acceptance as a partial moderator. That is, having both a direct influence and an indirect influence via a variable identified as *liquidity* (the number of buyers and sellers active in the EM at any one time). The influence of technology acceptance on the successful implementation of Web-based technology has been confined in studies by Lederer et al. (2000) and Lin and Lu (2000).

Further, causal network analysis indicated that Web page design and data quality influenced the acceptance of technology, in addition to the buyer–seller relationship (Matthyssens and Van de Butle, 1994). The importance of Web page design to the successful adoption of a Web-based system has been previously identified by Zhang and Von Dran (2002). Data/information quality has been identified as an important variable in the acceptance of Web-based information systems by Lederer et al. (2000).

EM business models in general are subject to declining revenues and margins due to their very nature and seem unable to capitalize on differentiated markets or the benefits they bring buyers (i.e. the *EM Paradox*). EM business performance is influenced by technological and customer turbulence, as well as competitive intensity. Acceptance of technology acts as an important partial moderator to business performance.

Causal network analysis identified several antecedent variables to business model success (including the retention of technical staff to ensure product quality standards) and, as a result, the model depicted in Figure 6.1 is proposed to describe the relationship between EM business models and business performance.

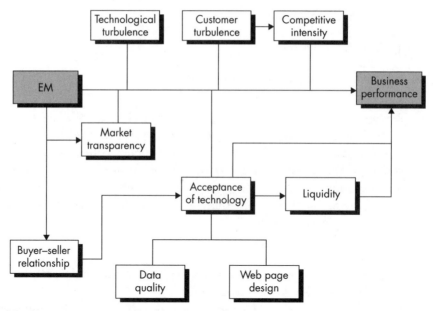

Figure 6.1: The EM paradox model.

Appendix 6A: Structured interview schedule

Structured interviews

Glossary
Definitions used in this research:

1 *EM*: An EM can be described as a marketplace of buyers and sellers brought together in the market by an information system that crosses organizational barriers (Bakos, 1997).

2 *Process map*: A diagram that documents, in sequence, the steps that departments go through to convert inputs to outputs for a specific process (Rummler and Brache, 1991).

3 *Process step*: A single activity box in the process map.

4 *Business model*: The goods and/or services a company offers to its customers; the means by which that company generates revenue and creates economic value (the difference between price and cost) (Porter, 2001).

5 *User acceptance*: The willingness of customers to use internet technology.

6 *Balanced scorecard*: A means of encompassing a wide variety of relevant performance measures.

7 *Performance measure*: How a business measures its success and how others measure that business' success.

Section 6A.1 Business model

Objective
Define the business model and validate process model.

Questions
1 Open discussion with the nature of the subject company's business objectives and a descriptive of the business model (revenue model and particularly in terms of value added product/services to customers)

2 Using a pre-prepared process map, discuss the following aspects:
   - How accurate is the map and what changes need to be made?
   - Which process steps differentiate the subject company from its competitors?
   - What are the main activities within these?
   - How would the subject company describe itself in one sentence?
   - Does a process map adequately represent the business model?
   - What are the particular challenges this business faces in terms of meeting its customers' demands?
   - Does the subject company believe that its current business model and processes will change significantly in the next 1–2 years?
   - If so, how?

Section 6A.2: Market conditions

Objective
Obtain perception of competitive environment.

Questions
1 Using the questionnaire developed for procurement professionals, ask the questions relating to market turbulence and competitive intensity (Section C).

2 Discuss the nature of competition in the subject company's market and solicit their view concerning the competitive environment over the next 1–2 years (e.g. main drivers and changes).

Section 6A.3: User acceptance

Objective
Understand the perception of customer/user acceptance of the technology/service.

Questions

1   Ask if any work has been conducted to collect feedback from users on the Web site and service offered.

2   Ask if work been conducted to find out why potential customers might not be using the Web site.

3   If any work has been carried out, explore the nature of it.

4   Explore the nature and results of customer feedback received about the Web site, its performance and quality.

Section 6A.4: Business performance

Objective

Identify the key business performance measures used, to understand why the company has chosen them and obtain measurements made YTD.

Questions

1   Identify the groups of performance measures that the subject company measures: For example, plot against the categories identified in the balanced scorecard: customer satisfaction, non-financials, learning and innovation and finance.

2   Identify the specific performance measures that are used within each category.

3   Ask why these specific measures were chosen and discuss the aspects of the business model they impact on.

4   Ask about targets and if they have been set for none/some/all of the measures.

5   What are the targets?

6   What is the performance against these targets (or in absolute terms) to date?

7   Discuss views on whether or not the performance measures used are the most appropriate/cover all relevant areas/are reviewed on a regular basis for suitability.

Administer the following questions on two specific aspects of performance:

1   Sales revenue

2   Return on sales (operating profit/turnover)

3   Profit before tax (PBIT)

4   Return on value added = (Sales − Cost of sales)/Sales (Mendelson, 2000)

5   Return on capital employed (ROCE) = PBIT/Total capital employed

6   Compound annual growth rate of sales.

END INTERVIEW

▨ Seek permission to come back to clarify any points.

▨ Clarify deliverables.

▨ Thank interviewee for their time.

Administration

1   Media: cassette tape, transcribed to Word 2000.

2   Manual notes, transcribed to Word 2000.

Appendix 6B

Figure 6.2 shows process model for Company A, 'integrated solutions provider'.
Figure 6.3 shows process model for Company B, purchasing portal.
Figure 6.4 shows process model of Company C, vertical industry portal.
Figure 6.5 shows process model for Company D, evolutionary model.

Appendix 6C: Causal network analysis

Figure 6.6 shows interview variables.

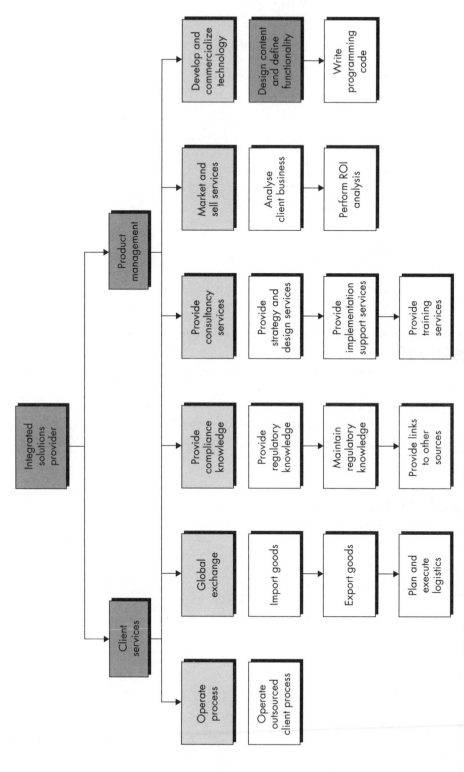

Figure 6.2: Process model for Company A, 'integrated solutions provider.'

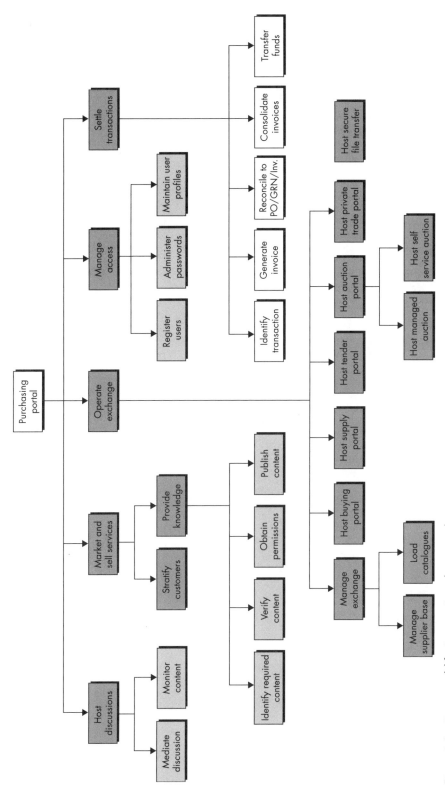

Figure 6.3: Process model for Company B, purchasing portal.

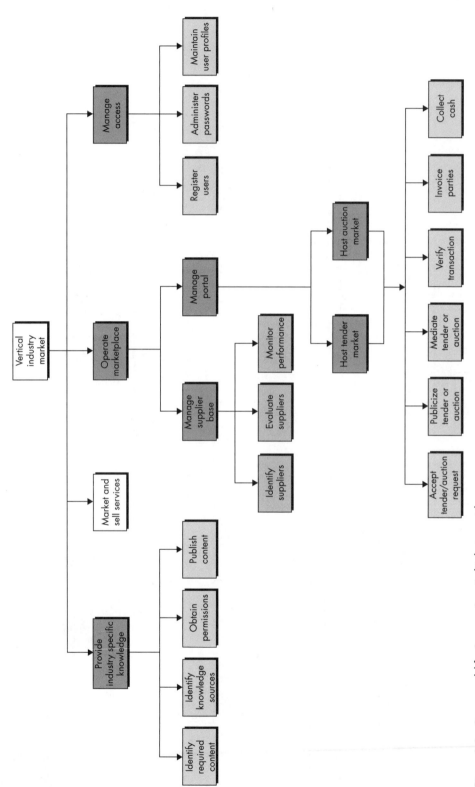

Figure 6.4:   Process model for Company C, vertical industry portal.

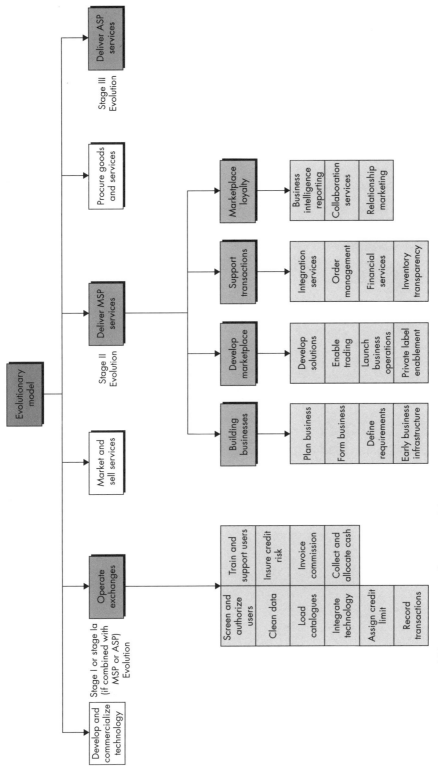

Figure 6.5: Process model for Company D, evolutionary model.

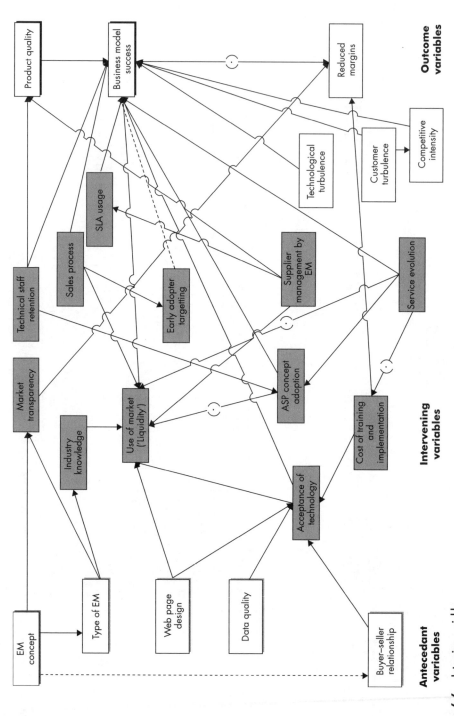

Figure 6.6: Interview variables.

References and Further Reading

Amit, R. and C. Zott (2001). 'Value Creation in eBusiness.' *Strategic Management Journal* **22**: 493–520.

Bakos, J. Y. (1991). 'A Strategic Analysis of Electronic Marketplaces.' *MISQ* **15**(3) September: 295–310.

Bakos, J. Y. (1997). 'Reducing Buyer Search Costs: Implications for Electronic Marketplaces.' *Management Science* **43**(12): 1676–1692.

Bakos, J. Y. and E. Brynjolfsson (1993). 'From Vendors to Partners: Information Technology and Incomplete Contracts in Buyer–Supplier Relationships.' *Journal of Organizational Computing* **3**(3): 301–328.

Barua, A., J. Pinnell, J. Shutter and A. B. Whinston (1999). Measuring Internet Economy: An Exploratory Paper. http://cism.bus.utexas.edu/works/articles/internet-economy.pdf

Bickman, L. and D. J. Rog (1998). *Handbook of Applied Social Research Methods.* Thousand Oaks, CA, Sage Publications Inc.

Choudhury, V., K. S. Hartzel and B. R. Konsynski (1998). 'Uses and Consequences of Electronic Markets: An Empirical Investigation in the Aircraft Parts Industry.' *MISQ* **22**(4) December: 471–507.

Clemons, E. and M. Row (1992). 'Information Technology and Industrial Cooperation: The Changing Economics of Coordination and Ownership.' *Journal of Management Information Systems* **9**(2): 9–28.

Clemons, E. K., S. P. Reddi and M. C. Row (1993). 'The Impact of Information Technology on the Organization of Production: The Move to the Middle Hypothesis.' *Journal of Management Information Systems* **10**(2): 435.

Daniel, E. and G. M. Klimis (1999). 'The Impact of Electronic Commerce on Market Structure: An Evaluation of Electronic Market Hypothesis.' *European Management Journal* **17**(3) June: 318–325.

Dai, Q. and R. J. Kauffman (2002). 'Business Models for Internet-Based B2B Electronic Markets.' *International Journal of Electronic Commerce* **6**(4): 41–72.

Davis, F. (1989). 'Perceived Usefulness, Perceived Ease-of-Use and User Acceptance of Information Technology.' *MISQ* **13**(3): 319–338.

Denzin, N. K. (1983). Interpretive Interactionism. G. Morgan (ed) *Beyond Method: Strategies for Social Research*. Beverley Hills, CA, Sage: 129–146.

Eisenhardt, K. M. (1989). 'Building Theories from Case Study Research.' *Academy of Management Review* **14**(4): 532–550.

Firestone, W. A. and R. E. Herriott (1983). 'The Formalization of Qualitative Research: An Adaptation of "Soft" Science to the Policy World.' *Evaluation Review* **7**: 437–466.

Garbade, K. (1982). Securities Markets, New York, McGraw Hill.

Grover, V. and P. Ramanlal (1999). 'Six Myths of Information and Markets: Information Technology Networks, Electronic Commerce and the Battle for Consumer Surplus.' *MISQ* **23**(4): 465–495.

Grover, V. and J. T. C. Teng (2001). E-commerce and the Information Market. Communications of the ACM, Vol. **44**(April 4): 79–86 cited in Denzin, K. and Y. S. Lincoln (1994) *Handbook of Qualitative Research*. Thousand Oaks, CA, Sage Publications Inc.

Guba, E. G. and Y. S. Lincoln (1994). Competing Paradigms in Qualitative Research.

Hagel III, J. and A. Armstrong (1997). *Net Gain: Expanding Markets through Virtual Communities*. Boston, Harvard Business School Press.

Hess, C. M. and C. F. Kemerer (1994). 'Computerized Loan Origination Systems: An Industry Case Study of Electronic Market Hypothesis.' *MISQ* 18(3): 251–280.

Imrie, R. and J. Morris (1992). 'A Review of Recent Changes in Buyer–Supplier Relationships.' *Omega Internetional Journal of Management Science* 20(5/6): 641–652.

Lederer, A. L., D. J. Maupin, M. P. Sena and Y. Zhuang (2000). 'The Technology Acceptance Model and the World Wide Web.' *Decision Support Systems* 29: 269–282.

Lee, H. G. (1998). 'Do Electronic Marketplaces Lower the Price of Goods?' *Communications of the ACM* 41(1): 73–80.

Lee, H. G. and T. H. Clark (1996). 'Market Process Re-engineering through Electronic Market Systems: Opportunities and Challenges.' *Journal of Management Information Systems* 13(3): 113–136.

Lin, J. C.-C., and H. Lu (2000). 'Towards an Understanding of the Behavioural Intention to Use a Website.' *International Journal of Information Management* 20: 197–208.

Lynd, R. S. and H. M. Lynd (1929). *Middletown: A study in American Culture*. New York, Harcourt, Brace.

Mahadevan, B. (2000). 'Business Models for Internet based e-Commerce.' *California Management Review* 42(4): 55–69.

Malone, T. W., J. Yates and R. I. Benjamin (1989). 'The Logic of Electronic Markets.' *Harvard Business Review* (May–June): 161–170.

Malone, T. W., K. Crowston, J. Lee and B. Pentland (1999). 'Tools for Inventing Organizations: Toward a Handbook of Organizational Processes.' *Management Science* 45(3): 425–443.

Manning, P. K. (1982). Analytic Induction. *Qualitative Data Analysis*. Miles & Huberman, 1994, Thousand Oaks, CA, Sage.

Matthyssens, P. and C. Van de Butle (1994). 'Getting Closer and Nicer: Partnerships in the Supply Chain.' *Long Range Planning* 27(1): 72–83.

Miles, M. B. and A. M. Huberman (1994). *Qualitative Data Analysis*, London, Sage.

Miller, S. I. (1982). 'Quality and Quantity: Another View of Analytic Induction as a Research Technique.' *Quality and Quantity* 16: 281–295.

Mowery, D. and D. Rosenberg (1989). *Technology and the Pursuit of Economic Growth*. New York, Cambridge University Press.

Pisano, G. P. (1989). 'Using Equity Participation to Support Exchange: Evidence from the Biotechnology Industry.' *Journal of Law, Economics and Organization* 5: 109–126.

Pisano, G. P., M. V. Russo and D. Teece (1988). Joint Ventures & Collaborative Agreements in the Telecommunications Equipment Industry. *International Collaborative Ventures in US Manufacturing*. David Mowery (ed), Cambridge MA, Ballinger: 23–70.

Porter, M. E. (2001). 'Strategy and the Internet.' *Harvard Business Review* (March): 63–78.

Rappa, M. (2000). Business Models on the Web. http://www.ecommerce.ncsu.edu/topics/models/models.html

Rummler, G. A. and A. P. Brache (1991). 'Improving Performance, San Francisco, Jossey Bass.

Salop, S. (1979). 'Monopolistic Competition with Outside Goods.' *Bell Journal of Economics* **10**: 141–156.

Seidemann, A. and E. Wang (1993). Electronic Data Interchange: Competitive Externalities and Strategic Implementation Policies. Simon School, University of Rochester Computers and Information Systems Working Paper 93–103.

Silver, M. (1984). Enterprise and the Scope of the Firm. Oxford, Martin Robertson Press.

Slater, S.F. and J.C. Narver (1994). 'Does Competitive Environment Moderate the Market-Orientation – Performance Relationships?' *Journal of Marketing* **58**(1): 46–55.

Smith, M. D., J. Bailey and E. Brynjolfsson (1999). Understanding Digital Markets: Review & Assessment. http://ecommerce.mit.edu/papers/ude

Teece, D. J. (1980). 'Economies of Scope and the Scope of the Enterprise.' *Journal of Economic Behaviour and Organization* **1**: 223–247.

Timmers, P. (1999). *Electronic Commerce: Strategies and Models for Business to Business Trading*. New York, John Wiley & Sons.

Weill, P. and M. R. Vitale (2001). *Place to Space – Migrating to eBusiness Models*, HBS Press.

Whyte, W. F. (1955). Street Corner Society: The Social Structure of an Indian Slum, 2nd edition. Chicago, University of Chicago Press.

Williamson, O. (1981). 'The Modern Corporation: Origins, Evolution, Attributes.' *Journal of Economic Literature* **19**: 1537–1568.

Yin, R. K. (1994). *Case Study Research, Design and Methods*, 2nd edition. Thousand Oaks, CA, Sage Publications.

Zhang, P. and G. M. Von Dran (2002). 'User Expectations and Rankings of Quality Factors in Different Website Domains.' *International Journal of Electronic Commerce* **6**(2): 9–33.

7 Knowledge management and e-Commerce: when self-service is not the sensible solution

Sue Newell and Jimmy Huang

7.1 Introduction

Contemporary accounts of organizations stress the importance of knowledge for sustainable competitive advantage (Drucker, 1988; Grant, 1996). Whether treated as a resource (knowledge) or as an activity (knowing), the effective creation and use of knowledge to develop and support products and services are crucial. This has led to a large body of literature on 'knowledge management' that both highlights the central importance of knowledge for organizational survival and examines ways in which organizations can better explore (create) and exploit (use) knowledge (March, 1991). And while 'knowledge management' as a term may fall out of fashion (Scarbrough and Swan, 2001), it is quite clear that the exploration and exploitation of knowledge has always been important. In this chapter, we adopt a knowledge perspective to examine aspects of e-Commerce and illustrate that such a perspective can help organizations better develop e-Commerce solutions that will add value. We also illustrate how being blind to such a knowledge lens can lead firms into adopting e-Commerce solutions that actually reduce rather than enhance their value-adding activities.

The chapter is organized as follows. First, we briefly introduce an e-Commerce framework and identify those aspects of e-Commerce that we intend to focus on in this chapter. Second, we provide an overview of some of the concepts, frameworks and theories within the knowledge management literature. Third, based on this literature, we apply a knowledge perspective on the e-Commerce issues that we have considered. In doing this, we develop a contingency account which suggests that there is no one best e-Commerce approach because what is best depends upon the particular situation. So, an organization should select its approach to e-Commerce by considering the knowledge demands of particular activities together with the strategic positioning of the organization. Finally, in the last section we draw out some general conclusions about the links between e-Commerce and knowledge management and summarize the main points of the chapter.

7.2 e-Commerce

Rayport and Jaworski (2001, p. 3) define e-Commerce as ... *technology-mediated exchanges between parties (individuals, organizations, or both) as well as the electronically based intra- or inter-organizational activities that facilitate such exchanges.* In other words, e-Commerce relates to the use of information and communication technologies (ICT) to support exchanges and transactions both within the organization and between the organization and its customers, suppliers, partners, shareholders and other stakeholders. Given this definition it is clear that virtually all business organizations have adopted some aspects of e-Commerce. Thus, it is undeniable that new types of ICT, in particular the Internet, Intranets and Extranets, have been widely adopted and are increasingly being used to support a wide variety of business activities. This includes:

1 *B2B activities*: For example, purchasing and procurement can now be done through the Internet with companies searching for and buying from suppliers through e-markets or e-hubs. One example is Covisint, formed jointly by a number of manufacturers, such as DaimlerChrysler, Renault, GM and Ford, for sourcing and procuring parts and components.

2 *B2C activities*: Many examples now exist that we are all familiar with, where as consumers we search for and buy products and even services using the Internet. Amazon.com is perhaps the most oft-cited example of a company that exploited Internet technology to develop a completely new way for us, as customers, to buy books (see below).

3 *C2C activities*: There are also examples of e-Commerce where the Internet has been successfully used to allow customers to exchange information and transact directly with each other. One of the best known examples here is eBay.com, but there are many others, including Monster.com for recruitment and Reunion.com to help in finding school friends.

4 *C2B activities*: This type of activity is perhaps the least prevalent, but is still very important. Here, customers can use ICT to aggregate their voices or purchase power, in order to make their voice heard or negotiate with the typically much larger and more powerful corporate enterprise. Pressure groups, for example Union of Concerned Scientists (Ucsusa.org), in particular, can use the Internet to build a network of support on a particular issue and then confront the organization with

a much stronger oppositional force than could have been achieved by individuals acting alone or at best in small local groups. Also, in the case of Goodenergy.com, consumers are aggregated to achieve economies of scale as a means of negotiating the price of electricity with suppliers.

In addition, there are all the internal e-Commerce transactions that are performed between individuals, departments and business units. Such transactions are now the predominant form of internal exchange and communication. In this chapter, we are looking at e-Commerce from the perspective of the organization in relation to its external customers and so will concentrate on B2C and B2B activities. This is not to deny the importance of internal, and C2C and C2B activities, but here we will focus on those external e-Commerce activities that the organization can directly control.

The important thing to recognize in relation to both B2B and B2C (and indeed to all types of transactions) is that ICT has opened up opportunities for more choice in terms of the media through which exchanges and transactions can occur. In other words, ICT has opened up the possibilities of adding new channels for B2C and B2B transactions – from only face-to-face to transactions using phone, mobile or Internet technologies. While some new so-called dot-com companies may only transact online, for most established 'bricks-and-mortar' organizations this has meant a move from accomplishing transactions in the traditional offline way to the inclusion of a variety of online transaction options. These new modes of transaction offer new choices, so that a firm can interact with its customers and business suppliers in different ways to suit their needs and circumstances. ICT has, thus, enabled organizations to develop new business models; that is new models for how to conduct business. Timmers (1999) defines a business model as the organization of product, service and information flows that form the foundation of revenues for suppliers and benefits for customers. More specifically, Weill and Vitale (2001, p. 34) define an e-Business model as *a description of the roles and relationships among a firm's consumers, customers, allies, and suppliers that identifies the major flows of product, information, and money, and the major benefits to participants.*

We can take the example of Amazon.com to consider this. In the past, the only real option for a person wishing to buy a book was to actually go to a shop and find the book. Shops could order books if the details were known and the book was in print. There was also the possibility of buying from a catalogue. The Internet, however, opened up the possibility of a completely different way of buying books – browsing books online and then purchasing directly and having the book delivered to the home within a very short period. In addition, the Internet could be used to encourage individuals to share their experiences of reading particular books so that before a person makes a purchase they can read reviews of the book. Of course, this was possible before – you could ask a friend about their experiences of reading a book, or you could read reviews that had been done by professional reviewers. However, the opportunity to more systematically read reviews from 'ordinary' readers was innovative. Moreover, data is collected through these online transactions, which allows the company to track the buying habits of particular individuals. This information can be used to tailor marketing material on particular books towards particular customers who have previously purchased related material. This, then, was a new business model for a book retailer. Not having to have a physical store and sales staff made the sale of books cheaper and this efficiency could be passed on to the customer. There was also a convenience factor for the customer, at least for those with access to the Internet (they could shop 24/7 and from their own home), and the opportunity for additional services to make book buying more interesting (e.g. the review service mentioned above).

A book is neither something that one really needs to see and feel before purchasing, nor is the decision to buy a particular book, one that typically relies on the expertise and advice of the sales staff. Most customers going into Barnes and Noble or W. H. Smith will not seek advice about which book to buy from the sales assistant; rather they will browse the books for themselves and make a decision based on this cursory view of the content. Of course, start-up costs for Amazon were high – the infrastructure had to be developed, the Web site created and maintained, and the customer base had to be built-up. Amazon for many years, therefore, made a loss and it was not until the 4th quarter of 2001 that its first profit was realized. However, the business model appeared to be one that could be viable and this is proving to be the case. This is evident in Wall Street financial analysts' confidence in Amazon, even though a loss was reported again during the 1st quarter of 2003.

Essentially Amazon.com is an example of automating the book-buying process and making it a self-service activity. The site is set up so that the reader can search for and find a particular book or type of book that they are interested in (indeed now at Amazon.com you can buy much more than just books). Individuals can then browse the book(s) and decide whether to purchase or not. Once the decision has been made the individual can then complete the purchase cycle online. So the traditional sales staff – who could advise customers of the location of a particular book, or take an order for an out-of-stock book, and/or complete the sales transaction – have been eliminated. Similarly, with B2B transactions, a firm can search for and purchase particular supplies online, without needing sales staff to locate and develop sales agreements with different suppliers. For instance, through Covisint, auto manufacturers such as GM and Renault, can form collaborative procurement arrangements to lower their transaction costs.

These, then, are examples of where ICT has transformed B2C and B2B transactions through using the Internet to directly connect to customers or other businesses, thus automating the process of buying a company's products and services. They are examples essentially based on a self-service philosophy – where the customers or business suppliers 'help themselves' or 'sell themselves'. This saves costs because sales staff are no longer needed. Rather the knowledge and expertise of these sales staff have been built into the system so that customers or other businesses are guided through an exchange or transaction automatically.

Many companies are adopting this self-service philosophy, attempting to use the Internet to 'cut out the middle man' and so reduce costs. For example, Moon and Frei (2000) reported that an online banking transaction cost just 2 cents, compared to 36 cents where an ATM was used and $1.15 for a teller-assisted transaction in a branch. However, we should remember that ICT is not the only, or necessarily the best, solution for all types of exchanges and transactions. Unfortunately, however, while the evolution of ICT has opened up possibilities for increasing the variety of exchange and transaction options, the reality in many business organizations is that they are trying to return to a narrower range of consumer choices as they recognize that the cost (measured in simple terms of the cost of the single transaction as reported above, rather than including the long-term cost of consumer satisfaction) of online transactions is significantly cheaper than the cost of offline transactions. In other words, we can see in many bricks-and-mortar organizations that there has been movement from purely offline (e.g. booking an air ticket through a visit to a travel agents) to a variety of online plus offline (e.g. booking an air ticket through a visit to a local travel agents or using the phone or through the Internet) to purely online (e.g. booking an air ticket on the Internet) transactions. Customers not wishing or unable to use the online transaction services are asked to pay a premium in an attempt to encourage this movement. For example, if you wish to book an airline ticket through British Airways, you now have to pay extra if you do not book your ticket online.

This move to pure online transactions saves costs, as seen. This is because the customer now has to do the work; so they involve self-service transactions where expert systems are designed to take the customer through a series of pre-defined steps that encompass the knowledge and expertise that previously resided in the sales person with whom the customer transacted directly. While in simple cost terms, as seen, this self-service strategy might appear to be most efficient, this strategy might not always be most effective, as Moon and Frei (2000) argue. To understand this, we can apply a knowledge perspective to explore the situations in which adopting a self-service e-Commerce strategy may actually be less effective. Before we consider this, we next turn to review the literature on knowledge management.

7.3 Knowledge management

In the knowledge management literature there is much debate about 'what knowledge is' (see e.g. Prusak, 1997; Newell et al., 2002). In particular, there are debates between those who argue that knowledge is something that is a resource that is possessed – by individuals, groups, organizations or even societies – and those who argue that knowledge (or rather knowing) is not so much possessed as embedded in practice and so inherently social (see e.g. Blackler, 1995). The knowledge as possession school views knowledge as an entity that can be made explicit and transferred from one person or group to another (e.g. Nonaka, 1994). So, one company appears to have developed some really good practices for managing its supply chain. The knowledge underpinning such practices can be made explicit and codified (written down) and transferred to another organization so that they can acquire this knowledge and begin to operate the same good supply-chain practices.

Those who adopt the view that knowledge is embedded in practice would argue that such direct knowledge transfer is not possible because knowledge is inherently sticky (Szulanski, 1996) and is always socially constructed (Tsoukas, 1996). In other words, knowledge is inherently social and embedded in practice (Weick, 1995). Transferring knowledge of any 'good practice' to another situation where those involved engage in different practices and so have developed different ways of knowing will not therefore be straightforwardly effective (Becker, 2001; Newell et al., 2003). For example, I 'know' that as a university teacher it is appropriate to have an independent third party check my grading to ensure that I am treating my students fairly. This I 'know' to be a fair and ethical system. However, having recently taught in a different country (the USA as opposed to the UK) I have come to realize that this practice is totally alien in other places and that in this new context this practice is 'known' to be a 'violation of academic freedom'. This makes it clear that any given work practice is culturally mediated, and therefore is the outcome of a web of knowledge that is the product of social participation and negotiated interpretations (Star, 1996). In the 'other' context, pre-existing ideas about normal practice will limit the absorptive capacity of those involved (Cohen and Levinthal, 1990). Absorptive capacity refers to the capacity of a recipient of knowledge to take in and use this knowledge. Most importantly, absorptive capacity is a function of pre-existing knowledge and practice.

While these two traditions (knowledge as something possessed versus knowing as something practiced) remain distinct, Cook and Brown (1999) have tried to bring them together, arguing that both are useful and simply represent two different, albeit related, epistemologies – the epistemology of possession (knowledge) and the epistemology of practice (knowing). It is the 'generative dance' between knowledge and knowing that, they argue, is important. So, knowledge as something possessed must be practiced in a specific context to be meaningful. In this sense, knowledge is a 'tool of knowing' (Cook and Brown, 1999), making knowledgeable action possible.

Another way of looking at this is to recognize that knowledge is always a combination of tacit and explicit knowledge (Polanyi, 1961). And while the knowledge as possession school tends to argue that tacit knowledge can be made explicit, Cook and Brown (1999) make it clear that tacit and explicit knowledge are inherently different and cannot simply be converted from one to the other. They use the example of learning to ride a bike to illustrate this. Tacit knowledge of riding a bike, for example that which enables one to maintain one's balance on the bike, will always remain tacit. Even if one explains balance in explicit terms, this knowledge will not, on its own, allow a person to learn to balance – knowing how to balance can only be acquired through practice. Tsoukas (1996) puts this another way when he argues that tacit and explicit knowledge are mutually constituted. We need both tacit and explicit knowledge to be able to complete any given activity or practice.

7.3.1 Different approaches to knowledge management

While in some of the literature on knowledge management we, therefore, see a fusion between the knowledge as possession and the knowing embedded in practice views; when we consider actual approaches to managing knowledge that are advocated, we continue to see the bifurcation. Indeed, there are several different typologies that have been developed by different authors which suggest two rather different approaches to knowledge management. In each case, these differences are clearly related to the two different epistemologies of knowledge discussed above. Table 7.1 summarizes some of these typologies of knowledge management.

We will briefly consider each of these different typologies in turn below. As we do this, and consider the different approaches to knowledge

Table 7.1: Different approaches to knowledge management

	Knowledge as possession	Knowing as embedded in practice
Hansen et al. (1999)	Codification strategy	Personalization strategy
Swan et al. (1999)	Cognitive view	Community view
Alavi (2000)	The repository model of knowledge management systems	The network model of knowledge management systems
McElroy (2000)	First-generation knowledge management	Second-generation knowledge management

management, it is useful to think about the links to our earlier consideration of e-Commerce. Offering online transactions is very much related to the approaches set out in the 'knowledge as possession' column of Table 7.1 (that is, to the codification strategy or cognitive model of knowledge management – first-generation knowledge management); while conducting transactions using face-to-face or even phone modes are related to the 'knowing as embedded in practice' column in the table (that is, to the personalization or community models of knowledge management – second-generation knowledge management). We will develop this analysis more fully after we have considered the different typologies themselves.

Hansen et al. (1999) observed two different strategies to knowledge management used by different companies. Companies using the codification strategy essentially attempt to make explicit all knowledge, store this on a database and encourage others to search this database in order to acquire knowledge from others rather than develop this knowledge themselves through experience. This strategy is obviously based on the knowledge as possession view. On the other hand, other companies use a personalization strategy, encouraging employees to develop networks with each other and use these networks to engage in discussion and dialogue. This strategy accepts that knowledge is closely tied to the person who developed it and so needs to be shared mainly through face-to-face contacts between people. From this perspective then, building social capital (Nahapiet and Ghoshal, 1998; Adler and Kwon, 2002) within an organization – that is, building interpersonal networks that can be used to share knowledge and understanding – is crucial since knowledge sharing is best encouraged through discussion and dialogue. This strategy is based more clearly in the knowing as embedded in practice view.

Swan et al. (1999) distinguish between a cognitive and community view of knowledge management. The cognitive view equates knowledge to objectively defined concepts and facts that can be transferred through text, using ICT. This approach is used to enhance the exploitation of knowledge, ensuring that knowledge is reused in different contexts across an organization, so that 'reinventing the wheel' is minimized. The community view, on the other hand, sees knowledge as socially constructed and based on experience. From this view, much knowledge will always remain largely tacit and so be shared through joint experiences in social networks and groups. This community approach focuses more on the creation or exploration of knowledge, seeing the transfer of knowledge as an inherently problematic idea. In particular, within this view, the emphasis is on creating and supporting communities of practice that can facilitate knowledge sharing and learning among those who are engaged in similar activities (Brown and Duguid, 2000). Such communities do not have any specific tasks to accomplish, unlike a project team, but members support each other more informally through sharing their experiences and insights. For example, when one community member is struggling to solve a problem, another community member can share their previously encountered experiences that may be relevant to solving this problem. For example, Orr (1990) demonstrated how xerox customer service representatives met informally between site visits and shared war stories about their experiences of difficult machines. These stories were an invaluable source of learning for this group, so that when management decided to put a stop to these informal meetings, viewing them as wasted time, the productivity of the representatives was significantly reduced. Again, then, the basic distinction between these two views (codification and community) of knowledge management resonates with the distinction we have already discussed between the knowledge as possession and knowing as practice views.

Alavi (1999) focuses explicitly on knowledge management systems – information technology (IT)-based systems developed to enhance knowledge exploitation and exploration. She distinguishes between two approaches to the development of such systems. The repository model of knowledge management systems, based on the knowledge as possession view, focuses on building knowledge repositories and retrieval technologies. In particular, the emphasis will be on the development of relational databases and document management systems, so that data, both internal and external, can be stored and searched. On the other hand, the network model of knowledge management systems, based on the socially constructed view of knowledge, focuses on using technology to connect or link people. For example, companies might develop a corporate 'yellow pages', which lists individuals and their expertise, or a 'knowledge map' of the organization, which depicts where certain expertise is located. The key difference between these two approaches, then, is that the network model focuses on providing information on the sources of knowledge while the repository model focuses on supplying the knowledge itself.

Finally, McElroy (2000) argues for a shift in thinking about knowledge management from strategies that emphasize dissemination, imitation and exploitation (that he terms first-generation knowledge management) to those that promote education, innovation and exploration (or second-generation knowledge management). In second-generation knowledge management the focus moves from the supply of knowledge to creating and maintaining the conditions required for the production of knowing. Second-generation knowledge management recognizes that knowledge is context dependent, since 'meanings' are interpreted in reference to a particular paradigm (Marakas et al., 2000). As Shariq (1999) notes, in order to make sense or create understanding, humans bring prior knowledge and context to the information. Without the human context the information by itself will have no meaning. Given differences in contexts, alternative interpretations or understandings are inevitable, even when people are presented with the same explicit knowledge. So, first-generation knowledge management is based on the knowledge as possession epistemology, while second-generation knowledge management is based on the epistemology of practice.

While these different typologies of knowledge management distinguish between approaches based on different epistemologies, as we have seen, it is useful to see knowledge as both something that is possessed and something that is embedded in practice. So, knowledge becomes the tool through which we can know and so practice any given task effectively. It is also possible to argue that tasks differ in the extent to which the mere possession of knowledge allows one to knowledgeably engage in the practice. As we saw in the bike riding example, this task is clearly one where the mere possession of the knowledge of 'how to ride a bike' does not allow one to simply go and pick up a bike and immediately be able to ride it. In this case, practice is paramount to develop the tacit knowledge that underpins this activity. Similarly, few of us would be comfortable performing some piece of intricate surgery on our mother, however much we read about the operation and so possessed the necessary explicit knowledge. We would want instead to have a skilled surgeon perform the operation – someone who was practiced in the performance of the operation and so had the requisite tacit understanding which must accompany the explicit knowledge about how and why to do certain things.

Lave and Wenger (1991) emphasize how such skill development involves a social process of learning. They consider how knowledgeable skills are acquired in a variety of situations including learning how to be a midwife, a butcher, a tailor and a quartermaster on a ship. In their analysis they emphasize the importance of situated learning as newcomers participate in the sociocultural practices of a community of practitioners and gradually learn the knowledgeable skills that will allow them to practice as experts. Formal or explicit knowledge is of less importance in the development of these skills than is active participation in the activities themselves within the particular sociocultural context. So for these tasks and activities the codification strategy of knowledge management would be less effective than the personalization or community strategy.

On the other hand, there are certain tasks where the possession of the knowledge allows one to accomplish the task fairly readily without having to develop unique tacit knowledge through extensive practice. For example, we can follow instructions and build a wardrobe from a set of pre-shaped and pre-prepared pieces; we can read our gas meter and work out how much gas we have used; we can follow the instructions in a recipe book and make a reasonably sophisticated meal for a dinner party. It is not that these types of activities do not contain any tacit knowledge. Of course, they do, but they contain the kind of tacit knowledge that most of us possess as an outcome of our daily life experiences. For such tasks, therefore, the codification or cognitive approach to knowledge management may be adequate. This suggests that a contingency approach to knowledge management is appropriate. For example, it is not that the community approach is inherently better than the cognitive approach (or vice versa) but that each approach is suited to different contexts. This indeed is an inherent assumption of the typologies discussed above.

7.3.2 Contingency versus 'best practice'

Most of the typologies discussed above are, thus, based on the idea that companies will adopt a mixture of the different approaches depending upon their particular context; in other words they advocate a contingency view of knowledge management. For example, Hansen et al. (1999) argue that companies should follow the 80/20 rule – focusing 80% of their efforts on, say, the codification strategy and the other 20% on personalization or vice versa. Which is the focus – codification or personalization – depends upon whether the firm's key strategic goal is efficiency or innovation/differentiation. In other words, the approach to knowledge management that should be adopted depends on characteristics of the situation and the tasks. In practice, however, the evidence suggests that most organizations have concentrated their knowledge management efforts on the codification/cognitive/repository strategy, developing IT systems able to store knowledge that can be reused at different places and times. For example, Ruggles (1998) found that the two most popular knowledge management initiatives in his sample of firms were creating an Intranet and data warehousing. Alavi and Leidner (2001) reported very similar findings.

In other words, the emphasis has been on ensuring that there is a stock or supply of knowledge that can be used by others as appropriate. For example, given the increasing use of project teams to accomplish organizational goals, organizations have been keen to ensure that lessons learned from a project are shared beyond the immediate project team, so that other project teams will not make the same mistakes or will take advantage of what was found to be a productive activity or method. Project teams are, therefore, required to complete reviews – either at intervals during a project or more commonly simply at the end of a project – where they must capture and write down the 'lessons learned'. These lessons are then input into a 'lessons learned database', so that theoretically others can learn from this. Such end-of-project learning review and capture practices could be considered to be 'best practice' since they are prescribed in most project management methodologies. Unfortunately, the research to date suggests that while such a knowledge management strategy does indeed lead to the accumulation of vast amounts of stored 'lessons', there is very little use of this knowledge by other project teams (Von Zedtwitz, 2002). For example, Keegan and Turner (2001), studying 18 different companies that used project-based work, found that all had this kind of end-of-project review practice in place, demanding that project members capture their learning experiences. However, they also report that *in no single company did respondents express satisfaction with the process* (p. 90).

So while the literature suggests that it might be relevant to adopt a contingency perspective and consider the two different views or strategies for knowledge management as applicable in different contexts depending on the particular situation, the reality is that most organizations have in fact put their efforts into the cognitive or codification strategy rather than the community or personalization strategy. This might be described as 'fashion following' (Benders and van Veen, 2001). Similarly, when we now turn to consider the approaches that organizations are adopting to e-Commerce we can see that there is a prevailing approach that is being followed – the self-service approach discussed above.

This self-service e-Commerce approach aligns with the dominant codification/cognitive knowledge management strategy. Thus, self-service assumes that knowledge underpinning a customer or supplier transaction can be made explicit and either embedded in the software or transferred to the customer. The problem is that this approach does not always fit the task and/or strategic orientation of the organization. Thus, in relation to e-Commerce, two particular aspects of the situation would appear to be important – the knowledge demands of the task and the value proposition of the organization. In terms of the former, this will encompass the amount of tacit knowledge embedded in the activity. In terms of the latter, this will encompass the amount of explicit knowledge that needs to be possessed to accomplish the activity and how far the organization can expect the customer or business supplier to have to invest the time and effort to acquire this explicit knowledge. We develop this contingency account in the next section.

7.4 Linking e-Commerce and knowledge management

Relating the different approaches to knowledge management to e-Commerce strategies, we can link the self-service orientation currently 'in vogue' to the knowledge as possession type of approach. So, the adoption of a self-service strategy is based on making all the knowledge that is needed to complete a particular transaction with a customer or other business explicit or codified. The customer or business can then complete the transaction on their own. On the other hand, the traditional face-to-face approach to transactions was much more based on the personalization strategy of knowledge management. Hansen et al. (1999)

argued that the personalization strategy, based on strong ties, was effective for sharing tacit knowledge while the codification strategy, based on weak ties, was effective for sharing explicit knowledge (e.g. see Granovetter, 1973). This suggests that which approach to transactions to adopt should be based on an examination of the knowledge demands of the task, rather than on a simple cost basis. It will also depend on the extent to which the organization thinks it is appropriate to 'make the customer do the work'. Each of these contingency aspects is considered next.

7.4.1 The knowledge demands of the task

Tasks and activities and products and services differ in the relative degree of tacit and explicit knowledge involved. Once we appreciate this, we may also be able to appreciate that, for some tasks and activities, it may not be possible or desirable to make all knowledge needed by the customer to complete a transaction explicit. For some tasks, therefore, attempting to codify all knowledge so that the customer can operate in a self-service mode may not be plausible. For example, e-learning is a growing trend – you can now get a degree through studying entirely online. The learning materials are made available on the Internet and you, as the learner, can work through this material at your own pace and then complete the various assignments or examinations to gain the necessary credits for the degree. This approach to learning assumes that all the knowledge that is needed to make one an expert in a particular field can be made explicit and transferred through text – an epistemology of possession. However, returning to our example of performing an operation on your mother, it seems implausible that one could become a qualified doctor simply through this e-learning mode. Similarly, becoming a biologist or a musician or an expert in any other field (e.g. the midwifes, butchers, tailors or quartermasters studied by Lave and Wenger (1991)) involves practice within a community of knowing, as well as the possession of a certain type of knowledge. Lave and Wenger (1991) refer to this as legitimate peripheral participation. The acquisition of 'community membership', according to Lave and Wenger, is as crucial as the acquisition of skill. In essence, legitimate peripheral participation indicates that receiving recognition from more experienced and competent practitioners is part of the learning process that can only be achieved through engagement and socialization.

It is interesting to note in this context that the Open University in the UK, which has always delivered distance education, and which now increasingly uses the Internet to deliver learning materials that signed up learners can self-serve from, nevertheless also insists that its students participate in face-to-face learning sessions, either during summer schools and/or periodic-term time seminars. On the other hand, the BBC, attempting to use the Internet to build on its traditional mode of communication through television programs, has attempted to develop

Web sites to teach viewers, for example, how to identify antiques or engage in do-it-yourself (DIY). There is no interaction here but just codified knowledge that is presented to viewers with the aim of making them experts in these areas. These sites, however, often provide viewers with the basic principles but fail to equip novices with sufficient skills to be able to apply the knowledge in action. For instance, in the BBC's DIY Web site (www.bbc.co.uk/homes/diy/diy_guide/factsheets/72.shtml), it is written: *Use spacers between the wall and the boards (no more than 9 mm) to allow the floor to expand with changes of temperature and to enable you to get the last strip in. If you don't use spacers, the floor may buckle later.* Without the actual experience of laying a laminate floor with an expert, however, viewers may encounter problems, such as how to fit in the last strip of flooring when the space to use the hammer is limited, or how the last strip should be cut, if the wall is uneven (this example is based on personal experience).

This discussion suggests that self-service e-Commerce approaches will not be universally applicable. In particular, where there is a lot of tacit knowledge, the self-service option is likely to be problematic. This is because, as we have discussed, it is very difficult to transfer tacit knowledge through ICT, given the situated nature of learning tacit knowledge.

7.4.2 The value proposition of the company

Not all transactions, however, necessitate a great deal of tacit knowledge, although tasks can differ in terms of the amount of explicit knowledge that a customer or business supplier needs to possess in order to complete the exchange or transaction. Indeed, for the execution of any kind of task, transferring the explicit knowledge to be able to accomplish the activity can be time-consuming for the receiver (i.e. the customer or supplier). Take the example above about building a wardrobe from a set of explicit instructions provided with the 'box of bits'. Few of us have not experienced the frustration of trying to follow these instructions once we have brought the box home from the DIY shop. We can do it, but it takes considerable time. Similarly, completing an online booking of an airline ticket takes longer than ringing the travel agent and asking them to fix this for us. This suggests that the self-service philosophy may not be appropriate in all situations and depends very much on the value proposition that underpins the quality of service that a firm is trying to offer to its customers. It is one thing for Tesco or Wal-Mart to move to self-service tills at checkouts, where the customer has to ring through their own purchases, but can you imagine Harrods introducing self-service tills!

Let us consider a specific B2C example. Any transaction process involves a series of steps: from the establishment of what the customer wants to purchase, through a search and evaluation of alternative options to satisfy this need, to a selection choice, and finally to the fulfillment of the order to satisfy the need. At each of these steps knowledge is needed. We can use the example of booking a holiday. The steps here might involve:

1   *Establishment of what the customer wants to purchase*: One might assume that this was straightforward but in reality customers are not always fully aware of what they want and so will need to be helped and encouraged to think through what they need and so what they want to buy to satisfy this need. For example, I want to book a holiday in August that will accommodate the needs of all members of my family. I have a rough idea of when I want to go, but I am flexible on this; I would like a holiday somewhere hot where I can sit by a pool, but my children want an activity-type holiday where they can do lots of different things and my partner wants to see some interesting historic sites; I have a budget in mind for this but this is somewhat flexible; I am happy to travel but have no specific location in mind. At the start of the process, however, I may not have articulated all of these criteria and in a traditional transaction it would be the job of the travel agent to 'pull' this information from me, using their past knowledge and experience to take me through an astute series of questions.

2   *Identification of alternative options*: Given the established criteria we can then move on to consider a number of options. Traditionally, the travel agent has used his/her knowledge to identify the various holiday options and propose these to the customer. So, we could go on a holiday where the children would be looked after in a holiday camp and have the opportunity to try out lots of different sports and activities under supervision, but in a location where there was historic interest and guaranteed sun. There may be many such options here. Or we could go on different holidays to serve our different needs. Or we could prioritize particular family needs and agree to accommodate other needs on the next holiday. These options would be presented to the customer and each discussed in turn, identifying positive and negative aspects of each.

3   *Selection and order fulfilment*: Once the options have been presented the customer can then make a decision. Traditionally, the customer might have the time to go and think about the various options and possibly discuss them with others – for example, in this case the other family members. Once a decision has been made, the holiday can be booked. Traditionally, once the customer has made the decision, the travel agent will do all the booking and confirming of the reservations, with the customer simply handing over the money to pay for the holiday and getting the tickets in return.

Now, with e-Commerce, this entire process can be automated, getting rid of the travel agent, and allowing the customer to search the options for him/herself, evaluate which best suits all his/her needs, make a decision and book the holiday online. Getting rid of the travel agent can, of course, reduce costs. But there is a price to pay for this – the customer now has to do much more work for him/herself and acquire the knowledge that previously resided with the travel agent, understand his/her own needs, locate all the various options, search out different companies and different package deals, learn how to and spend time actually completing the transaction, etc.

Whether or not this self-service option is the most sensible strategy to adopt will depend on the value proposition of the organization. If the value proposition is to provide customers with the cheapest holiday then the self-service mode of transaction will achieve this – as with low cost airlines, such as Easyjet.com or Ryanair.com. On the other hand, if the value proposition is to provide a differentiated service based on high-quality customer service and interaction then this is unlikely to be the best option. For example, British Airways (BA) has not traditionally been the cheapest airline but has thrived on the basis of a high-quality service and high levels of customer service. Its move to Internet ticketing – making the customer do more of the work or at least charging them a premium on top of the premium cost they are already paying – may not be the most successful long-term strategy given the company's overall business strategy.

Again, this discussion suggests that the self-service approach to e-Commerce is not going to be universally successful. Where customers are paying a premium for a service or where there is a desire to develop trust-based relations with suppliers, self-service is unlikely to be appropriate, at least as the only transaction option.

7.5 A contingency approach to e-Commerce

Based on a knowledge perspective, we therefore arrive at a contingency view of e-Commerce that takes into account:

1 the complexity of the knowledge underpinning the task to be performed – in particular the level of tacit knowledge that is involved,

2 the underlying value proposition of the firm (cost minimization or differentiation) and so the extent to which the firm can expect the customer or supplier to invest in acquiring the explicit knowledge needed (this is illustrated in Figure 7.1).

Taking each of these quadrants in turn we can consider some examples.

7.5.1 Low complexity of knowledge and value proposition based on low cost

In such situations the most sensible e-Commerce strategy to adopt is likely to be the online-only option, that is, using the pure self-service mode of transaction. Many dot.com companies were essentially started from this premise – that services or products could be delivered more

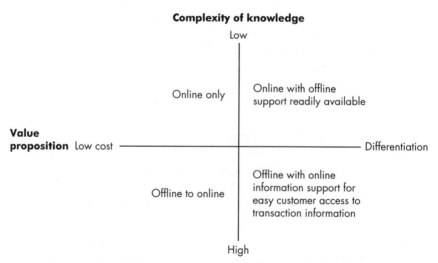

Figure 7.1: A contingency model of e-Commerce based on the knowledge requirements of activities and the organization's value proposition.

cheaply if you cut out the direct customer interface and allowed the customer to serve him/herself. Examples include the many sites that offer comparison of different products; for example, mortgages, loans or credit, flight tickets, hotels, car hire, etc. Specific examples include cheaptickets.com (for purchasing airline tickets), eBay.com (for selling between customers), Google.com (for performing search functions). This is also true for some of the supplier e-markets or e-hubs, such as Covisint.

7.5.2 High complexity of knowledge and value proposition based on low cost
In such situations, while the desire may be to get the customer to complete transactions online in order to reduce costs, the complexity of the knowledge needed may mean that some offline input is needed in order to ensure that customers acquire the necessary tacit as well as explicit knowledge. Here the best e-Commerce approach to adopt may therefore involve a blend of offline and online transactions. For example, the Open University, as discussed previously, uses a combination of online delivery of educational materials and offline activities where students can use the knowledge to engage in practical exercises that will help them develop knowledgeable skills. Other educational providers attempt to educate students through only online transactions. Given the situated nature of learning and the extent of tacit knowledge under-pinning most knowledgeable action, this e-Commerce strategy is of dubious merit, albeit the education can be delivered cheaply.

7.5.3 Low complexity of knowledge and value proposition based on differentiation
Here the knowledge needed to complete a transaction is relatively straightforward so that customers can easily complete transactions

online and may prefer to do this because it is more convenient. However, given that the value proposition is based on differentiated service and quality, there needs to be much more opportunity for offline support. Indeed, given the value proposition of differentiation, the reduced costs of online transactions may sensibly be plowed back into the development of more supportive offline services to enhance the quality of customer service. So, rather than having to search for a long time to find the contact phone number on the Web site where a person can get directly in touch with a company representative, the phone contact details are readily available. For example, at Schwab.com online banking is provided, but with offline support when needed. Similarly, Capital One offers online banking, but with an offline option. BA, on the other hand, which might fit into this quadrant, makes it very difficult to find the direct contact information on its Web site and, as discussed, enforces a penalty on customers who do not book tickets online, rather than using the cost savings of online booking to enhance the offline support services.

7.5.4 High complexity of knowledge and value proposition based on differentiation
In this situation, given the complexity of the knowledge needed to complete the transaction and the strategy of offering a differentiated service, the best option might be to encourage offline transactions but with online information support for easy customer access to transaction information. For example, IT outsourcing firms, such as IBM and EDS, deliver their services primarily offline. Yet, online access is provided to their clients to obtain information from some of the databases that are not available to other users.

7.6 Conclusions
In conclusion, we have considered how a knowledge management perspective can shed light on how a company might want to make use of the new transaction opportunities afforded by developments in ICT. In particular, we have argued that a firm's e-Commerce strategy should not mindlessly follow the latest fashion and encourage/demand all customers or business partners transact with them through an online, self-service mode. Rather, a company needs to develop transaction choices that take into consideration the knowledge requirements underpinning a particular transaction, both tacit and explicit, together with the underlying value proposition that is driving the company's overall strategic plan. This is likely to suggest that for some companies the self-service-only mode of transaction is not the best long-term e-Commerce strategy, even if this is the strategy that is currently being adopted.

References and Further Reading

Adler, P. and S.-W. Kwon (2002). 'Social Capital: Prospects for a New Concept.' *Academy of Management Review* **27**(1): 17–40.

Alavi, M. (2000). Managing knowledge. In: *Framing the Domain of IT Management*. R. Zmud (ed.), Cincinnati, Ohio: Pinnoflex Educational Resources Ltd. pp. 15–28.

Alavi, M. and D. E. Leidner (1999). Knowledge management systems: issues, challenges and benefits. *Communications of the Association for Information Systems*, **1**, Article 7.

Alavi, M. and D. E. Leidner (2001). 'Review: Knowledge Management and Knowledge Management Systems: Conceptual Foundations and Research Issues.' *MIS Quarterly* **25**: 107–136.

Becker, M. (2001). 'Managing Dispersed Knowledge: Organizational Problems, Managerial Strategies and Their Effectiveness.' *Journal of Management Studies* **38**(7): 1037–1051.

Benders, J. and K. van Veen (2001). 'What's in a Fashion? Interpretive viability and Management Fashions.' *Organization* **8**(1): 17–32.

Blackler, F. (1995). 'Knowledge, Knowledge Work and Organizations: An Overview and Interpretation.' *Organization Studies* **16**(6): 1021–1046.

Brown, J. and P. Duguid (2000). *The Social Life of Information*. Boston, MA, Harvard Business School Press.

Cohen, M. and D. Levinthal (1990). 'Absorptive Capacity: A New Perspective on Learning and Innovation.' *Administrative Science Quarterly* **35**: 128–152.

Cook, S. and J. Brown (1999). 'Bridging Epistemologies: The Generative Dance between Organizational Knowledge and Organizational Knowing.' *Organization Science* **10**: 381–400.

Drucker, P. (1988). 'The Coming of the New Organization.' *Harvard Business Review* Summer: pp. 53–65.

Granovetter, M. (1973). 'The Strength of Weak Ties.' *American Journal of Sociology* **78**: 1360–1380.

Grant, R. (1996). 'Prospering in Dynamically Competitive Environments: Organizational Capability as Knowledge Integration.' *Organization Science* **7**(4): 375–387.

Hansen, K., W. Weiss and S. Kwak (1999). 'Allocating R&D Resources: A Quantitative Aid to Management Insight.' *Research Technology Management* **42**: 44–50.

Keegan, A. and R. Turner (2001). 'Quantity versus Quality in Project-Based Learning Practices.' *Management Learning* **32**(1): 77–98.

Lave, J. and E. Wenger (1991). *Situated Learning: Legitimate Peripheral Participation*. Cambridge, Cambridge University Press.

Marakas, G. M., R. D. Johnson and J. W. Palmer (2000). 'A Theoretical Model of Differential Social Attributions toward Computing Technology: When the Metaphor becomes the Model.' *International Journal of Human Computer Science* **4**: 719–750.

March, J. G. (1991). 'Exploration and Exploitation in Organizational Learning.' *Organization Science* **2**: 71–87.

McElroy, M. (2000). 'Integrating Complexity Theory, Knowledge Management and Organizational Learning.' *Journal of Knowledge Management* **4**: 195–203.

Moon, Y. and F. X. Frei (2000). 'Exploding the Self-Service Myth.' *Harvard Business Review* **78**: 26–27.

Nahapiet, J. and S. Ghoshal (1998). 'Social Capital, Intellectual Capital, and the Organizational Advantage.' *Academy of Management Review* **23**: 242–266.

Newell, S., M. Robertson, H. Scarbrough and J. Swan (2002). *Managing Knowledge Work*. Houndsmills, Palgrave.

Newell, S., L. Edelman, H. Scarbrough, J. Swan and M. Bresnen (2003). 'The Inevitability of Reinvention in Project-Based Learning.' *Journal of Health Services Management* **16**: 1–12.

Nonaka, I. (1994). 'A Dynamic Theory of Organizational Knowledge Creation.' *Organization Science* **5**(1): 14–37.

Orr, J. (1990). Sharing Knowledge, Celebrating Identity in War Stories and Community Memory in a Service Culture. In: *Collective Remembering: Remembering in a Society*. D. Middleton and D. Edwards (eds). Beverly Hills, CA, Sage.

Polanyi, M. (1961). *Personal Knowledge*. Chicago, University of Chicago Press.

Prusak, L. (1997). *Knowledge in Organizations*. Oxford, Butterworth-Heinemann.

Rayport, J. F. and B. J. Jaworski (2001). *E-commerce*. London, McGraw-Hill.

Ruggles, R. (1998). 'The state of the notion: knowledge management in practice.' *California Management Review*, **40**(3): 80–89.

Scarbrough, H. and J. Swan (2001). 'Explaining the Diffusion of Knowledge Management: The Role of Fashion.' *British Journal of Management* **12**(1): 3–18.

Shariq, S. (1999). 'How Does Knowledge Transform as It is Transferred? Speculations on the Possibility of a Cognitive Theory of Knowledge Escapes.' *Journal of Knowledge Management* **3**: 243–251.

Star, S. L. (1996). Working Together: Symbolic Interactionism, Activity Theory and Information Systems. In: *Cognition and Communication at Work*. Y. Engestrom and D. Middleton (eds). Cambridge, UK, Cambridge University Press: pp. 296–318.

Swan, J., S. Newell, H. Scarbrough and D. Hislop (1999). 'Knowledge Management and Innovation: Networks and Networking.' *Journal of Knowledge Management* **3**: 262–275.

Szulanski, G. (1996). 'Exploring Internal Stickiness: Impediments to the Transfer of Best Practice within the Firm.' *Strategic Management Journal* **17**: 27–43.

Timmers, P. (1999). *Electronic Commerce: Strategies and Models for Business-to-Business Trading*. Chichester, John Wiley.

Tsoukas, H. (1996). 'The Firm as a Distributed Knowledge System: A Constructionist Approach.' *Strategic Management Journal* **17**: 11–25.

Von Zedtwitz, M. (2002).'Organizational Learning through Post-Project Reviews in R & D.' *R & D Management* **32**(3): 255–268.

Weick, K. (1995). *Sense-Making in Organizations*. Thousand Oaks, CA, Sage.

Weill, P. and M. R. Vitale (2001). *Place to Space: Migrating to eBusiness Models*. Cambridge, MA, Harvard Business School.

8 Perceptions of strategic value and adoption of e-Commerce: a theoretical framework and empirical test

Elizabeth E. Grandón and J. Michael Pearson

8.1 Introduction

The extraordinary growth in Internet-based business has triggered the need to better understand the characteristics of specific business models adopted by successful organizations. As Colvin (2001) reported and reiterated by Bienstock et al. (2002) 'the recent rash of failed dot.com companies consist primarily of startups with dumb business models' (p. 174). Thus, business models seem to play an important role in the failure/success of Internet initiatives, such as e-Commerce. However, in spite of its important role, there have been few attempts to provide a consistent definition of a business model (Mahadevan, 2000). In general terms, Timmers (1998) defined a business model as the way a firm makes money. Betz (2002) defined it as 'abstracts about how inputs to an organization are transformed to value-adding outputs' (p. 21). More specifically, Osterwalder and Pigneur (2002) defined a business model as the value a company offers to customers and the architecture of the firm and its network of partners for creating, marketing, and delivering this value in order to generate profitable and sustainable revenue streams.

Attempts to classify business models in the context of e-Business/e-Commerce abound in current popular press and scholarly journals. For example, Timmers (1998) identified eleven business models and classified them on the basis of innovation and the requirements of functional integration. Bienstock et al. (2002) proposed a taxonomy of Web business models for both business-to-consumer and business-to-business e-Commerce. Based upon a review of marketing literature, Bienstock et al.'s (2002) taxonomy identified four key dimensions of exchange: number of buyers, number and type of sellers, nature and frequency of product offering, and price mechanism. Similarly, Bartelt and Lamersdorf (2001) developed a multi-criteria taxonomy of business models in e-Commerce. Based on the work of Timmers (1998), the criteria to classify business models were based on: (a) the type of business subjects (suppliers, customers, and mediators) and their active or passive role as initiators of a business model, and (b) the breakdown of the concept of e-Commerce.

For the purpose of this chapter, we have focused on the comprehensive definition and classification of business models given by Mahadevan (2000). He argued that business models are a unique blend of three streams that are critical to the business: value, revenue, and logistical. The value stream identifies the value proposition for the buyers, sellers, and business partners. The revenue stream is a plan for assuring revenue generation for the business. Finally, the logistical stream addresses various issues related to the design of the supply chain for the business. In this chapter, we have centered our attention on the value stream of Mahadevan's (2000) study to understand the value proposition of e-Commerce from the seller perspective, particularly top managers of small- and medium-sized organizations.

The purpose of this chapter is three-fold: (a) to summarize current research in strategic value and adoption of e-Commerce and suggest future research areas, (b) to present a theoretical framework that explains the factors associated with the perceptions of strategic value of e-Commerce and e-Commerce adoption as well as the relationship between these two, and (c) to empirically test the validity of the proposed theoretical framework in field studies. To accomplish this, we conducted survey research in two different countries involving a total of 183 subjects.

In the next section, we provide an overview of e-Commerce, the core concept of this chapter. In the following section, we survey the current literature related to the two research streams – strategic value and adoption of e-Commerce – and present the proposed theoretical framework. Then, we describe the survey research and discuss the results generated from each independent study and the implications obtained from both. We close the chapter with a discussion of the validation of the proposed theoretical framework and suggestions for future academic research.

8.1.1 e-Commerce: an overview

e-Commerce is defined as 'business activities conducted using e-data transmission via the Internet and the World Wide Web' (Schneider and Perry, 2000). e-Commerce can provide many benefits to both buyers and sellers. For instance, Napier et al. (2001) suggested that by using e-Commerce, sellers could access narrow market segments that may be geographically dispersed, thereby extending their reach globally. Buyers could also benefit from accessing global markets thereby having larger product availability from a wider variety of sellers.

It is also been suggested that e-Commerce reduces costs. For example, Schneider and Perry (2000) cited the example of Cisco Systems which sold 72% of its computer equipment via the Web in 1998. Since no customer service representatives were involved in these sales, Cisco estimated that it avoided handling 500,000 calls per month, for an annual savings of over $500 million. Improvement in product quality and the creation of new ways of selling existing products are other benefits cited in the literature (Napier et al., 2001; Chaudhury and Kuilboer, 2002; Saloner and Spence, 2002). All these benefits can be achieved by sellers and buyers after e-Commerce adoption.

8.2 Theoretical framework

The e-Commerce adoption framework proposed in this chapter represents a fusion of two independent research streams developed over the last decade. The first stream can be characterized as identifying the strategic value of certain information technologies (IT) as perceived by top managers. The second stream identifies factors that influence the adoption of various IT. The former has been studied by Subramanian and Nosek (2001) and others (e.g. Barua et al., 1995; Tallon et al., 2000), while the latter has been investigated by Davis (1989) and others (e.g. Adams et al., 1992; Venkatesh and Davis, 1996; Lederer et al., 2000). The proposed framework connects these two research streams via a causal link that theorizes that individual perceptions influence behavior. Specifically, we theorize that managers' perceptions of strategic value of e-Commerce influence e-Commerce adoption. Support for this causal link comes from psychology theories, such as the theory of planned behavior (TPB) (Ajzen, 1991), theory of reasoned action (Fishbein and Ajzen, 1975), and the technology acceptance model (TAM) (Davis, 1989).

We begin by surveying previous literature regarding strategic value of IT in general and e-Commerce in particular. Similarly, we then examine prior research regarding adoption of IT in general and e-Commerce in particular. This literature review is intended to help us to devise the theoretical framework to better understand managers' perceptions about the strategic value of e-Commerce and the factors that influence its adoption.

8.2.1 Perceived strategic value of IT

A number of studies regarding strategic value of IT have been carried out over the past decade. To obtain insights into the factors that create strategic value of e-Commerce, we have classified prior research into two unique categories. The first category considers those studies that have focused on the relationship between IT investment and firm performance. In these studies, the value that IT may create is assessed through performance indexes, such as return on IT investment (ROI) or return on assets (ROA). This body of research is closely associated with the 'IT productivity paradox problem' (Brynjolfsson, 1993; Brynjolfsson and Hitt, 1996; Dewan and Min, 1997; Lee, 2001). The second category focuses on studies that have investigated executives' perceptions of the strategic value IT may provide to their firms. In this body of research, perceptions are assessed by using less tangible measures, such as personal experience and novelty.

Value of IT: investment and firm performance assessment

A common method to determine how IT creates value for the firm is measuring performance after IT implementation. Performance has typically been measured by using productivity and/or profitability indexes (Lee, 2001). For example, Hitt and Brynjolfsson (1996) investigated how IT affects productivity, profitability, and consumer surplus. They found that IT increases productivity and consumer surplus but does not necessarily increase business profits. They suggested that IT could create strategic value but negatively impact profits. This interesting finding leads us to conclude that IT investments are important to maintain competitive parity but do not necessarily support competitive advantage. Similar results were found in Barua et al.'s (1995) study where they concluded that the productivity gains from IT investments have been neutral or negative.

In order to validate previous research dealing with the impact of IT investment and firm performance in US companies, Tam (1998) conducted a study on four newly industrialized economies: Hong Kong, Singapore, Malaysia, and Taiwan. Similar to the findings on US firms, Tam (1998) found that IT investment is not correlated with shareholder's return and specifically, there is no consistent measurement of IT investment as indicated by the mixed results across different performance ratios.

The majority of the above research has proposed a direct causal link between IT investment and firm performance. Some exceptions are the work by Li and Ye (1999) and Lee (2001). Li and Ye (1999) empirically tested the moderating effects of environmental dynamism, firm strategy, and CIO/CEO relationship on the impact of IT investment on firm performance. They found that IT investment appears to have a stronger positive impact on financial performance when there are greater environmental changes, the strategy of the company is more proactive, and closer CIO/CEO ties.

In a similar line of inquiry, Lee (2001) created a multi-level value model that connects the use of IT to a firm's profit. She pointed out that the effect of incorporating IT should not be considered alone. As in the case of Li and Ye (1999), Lee (2001) argued that there are other variables that may influence the relationship between IT investment and performance. She created an IT business value model by adopting the grounded theory approach and studying seven mortgage firms. The value model incorporated other variables, such as origination cost, cycle time, loan officer retention, control over external partners, and marketing effort. The results of her study showed that IT can reduce cycle time and cost, and change the way business is run. She concluded that due to the complementarily nature of IT with many other variables, 'one has to know what other variables to manage and how to manage them in order to make IT investments profitable' (p. 208).

Models have also been devised to identify e-Commerce opportunities to create value. For instance, by combining five dimensions of e-Commerce (time, distance, relationships, interaction, and product) and three types of value generated by e-Commerce (efficiency, effectiveness, and strategic), Riggins (1999) created a model to identify 15 areas in which managers could use e-Commerce to add business value. Riggins' model, called the 'e-Commerce value grid', is very prescriptive in the sense that managers can locate their specific firm in a particular cell of the value grid and take actions toward increasing business value to their customers.

Value of IT: perceptual assessment

Now we turn our attention to studies that have focused on managers' perceptions of strategic value of IT, particularly of e-Commerce. Tallon et al. (1998, 2000) measured IT payoffs through perceptual measures. They concluded that despite significant progress in evaluating the productivity impacts from IT investment, the inability of traditional economic measures to fully account for intangible impacts has led to a call for a more comprehensive approach to measure IT business value. They argued that executives rely on their perceptions in determining whether or not a particular IT investment creates value for the firm. Personal experience and peer evaluations were found to be important determinants of IT value.

The work by Amit and Zott (2001) is another example of studies that have focused on determining the perceptions of top management regarding strategic value of e-Commerce. Even though they focused their analysis on e-Business, their results can be generalized to e-Commerce since e-Commerce is viewed as part of e-Business (Huff et al., 2000). Based on a review of literature in entrepreneurship and strategic management and on data obtained from case study analyses, Amit and Zott (2001) developed a value-drivers model which includes four factors found to be sources of value creation of e-Business: transaction efficiency, complementarities, lock-in, and novelty. They also pointed out that 'the greater the transaction efficiency gains that are enabled by a particular e-Business, the lower the cost and hence the more valuable it will be' (p. 503). Some of these factors were also confirmed in Saloner and Spence's (2002) work. For example, they pointed out that the most important area in which e-Commerce can create value is in reducing transaction costs involved in bringing buyers and sellers together.

Bringing together both areas of research, investment/performance and perceptual assessment of value, Subramanian and Nosek (2001) created an instrument to validate the strategic value that an information system (IS) may provide. From Parker et al. (1988) and as cited by Subramanian and Nosek (2001), it can be seen that 'management use their own value system and acts as interpreters of the organization's value system in judging cost, benefits, and risk during resource allocation decisions' (p. 2). Through an empirical study of 73 firms, Subramanian and Nosek (2001) identified three factors that were found to create strategic value of IS: operational support, managerial productivity, and strategic decision aid. In each of these constructs, they utilized different items that were found to have high convergent validity and reliability. The factors tested in Subramanian and Nosek's (2001) work seem to be applicable to other IT, especially to e-Commerce. Therefore, and due to the lack of current research identifying factors that create strategic value of e-Commerce, we incorporated these constructs into our theoretical framework.

8.2.2 IT adoption

We surveyed current literature on IT adoption in order to obtain insights on the factors that influence the adoption of e-Commerce. IT adoption has been studied by the management information systems (MIS) community via different approaches. For the purpose of this literature review, we have grouped the existing research by the type of technology addressed: application programs, Computer-Aided Software Engineering (CASE), Group Support Systems (GSS), E-Data Interchange (EDI), the Internet/WWW and corporate Web sites, and e-Commerce. A description of the factors involved in each of these technologies follows.

Application programs

The seminal work of Davis (1989) has set the basis for later studies in the area of IT adoption. He proposed the technology acceptance model (TAM), which posits two antecedents of user acceptance of IT: perceived usefulness and perceived ease of use. He defined perceived usefulness as 'the degree to which a person believes that using a particular system would enhance his or her job performance' (p. 320). Perceived ease of use is defined as 'the degree to which a person believes that using a particular system would be free of effort' (p. 320). Perceived usefulness and perceived ease of use are hypothesized to influence attitudes which, in turn, influence intention and behavior. In order to test his proposed model, Davis (1989) conducted two independent studies involving a total of 152 subjects and four application programs. He found that these two antecedents explain a high percentage of system usage. This model has been tested in numerous studies (e.g. Adams et al., 1992; Hendrickson et al., 1993; Szajna, 1994; Igbaria et al., 1997; Straub et al., 1997; Subramanian, 1998) and has been found to explain a significant amount of the variance in intentions to use a technology and/or actual use of the technology.

CASE

Adoption of CASE has also been addressed in the IT adoption literature. Premkumar and Potter (1995) examined the impact of various organizational and technology characteristics on the adoption of CASE tools. Within the organizational factors, they considered top management support, product champion, and IS expertise. The variables included in the technical factor were relative advantage, cost, complexity, technical compatibility, and organizational compatibility. Ninety IS managers participated in the field survey. Results revealed that the existence of a product champion, strong top management support, lower IS expertise, relative advantage of CASE technology over other alternatives, and a conviction of the cost effectiveness of the technology were found to be strong indicators of the adoption of CASE tools.

GSS

Chin and Gopal (1995) studied the relative importance of beliefs in the adoption of GSS. They examined how relative advantage, ease of use, compatibility, and enjoyment influenced the intention to adopt GSS. Similar to Premkumar and Potter (1995), relative advantage incorporated the concept of technology assessment relative to another technology that was currently used. To assess relative advantage, Chin and Gopal (1995) included the items to measure perceived usefulness defined by Davis (1989). Compatibility was a construct taken from Moore and Benbasat's (1991) study and defined as the degree to which an innovation is perceived as being consistent with the existing values, needs, and past experiences of potential adopters. Enjoyment, however, was considered as a new factor influencing the intention to adopt GSS. They drew upon Davis et al. (1992) work to define enjoyment: 'the extend to which the activity of using the computer is perceived to be enjoyable in its own right, apart from any performance consequences' (p. 47). They found that beliefs about technology were also effective in explaining GSS intention to adopt. The factor found to be the most influential in GSS adoption was relative advantage: 'the extent to which an innovation is perceived as being better than its precursor' (p. 47).

EDI

Iacovou et al. (1995) studied the factors influencing the adoption of EDI. They considered seven organizations in different industries that were pursuing EDI initiatives. Among the factors included were perceived benefits, organizational readiness, and external pressure. To measure perceived benefits, they used awareness of direct and indirect benefits. Variables measuring organizational readiness were financial and technological resources. In order to measure external pressure, they considered competitive pressure and imposition by partners. They found that the relationship between perceived benefits and adoption as well as between organizational readiness and adoption was moderated. However, the relationship between external pressure and adoption of EDI was found to be strong.

In another study, Chwelos et al. (2001) considered similar factors as influencing the adoption of EDI. The variables measuring the main constructs were slightly different, however. For example, they considered the trading partner as influencing external pressure and readiness. External pressure was considered to be influenced by the dependency on the trading partner and enacted trading partner power. In this study, all three determinants were found to be significant predictors of the intention to adopt EDI, with external pressure, and readiness being considerably more important than perceived benefits. In a similar line of inquiry, Kuan and Chau (2001) determined the factors influencing the adoption of EDI in small businesses using a technology, organization, and environment framework. The technology factor, as in Iacovou et al.'s (1995) study, incorporated perceived direct and indirect benefits of EDI. The organization factor corresponded to organizational readiness in Iacovou et al.'s (1995) study and consisted of perceived financial cost and perceived technical competence. The environment factor included industry and perceived government pressure (in Iacovou et al.'s (1995) study this factor was labeled 'external pressure'). As in the case of Chwelos et al. (2001), Kuan and Chau (2001) found that all three factors had significant influences on EDI adoption by small businesses, with organizational readiness and external pressure being the most important. Yet, the perceived indirect benefits variable was found to be non-significant.

The Internet/WWW and corporate Web sites

In a study by Chang and Cheung (2001), the determinants of the intention to use the Internet/WWW were established. Instead of investigating the factors affecting adoption, they studied those affecting the intention to use the Internet/WWW. Among the factors considered were near and long-term consequences, complexity, affect, social factors, and facilitation conditions. Complexity and long-term consequences were not found to influence the intention to adopt the Internet/WWW. In a similar inquiry, Beatty et al. (2001) studied the factors influencing corporate Web site adoption. They found that the factors involved in the adoption process differ depending on the time at which the technology has been adopted. In their empirical study of 286 medium-to-large US firms, they found that early adopters placed significantly more emphasis on perceived benefits for having a Web site than late adopters. The early adopters viewed using the Web as being more compatible with their current organizational processes and their existing technological infrastructures. In addition, early adopters had greater top manager support for a Web site than did late adopters. Firms that adopted corporate Web sites later appear not to have placed as much emphasis on benefits, and adopted them in spite of the lack of compatibility between the Web and their existing technology and organizational norms. This fact suggests that external pressure of peers, industry, or government may play a role in the decision to adopt an IT at least for later adopters. Finally, there were no significant differences among firms' perceptions of complexity of Web technologies regardless of when adoption occurred.

e-Commerce

The study of e-Commerce adoption has not been investigated as thoroughly. Mirchandani and Motwani (2001) investigated factors that differentiate adopters from non-adopters of e-Commerce in small businesses. As in the case of Chin and Gopal (1995) and Premkumar and Potter (1995), the relevant factors included compatibility of e-Commerce with the work of the company and relative advantage perceived from e-Commerce. In addition, knowledge of the company's employees about computers and enthusiasm of top managers were discriminant factors between adopters and non-adopters of e-Commerce. The degree of dependence of the company on information, managerial time required to plan and implement the e-Commerce application, the nature of the company's competition, as well as the financial cost of implementing and operating the e-Commerce application were found not to be influencing factors.

By using the theory of planned behavior (Ajzen, 1991), Riemenschneider and McKinney (2001–2002) analyzed the beliefs of small business executives regarding the adoption of e-Commerce. They found that all the component items of the normative and control beliefs differentiated between adopters and non-adopters of e-Commerce. In the behavioral beliefs (attitude) group, however, only some items (*e-Commerce enhances the distribution of information, improves information accessibility, communication, and the speed with which things get done*) were found to differentiate adopters from non-adopters of e-Commerce. Table 8.1 summarizes the factors that influence IT adoption according to the previous literature review.

8.2.3 Proposed framework

In building our theoretical framework, we surveyed the current literature and found perceptual factors that create strategic value of IS as well as factors that influence IT adoption, including e-Commerce. However, one piece of the puzzle is still missing: the link between these two research streams. We postulate that top managers/owners who perceive that e-Commerce provides strategic value to their firms will have a positive attitude towards its adoption. Thus, these two main constructs, perceptions of strategic value and adoption, are tied together

Table 8.1: Summary of relevant factors associated with the adoption of different technologies

Technology	Relevant factors	Source
Application programs	Perceived ease of use Perceived usefulness	Davis (1989)
CASE	Technology (relative advantage, cost, complexity, technical and organizational compatibility) Organizational (top management support, product champion, IS expertise)	Premkumar and Potter (1995)
GSS	Relative advantage Ease of use Compatibility Enjoyment	Chin and Gopal (1995)
EDI	Perceived benefits Organizational readiness External pressure	Iacovou et al. (1995) Chwelos et al. (2001)
EDI	Technology Organization Environment	Kuan and Chau (2001)
Internet/WWW	Near, long-term consequences Complexity Affect Social factors Facilitating conditions	Chang and Cheung (2001)
Corporate Web site	Organizational compatibility Technical compatibility Perceived benefits Top management support Complexity	Beatty et al. (2001)
e-Commerce	Relative advantage Compatibility with company Knowledge of computers within the company Enthusiasm of top managers	Mirchandani and Motwani (2001)
e-Commerce	Behavioral beliefs Normative beliefs Control beliefs	Riemenschneider and McKinney (2001–2002)

through a direct causal link. Support for the causal link between perceptions of strategic value and adoption comes from different research studies that associate individual perceptions and behavior. Borrowing from social psychology, MIS researchers have used intention models to explain and predict IT adoption and usage. The theory of planned behavior (Ajzen, 1991), for example, is an especially well-established intention model that has been proven successful in predicting and explaining behavior across a wide variety of domains, including the use of IT (e.g. Taylor and Todd, 1995; Harrison et al., 1997; Hausenblas et al., 1997; Chang, 1998; Johnson et al., 1999; Riemenschneider et al., 2003). The TPB establishes that perceptions influence intentions which in turn influence the actual behavior of the individual. By considering the intention to adopt e-Commerce as the target behavior in question, the use of intention models, such as the TPB, theoretically justify the causal link between perceptions and adoption of e-Commerce. In general terms, the more favorable the attitude toward the behavior in question, the more likely will be its achievement. In particular, the more favorable the attitudes and beliefs of managers/owners toward the perceived strategic value of e-Commerce, the more likely they will adopt it.

In addition, this causal link has been studied in other researches that have shown that managers' perception and attitudes towards other types of IT are strongly associated with an organization's progressive use of IT. For example, some of the hypotheses developed by Jarvenpaa and Ives (1991) were whether a CEO's high involvement in IT and CEO's active personal participation in IT management were associated with a firm being highly progressive in its use of IT. They defined involvement as 'CEO's perceptions and attitudes concerning IT' (p. 206) and participation as 'the CEO's activities or substantive personal interventions in the management of IT' (p. 206). In order to test these hypotheses, they conducted a survey study involving 83 firms from four different industries. They found strong support for the relationship between involvement (favorable perceptions of IT) and progressive use of the IT. However, the link between CEO's participation in IT management and progressive use of the IT was found to be moderate. Similar research in this line of inquiry are those by Sanders and Courtney (1985), Reich and Benbasat (1990), and Bush et al. (1991).

For the purpose of our research, we grouped the factors (according to their similarity and face validity) found to be significant in influencing the adoption of different IT and considered them as potential factors that determine e-Commerce adoption (*organizational readiness, external pressure, perceived ease of use, and perceived usefulness*). In order to explain whether perceptions of strategic value of e-Commerce influence its adoption we have proposed the following theoretical framework (Figure 8.1).

The three factors that were found to create strategic value of IS (*operational support, managerial productivity, and strategic decision aid*) considered by Subramanian and Nosek's (2001) study have been customized to this current study to determine whether they create strategic value for e-Commerce. Table 8.2 below describes the constructs and identifies the original source of the construct. Table 8.3 summarizes the four factors considered in the adoption of e-Commerce construct (*organizational readiness, external pressure, perceived ease of use, and perceived usefulness*) with an indication of the previous studies that

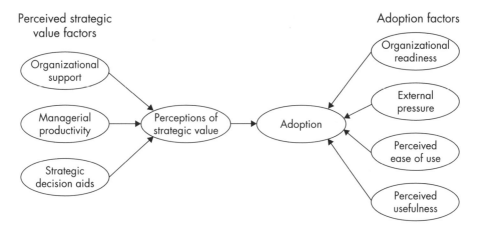

Figure 8.1: Theoretical framework to study perceptions of strategic value and adoption of e-Commerce.

Table 8.2: Hypothesized factors that create strategic value in e-Commerce

Construct	Description/source	Derived from
Operational support	Managers' perceptions of an operational support value for e-Commerce. It includes support to decision-making, cooperative partnerships in the industry, transaction cost reduction, improved customers service, and improved distribution channels (adapted from Subramanian and Nosek, 2001)	'Vision to automate', Segars and Grover, 1998; Weill, 1992
Managerial productivity	Managers' perceptions that e-Commerce provides better access to information, helps in the management of time, improves communication among managers, and improve productivity of managers (adapted from Subramanian and Nosek, 2001)	'Vision to informate up', Segars and Gover, 1998; Weill, 1992
Strategic decision aid	Managers' perceptions that e-Commerce supports strategic decisions of managers, provides information for strategic decisions, and enhances relationships between customers and suppliers (adapted from Subramanian and Nosek, 2001)	'Vision to transform', Segars and Grover, 1998

have included these constructs as determinants of IT adoption. The customized definition of each construct is also given.

8.3 Empirical evidence from the field

We have developed a theoretical framework that we believe will explain whether managers'/owners' perceptions of strategic value of e-Commerce influence their decision to adopt it. If the framework is valid,

Table 8.3: Hypothesized factors that determine e-Commerce adoption

Factor in the current theoretical framework and definition	Factors in previous studies	Source
Organizational readiness Availability of the financial and technological resources to adopt e-Commerce (adapted from Iacovou et al., 1995)	Organizational compatibility	Beatty et al. (2001); Premkumar and Potter (1995)
	Technical compatibility	Beatty et al. (2001); Premkumar and Potter (1995)
	Organizational readiness	Iacovou et al. (1995); Chwelos et al. (2001)
	Organization	Kuan and Chau (2001)
	Compatibility with company	Mirchandani and Motwani (2001)
	Facilitating conditions	Chang and Cheung (2001)
	Technological context	Ryan and Prybutock (2001)
	Control beliefs	Riemenschneider and McKinney (2001–2002)
External Pressure Direct or indirect pressure exerted by competitors, social referents, other firms, the government, and the industry to adopt e-Commerce (based on Iacovou et al., 1995)	External Pressure	Iacovou et al. (1995); Chwelos et al. (2001)
	Environment	Kuan and Chau (2001)
	Social factors	Chang and Cheung (2001)
	Environmental context	Ryan and Prybutock (2001)
	Normative beliefs	Riemenschneider and McKinney (2001–2002)
Perceived ease of use The degree to which an individual believes that using e-Commerce would be free of effort (based on Davis, 1989)	Perceived ease of use	Davis (1989); Chin and Gopal (1995)
Perceived usefulness The degree to which a person believes that using e-Commerce would enhance his or her job performance (based on Davis, 1989)	Perceived usefulness	Davis (1989)

interventions to change managers'/owners' perceptions toward e-Commerce adoption can be developed. However, before suggesting interventions or guidelines to help managers'/owners' understanding about e-Commerce adoption issues, it is necessary to collect empirical evidence from the field to support our theoretical framework. To accomplish this, we conducted two studies in two different countries. Finding support for the theoretical framework by empirically testing it in two disparate countries (developed versus developing) would provide a solid grounding for the suggested theoretical model.

We wanted to obtain empirical evidence from developed countries (US), where research concerning IT has been extensively carried out, and compare and contrast the results with empirical evidence from developing countries (Chile), where there is a lack of research concerning the same topic. As a matter of fact, in two separate literature reviews (Thompson and Rose, 1994; Prescott and Conger, 1995) that covered 100 studies concerning IT adoption, none of the studies took place in developing countries. This can be explained partly by the fact that the majority of research/academic institutions are located in developed countries, such as US, Canada, and the UK. The need for understanding perceptions of strategic value and adoption of e-Commerce by developing countries, which account for 85% of the worldwide population, is an important area of study that deserves attention.

The lack of research centered on developing countries is not the only motivation for this study. Among the studies that have focused on technology adoption, only a small percentage has been devoted to the adoption and use of e-Commerce in small- and medium-sized enterprises (SMEs) (e.g. Mirchandani and Motwani, 2001; Riemenschneider and McKinney, 2001–2002). The contribution of SMEs is extremely important to the economy of both developed and developing countries. For example, SMEs represent 99% of businesses, employ more than half of the American work force, and create two-thirds of the new jobs in the US (Small Business Administration, 1999–2000). In Chile, on the other hand, 80% of the economy is represented by SMEs (http://www.genexiachile. com/pymes/pymes1.htm)*, while 49% of the employment is generated by SMEs (http://cowles.econ.yale.edu/~engel/arts/pymeweb.pdf)*. In a literature review conducted by Lee and Runge (2001), only eight articles published in the last 10 years were directly concerned with SMEs and IT adoption. Surprisingly, none of them were devoted to the study of the adoption of e-Commerce.

Although there are many potential advantages, the adoption of e-Commerce by SMEs remains limited. According to a survey by The Gallup Organization (http://www.gallup.com) small businesses are establishing Web sites primarily to advertise and promote their business, rather than to conduct e-Commerce. The number of small firms that established a Web site to advertise and promote their business increased 123% from 1999 to 2000, while small businesses establishing Web sites primarily to sell products decreased 48% during the same period (Second Annual Small Business Internet Survey, http://superpages.com/about/press/press10.html). Moreover, according to the US Small Business Administration, only 1.4% of Internet use among SMEs is directed toward e-Commerce sales. These findings are quite interesting. While top managers and owners of SMEs seem to recognize the importance of

---

*In Spanish.

having an Internet presence (Cyber Atlas, 2001; OPEN Small Business Network 2002 Monitor), only a small percentage of them use the Internet for commercial purposes. Does this mean that top managers/owners of SMEs do not realize the strategic value e-Commerce may provide to their businesses? In the hypothetical scenario that top managers recognize the strategic value in e-Commerce, does this mean that they encounter significant barriers to implement e-Commerce? Thus, we were motivated to investigate further whether the perceptions of strategic value of e-Commerce influence top manager's decision to adopt e-Commerce.

In order to test our theoretical framework, we conducted two studies during Spring 2002: Study 1 in a developed country (US) and Study 2 in a developing country (Chile) where the requisite resources to implement or adopt e-Commerce may differ considerably from those available in developed countries. A general description of the methodology utilized in both studies follows.

8.3.1 Subjects

In Study 1, we targeted top managers/owners of SMEs in the Midwest region of the USA. In Study 2, we targeted top managers/owners of SMEs in the Bío-Bío region of Chile. The Bío-Bío region of Chile, which is located 328 miles south of Santiago, is the second largest in terms of population. It is also the second most important region in terms of its contribution to the national economy (http://www.bcn.cl/pags/regional/cont/pags/20010103170558.html)*.

Different criteria have been utilized to determine a small- or medium-size business. In our studies, we considered the number of employees as the principal criteria since other categorizations such of those involving revenue, total capital and/or other types are more difficult to obtain and can result in misleading classifications of organizations. The number of employees considered in a SME varies according to the agency providing the definition. For example, the US Small Business Administration (http://www.sba.gov) uses a cutoff of fewer than 500 employees. Morales (1990) and Cabrera (1994) used a cut-off value of less than 100 employees. Harrison et al. (1997) as well as Iacovo et al. (1995) utilized a cutoff of 200 employees. In order to make reasonable comparisons among SMEs in the two countries surveyed in these studies, we used the cutoff for small and medium-size businesses suggested by the US Small Business Administration (less than 500 employees) for both Study 1 and 2.

8.3.2 Data collection

Data for Study 1 were gathered by means of an e-survey. The data gathering process was carried out in three steps. First, a sample of 1069

---

*In Spanish.

small and medium-size businesses were identified from various sources that focus on small and medium-sized business organizations. From these sources, we identified the company name, a contact person, an e-mail address for that person, an address and a telephone number. The contact person identified was typically the owner of the business or a top-level manager in the organization. Second, an initial mailing, which identified the purpose of the study, a request to participate and an opt-out feature, was sent to all 1069 potential respondents. One hundred and thirty-six of these e-messages were returned due to an incorrect e-mail address or the organization no longer being in business. An additional 101 individuals indicated they were unable or were unwilling to participate in this study. Thirdly, approximately 1 week after the initial mailing, a second e-mailing was sent to the remaining 832 potential respondents. This e-message directed these individuals to the Web site where the survey instrument was located. As a result of this procedure, 100 individuals completed the survey for a response rate of 12%.

Data for Study 2 were gathered by means of a mail survey. In this case, the gathering process was carried out in two steps. First, a sample of 130 small- and medium-size businesses in the Bío-Bío region of Chile was selected from a guide of enterprises of the Bío-Bío region (GEEP, 2001). Follow-up telephone calls were made in order to ensure that the surveys were received by targeted mail addresses. During this first step, we realized that not all the surveys had been delivered due to changes in mail addresses. Therefore, we resent 30 surveys to those organizations that did not receive the survey via the first mailing.

During the second step, 80 more surveys were mailed to different companies randomly selected from the same enterprise guide (GEEP, 2001). The same procedure was followed to ensure that the surveys were delivered and to ascertain top managers' willingness to participate. In addition, through one author's personal contacts, it was possible to send 30 more surveys to other firms that were not targeted either in the first or second mailing. A total of 240 surveys were sent. Eighty-three companies provided usable data which represents a 34% response rate.

8.3.3 Instrument development

The instrument utilized in both studies was identical. Three top managers participated in a pilot of the survey instrument. One of the authors observed the pilot subjects as they completed the survey. Feedback from the subjects resulted in minor changes to survey instructions and questions. Respondents were required to complete the survey that had the following major sections:

- Seven demographic questions about the respondent's gender, age, education, years of work in present position, and years of work within present firm.

■ Two general questions about the firm: total number of employees and industry in which the firm operates.

■ Four questions about the technology in the organization: number of PCs, presence of Internet server provider, presence of Web site, and utilization of e-Commerce.

■ Fifteen questions asking the extent to which e-Commerce is perceived as contributing to strategic value of the firm.

■ Twenty-three questions to measure the factors involved in e-Commerce adoption.

A seven-point Likert scale (from strongly disagree to strongly agree) was utilized to measure the questions regarding perceived strategic value and adoption of e-Commerce. The survey included a brief definition of e-Commerce in order to clarify the concept.

8.3.4 General statistical procedure

In both studies the statistical analysis was conducted in two stages. The first step employed confirmatory factor analysis to determine whether the number of factors and loadings of items involved in the two main constructs of the theoretical framework (perceived strategic value and adoption) conformed to the model. The factor analysis used principal components in order to extract the maximum variance from the items. To minimize the number of items which have high loadings on any given factor, a varimax rotation was utilized. Eigenvalues above 1 were considered to test the factor structure of the two main constructs.

Since we were also interested in exploring how the perceptions of strategic value influence the decision to adopt e-Commerce, canonical analysis was utilized in the second step. Canonical analysis is a multivariate statistical technique that studies the interrelationships among sets of multiple dependent and independent variables (Hair et al., 1998; Johnson and Wichern, 1998; Stevens, 2002). By simultaneously considering both multiple dependent and independent variables, it is possible to control for moderator or suppressor effects that may exist among various dependent variables (Mahmood and Mann, 1993). MIS research has benefited from the use of this multivariate technique (e.g. Koh and Watson, 1998; Byrd and Turner, 2001).

In canonical analysis, there are r-criterion variables (dependent variables) and s-predictor variables (independent variables). The maximum number of canonical correlations (functions) between these two sets of variables is the number of variables in the smaller set (Green et al., 1966; Johnson and Wichern, 1998; Stevens, 2002). In our proposed theoretical framework the number of variables for the perception of strategic value is three (*organizational support, managerial productivity, and decision aids*) while the number of variables in the adoption construct is four (*perceived usefulness, perceived ease of use, external pressure, and organizational readiness*). Thus, the number of canonical functions extracted from the analysis is three which correspond to the smallest set of variables. To test the significance of the canonical correlations we looked at two different measures: (a) the significance of the *F*-value given by Wilk's lambda, Pillai's criterion, Hotteling's trace, and Roy's gcr (Hair et al., 1998) and (b) the measures of overall model fit.

The following sections in this chapter summarize the findings of both studies. Interested readers may refer to more detailed coverage of these studies in the original papers published separately (Grandón and Pearson, 2003, 2004).

8.4 US and Chile studies

8.4.1 The case of US

Demographics: Study 1

The results indicate that top managers in the Midwest region of US are well educated with over 64% holding a 4-year college degree or Masters. The majority of them are male (64%) and 36% were between 41 and 50 years of age. Table 8.4 shows other demographics associated with the respondents of this study.

Confirmatory factor analysis: Study 1

Perceived strategic value construct. Using the Kaiser eigenvalues criterion, we extracted three factors (*organizational support, managerial productivity, and decision aids*) that collectively explained 79.43% of the variance in all items. Hair et al. (1998) provide guidelines for identifying significant factor loadings based on sample size. In order to obtain a power level of 80% at 0.05 significant level, and standard errors assumed to be twice those of conventional correlation coefficient, a factor loading of 0.55 or higher should be considered as a cut-off value. The rotated factor matrix showed that all the items loaded cleanly on their intended factors with loadings greater than 0.69.

Convergent and discriminant validity was assessed via factor analysis. All items have loading greater than 0.55 and load stronger on their associated factors than on other factors. Thus, convergent and discriminant validity are demonstrated. Construct reliability or internal consistency was assessed using Cronbach's alpha. The values for alpha varied from 0.88 to 0.95. The scale reliabilities for the perceived strategic value construct in this study are unusually good compared to the acceptable 0.7 level for field research (Nunnally, 1978).

Table 8.4: Demographic information for Study 1

Study 1: US		
Gender	Male: 64%	Female: 36%
Age	10% between 18 and 30	36% between 41 and 50
	25% between 31 and 40	26% more than 50
Years of work in present position	Average: 8.03	SD: 7.1
Years of work with present firm	Average: 8.12	SD: 7.6
Education	High school	12%
	2-year college	17%
	4-year college	35%
	Master degree	21%
	Other (JD, 3-year college, etc.)	11%
Industry	Education	8%
	Finance	2%
	Wholesale	2%
	Retail	12%
	Healthcare	2%
	Construction	5%
	Insurance	1%
	Other	48% (consulting, marketing service, advertising, etc.)
Internet service provider already in place	Yes	94%
	No	6%
Firm Web site	Yes	85%
	No	15%
e-Commerce already in place	Yes	64%
	No	36%

Adoption construct.   The adoption construct was initially comprised of 23 items. In order to test how these items loaded, another factor analysis was run. Different from our hypothesized framework that posited four factors as influencing e-Commerce adoption, the results of this confirmatory factor analysis resulted in five factors loading cleanly with a total explained variance of 74.9%. The items considered in the fifth factor, which we named 'compatibility', were originally included in the organizational readiness factor during the first run of the factor analysis. However, the empirical evidence suggested that compatibility is an important factor to be considered independent from organizational readiness. Thus, we revised the proposed theoretical framework to better describe the items used.

As in the case of the perceived strategic value construct, convergent, and discriminant validity was assessed via factor analysis. All adoption items had loading greater than 0.59 and loaded stronger on their associated factors than on other factors. The values for alpha varied from

Table 8.5: Measures of overall model fit

Canonical function	Canonical correlation	Canonical R^2	F statistic	Probability
1	0.644	0.415	4.02864	0.000
2	0.266	0.071	0.98655	0.448
3	0.122	0.015	0.44634	0.720

0.76 to 0.95. Therefore, the reliability of the adoption construct for Study 1 turned out to be very high.

Canonical analysis: Study 1

Even though the multivariate test of significance showed that the canonical functions, taken collectively, are statistically significant at the 0.01 level, from the overall model fit (Table 8.5) it can be concluded that only the first canonical function is significant $(P < 0.01)$. This conclusion is consistent with the canonical R^2-values showed in Table 8.5. For these data, in the first canonical function the independent variables explain 42% of the variance in the dependent variables; the second canonical function explains 7%, and the third one explains only 1.5%. This is not unusual since typically the first canonical function is far more important than the others (Campbell and Taylor, 1996; Johnson and Wichern, 1998).

In order to interpret the selected canonical function, two methods were employed: canonical weights and canonical loadings. Due to the pattern of results in canonical weights and canonical loadings, we opted to interpret the results based on the canonical loadings. The rationality of this choice is the fact that the interpretation of canonical weights is subject to some criticism (Thompson, 1991). For example, Hair et al. (1998) stated, 'a small weight may mean either that its corresponding variable is irrelevant in determining the relationship or that it has been partialed out of the relationship because of a high degree of multicollinearity' (p. 453). Canonical weights are also considered to have low stability from one sample to another (Hair et al., 1998).

The canonical loadings measure the linear correlation between the independent variables and their respective canonical variates. These can be interpreted like factor loadings (Hair et al., 1998). Table 8.6 shows that all the canonical loadings are significant for the dependent and independent variables (cut-off > 0.3 according to Ma and Bateson (1999) and Byrd and Turner (2001)) with the exception of organizational readiness. The rank order of importance (determined by the absolute value of the canonical loadings) for the perceived strategic value of e-Commerce is organizational support, managerial productivity, and decision aids. Similarly, the rank of importance for the adoption construct

Table 8.6: Standardized canonical coefficients and canonical loadings for perceived strategic value and adoption

Construct	Variable	Canonical weights	Canonical loading
Perceived strategic value			
	OS	−0.854	−0.982
	MP	−0.267	−0.744
	DA	0.056	−0.674
Adoption			
	OR	0.179	−0.120
	CC	−0.206	−0.563
	EP	0.070	−0.482
	EU	−0.132	−0.630
	PU	−0.881	−0.972

contributing to the first canonical function is perceived usefulness, ease of use, compatibility, and external pressure. Organizational readiness seems to be a non-important factor in the adoption construct.

8.4.2 The case of Chile

Demographics: Study 2

The results indicate that the majority of Chilean top managers (90%) are owners or CEOs of small- and medium-size businesses. These individuals are well educated with over 68.67% holding a 4-year college degree. The majority are male (94%) with an average age of 41 years. Table 8.7 shows these and other demographics of the Chilean respondents.

Confirmatory factor analysis: Study 2

Perceived strategic value construct.   The results of the confirmatory factor analysis for Study 2 resulted in three factors (*managerial productivity, decision aids, and organizational support*) loading cleanly with a total explained variance of 73.73%. As in the case of Study 1, convergent and discriminant validity were assessed using factor analysis. All items loaded stronger on their associated factors than on other factors. Thus, convergent and discriminant validity are demonstrated. Construct reliability or internal consistency was assessed using Cronbach's alpha. The alpha values ranges from 0.72 to 0.85. Construct reliability is deemed to be sufficient for all factors.

Adoption construct.   As in the case of Study 1, the results of the confirmatory factor analysis for the adoption construct showed five factors loading cleanly with a total explained variance of 76%. Again, we found support to revise the proposed theoretical framework and considered a fifth factor, which we named 'compatibility', that better

Table 8.7: Demographic information for Study 2

Study 2: Chile

Gender	Male: 94%	Female: 6%
Age	Average: 40.67	SD: 9.87
Years of work in present position	Average: 9.55	SD: 7.89
Years of work with present firm	Average: 11.07	SD: 9.35
Education	High school	4.82%
	2-year college	26.51%
	4-year college	62.65%
	Master degree	4.82%
	Doctoral degree	1.2%
Industry	Manufacturing	4.82%
	Wholesale	20.48%
	Retail	21.69%
	Healthcare	4.82%
	Construction	13.25%
	Transportation	1.20%
	Other (forestry, fishing, services, and others)	33.73%
Hardware platform	Mainframe	3.61%
	Mini	1.2%
	PC	65.06%
	Mixture	25.30%
	Other	4.82%
Internet service provider already in place	Yes	87.95%
	No	12.05%
Firm Web site	Yes	48.19%
	No	51.81%
e-Commerce already in place	Yes	15.66%
	No	84.34%

described the items used. Again, convergent and discriminant validity were assessed using factor analysis. As in the case of Study 1, all items in the adoption construct had loadings greater than 0.55 with alpha values between 0.72 for external pressure and 0.95 for perceived usefulness.

Canonical analysis: Study 2

Table 8.8 shows the measures of overall model fit in the three canonical functions for the Chilean data. Note that the strength of the relationship between the canonical covariates is given by the canonical correlation (Hair et al., 1998).

As in the case of Study 1, even though the multivariate test of significance showed that all the tests (Wilk's lambda, Pillai's criterion,

Table 8.8: Measures of overall model fit

Canonical function	Canonical correlation	Canonical R²	F statistic	Probability
1	0.692	0.478	4.27883	0.000
2	0.277	0.077	0.90671	0.513
3	0.115	0.013	0.34255	0.795

Table 8.9: Standardized canonical coefficients and canonical loadings for perceived strategic value and adoption

Construct	Variable	Canonical weights	Canonical loading
Perceived Strategic Value			
	OS	0.081	0.570
	MP	0.483	0.906
	DA	0.558	0.925
Adoption			
	OR	0.201	0.449
	CC	0.560	0.825
	EP	0.032	0.616
	EU	−0.128	0.239
	PU	0.565	0.813

Hotteling's trace, and Roy's gcr) are statistically significant at the 0.05 level, from the overall model fit we concluded that only the first canonical function represents a significant value ($P < 0.01$). For the Chilean data, in the first canonical correlation, the independent variables explain 48% of the variance in the dependent variables; the second canonical correlation explains 8%, and the third one explains only 1%. This finding indicates that the perception of strategic value, as perceived by Chilean managers, and the adoption of e-Commerce were significantly connected via the first canonical function. Thus, as the case of Study 1, the rest of the study is based on the interpretation of this first canonical function.

To make reasonable comparisons between both studies, we opted to interpret the final results based on the canonical loadings. Table 8.9 shows that all the canonical loadings are significant for the independent variables (cut-off > 0.3). The rank order of importance for the perceived strategic value of e-Commerce is decision aids, managerial productivity, and organizational support. Similarly, the rank of importance for the adoption construct contributing to the first canonical function is compatibility, perceived usefulness, external pressure, and organizational readiness. Ease of use of e-Commerce seems to be a non-important factor in the adoption construct.

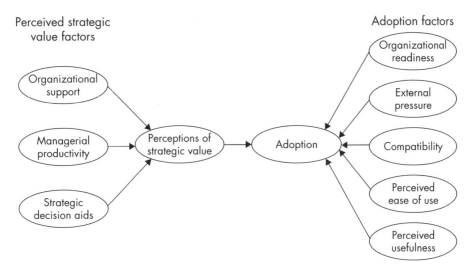

Figure 8.2: The revised theoretical framework.

8.5 Implications of the two studies

Results from the factor analysis conducted for the strategic value construct resulted in three factors (*operational support, managerial productivity, and decision aids*) loading cleanly on the hypothesized factors for both Studies 1 and 2. Surprisingly, and common to both studies, the results from the factor analysis conducted for the adoption construct resulted in five factors instead of the four initially hypothesized (*organizational readiness, external pressure, perceived ease of use, and perceived usefulness*). Thus, we revised the proposed theoretical framework and considered a fifth factor, which we named 'compatibility', that better described the items used (Figure 8.2 shows the revised theoretical framework). The results from these factor analyses are quite interesting. Previous research found compatibility an important factor that influenced the adoption of IT (Chin and Gopal, 1995; Premkumar and Potter, 1995; Beatty et al., 2001; Mirchandani and Motwani, 2001;). In our research, compatibility emerged freely as a significant independent factor in both studies. This suggests that compatibility, or how e-Commerce fits within the organization, should be considered in future studies related to e-Commerce adoption. The revised theoretical framework was the basis to further analyze whether perceptions of e-Commerce influence the adoption of it.

Results from the canonical correlation analysis revealed a significant relationship between the perceived strategic value of e-Commerce variables and the factors that influence e-Commerce adoption in SMEs. This means that those top managers, either Chilean or American, who perceived e-Commerce as adding strategic value to the firm have a positive attitude toward its adoption. From the canonical loadings we conclude that the three factors proposed as determinants of perceived strategic value of e-Commerce have significant impact on managers' attitudes toward e-Commerce adoption.

It seems that top managers/owners, independent of their country of origin, perceive organizational support, managerial productivity, and decision aids as factors that create strategic value of e-Commerce. However, the order of importance they assigned to each factor is different. For example, American managers think that e-Commerce creates value for their firms primarily through the organizational support e-Commerce may provide to their businesses. This result is corroborated by the fact that for Study 1 most of the items measuring organizational support (six out of seven) were found to be significant while for Study 2 only three items (out of the same seven) were found to be significant. In other words, and different from Chilean managers, American managers think that e-Commerce reduces costs of business operations, provides effective support role to operations, and reap operational benefits. These items, as a whole, are the most important sources of value creation of e-Commerce as perceived by top managers/owners of American SMEs. Chilean managers, on the other hand, think that e-Commerce creates value to their firms but primarily through the decision aids e-Commerce may provide. They think that e-Commerce supports strategic decisions for managers, helps making decisions, and provides information for strategic decisions and these items, as a whole, are the most important sources of value creation of e-Commerce.

Similarly, it seems that top managers/owners, independent of their country of origin, think that perceived usefulness, ease of use, compatibility, external pressure, organizational readiness, and ease of use are important determinants of e-Commerce adoption. However, as in the case of the perceived strategic value construct, the order of importance differs for American and Chilean managers. American managers believe that perceived usefulness, ease of use, compatibility, and external pressure are the factors that influence e-Commerce adoption in that order. Chilean managers, on the other hand, think that compatibility, perceived usefulness, external pressure, and organizational readiness are important factors when making the decision to adopt the same business model (in that order of importance). In addition, from the canonical loadings, it can be concluded that American managers do not consider organizational readiness as an influential factor at all, while Chilean managers believe that ease of use is not important when deciding to adopt e-Commerce in their companies.

8.6 Conclusions and future research

Throughout this chapter we have attempted to build a theoretical framework that explains how perceived strategic value of e-Commerce influences manager's attitude toward e-Commerce adoption. Through studying two different streams of research, and empirically testing the theoretical framework in two different countries, we have validated a framework that suggests three factors that provide strategic value to the organization through of e-Commerce and five determinant factors of e-Commerce adoption in SMEs.

The canonical results from both studies reveal a significant relationship between the perceived strategic value of e-Commerce variables and the factors that influence e-Commerce adoption in SMEs. This means that those top managers who perceived e-Commerce as adding strategic value to the firm have a positive attitude toward its adoption. In addition, the confirmatory factor analysis corroborated Subramanian and Nosek's (2001) results in the sense that all the variables considered in the perception of strategic value construct were found to be significant for both American and Chilean managers/owners of SMEs.

Perceived usefulness was found to be the most influential factor to determine e-Commerce adoption by top American managers/owners and the second most influential as perceived by top Chilean managers/owners. This result corroborates the TAM model of Davis (1989) which states that perceived usefulness is a strong determinant of system usage. However, the TAM was only partially supported for the ease of use construct: American managers ranked ease of use the second most influential factor in the adoption of e-Commerce while Chilean managers ranked it last. As a matter of fact, the data from Study 2 revealed that ease of use does not contribute to the linear combination of variables in the adoption of e-Commerce construct, since its canonical loading is small. In other words, when considered together with perception of strategic value variables, ease of use does not play a role in the canonical correlation for Chilean managers. However, the confirmatory factor analysis indicated that ease of use is an important factor that determines e-Commerce adoption given the high loadings found in the analysis. This suggests that Chilean managers do consider ease of use of e-Commerce as a determinant factor of its adoption, however, even though managers may consider that e-Commerce adds value to their firms that does not necessarily imply that they find e-Commerce easy to use.

Compatibility between e-Commerce and firm's culture, values, and preferred work practices turned out to be the most influential factor that determines e-Commerce adoption as perceived by Chilean managers. American managers ranked compatibility third after ease of use and perceived usefulness. Results from the factor analysis confirmed the work of Mirchandani and Motwani (2001), Chwelos et al. (2001), Chin and Gopal (1995), and Premkumar and Potter (1995) in which compatibility is considered an important factor that determines adoption of IT.

Regarding the findings on external pressure, our study validated previous research that have dealt with other IT adoption issues (e.g. Iacovou et al., 1995; Chwelos et al., 2001). In these studies, external pressure was found to be a strong determinant of the adoption of IT. In our studies, we noticed the same trend with slightly differences in the level of importance managers assigned to this factor. Chilean managers gave more importance to external pressure (ranked third) than American managers did (ranked fourth). This can be explained by the fact that Chilean managers seem to be more sensitive to social norms than those of American managers.

Organizational readiness, which includes the financial and technological resources to adopt e-Commerce, turned out to be more important for Chilean managers than for American managers when ranking the determinant factors that influence e-Commerce adoption. This could be explained by the fact that in a developing country, such as Chile, the lack of financial and technological resources available to managers/owners of SMEs may, to certain extent, dictate the likelihood of behavioral achievement. Therefore, Chilean managers/owners give more emphasis to this factor than American managers of SMEs do.

Overall, the discrepancies in the order of importance managers assign to different factors determining perceived strategic value and adoption of e-Commerce can also be explained by cultural differences between managers/owners of SMEs in both countries. According to the Hofstede's model (Hofstede, 1980a,b), five dimensions can be distinguished among different cultures: power-distance, uncertainty avoidance, masculinity–femininity, individualism–collectivism, and long- versus short-term patterns of thought. US and Chile differ considerably on these dimensions, especially in uncertainty avoidance and individualism–collectivism (see, Hofstede, 2001, pp. 151 and 215). Therefore, it seems logical to find differences in the weights managers/owners assign to each factor.

8.6.1 Future research

The uniqueness of this study, gathering together two different streams of research, generates many opportunities for future inquiries. First, in order to corroborate the results of this study and to create a broader, cumulative knowledge of the relationship between perceived strategic value and adoption of e-Commerce, it would be desirable to reproduce this research. As Adams et al. (1992) pointed out 'the tendency of IS researchers to become complacent or discouraged with progress in a specific area after conducting what would be considered a limited number of studies in other domains should be challenged. We should begin to focus on replication, refinement, and development of models and measures' (p. 245). Thus, by using the revised theoretical framework, this research should be replicated using a sample from other regions of the US and in other developing countries.

Second, a discriminatory analysis to identify the factors that differentiate between adopters from non-adopters of e-Commerce in small- and medium-sized companies could also be conducted in the future. The results from this suggested analysis could be compared with previous research that have tried to determine discriminant factors between adopters and non-adopters in other IT. Third, it would be also interesting to extend this study to determine the relationship between the total number of employees, budget allocated to IS, and number of employees in the IS department (if any) and the extent to which the firms have adopted e-Commerce. Findings regarding this proposed study could help to determine the state-of-the-art in which SMEs are regarding e-Commerce adoption according to these variables and determine what will be the tendency of e-Commerce adoption in the future. Finally, this study can be extended by incorporating other factors that might influence the perceptions of strategic value and adoption of e-Commerce. Specifically, future research can focus on directly measuring the cultural dimensions of Hofstede's model (Hofstede, 1980a,b) to investigate the extent to which managers' perceptions toward the strategic value and adoption of e-Commerce differ due to both organizational and national cultural differences.

References and Further Reading

Adams, D. A., R. R. Nelson and P. A. Todd (1992). 'Perceived Usefulness, Ease of Use, and Usage of Information Technology: A Replication.' *MIS Quarterly* 16: 227–247.

Ajzen, I. (1991). 'The Theory of Planned Behavior.' *Organizational Behavior and Human Decision Processes* 50: 179–211.

Amit, R. and C. Zott (2001). 'Value Creation in e-Business.' *Strategic Management Journal* 22: 493–520.

Bartelt, A. and W. Lamersdorf (2001). A Multi-criteria Taxonomy of Business Models in Electronic Commerce. *Proceedings of the IFIP/ACM International Conference on Distributed Systems Platforms, WS on Electronic Commerce*, Springer-Verlag 193–205.

Barua, A., C. H. Kriebel and T. Mukhopadhyay (1995). 'Information Technology and Business Value: An Analysis and Empirical Investigation.' *Information Systems Research* 6(1): 3–23.

Beatty, R. C., J. P. Shim and M. C. Jones (2001). 'Factors Influencing Corporate Web Site Adoption: A Time-Based Assessment.' *Information and Management* 38: 337–354.

Betz, F. (2002). 'Strategic Business Models.' *Engineering Management Journal* 14(1): 21–27.

Bienstock, C. C., M. L. Gillerson and T. C. Sanders (2002). 'The Complete Taxonomy of Web Business Models.' *Quarterly Journal of Electronic Commerce* 3(2): 173–182.

Brynjolfsson, E. (1993). 'The Productivity Paradox of Information Technology.' *Communications of the ACM* 35(12): 66–77.

Brynjolfsson, E. and L. Hitt (1996). 'Paradox Lost? Firm-Level Evidence on the Returns to Information Systems Spending.' *Management Science* **42**(4): 541–558.

Bush, E. A., L. Jarvenpaa, N. Tractinsky and W. H. Glick (1991). 'External Versus Internal Perspectives in Determining a Firm's Progressive Use of Information Technology.' J. I. DeGross, I. Benbasat, G. DeSanctis and C. M. Beath (eds). *Proceedings of the Twelve International Conference on Information Systems*, New York, NY, 239–250.

Byrd, T. A. and D. E. Turner (2001). 'An Exploratory Examination of the Relationship between Flexible IT Infrastructure and Competitive Advantage.' *Information and Management* **39**: 41–52.

Cabrera, G. S. (1994). PYME, un desafío a la modernización productiva. Corfo (ed.). Santiago de Chile, Corfo: 1–2.

Campbell, K. T. and D. L. Taylor (1996). 'Canonical Correlation Analysis as a General Linear Model: A Heuristic Lesson for Teachers and Students.' *The Journal of Experimental Education* **64**(2): 157–171.

Chang, M. K. (1998). 'Predicting Unethical Behavior: A Comparison of the Theory of Reasoned Action and the Theory of Planned Behavior.' *Journal of Business Ethics* **17**: 1825–1834.

Chang, M. K. and W. Cheung (2001). 'Determinants of the Intention to use Internet/WWW at Work: A Confirmatory Study.' *Information and Management* **39**: 1–14.

Chaudhury, A. and J. P. Kuilboer (2002). *E-Business and E-Commerce Infrastructure*. Boston, MA, McGraw-Hill.

Chin, W. W. and A. Gopal (1995). 'Adoption Intention in GSS: Relative Importance of Beliefs.' *Data Base* **26**(2–3): 42–64.

Chwelos, P., I. Benbasat and A. Dexter (2001). 'Research Report: Empirical Test of an EDI Adoption Model.' *Information Systems Research* **12**(3): 304–321.

Colvin, G. (2001). 'It's the Business Model, Stupid!' *Fortune* **123**: 54.

Cyber Atlas (November 2001). Small businesses use net for customer service, communications. Retrieved March 2003, from http://cyberatlas.internet.com/markets/smallbiz/article/0,10098_921821,00.html

Davis, F. D. (1989). 'Perceived Usefulness, Perceived Ease of Use, and User Acceptance of Information Technology.' *MIS Quarterly* **13**(3): 319–340.

Davis, F. D., R. P. Bagozzi and P. R. Warshaw (1992). 'Extrinsic and Intrinsic Motivation to Use Computers in the Workplace.' *Journal of Applied Social Psychology* **22**: 1111–1132.

Dewan, S. and C. Min (1997). 'The Substitution of Information Technology for Other Factors of Production: A Firm Level Analysis.' *Management Science* **43**(12): 1660–1675.

Fishbein, M. and I. Ajzen (1975). *Belief, Attitude, Intention and Behavior: An Introduction to Theory and Research*. Reading, MA, Addison-Wesley.

GEEP (2001). *Guide of Enterprises, Executives, and Products of Bío-Bío Region*.

Grandón, E. and J. Pearson (2003). 'Strategic Value and Adoption of Electronic Commerce: An Empirical Study of Chilean Small and Medium Businesses.' *Journal of Global Information Technology Management* **6**(3): 22–43.

Grandón, E. and J. Pearson (2004). 'Electronic Commerce Adoption: An Empirical Study of Small and Medium US Businesses.' *Information and Management*, in press, http://www.sciencedirect.com/science/journal/03787206.

Green, P. E., M. H. Halbert and P. J. Robinson (1966). 'Canonical Analysis: An Exposition and Illustrative Application.' *Journal and Marketing Research* 3: 32–39.

Hair, J. F., R. E. Anderson, R. L. Tatham and W. C. Black (1998). *Multivariate Data Analysis*. NJ, Prentice Hall.

Harrison, D. A., P. P. Mykytyn and C. K. Riemenschneider (1997). 'Executive Decisions About Adoption of Information Technology in Small Business: Theory and Empirical Tests.' *Information Systems Research* 8(2): 171–195.

Hausenblas, H., A. Carron and D. Mack (1997). 'Application of the Theories of Reasoned Action and Planned Behavior to Exercise Behavior: A Meta-analysis.' *Journal of Sport and Exercise Psychology* 19: 36–51.

Hendrickson, A. R., P. D. Massey and T. P. Cronan (1993). 'On the Test–Retest Reliability of Perceived Usefulness and Perceived Ease of Use Scales.' *MIS Quarterly* 17(2): 227–230.

Hitt, L. M. and E. Brynjolfsson (1996). 'Productivity, Business Profitability, and Consumer Surplus: Three Different Measures of Information Technology Value.' *MIS Quarterly* 20(2): 121–142.

Hofstede, G. H. (1980a). *Culture's Consequences: International Differences in Work-Related Values*. CA, Sage Publications Inc.

Hofstede, G. H. (1980b). 'Motivation, Leadership and Organization: Do American Theories Apply Abroad?' *Organizational Dynamics* 2: 42–63.

Hofstede, G. H. (2001). *Culture's Consequences: Comparing Values, Behaviors, Institutions, and Organizations Across Nations*. CA, Sage Publications, Inc.

Huff, S. I., M. Wade, M. Parent, S. Schneberger and P. Newson (2000). *Cases in Electronic Commerce*. Boston, McGraw-Hill.

Iacovou, A. L., I. Benbasat and A. Dexter (1995). 'Electronic Data Interchange and Small Organizations: Adoption and Impact of Technology.' *MIS Quarterly* 19(4): 465–485.

Igbaria, M., N. Zinatelli, P. Cragg and A. Cavaye (1997). 'Personal Computing Acceptance Factors in Small Firms: A Structural Equation Model.' *MIS Quarterly* 21(3): 279–302.

Jarvenpaa, S. L. and B. Ives (1991). 'Executive Involvement and Participation in the Management of IT.' *MIS Quarterly* 15(2): 205–227.

Johnson, R. A. and D. W. Wichern (1998). *Applied Multivariate Statistical Analysis*. NJ, Prentice Hall.

Johnson, R. A., B. C. Hardgrave and E. R. Doke (1999). 'An Industry Analysis of Developer Beliefs About Object-Oriented Systems Development.' *Data Base* 30(1): 47–64.

Koh, A. E. and H. J. Watson (1998). 'Data Management in Executive in Executive Information Systems.' *Information and Management* 33: 301–312.

Kuan, K. and P. Chau (2001). 'A Perception-Based Model of EDI Adoption in Small Businesses Using Technology–Organization–Environment Framework.' *Information and Management* 38: 507–521.

Lederer, A. L., D. J. Maupin, M. P. Sena and Y. Zhuang (2000). 'The Technology Acceptance Model and the World Wide Web.' *Decision Support Systems* 29: 269–282.

Lee, C. S. (2001). 'Modeling the Business Value of Information Technology'. *Information and Management* 39: 191–210.

Lee, J. and J. Runge (2001). 'Adoption of Information Technology in Small Business: Testing Drivers of Adoption for Entrepreneurs.' *Journal of Computing Information Systems* 42(1): 44–57.

Li, M. and L. R. Ye (1999). 'Information Technology and Firm Performance: Linking with Environmental, Strategic and Managerial Contexts.' *Information and Management* 35: 43–51.

Ma, X. and D. J. Bateson (1999). 'A Multivariate Analysis of the Relationship between Attitude Toward Science and Attitude Toward Environment.' *The Journal of Environmental Education* 31: 27–32.

Mahadevan, B. (2000). 'Business Models for Internet-Based e-Commerce.' *California Management Review* 42(4): 55–69.

Mahmood, M. A. and G. J. Mann (1993). 'Measuring the Organizational Impact of Information Technology Investment: An Exploratory Study.' *Journal of Management Information Systems* 10(1): 97–122.

Mirchandani, A. A. and J. Motwani (2001). 'Understanding Small Business Electronic Commerce Adoption: An Empirical Analysis.' *Journal of Computer Information Systems*, Spring 70–73.

Moore, G. C. and I. Benbasat (1991). 'Development of an Instrument to Measure the Perceptions of Adopting an Information Technology Innovation.' *Information Systems Research* 2(3): 192–222.

Morales, O. J. (1990). Promoción y desarrollo de la PYME en Chile: propuestas específicas. Cefope (ed.), *Propuesta para el desarrollo de la pequeña y mediana industria en Chile*. Santiago de Chile, Cefope: 7–14.

Napier, H. A., P. J. Judd, O. N. Rivers and S. W. Wagner (2001). *Creating a Winning E-business*. Boston, MA, Course Technology.

Nunnally, J. C. (1978). *Psychometric Theory*. New York, McGraw-Hill.

OPEN Small Business Network 2002 Monitor. URL: http://www.americanexpress.com/homepage/smallbusiness.shtml?mtpers_home=smbustab

Osterwalder, A. and Y. Pigneur (2002). 'An e-Business Model Ontology for Modeling e-Business.' *Proceedings of the 15th Bled Electronic Commerce Conference*. e-Reality: Constructing the e-Economy. Bled, Slovenia, June 17–19.

Parker, M. M., R. J. Benson and H. E. Trainor (1988). *Information Economics: Linking Business Performance to Information Technology*. Englewood Cliffs, NJ, Prentice Hall.

Premkumar, G. and M. Potter (1995). 'Adoption of Computer Aided Software Engineering (CASE) Technology: An Innovation Adoption Perspective.' *Data Base* 26(2–3): 105–123.

Prescott, M. B. and S. A. Conger (1995). 'Information Technology Innovations: A Classification by it Locus of Impact and Research Approach.' *Data Base* 26(2–3): 20–41.

Reich, B. H. and I. Benbasat (1990). 'An Empirical Investigation of Factors Influencing the Success of Customer-Oriented Strategic Systems.' *Information Systems Research* 1(3): 325–347.

Riemenschneider, C. K. and V. R. McKinney (2001–2002). 'Assessing Belief Differences in Small Business Adopters and Non-Adopters of Web-Based e-Commerce.' *Journal of Computer Information Systems* 42(2): 101–107.

Riemenschneider, C. K., D. A. Harrison and P. P. Mykytyn (2003). 'Understanding IT Adoption Decisions in Small Business: Integrating Current Theories.' *Information and Management* 40: 269–285.

Riggins, F. J. (1999). 'A Framework for Identifying Web-Based Electronic Commerce Opportunities.' *Journal of Organizational Computing and Electronic Commerce* **9**(4): 297–310.

Ryan, S. D. and V. R. Prybutock (2001). 'Factors Affecting the Adoption of Knowledge Management Technologies: A Discriminative Approach.' *Journal of Computer Information Systems* **41**(4): 31–38.

Saloner, G. and A. M. Spence (2002). *Creating and Capturing Value, Perspectives and Cases on Electronic Commerce*. NY, Wiley.

Sanders, G. L. and J. F. Courtney (1985). 'A Field Study of Organizational Factors Influencing DSS Success.' *MIS Quarterly* **9**(1): 77–93.

Schneider, G. and J. T. Perry (2000). *Electronic Commerce*. Cambridge, MA, Course Technology, Thomson Learning, Inc.

Segars, A. H. and V. Grover (1998). 'Strategic Information Systems Planning Success: An Investigation of the Construct and its Measurement.' *MIS Quarterly* **22**(2): 139–163.

Small Business Administration (1999–2000). The State of Small Businesses. A Report of the President 1999–2000. Together with the Office of Advocacy's Annual Report on Small Business and Competition. URL: http://www.sba.gov/advo/stats/stateofsb99_00.pdf

Stevens, J. P. (2002). *Applied Multivariate Statistics for the Social Sciences*. London, Lawrence Erlbaum Associates, Publishers.

Straub, D., M. Keil and W. Brenner (1997). 'Testing the Technology Acceptance Model Across Cultures: A Three Country Study.' *Information and Management* **33**: 1–11.

Subramanian, G. H. (1998). 'A Replication of Perceived Usefulness and Perceived Ease of Use Measurement.' *Decision Science* **25**(5–6): 863–874.

Subramanian, G. H. and J. T. Nosek (2001). 'An Empirical Study of the Measurement and Instrument Validation of Perceived Strategy Value of Information Systems.' *Journal of Computer Information Systems* **41**(3): 64–69.

Szajna, B. (1994). 'Software Evaluation and Choice: Predictive Validation of the Technology Acceptance Instrument.' *MIS Quarterly* **18**(3): 319–324.

Tallon, P. P., K. L. Kraemer and V. Gurbaxani (1998). Fact or Fiction: The Reality Behind Executive Perceptions of IT Business Value. Irvine, Working paper, University of California.

Tallon, P. P., K. L. Kraemer and V. Gurbaxani (2000). 'Executives' Perceptions of the Business Value of Information Technology: A Process-Oriented Approach.' *Journal of Management Information Systems* **16**(4): 145–173.

Tam, K. Y. (1998). 'The Impact of Information Technology Investments on Firm Performance and Evaluation: Evidence from Newly Industrialized Economies.' *Information Systems Research*, **9**(1): 85–98.

Taylor, S. and P. Todd (1995). 'Understanding Information Technology Usage: A Test of Competing Models.' *Information Systems Research* **6**(2): 144–176.

Thompson, B. (1991). 'A Primer on the Logic and Use of Canonical Correlation Analysis.' *Measurement and Evaluation in Counseling and Development* **24**(2): 80–96.

Thompson, R. and G. Rose (1994). Information Technology Adoption and Use. *Proceedings of Administrative Sciences Association of Canada (ASAC) Annual Conference*, Halifax, Nova Scotia, Canada, pp. 16–26.

Timmers, P. (1998). 'Business Models for Electronic Markets.' *Journal on Electronic Markets* **8**(2): 3–8.

Venkatesh, V. and F. D. Davis (1996). 'A Model of the Antecedents of Perceived Ease of Use: Development and Test.' *Decision Sciences* **27**(3): 451–481.

Weill, P. (1992). 'The Relationship between Investment in Information Technology and Firm Performance: A Study of the Valve Manufacturing Sector.' *Information System Research* **3**(4): 307–333.

Part Three

e-Business Performance Measurement and Value Creation

9 Value creation from corporate Web sites: how different features contribute to success in e-Business

Nils Madeja and Detlef Schoder

9.1 Introduction

The Worldwide Web exhibits specific media characteristics or so-called 'Web features' that distinguish it from other types of media (e.g. TV, radio or newspaper). These media characteristics encompass several dimensions ranging from technical features, content-related criteria, features related to user interaction, to the management of information on the Web or even social or community-related aspects. It is often reasoned that in order to be successful, companies should make implementations on their Web sites or in related business processes, such as to properly address the Web features, thus 'implement them'. However, as corporate Web sites can be viewed as a technical or communications interfaces, they are mostly evaluated under technical, or other aspects of very limited conceptual breadth, with which 'success' is measured, for example design, usability, features, acceptance of Web pages, trust aspects, customer satisfaction, etc. (Bennett, 2002; Post et al., 2002; Shim et al., 2002). Related research on Web features and Web sites has often focused on certain markets, industries or business models (e.g. Barnes and Vidgen, 2001; Christ et al., 2002). Much of this research has been undertaken in the context of Electronic Commerce Customer Relationship Management (ECCRM) (Romano and Fjermestad, 2002). There has been only little work on how, and if at all, the implementation of measures on companies' Web sites in order to make use of the above Web features contributes to corporate success in general and from a comprehensive perspective (Dewan et al., 2002). Therefore, the business benefit on the corporate level or the business value from implementing Web features on companies' Web sites remains difficult to assess, especially for corporate decision makers.

In this chapter, we present results from a broad empirical investigation studying the effectiveness of implementing the Web features for corporate performance. The empirical investigation has been based on a large-scale survey comprising 469 cases in the German-speaking market, which is one of the key international e-Business markets. Thereby, we address the research gap diagnosed above and provide practical advice for corporate decision makers. The remainder of this article is structured as follows. In the next section, we give a practical overview of the Web features and a review of the background of related literature. The research model is developed in the third section. In the fourth section, the survey is introduced, and the results of the statistical analysis are presented. In the fifth section, the findings are summarized and discussed. Finally, we derive implications from our work for further research and for practice in the sixth section.

9.2 Understanding the media characteristics of the Worldwide Web

9.2.1 Web features: definitions and practical implementations

For the purposes of this chapter, we employ the Web features as they have been listed in Schoder (2000, pp. 114–116). They have been extracted from earlier conceptual work on the use of the WWW and e-Commerce, such as Bloch et al. (1996) and Breitenbach and Van Doren (1998). We exclude two factors listed in Schoder (2000): interoperability (direct and transparent integration of customers' information technology (IT) infrastructure with one's own) and ubiquity or 'pervasiveness' (geographical omnipresence of the Internet as an access medium), since they constitute features, which companies cannot control sufficiently by themselves or in the general case. The remaining eight Web features are considered sufficient for characterizing Web sites because they cover a broad range of theoretical dimensions and the main factors governing user interaction with Web sites: technical criteria, single-user applications, multi-user applications, content and functionalities as well as multimedia aspects. They are discussed in the following.

Interactivity.   It enables customers to communicate with the company or organization which is operating a Web site by offering them a feedback channel. Such a feedback channel can be implemented via e-mail in the simplest case, more sophisticated solutions may employ Internet or even regular telephony in connection with the Web site. Advanced solutions might even incorporate video conferencing via the Internet. Depending upon the time criticality and complexity of the problem to be solved as well as the service level, which is to be fulfilled, the requirements for the technical solution may differ. In simple cases, for example for soliciting customers' opinion or inquiries, the e-mail solution is probably sufficient. In a more complex application, an agent in a Web call centre might assist a customer in filling out an online form, for example for reservations, travel bookings or financial transactions. Both the customer and the agent can view the same material on their respective computer screen and the agent can literally 'show' the customer his way through the process.

A key issue concerning this Web feature is that simply installing a technical feedback channel alone is not enough. Yet it must be sufficiently staffed with qualified and service and support personnel for the customer to have a productive and pleasant interactive experience. A seldom monitored e-mail alias or poorly administered online forms, where the information entered is routed, disappears into the digital Nirvana, provides customers with a poor interactive experience, which can easily affect their overall satisfaction with the respective company.

Immediacy.   The opportunity to transmit and receive content as well as to update and react to new content without any significant delay. For customers on the Web, especially the aspect of *receiving* new content quickly is important. To match customers' expectations with respect to the immediacy of the Web site content, companies should update their Web site accordingly. Depending on the type of the company or organization, the purpose of the Web site and on the information to be displayed, the interpretation of what 'new' means may differ greatly. For example, in an online trading environment, customers will typically expect that they can access quotes and place orders in real time. Or from a typical news Web site, most visitors would expect that the news headlines are updated hourly. For a travel Web site, selling last-minute airline tickets and tour packages, it is probably enough to update the content on a daily basis. In other industries (e.g. utilities or manufacturing), where the currency of the information about products and services offered is not so critical, it may be enough to update corporate Web sites weekly, monthly or in even larger time intervals. It must be noted, however, that even in these industries, many companies have incorporated elements in their Web site which they update several times a week (such as company news and press releases) or more often (such as a real-time stock quote of the respective company). Although these elements are not directly related to the products and services, they preserve an up-to-date appearance of the Web site.

Connectivity.   The formation of collective interactive spaces for communication and collaboration, for example in terms of so-called community functionalities or discussion forums. These interactive spaces can fulfill several functions and offer benefits for customers as well as the company who operates them.

For the customers, they can offer information about products and services, which may be invaluable for their purchase decisions. Consider, for example, the case of a travel agency specializing in a certain country. That travel agency offers a community functionality on its Web sites, where visitors, regardless of whether they are customers or not, can rate and provide detailed feedback about the hotels in that particular country. Especially in the case tour packages, customers quite often feel that their expectations based on catalogue descriptions of the hotels and services are not fulfilled once they have reached their destination and once they actually experience the hotels and services booked. Yet once they are on site, these tourists have little practical chance to improve their situation, for example by changing hotels or moving to another destination, as switching costs are often prohibitively high. Therefore, considering the feedback from other customers prior to the booking decision may save prospective customers from a lot of disappointment. Or consider the often-cited case of an online bookstore where visitors can write reviews for all the books. Even after the actual purchase, the collective interactive spaces may provide valuable help for customers, for example product support information from customer experience. Consider the case of a large vendor for e-Commerce software who operates a mailing list for all developers using their software packages, including its internal developers who build them. Customers can share experiences with other customers, and they can also obtain support from the internal developers.

For the companies who operate them, virtual communities constitute a low-cost channel for providing product support and obtaining customer feedback (cf. the 'interactivity' feature). For example, the software vendor discussed above can provide after-sales support and incorporate customer feedback at the same time via his mailing list. Virtual communities exhibit network externalities, which may be coupled to a certain company or its products and services. Online shoppers may prefer a certain virtual bookstore because of the book reviews offered. Therefore, the virtual community of reviewers serves other customers at next-to-zero extra-cost for the bookstore, which is a favourable case. Under other circumstances, the dynamics of a virtual community may have detrimental effects on a company's standing, that is if that company or its products are badmouthed in an online forum or simply if cases of customers reporting negative experiences related to that company or its products become frequent.

To conclude, virtual communities can increase the value of companies' products and services at practically no extra-cost. Yet (as can be seen from the example of the online travel agency) they can also contribute to reducing the possible information asymmetry between companies and their customers, thus strengthening the position of the customer. Companies can do only very little to avert damage once an *external* virtual community has turned against them, for example a forum where negative feedback concerning its products and services accumulate or an investors' forum where the voice of disgruntled stockholders grows louder. Yet companies can do a lot to prevent similar situations if they operate and manage their own *internal* virtual community, where they can respond to and edit certain destructive opinions.

Media richness and variety.   The opportunity to link different types of information, for example text, graphics, audio, pictures and video, and display them together as a multimedia object. Thanks to the availability of different types of media, companies can present content in different depth and style, depending upon the target group and the featured information. Thereby, they can address many different target groups and provide different service levels on their Web sites, from which additional opportunities for generating revenues may appear, for example a news Web site can offer news as text-only messages, test with pictures, audio reports or video documentations. While it might offer the text-based messages for free, it might charge for the audio and video content.

Availability.   The temporal omnipresence of the Internet as an access medium. Being accessible practically all the time, today's Internet has reached a very high degree of availability, at least in the industrialized nations. Companies' Web sites as well as the content and functionalities they offer, however, may not be accessible all the time or under all circumstances. For example, the Web sites or parts of it might be down because of technical problems, for maintenance or redesign. Many system vendors try to push their products by stressing the necessity for having (usually expensive) high-availability solutions. Yet the business need for having a high-availability Web site may vary very greatly with the type of company and the business model. While the need may seem to be clear for an online trading or banking environment, what damage does it do to an small and medium-sized enterprises (SME) with predominantly local and regional customers if it switches off (parts of) its Web site for maintenance?

The size of companies' Web sites may be another reason why some of them are not accessible all the time or from certain terminals. Even today, many users are connected to the Internet via slow modem connections or congested company networks. If Web sites exceed a certain size, this group of users cannot access parts of it.

Information richness.   The opportunity to compile different types of content and content of different quality. Similar to the 'media richness' feature, the information richness enables companies to present their content in different service levels and for different target groups, from which additional business opportunities may be generated. Yet, as there is practically no limit with respect to the amount of information, which can be presented on a corporate Web site, companies can try to compile all of the information which they believe to be of interest for their customers on their Web site. So far, this is not possible for any other communications medium. For example, portal sites follow this approach, trying to become their visitors' single point of access for the Worldwide Web and dominate their visitors' whole online experience. Less ambitious companies in manufacturing or high technology might post all of their product catalogues, technical specifications, data sheets and support information on their Web sites.

Ease of use. Users' ability to browse multimedia content and distributed information transparently, that is without being involved in technical or organizational aspects of accessing distributed information, using dedicated communication and navigation services. Generally, the ease of use is a factor of paramount importance in the acceptance of any information system (IS) (cf. the literature review below). In case of Web sites, the ease of use practically refers to two issues: how information or content is organized and how it is presented.

The first issue is mostly independent from the type of content or from technical issues. It refers to the clarity and consistency of a Web site, for example the quality of the menu structure or the availability and quality of search and navigation functions. The second issue may be very closely related to design or technical details. For example, can the content be displayed on every standard Web browser? Are additional plug-ins or updates necessary to view the content? How legible is the content? Can the information be browsed quickly and comfortably?

Individualization and customization. The opportunity to compose individual information or content according to individual preferences or user profiles. Companies can employ their Web sites as an individual interface for personally addressing every customer and delivering individual service. In simple cases, only the displayed information is personalized, for example on 'my-xyz.com'-type Web sites. In more complex applications, corporate Web sites may be used as frontends for integrated e-Business concepts, such as ECCRM or one-to-one marketing. Then, also the product and service offerings as well as the pricing may be individualized.

9.2.2 Literature review

The implementation and user acceptance of the Web features on corporate Web sites can be considered as a specific case of IS/IT adoption. Analogously, its impact on corporate success in e-Business is linked to the issue of IS/IT success and business value. Finally, the Web features are related to the issue of Web evaluation and effectiveness. As there is a rich body of literature available on each of these subjects, we will, in the following overview, discuss a selection of previous works from relevant traits of research in the IS/IT discipline and e-Business.

IS/IT adoption and the role of ease of use

In their recent meta-analysis, Mahmood et al. (2001) aggregate the factors affecting the adoption or use of IT investigated in previous studies to a single model. They propose that the use of IT is determined by the following four dimensions of factors: the perceived benefits which an end user expects from using a particular IS, the individual characteristics of an end user, the IT maturity of the organization in which a particular IS is employed and the characteristics of that organization (such as size and the degree of support for IS usage). They find that the perceived benefits which an end user expects is the key determinant for the usage of a particular IS. This dimension of factor has been introduced by Davis (cf. Davis, 1989, or Davis et al., 1989) as a part of the Technology Acceptance Model (TAM), proposing that the perceived ease of use of an IS influences the perceived usefulness and, in turn, that both of these factors determine an end user's usage decision. Davis' study has since been the subject of a multitude of replication studies for many different IS.

The link between adoption of IS/IT and corporate success

DeLone and McLean (1992) developed a taxonomy of different stages of IS success, covering system quality, information quality, use, user satisfaction, individual impact and organizational impact. They derive this broad spectrum ranging from system- to top-level constructs from a 'series of influence events' occurring 'at the receiving end of an IS', thus establishing the conceptual link between these stages of IS success. For every stage, they review a number of previous studies employing IS success measures from the respective stage. They conclude that 'not enough MIS field study research attempts to measure the influence of the MIS effort on organizational performance.' Recently, DeLone and McLean (2003) have reviewed past works based on their model and made some extensions to it, for example service quality or the application to e-Commerce. They introduce net benefits as the new top-level construct to substitute individual and organizational impacts, again strengthening the importance of this stage of measures.

The business value of IT

The issue of the business value of IT addresses the last stage of IS success in the DeLone and McLean model. Many studies have been undertaken to find empirical evidence for the business value of IT, yet their results have been inconsistent. The results of several works even suggest that IT might have a negative impact on business performance, leading to the so-called productivity paradox (Brynjolfsson, 1993). In an attempt to resolve this paradox, Brynjolfsson and Hitt (1996) separate the organizational impact of IT into three dimensions: productivity, consumer value and business productivity. While they find evidence that IT spending increases productivity and consumer value, their results do not support the hypothesis that IT spending drives business productivity. For a more recent and comprehensive discussion of related literature, see the discussion in Chircu and Kauffmann (2000).

The Web features and the quality of Web sites

Armstrong and Hagel (1996) make a very strong statement in favour of online communities and, thus, the above 'connectivity' feature, stressing the importance of online communities for customer loyalty and showing four sources of value generation within communities. Trepper (2000) points out the importance of content currency for Web site success, thus supporting the assumption that 'immediacy' is a success factor. Similarly, Nielsen and Norman (2000) highlight the importance of ease of use. Some of the Web features and their applicability for Internet marketing are also explained in Strauß and Schoder (2002, p. 103) and, in more detail, in Timmers (1999).

Liu and Arnett (2000) derive six criteria for the design quality of Web sites (information quality, learning capability, playfulness, system quality, system use and service quality), which they implement as broad multi-item measures. They find support for four success factors of Web sites (quality of information and service, system use, playfulness and system design quality). However, essentially, their definition of Web site success is also narrow and focused on customer satisfaction and loyalty. Koufaris et al. (2001) study the effects that the features of a B2C-Commerce site have on shopping enjoyment, and thereby on customer retention and repatronage decisions.

Finally, Böing presents an investigation with a similar research methodology and approach as ours (Böing, 2001, pp. 192–198). He investigates the impact of design elements of B2C-Web pages on overall corporate success (which he operationalizes as a single-score value). Böing hypothesizes two design elements, the Web feature 'immediacy' (measured directly with one indicator variable recording the update frequency) and a complex construct he terms 'integrated elements', comprising a subdimension called 'additional information', a subdimension for transaction-related functionalities, and a third one composed of the two Web features 'connectivity' and 'individualization and customization'. Although numerical support for the influence of 'integrated elements' on corporate success is obtained, no support can be found for the hypothesis that the Web feature 'immediacy' is also a success factor.

9.3 Research model

9.3.1 Research aim and model perspective

The aim of our empirical study is to investigate the role of the Web features as explanatory factors for corporate success in e-Business. Therefore, the dependent construct in our analysis corresponds to the last stage of IS success in the DeLone and McLean model. We assume an integrated perspective and choose the corporate level as the level of analysis for our model and, hence, the whole company as the object under study. Moreover, although there may certainly be factors, which have more impact on corporate success in e-Business than the features that characterize a company's Web sites (or which might even be the *cause* for the implementation of these features), we limit the explanatory factors in our model to the Web features.

Viewing the implementation of Web features on companies' Web sites as investments in e-Commerce technology, the payoffs from these investments can be assessed qualitatively once the effectiveness of a single Web feature or of the Web features as a whole for corporate success has been determined. Similarly, conclusions can then be made with respect to the economic value of corporate Web sites.

9.3.2 Conceptualizing corporate success in e-Business

We choose to focus our view of the concept of corporate success in e-Business on the shareholders' perspective. The concept is viewed and implemented as a complex construct comprising several theoretical subdimensions so as to accommodate the major theories on competitive advantage, value creation and firm performance (Amit and Zott, 2001):

1 *Hard factors*: This reflects economic performance indicated by economic quantities or coefficients, for example revenue and profit growth.

2 *Soft factors*: This accounts for a company's achievement(s) in relation to, or by perception of, its customers, for example increased loyalty, improvement of the corporate image or increased customer satisfaction.

3 *Cost reduction*: This indicates a company's improvement(s) in process efficiency as well as procurement conditions, for example reduced purchasing or marketing costs, therefore covering firm performance from a transaction-cost economical perspective.

4 *Innovation*: This measures the extent by which a company has strengthened its competitive position from the perspective of Schumpeterian theory, that is by being innovative, for example by offering new services and by developing new markets.

5 *Increased corporate value*: A company's valuation not only depends on its economic or overall performance, but also (mostly) on the way it is perceived by third parties, such as investors. Therefore, this final subdimension is the broadest and most susceptible to external influential factors (micro- and macroeconomic, psychological, etc.).

9.3.3 Derivation of hypotheses

Considering the literature review, we now generate eight hypotheses from the Web features as listed above by assuming in each case that utilizing the respective feature by making a corresponding implementation either directly on or in the context of corporate Web sites (e.g. site management or operation, related business processes, etc.) positively impacts overall corporate success in e-Business. Based on the DeLone and McLean model, we argue in every case that through the use of a particular feature, corporate Web sites become more efficient interfaces in the sense of the media characteristics of the WWW, which leads to more user interaction, more business transactions and, therefore, to increased success in e-Business for the respective company.

9.4 Method

The research model comprises the eight hypotheses as presented above, each hypothesis is a single factor influencing the dependent construct of corporate success in e-Business. It is implemented as a path model and tested with numerical data obtained from a large-scale survey. The numerical results are summarized and evaluated to establish if they give support for the single hypothesis.

9.4.1 The survey

The numerical data used in the statistical analysis of this model has been collected in a large survey that was conducted from May to June 2000 and which has been published as the 'e-reality 2000 study' in September 2000 (Strauß and Schoder, 2000). This survey was targeted at decision makers of companies in the German-speaking area (Germany, Austria and Switzerland). To gather data, market research professionals conducted personal interviews with upper- to top-level executives from 1308 companies. The companies for conducting the interviews were explicitly selected according to a superset of company data, such as to render the survey representative with respect to general company size and industry in the German-speaking market. In case that an interview could not be conducted as planned, a replacement was determined from the same superset in order to maintain the representation of the sample.

Aggregation of survey data

Prior to the statistical analysis, the gathered raw data is reduced and condensed to an essential subset as follows. At first, we concentrate on companies who had a Web page online at the time of the survey, reducing the original data set of 1308 cases to 730 cases (or 55.8%). (Another 171 companies, or 13.0%, were still planning to launch their site within the next 12 months.) In a second step, we focus on companies who specified that they had yet gained sufficient online experience, such as to provide information on the success of their company's e-Business activities, leaving a total of 469 valid cases for the numerical analysis.

Descriptive analysis

As in the original survey, the remaining cases constitute a heterogeneous selection of companies from all industry backgrounds, company sizes and business models; although the original claim that it is a representative selection of the German-speaking market that must be relaxed. Grouped according to the US Standard Industrial Classification (SIC), the 469 companies in our numerical base are structured as follows: 23.1% (108, as an absolute figure) of the remaining companies operate in the manufacturing sector; 5.8% (27) in transportation, communication and utilities; and 9.8% (46) in construction. A large percentage of 25.3% (119) are active in the trade sector, and 12.0% (56) are in finance, insurance or real estate. Further, 18.0% (89) belong to the service industry. Finally, 1.1% (5) of businesses are in the public administration segment. (Possibly remaining cases or fractions in this subsection cannot be classified due to missing values in the respective structural variable.)

There are 101 large companies (21.5%) with 50 or more employees, 203 medium-sized companies (43.3%) with between 20 and 49 employees, and 142 small companies (30.3%) with fewer than 20 employees. To conclude the grouping of the companies, 225 (48.0%) had up to 2 years of experience on the Web at the time of the survey, while 241 (51.4%) had been on the Web for 2 years or more.

The vast majority (95.8%, corresponding to 450 cases) of companies are traditional 'brick-and-mortar' enterprises. Only 2.3% (11 cases) are spin-offs, and only 0.6% (2 cases) are e-Commerce startups. Also, 27.3% (128 cases) of the represented companies generate 50% or more of their revenue from selling services. A respectable fraction of 15.8% (74 cases) of the businesses generate 10% or more of their revenue online and can thus be regarded as 'true e-Businesses' (Amit and Zott, 2001). Moreover, 53.1% (249 cases) offer consumers the opportunity to place orders online.

Finally, 224 companies (or 47.6%) specify consumers as their main customer segment, 215 companies (or 45.8%) stated that they mainly serve businesses. Another 18 (or 3.7%) mainly serve administrations, thus consider themselves as B2A-companies. Therefore, the data set obtained from the survey can be considered appropriate for testing hypotheses about the *general* effectiveness of mastering the media characteristics of the WWW, and nearly ideal for performing a separate analysis of B2B- and B2C-enterprises.

Statistical analysis and hypothesis testing

For testing the hypotheses in our research model, we employ the path analysis method. We perform the statistical analysis in two steps. In the first step, we analyse the case of all 469 general companies, without differentiating between any particular industry or company size. In the second step, we concentrate on the 215 companies primarily operating in

Table 9.1: Numerical results for the hypothesized effectiveness of the web features

Web features	General case	Separated according to main customer segments	
		B2B	B2C
Interactivity	+	++	○
Immediacy	++	++	○
Connectivity	○	○	○
Media richness and variety	+	○	++
Availability	○	○	++
Information richness	++	○	+
Ease of use	+	○	++
Individualization and customization	○	○	○

'++' indicates strong support, '+' indicates support and '○' indicates no support.

the B2B-segment (B2B-companies) and, separately, on the 224 companies primarily operating in the B2C-segment (B2C-companies).

9.4.2 Summary of the results

The numerical results for our research model are displayed in Table 9.1.

In the general case, five Web features prove to be success factors. Strong statistical support is found for the assumption that immediacy and information richness of companies' Web sites positively impact corporate success. We obtain support for the hypothesized influence of interactivity, ease of use and media richness and variety on corporate success. For B2B-companies, only the hypothesized effectiveness of the two Web features interactivity and immediacy can be backed from our numerical analysis. However, they receive strong numerical support.

In the case of B2C-companies, our model leads to the identification of four success factors among the Web features. There is strong statistical support for the assumed positive impact of media richness and variety, availability and ease of use on corporate success. Further, support is found for the hypothesized impact of information richness on corporate success.

9.5 Discussion

9.5.1 Explanation of the findings

Comparing the statistical analysis for the case of general companies with the two separate analyses for each customer segment, it is apparent that the Web features which significantly load on corporate success in the former can be interpreted as the combination of the Web features found to have significant impact on corporate success in the latter two analyses. The Web features that are drivers for corporate success are disjoint in the specific case of each B2B- or B2C-companies only. Therefore, in the general model they receive weaker numerical support. Information richness seems to be just the opposite of this rule – it receives the strongest numerical support in the general model.

In summary, a general corporate Web site is found to be a success driver mostly if it is rich in information (content) and updated frequently. These two factors are the key factors for attracting and retaining surfers, maintaining a continuous level of visits to the site, thus making it an effective interface for communication and business. In addition, a general corporate Web site contributes to corporate success in e-Business if it also offers interactive features, content from a variety of media and if it is easy to use.

In the case of companies with business customers, interactivity of the Web site and frequent updates are the only two, but very strong success factors among the Web features. Web users who surf for professional reasons typically view a Web site as an interface for engaging in business activities. They expect to find information about products and services which is up to date and they want to interact with the company 'behind' the site, as they need service and consulting. In practice, these B2B-customers are referred to as 'buyers, not browsers.' While other features may be nice to have as 'add-ons' they are not critical and of less importance for business users when they make purchase decisions.

On the contrary, consumers typically expect from a corporate Web site that it integrates content from different types of media. For consumers, the benefit from accessing a Web site consists in that it readily offers a variety of pre-selected and aggregated content and functionalities all in one interface such that they do not have to research and filter the content themselves. Plus, a Web site must be easy and convenient to use. These are the reasons explaining the success of some portal sites, such as yahoo.com. Additionally, as the Internet connection is a real bottleneck for most consumers since they do *not* have high-speed Internet access (which was especially true in the German-speaking market at the time of the survey) it is essential that Web sites are designed for short download times and kept available (even in situations where the Web is slow due to a high traffic load, e.g. in the evening hours).

9.5.2 Interpretation of selected results

Evaluating those Web features which do not prove to be significant in one or all of the three numerical analyses, there are generally two possible interpretations. Individually, the respective Web feature may have a positive impact on corporate success, but as most of the companies in the segment-specific or in the general context have already successfully implemented this Web feature, no discriminatory power can be attributed to this feature anymore. Or the respective Web feature might be a 'must have'. For example, a pre-requisite, which constitutes no particular benefit if present, but whose absence can be a strong inhibitor for Web-based transactions, such as trust (Böing, 2001, p. 192).

9.6 Future trends and conclusion

9.6.1 Research opportunities

Weighing the contributions of our study against its limitations and shortcomings, it is clear that our contribution must be viewed as a first-level analysis – as a 'snapshot'. It leaves a number of issues open for future empirical research. Some suggestions are: the survey should be repeated in a similar manner in order to assess how the identified interrelations change with time – especially as e-Business slowly matures – and vary in different markets. Moreover, the Web features investigated in this paper represent the media characteristics of corporate Web sites merely viewed as a customer interface. Therefore, in future research, the effectiveness of Web features should be researched in combination with strategies for online selling, Internet marketing or integrated e-Business concepts, such as ECCRM, one-to-one marketing or mass customization.

9.6.2 Implications for managerial practice

The results of our research provide practical help for IT managers and executives on how to direct and prioritize their investment decisions with respect to the features and functionalities of their corporate WWW-presence, although, naturally, certain minimum levels must be fulfilled for most features simply in order to ensure site operation and minimum user acceptance. Based on the main customer segment that a company targets with its Web site, decision makers should channel their investments as follows.

If the company operates a Web site directed at a general user audience, executives should, as a first step, ensure information and functionality richness of the site and that it be kept up to date. As a second step, they might consider implementing interactive features, that is a 'feedback channel' for their customers. Further, they should consider cooperating with other companies in order to be able to offer various content on their Web site. If the company operates a B2B-Web site, the message to its executive in charge is simple and clear: they should keep the Web site up to date and ensure that it is a transparent interface making it easy for their customers to communicate with their company.

If the Web site is directed at consumers, it should offer a variety of pre-selected and aggregated content and, to a lesser extent, functionalities all in one interface. Plus, navigating the site must be kept simple and intuitive. Also, as most consumers still do *not* have broadband Internet access, the site design should accommodate for slow Internet connections, and executives should ensure that the site remains accessible even during traffic peaks.

References and Further Reading

Amit, R. and C. Zott (2001). 'Value Creation in eBusiness.' *Strategic Management Journal* **22**: 493–520.

Armstrong, A. and J. Hagel (1996). 'The Real Value of On-line Communities.' *Harvard Business Review* **74**(3): 134–141.

Barnes, S. J. and R. T. Vidgen (2001). Assessing the Quality of Auction Web Sites. *Proceedings of the 34th Hawaii International Conference on System Sciences*, Hawaii.

Bennett, R. (2002). 'Use of Curiosity Arousing Web Sites for Business-to-Business Internet Marketing.' *Quarterly Journal of Electronic Commerce* **3**(2): 125–134.

Böing, C. (2001). *Erfolgsfaktoren im Business-to-Consumer-E-Commerce*. Gabler Verlag, Wiesbaden.

Bloch, M., Y. Pigneur and A. Segev (1996). On the Road of Electronic Commerce – A Business Value Framework, Gaining Competitive Advantage and Some Research Issues. *Proceedings of the Ninth International EDI-IOS Conference*, Bled, Slovenia.

Breitenbach, C. S. and D. C. Van Doren (1998). 'Value-Added Marketing in the Digital Domain: Enhancing the Utility of the Internet.' *Journal of Consumer Marketing* **15**(6): 558–575.

Brynjolfsson, E. (1993). 'The Productivity Paradox of Information Technology.' *Communications of the ACM* **36**(12): 67–77.

Brynjolfsson, E. and L. Hitt (1996). 'Productivity, Business Profitability, and Consumer Surplus: Three Different Measures of Information Technology Value.' *MIS Quarterly* **20**(2): 121–142.

Chircu, A. M. and R. J. Kauffmann (2000). 'Limits to Value in Electronic Commerce-Related IT Investments.' *Journal of Management Information Systems* **17**(2): 59–80.

Christ, M., R. Krishnan, D. Nagin and O. Günther (2002). Measuring Web Portal Utilization. *Proceedings of the 35th Hawaii International Conference on System Sciences*, Hawaii.

Davis, F. D. (1989). 'Perceived Usefulness, Perceived Ease of Use, and User Acceptance of Information Technology.' *MIS Quarterly* **13**(3): 318–340.

Davis, F. D., R. P. Bagozzi and P. R. Warshaw (1989). 'User Acceptance of Information Technology: A Comparison of Two Theoretical Models.' *Management Science* **35**(8): 982–1003.

DeLone, W. H. and E. R. McLean (1992). 'Information Systems Success: The Quest for the Dependent Variable.' *Information Systems Research* **3**(1): 60–95.

DeLone, W. H. and E. R. McLean (2003). 'The DeLone and McLean Model of Information Systems Success: A Ten-Year Update.' *Journal of Management Information Systems* **19**(4): 9–30.

Dewan, R., M. Freimer and J. Zhang (2002). Managing Web Sites Managing Web Sites for Profitability: Balancing Content and Advertising. *Proceedings of the 35th Hawaii International Conference on System Sciences*, Hawaii.

Koufaris, M., A. Kambil and P. A. LaBarbera (2001). 'Consumer Behavior in Web-Based Commerce: An Empirical Study.' *International Journal of Electronic Commerce* **6**(2): 115–138.

Liu, C. and K. P. Arnett (2000). 'Exploring the Factors Associated with Web Site Success in the Context of Electronic Commerce.' *Information and Management* **38**(1): 23–33.

Mahmood, M. A., L. Hall and D. L. Swanberg (2001). 'Factors Affecting Information Technology Usage: A Meta-Analysis of the Empirical Literature.' *Journal of Organizational Computing and Electronic Commerce* **11**(2): 107–130.

Nielsen, J. and D. A. Norman (2000). 'Usability on the Web Isn't a Luxury.' *Informationweek* **773**: 65–73.

v. Post, G., A. Kagan, T. J. Burkink and T. G. Schmitz (2002). 'Analyzing Consumers' Preferences on Commercial Web Site Attributes.' *Quarterly Journal of Electronic Commerce* **3**(2): 111–123.

Romano Jr., N. C. and J. Fjermestad (2002). 'Electronic Commerce Customer Relationship Management: An Assessment of Research.' *International Journal of Electronic Commerce* **6**(2): 61–113.

Schoder, D. (2000). *Die ökonomische Bedeutung von Intermediären im Electronic Commerce*, Wirtschaftswissenschaftliche Fakultät der Universität Freiburg i.Br.

Shim, J. P., Y. B. Shin and L. Nottingham (2002). 'Retailer Web Site Influence on Customer Shopping: An Exploratory Study on Key Factors of Customer Satisfaction.' *Journal of the Association for Information Systems* **3**: 53–76.

Strauß, R. and D. Schoder (2000). *e-Reality 2000 – Electronic Commerce von der Vision zur Realität: Status, Entwicklung, Problemstellungen, Erfolgsfaktoren Sowie Management-Implikationen des Electronic Commerce*, ISBN: 3-00-006870-8, Consulting Partner Group, Frankfurt a. M.

Strauß, R. and D. Schoder (2002). *eReality – Das EBusiness Bausteinkonzept. Strategien und Erfolgsfaktoren für das EBusiness-Management*, F.A.Z.-Institut für Management-, Markt- und Medieninformationen, Frankfurt a. M.

Timmers, P. (1999). *Electronic Commerce – Strategies and Models for Business-to-Business Trading*. Chichester, John Wiley & Sons.

Trepper, C. (2000). 'Content Currency is Key to a Successful Web Site.' *Informationweek* June 12: 108–112.

10 Evaluating the quality of e-Business implementation with E-Qual

Stuart Barnes and Richard Vidgen

10.1 Introduction

It is essential that organizations be able to make an assessment of the quality of their e-Business offering if they are to survive in a competitive environment. However good the e-Business model in abstract terms, if it is poorly implemented then it is unlikely that the organization will be able to prosper and thrive. Whereas e-Commerce is typically defined as being concerned with electronic transactions conducted via a Web site, e-Business constitutes a broader sense of value and impinges on many, if not all, aspects of an organization's activity. Over the last few years the E-Qual instrument (formerly known as 'WebQual') has been developed as a means of making a quantifiable assessment of subjective customer perceptions of e-Business implementation quality. E-Qual has been refined through many iterations and through application in different domains, both profit and not-for-profit. In this chapter we explicate the E-Qual approach to e-Business evaluation and show how E-Qual has been applied in one particular setting to evaluate a cross-national e-government community, the Forum on Strategic Management Knowledge Exchange (FSMKE).

10.2 The provenance of E-Qual

10.2.1 E-Qual 1.0

The first version of the E-Qual instrument was developed in the domain of UK business schools (Barnes and Vidgen, 2000). The development methodology for the instrument was to use quality function deployment (QFD), which is a 'structured and disciplined process that provides a means to identify and carry the voice of the customer through each stage of product and/or service development and implementation' (Slabey, 1990). The starting point for QFD is to articulate the 'voice of the customer' and to this end we ran a quality workshop in August 1998 with six postgraduate (Masters) students. Bossert (1991) recommends a three-stage process for a quality workshop: establish a single issue for discussion; collect quality requirements and functions using post-it notes; and, use affinity grouping to gather requirements into categories that make sense to the customer. The single issue for discussion was: 'What are the qualities of an excellent business school Web site?' Delegates worked individually writing out their ideas onto post-it notes and were encouraged to put down a brief phrase together with a longer sentence to explain the rationale for the proposed quality. The delegates were then allocated to two teams and asked to combine their qualities into affinity groups (a tree-structured list), initially working in silence, moving the post-it notes around to create headings as they felt appropriate. Finally, the two teams were brought back together to produce a single consolidated list of demanded qualities. By the end of the session 54 raw qualities had been collected that were structured hierarchically into affinity groupings.

From the raw qualities a pilot questionnaire with 35 questions was developed. This was completed by the six attendees of the workshop and used to refine the questions. An immediate outcome of the pilot was the recognition that the questionnaire was too long – to answer 35 questions for each of four business school Web sites would involve each respondent in 140 assessments, plus a further 35 assessments of the importance of each quality. Using the literature on information quality, particularly Bailey and Pearson (1983), DeLone and McLean (1992), Strong et al. (1997), and looking carefully for overlap of qualities, the questionnaire was reduced to a more manageable 24 questions. Wherever possible, questions that referred directly to characteristics, functions, or parts of the Web site, were removed since these represent the supplier perspective rather than the subjective user experience.

Following standard practice in QFD, respondents were asked to rate each business school Web site in terms of the 24 qualities using a 5-point scale. The respondents were also asked to indicate how important each quality was to them, also using a 5-point scale. Analysis of the collected data led to the removal of one question. Based on reliability analysis, the remaining 23 questions were clustered into four major dimensions: ease of use, experience, information, and communication and integration. Analysis of the data collected using the E-Qual 1.0 instrument allowed the four business school sites to be differentiated and their relative strengths and weaknesses to be assessed, but the major value of the application of E-Qual 1.0 was the beginning of an understanding of how users perceive Web site quality.

10.2.2 E-Qual 2.0

In applying E-Qual to business-to-consumer (B2C) Web sites it became clear that the interaction perspective of quality was largely missing from

E-Qual 1.0. Bitner (1990) adopts Shostack's (1985) definition of a service encounter as 'a period of time during which a consumer directly interacts with a service' and notes that these interactions need not be interpersonal – a service encounter can occur without a human interaction element. Bitner (1990) also recognizes that 'many times that interaction is the service from the customer's point of view' (p. 71). This suggests that interaction quality may also be as important to the success of e-Businesses as it is to 'bricks and mortar' organizations (and possibly more so given the removal of the interpersonal dimension). In E-Qual 2.0 we therefore extended the interaction aspects by adapting and applying the work on service quality, chiefly SERVQUAL (Parasuraman et al., 1985, 1988, 1995; Zeithaml et al., 1990, 1993) and information system (IS) SERVQUAL (Pitt et al., 1995, 1997; Kettinger and Lee, 1997; Van Dyke et al., 1997), to an evaluation of online bookshops.

As with E-Qual 1.0, quality workshops were conducted to elicit customer online service requirements, this time in the domain of Internet bookshops (Barnes and Vidgen, 2001b). The instrument was refined and piloted and then tested with students at the University of Bath. Fifty-four questionnaires were collected with each respondent assessing three Internet bookshops – Amazon, Bertelsmann Online (BOL), and the Internet Bookshop (IBS) – using a 5-point scale. Respondents also rated the importance of the qualities in this context using a 5-point scale. The analysis of the results yielded five categories of quality: tangibles (e.g. site navigation); reliability; responsiveness; assurance (e.g. security); and empathy (e.g. understanding the individual). The results of the evaluation showed that Amazon literally ran rings around the competition, scoring more highly on every item of evaluation.

10.2.3 E-Qual 3.0

While E-Qual 1.0 was strong on information quality, it did not address service interaction. Similarly, where E-Qual 2.0 had been developed to test service interaction quality it lost some of the information quality richness of E-Qual 1.0. Both instruments contained a range of qualities concerned with the Web site as a software artefact. In reviewing the instruments we found that all of the qualities could be categorized into three distinct areas: site quality, information quality, and service interaction quality. This new version of E-Qual 3.0 was tested in the domain of online auctions (Barnes and Vidgen, 2001a) where Amazon, eBay, and QXL were evaluated. The quantitative analysis showed clearly that Amazon scored most highly in terms of user-perceived quality. While eBay was a close second, the QXL site fared less well by a significant margin. The strength of Amazon may be in part due to brand image. One of the respondents commented:

> *I really did not like the QXL Web site, it takes an hour to register, the*
> *icons are so small I practically needed a magnifier to see them, not a*

good experience ... I loved Amazon though!!!! But then again, I might be biased towards it because of its reputation. I guess advertising and the name are very important.

The QXL site fared particularly badly in terms of customer relationships and trustworthiness. This led us to move away from the more limited notion of Web site and e-Commerce quality to a broader notion of e-Business quality where the quality of the site is but one dimension of user satisfaction.

10.2.4 E-Qual 4.0

Analysis of the results of E-Qual 3.0 led to the confirmation of three dimensions of e-Business quality: usability, information quality, and service interaction quality. The core qualities of E-Qual 4.0 are shown in Table 10.1, along with primary and secondary literature support. Lastly, a 7-point scale was adopted in E-Qual 4.0 (as in SERVQUAL; see Zeithaml et al. (1990)) where the anchors are $1 =$ 'strongly disagree' and $7 =$ 'strongly agree'. The importance scale was anchored with $1 =$ 'least important' and $7 =$ 'most important' (as recommended in the QFD literature; see King (1989)).

Table 10.1: The E-Qual 4.0 instrument

Category	E-Qual 4.0 questions
Usability	1. I find the site easy to learn to operate
	2. My interaction with the site is clear and understandable
	3. I find the site easy to navigate
	4. I find the site easy to use
	5. The site has an attractive appearance
	6. The design is appropriate to the type of site
	7. The site conveys a sense of competency
	8. The site creates a positive experience for me
Information	9. Provides accurate information
	10. Provides believable information
	11. Provides timely information
	12. Provides relevant information
	13. Provides easy to understand information
	14. Provides information at the right level of detail
	15. Presents the information in an appropriate format
Service interaction	16. Has a good reputation
	17. It feels safe to complete transactions
	18. My personal information feels secure
	19. Creates a sense of personalization
	20. Conveys a sense of community
	21. Makes it easy to communicate with the organization
	22. I feel confident that goods/services will be delivered as promised
	23. Overall impression

Usability replaced site quality in E-Qual version 4.0 because it keeps the emphasis on the user and their perceptions rather than on the designer and the idea of a Web site as simply a context-free software artefact. The term usability is also more consistent with the level of abstraction of the other two dimensions of E-Qual – information and service interaction. In E-Qual 4.0 the usability dimension draws from literature in the field of human computer interaction (Davis, 1989, 1993; Nielsen, 1993) and more latterly Web usability (Nielsen, 1999, 2000; Spool, 1999). Usability is concerned with the pragmatics of how a user perceives and interacts with a Web site: is it easy to navigate?; is the design appropriate to the type of site? It is not, in the first instance, concerned with design principles such as the use of frames or the percentage of white space, although these are concerns for the Web site designer who is charged with improving usability.

Thus, E-Qual has evolved using quality workshops, factor analysis to identify question groupings, and literature from three core research areas: information quality from mainstream IS research; service interaction quality from marketing (as well as some IS and e-Commerce sources); and usability from human–computer interaction. We ran quality workshops at every stage of E-Qual's development to ensure that the qualities were relevant, particularly where they relate to pre-Internet literature, such as SERVQUAL, and new industries, such as online auctions. E-Qual is thus an instrument for the evaluation of e-Business quality – Web site quality is one dimension of this, but the service-related questions are concerned with perceptions of the organization behind the Web site. We can illustrate this important distinction through the application of E-Qual 4.0 to Internet bookstores.

10.2.5 Internet bookstores – it's not just about the Web site

Buying books over the Internet is one of the early applications of B2C e-Commerce and has matured to become relatively stable, at least in Internet terms, with 5.4% of total global book sales in 1999. E-Qual was implemented using an online questionnaire targeted at users of the three largest UK online bookshops: Amazon, BOL, and IBS and resulted in 280 usable responses (Barnes and Vidgen, 2002). As well as rating a site for each of the qualities in the instrument, respondents are asked to rate the importance of the quality to them in this context using a 1 to 7 scale. Table 10.2 shows the top six questions in terms of importance to respondents. Those considered most important are heavily tied to information accuracy, usability, and issues of trust. Such questions concern security and reliability regarding completion of transactions, receipt of goods and personal information, accuracy of content, as well as ease of site use and navigation.

To provide an overall benchmark for the three e-Commerce operations the total weighted score is indexed against the total possible score, thus

Table 10.2: The most important qualities for users of Internet bookshops

Item	Quality
9	Provides accurate information
17	It feels safe to complete transactions
22	I feel confident that goods/services will be delivered as promised
18	My personal information feels secure
3	I find the site easy to navigate
4	I find the site easy to use

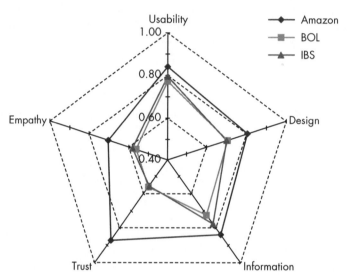

Figure 10.1: Radar chart of E-Qual 4.0 subcategories for online bookshops (Barnes and Vidgen, 2002).

allowing an E-Qual Index (EQI) to be calculated. Amazon achieved the highest EQI at 72%, followed by BOL (70%) and IBS (67%). Factor analysis showed the presence of five constructs. The usability questions contained two constructs: *usability* and *design*. Service interaction subdivided into *trust* and *empathy*, while information questions group together in a single construct. These dimensions indicate how site users perceive e-Commerce quality in the online bookshop domain. Figure 10.1 demonstrates clearly that the Amazon UK site out-performs its two rivals in all five constructs. The indices for the Amazon subcategories make a clear circle around the other two sites, with Trust rating particularly well. Other areas are less strong, in relative terms. Empathy has the lowest EQI for Amazon. The scores of the two other bookshops are close. Information quality presents the largest discrepancy with IBS leading BOL. IBS also score marginally higher for empathy and usability.

The survey indicates that the differences in usability between the sites are small, suggesting that once a basic level of usability is achieved then site design is unlikely to be a differentiating competitive factor. With regard to design, the difference is more marked, indicating that the Amazon site is preferred, although this may be due in part to respondents being more familiar with the Amazon site.

10.3 Applying E-Qual to the FSMKE

To illustrate the E-Qual 4.0 approach to e-Business evaluation in detail we report on the application of the method to the assessment of a cross-national Web site provided via the Organization for Economic Cooperation and Development (OECD). The Web site is that of the FSMKE – a site relating to international tax policy and administration. The FSMKE offering was evaluated before and after a process of redesign, allowing E-Qual to be used to assess the effectiveness of the redesign initiative (Barnes and Vidgen, 2003).

10.3.1 The e-government context

Recently, government services have begun to be provided via the Web in countries such as the US, UK, Australia, New Zealand, Italy, Singapore, and Portugal. In addition, cross-national organizations such as the OECD, World Trade Organization (WTO), and United Nations have started to develop Web offerings aimed at recipients in many and varied countries. Digital government – or electronic (e)-government as it is often called – has huge potential benefits. Government transcends all sectors of society, and not only provides the legal, political, and economic infrastructure to support other sectors, but also exerts considerable influence on the social factors that add to their development (Elmagarmid and McIver, 2001). e-Government thus has the potential to profoundly transform people's perceptions of civil and political interactions with their governments. Even though we may see further convergence of e-Commerce and e-government services (Kubicek and Hagen, 2001), unlike e-Commerce, e-government services must – in most societies – be accessible to all. Through the Web, expectations of the service levels that e-government sites must provide have been raised considerably (Cook, 2000).

While e-government can provide communication, transaction, and integration of administrative services, most countries are not making extensive use of the Web. According to the Cyberspace Policy Research Group (CyPRG) the 1999 global average score for information transparency was less than 50% and for interactivity it was less than 25% (La Porte et al., 2001). Although there appears to be less progress with transaction-based services, a Gartner (2001) Research survey of European countries showed that the demand by citizens for information massively outweighs the demand for interactivity. The offerings examined in this research are quite basic, defined by the Economist (2000) as first or entry-level services, provided largely for one-way communication.

10.3.2 The FSMKE

A project to evaluate the quality of the FSMKE Web site was initiated by the Tax Management Research Network (TMRnet) in the early part of 2001. TMRnet is a network of academic researchers and tax practitioners that was launched in 2000 to undertake joint research related to the interface between national tax policy and the practical management of national tax regimes. The aim is to further understand, how to manage taxation departments: i.e. to improve tax administration and customer service, including the exploration of opportunities afforded by new technologies, such as the Internet. The TMRnet Steering Group includes academics from the Universities of Bath and Nottingham, senior members of the UK Inland Revenue and H.M. Customs and Excise and members of the Fiscal Affairs Division of the OECD.

10.3.3 Research design

The evaluation of the FSMKE Web site was undertaken using the E-Qual instrument shown in Table 10.1 (but with the transaction-oriented questions removed 17, 18, 22) since the site is concerned with communication and knowledge sharing. The assessment was carried out in two parts. The FSMKE Web site was first evaluated in April through May 2001 and then, following a Web site redesign exercise, the new site was re-evaluated in the period July to September 2001. We present the results of the evaluation and compare perceptions of the FSMKE Web site before and after the redesign exercise. The quantitative results produced through analysis of the E-Qual data are supplemented by qualitative comments of the respondents to provide triangulation of the results and a deeper insight into user attitudes.

10.3.4 Survey implementation

The survey of e-government quality for FSMKE was conducted using an Internet-based questionnaire. The home page of the questionnaire had instructions and guidelines for completion of the instrument. The home page would then open a separate window (control panel) containing the Web site qualities to be assessed (see Figure 10.2). The control panel allowed the user to switch the contents of the target window between the instruction page, the FSMKE Web site, and the quality dictionary. Having the quality dictionary online and linked to the question number made it easy to get more details of a particular quality. Users were asked

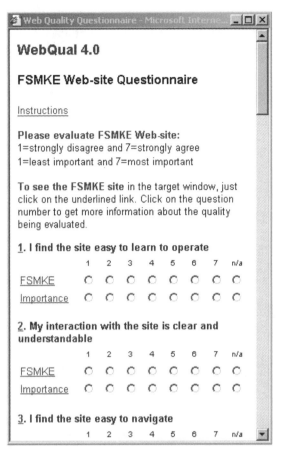

Figure 10.2:   The E-Qual questionnaire interface (see www.webqual.co.uk/demonstration.htm).

to rate the FSMKE site for each quality using a scale ranging from 1 (strongly disagree) to 7 (strongly agree). Users were also asked to rate the importance of the quality to them, again using a 1 (least important) to 7 (most important).

The first phase of the valuation was conducted in the period April to May 2001 and resulted in 65 questionnaire responses. The original Web site is shown in Figure 10.3. The second phase, conducted in August to September of 2001 after the Web site redesign, resulted in 59 responses. The redesigned site is illustrated in Figure 10.4. Demographic and other respondent information are shown in Table 10.3. The respondents were typically experienced and intensive users of the Internet, although not intensive or experienced users of the FSMKE Web site. The majority of respondents were also male, of typical working age, but located in a variety of FSMKE countries, particularly Japan, Australia, the UK, and Canada.

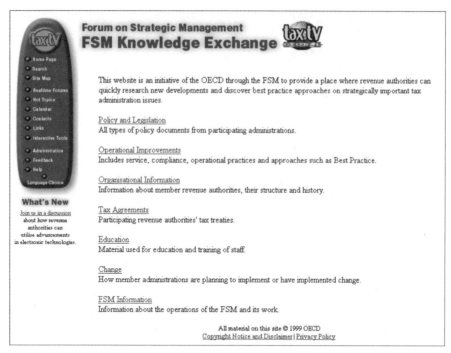

Figure 10.3: The FSMKE site prior to redesign.

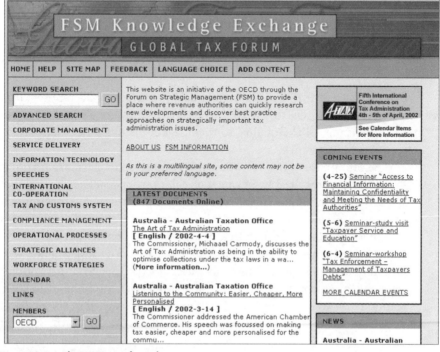

Figure 10.4: The FSMKE site after redesign.

Table 10.3: Respondent demographics and experience

Question	Response	Before (%)	After (%)
Country of origin	Australia	29.0	25.6
	Canada	16.2	7.0
	Denmark	0.0	0.0
	Eire	0.0	0.0
	Japan	27.4	31.6
	The Netherlands	0.0	5.2
	United Kingdom	14.5	12.3
	United States	0.0	0.0
	Other	12.9	19.3
Sex	Male	67.2	71.9
	Female	32.8	28.1
Age	Under 26	6.8	3.7
	26–35	22.0	24.1
	36–45	50.9	46.3
	46–55	20.3	25.9
	Over 55	0.0	0.0
Internet experience	Less than 6 months	0.0	1.8
	6 months to 1 year	1.7	0.0
	1–2 years	16.6	8.9
	2–3 years	16.7	21.4
	More than 3 years	65.0	67.9
Internet usage	Less than once a month	1.7	0.0
	Once a month	1.6	0.0
	Once a fortnight	1.7	0.0
	Once a week	10.0	21.4
	Two or three times a week	1.7	3.6
	Once a day	18.3	21.4
	More than once a day	65.0	53.6
FSMKE experience	Less than 3 months	70.7	45.3
	3–6 months	8.6	18.9
	6 months to 1 year	8.6	18.8
	1–2 years	10.4	13.2
	More than 2 years	1.7	3.8
FSMKE usage	Less than every 3 months	54.5	27.5
	Once every 3 months	18.2	27.5
	Once a month	12.8	21.6
	Once a week	3.6	3.9
	Two or three times a week	7.3	13.7
	Daily	3.6	7.8

10.4 The FSMKE evaluation

The data collected before and after site redesign are summarized in Tables 10.4 and 10.5. Note that at this stage, we have not presented any categories for the questions (this is discussed below). The importance scores give the average importance ranking for each question based on all of the responses received before site redesign and then again for all of the responses after site redesign. In addition, the per question average scores for each of the classifications is given along with the standard error of the mean.

10.4.1 Perceptions of importance

Referring to Table 10.4, we see some interesting patterns in the data. In terms of the importance ratings of particular questions, there are some useful groupings to note. Let us consider the perceptions of important qualities both before and after the redesign of the site. Before site design, overall, those questions considered most important, e.g. above upper quartile of 5.88, are all about ease of use and accurate, trusted, and pertinent information. Here we find, in descending order of importance, questions 9, 10, 12, 1, and 4. At the other end of the spectrum, those questions considered least important, e.g. below the overall 5.20 lower quartile, are based around the look and feel of the site in terms of user empathy and site design. Specifically, questions 17, 18, 5, 6, and 19 are in ascending order of importance. Other questions are in between, and the median is 5.49.

The results suggest that there are specific priorities in the qualities demanded from the FSMKE Web site by users. Getting easy access to 'good' information appears paramount, whilst certain other aspects which may be important for some commercial sites, such as building a networked community experience for users to return to, is not so important. Intuitively, such trends make sense, particularly when we consider that the primary focus seems to be on information orientation rather than business transactions.

Once site redesign was completed, the resultant data on site quality yield some similar importance rankings. However, there were some changes in priorities for questions at the margins. Overall, question 1 slips out of the upper quartile range (6.07 and above), whilst questions 11 and 13 are added. At the other end of the scale, question 6 is promoted from the lower quartile (5.28), whilst question 16 now falls into this zone. Notwithstanding, the picture remains the same, with important questions all referring to 'good' information and the ease of use of the site. The least important questions refer to soft issues of service, empathy, and aesthetics.

10.4.2 Weighted scores and the EQI

Overall, the ratings of the redesigned site appear consistently higher than that of the original. However, for the raw data, it is difficult to see

Table 10.4: Summary of the data – mean, standard error (SE), and standard deviation (SD)

No.	Description	Importance (before)			Before			Importance (after)			After		
		Mean	SE	SD	Mean	SE	SD	Mean	SE	SD	Mean	SE	SD
1	I find the site easy to learn to operate	5.94	0.16	1.27	4.29	0.21	1.68	6.05	0.14	1.06	5.73	0.12	0.94
2	My interaction with the site is clear and understandable	5.49	0.19	1.55	4.03	0.20	1.62	5.80	0.14	1.08	5.37	0.14	1.07
3	I find the site easy to navigate	5.87	0.19	1.54	3.85	0.23	1.86	6.07	0.13	0.96	5.51	0.15	1.18
4	I find the site easy to use	5.89	0.18	1.49	3.85	0.23	1.82	6.20	0.12	0.94	5.46	0.16	1.21
5	The site has an attractive appearance	4.94	0.17	1.40	3.78	0.19	1.57	5.15	0.20	1.51	5.19	0.18	1.37
6	The design is appropriate to the type of site	5.02	0.17	1.39	3.88	0.22	1.72	5.31	0.19	1.45	5.50	0.16	1.23
7	The site conveys a sense of competency	5.34	0.18	1.42	3.97	0.19	1.53	5.59	0.17	1.34	5.39	0.14	1.08
8	The site creates a positive experience for me	5.31	0.18	1.43	3.60	0.22	1.72	5.47	0.15	1.12	5.07	0.18	1.36
9	Provides accurate information	6.45	0.16	1.26	4.18	0.25	1.75	6.40	0.13	1.00	5.50	0.16	1.15
10	Provides believable information	6.30	0.16	1.32	5.02	0.22	1.65	6.39	0.14	1.05	5.75	0.14	1.08
11	Provides timely information	5.77	0.21	1.64	3.80	0.24	1.70	6.07	0.13	1.02	4.85	0.19	1.38
12	Provides relevant information	6.06	0.16	1.26	4.25	0.20	1.52	6.19	0.13	1.03	5.14	0.18	1.41
13	Provides easy to understand information	5.82	0.16	1.31	4.20	0.20	1.57	5.81	0.14	1.07	5.17	0.15	1.15
14	Provides information at the right level of detail	5.61	0.17	1.32	4.02	0.22	1.59	5.73	0.13	0.98	5.02	0.18	1.36
15	Presents the information in an appropriate format	5.35	0.16	1.33	4.40	0.19	1.50	5.61	0.16	1.22	5.24	0.16	1.24
16	Has a good reputation	5.26	0.22	1.63	3.31	0.31	1.83	5.25	0.24	1.76	4.68	0.23	1.47
17	Creates a sense of personalization	4.11	0.20	1.48	2.84	0.20	1.50	3.84	0.23	1.68	3.89	0.22	1.63
18	Conveys a sense of community	4.35	0.19	1.51	3.67	0.22	1.70	4.59	0.24	1.74	4.72	0.20	1.45
19	Makes it easy to communicate with the organization	5.14	0.20	1.59	4.17	0.21	1.66	5.10	0.17	1.32	4.95	0.18	1.37
20	What is your overall view of this Web site	—	—	—	3.83	0.19	1.56	—	—	—	5.24	0.14	1.08

Table 10.5: Weighted scores and E-Qual indices (WQI) – before and after redesign

No.	Description	Max. score (before)	Before		Max. score (after)	After	
			Wgt. score	WQI		Wgt. score	EQI
1	I find the site easy to learn to operate	41.56	26.23	0.63	42.36	35.07	0.83
2	My interaction with the site is clear and understandable	38.45	22.88	0.60	40.58	31.54	0.78
3	I find the site easy to navigate	41.11	24.00	0.58	42.47	33.93	0.80
4	I find the site easy to use	41.25	23.31	0.57	43.42	34.17	0.79
5	The site has an attractive appearance	34.57	18.75	0.54	36.07	27.59	0.77
6	The design is appropriate to the type of site	35.11	19.40	0.55	37.17	30.29	0.81
7	The site conveys a sense of competency	37.41	21.25	0.57	39.15	30.75	0.79
8	The site creates a positive experience for me	37.15	19.24	0.52	38.32	28.38	0.74
9	Provides accurate information	45.17	26.84	0.59	44.82	35.61	0.79
10	Provides believable information	44.08	32.26	0.73	44.73	37.14	0.83
11	Provides timely information	40.42	21.76	0.54	42.48	30.00	0.71
12	Provides relevant information	42.44	25.73	0.61	43.31	32.12	0.74
13	Provides easy to understand information	40.71	24.65	0.61	40.69	30.53	0.75
14	Provides information at the right level of detail	39.25	23.06	0.59	40.10	29.24	0.73
15	Presents the information in an appropriate format	37.48	24.08	0.64	39.27	30.37	0.77
16	Has a good reputation	36.85	15.77	0.43	36.72	25.76	0.70
17	Creates a sense of personalization	28.74	12.05	0.42	26.85	17.34	0.65
18	Conveys a sense of community	30.48	17.51	0.57	32.15	23.44	0.73
19	Makes it easy to communicate with the organization	35.98	22.75	0.63	35.72	26.27	0.74
	Totals	728.19	421.52	0.58	746.39	569.54	0.78

where the perceptions have changed most (especially in the context of the areas of quality considered most important). The importance ratings filter through to the weighted results of the data set. Unweighted results for individual questions in Table 10.4 show some varying results.

Weighted results serve to accentuate these differences in the direction of user priorities. These are shown in Table 10.5.

One key aim of this approach is to achieve some overall quality rating for the Web site so that we may benchmark the effect of site redesign. Total average scores for the unweighted data showed an overall increase of 24.43, from 78.93 to 103.36. Weighting these scores by the importance ratings provides a similar picture, with the total average weighted score increasing from 421.52 to 569.54.

However, the total scores make it difficult to give a standard benchmark for the two Web sites. One way to achieve this is to index the total weighted score for each site against the total possible score in that time period (i.e. the total importance for all questions multiplied by 7, the maximum rating for a site). The result is expressed as an index from zero to one (which, when multiplied by 100, may also be considered as a percentage). A summary of these calculations and totals are given in Table 10.5. Overall, we can see quite clearly that the redesigned site is benchmarked well above the original site, increasing by 20% in the EQI from 58% to 78%. Perhaps more interesting is some assessment of how the Web sites differ in quality. To this end, the next section uses a number of reliable subgroupings and applies them to the analysis.

10.4.3 Analysing the differences in the sites

The data indicates that the new Web site surpasses the old in terms of E-Qual site quality. Here we examine where these perceived improvements have occurred. The Internet bookstore application of E-Qual described above (Figure 10.1) led to a number of valid and reliable question subgroupings. In the adapted E-Qual 4.0 instrument used in this research they can be explained as follows (question numbers in brackets as per Table 10.5):

■ Usability (questions 1–4). Qualities associated with site usability; e.g. ease of use and navigation.

■ Design (questions 5–8). Qualities associated with site design; e.g. appearance and the image conveyed to the user.

■ Information quality (questions 9–15). The quality of the content of the site: the suitability of the information for the user's purposes, e.g. accuracy, format, and relevancy.

■ Service quality (questions 16–19). The quality of the service interaction experienced by users as they delve deeper into the site (embodied by trust and empathy in Figure 10.1); e.g. issues of reputation, personalization, and communication with the site owner.

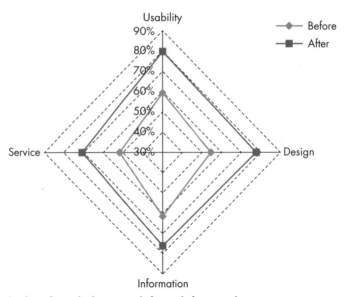

Figure 10.5: Radar chart of E-Qual subcategories before and after site redesign.

These categories provide some useful criteria by which to assess the Web sites before and after redesign. Using the question groupings, we can build a profile of an individual Web site that is easily compared to others. We are now in a position to examine why the redesigned site fared better than original site on the EQI.

As a starting point, the data was summarized around the questionnaire subcategories. Then, and similarly to the EQI in Table 10.5, the total score for each category was indexed against the maximum score (based on the importance ratings for questions multiplied by 7). Figure 10.5 is the result, which rates the two Web sites using these criteria. Note that the scale has been adjusted to between 30% and 90% to allow for clearer comparison. Clearly the new site is rated more highly than its predecessor, out-performing the old site in all four dimensions. As we can see, most improved in the new site are usability and design – up 20% and 23%, respectively. Close behind is service – up 19%. Least improved is information quality – the highest rated quality before site design – although still up 15%. Apparently, the new site has greater ease of use and more aesthetic appeal, with better service and access to information.

10.4.4 Differences in perception among respondent groups

In absolute terms, whilst the new site has most categories rating quite highly at between 76% and 80%, one is still low in absolute terms – service (71%). This indicates that although this area is vastly improved, there is still considerable work to be done in building relationships with users. This result is also borne out in an analysis of variance of the data by the country of respondent (with Bonferroni correction). Although the samples are not large, the test reveals some significant discrepancies in the views of different FSMKE members. For the original site, questions 1, 4, 13, and 19 indicated significant differences between the views of UK users, Japan, and others at the 5% level. These questions are varied, indicating differences in terms of ease of use, understanding information, and ease of communication within FSMKE. This may indicate some cultural and language issues associated with the original site, as well as regional variations in site use and contribution.

For the redesigned site, significant differences were revealed between the views of Australian users, Japan, and others for questions 2, 3, 7, and 15. These are different questions to those involving differences in perceptions for the first site. However, they are likely to be indicative of the changing perceptions of individuals in the various member countries. One of the areas of disagreement is ease of use/navigation, which was also an area of difference for the original site. Other areas are competency and information format. Again this could point to some clear differences in the interpretation of the site by different national identities, both in terms of cognitive issues of language and culture, and differences in expectations, interaction and commitment of the various members. Further, this is underlined by the assessment of the two sites by the same respondents – more than 50% evaluated both sites.

Overall, the results point to some apparent differences in perceptions among FSMKE member countries. This obviously has implications for the difficulties in designing a multinational Web site that appeals to all FSMKE member countries. Some of these issues are surfaced more clearly in the qualitative results.

10.4.5 Qualitative data

At an interpretive level, many of the features drawn out in the quantitative findings are supported in the qualitative data drawn from the open comments of respondents. This also adds richness and helps to explain the 'why?' behind some of these patterns in the quantitative data.

Before site redesign

As indicated in Figure 10.3, numerous areas were open to criticism in the initial FSMKE Web site. In terms of site design and usability, broken links, difficult navigation and aesthetics appeared common complaints. Comments included:

> *There is a broken link on Customs page Dutch Tax & Customs Admin. There are too many stages to drill down; the rule of three in navigation is broken. The site looks poor because of the bad choice of serif fonts, i.e. it looks like a typed document. The navigation gif is not cached and at times*

takes more than 8 seconds to rendering full – the turn off time for most users. Can this be compressed further or sliced so that it is rendered quickly in the browser.

The site is completely text based. There are few pictures. There could be more pop up screens or interesting features such as moving reminder banners or something with more pizzazz. This should be a showpiece and is not. Given the subject matter, I would have expected more imagination and technology woven into the site.

Far too many areas where links lead me to no content. This creates a very negative impression. Why have links leading nowhere?

Broken links, and Times Roman fonts are not good!

Not a bad effort but make it more attractive.

I found the site bland and boring. (Sorry. It is not a site I would use unless I absolutely had to.) The information/content seemed to be good, and interesting, but I wasn't enticed to stay or visit again.

The quality of the content provided was another concern, with a number of respondents criticizing the volume, language translation, relevance, and currency of material:

Also, all documents should be fully translated. There is no point putting in documents that not everyone can read. Best practices should be available to all, not just the select few who can read and understand the language.

I could not read Asian Languages.

A lot of the content appears dated. I did not find all titles very helpful – e.g. where would I find Internet initiatives?

I could not find any information that I searched for in the 15 minutes I used the site. Every time, the results turned out 'o documents met your search criteria.' Maybe it was just my bad luck that the topics I selected had no documents input as of yet. I also found that there were a lot of very broad topics (such as 'advice' or 'reporting' or 'research') which I didn't find too helpful in selecting what to search. I hope there will be more info on Information Management specific practices, as there doesn't seem to be anything yet. I also found that there were a lot of acronyms with which I was not familiar.

There were fewer comments on the service aspects of the site, partly because respondents saw this area as less important. However, some respondents clearly thought service aspects such were lacking; there were criticisms regarding the purpose of the site, participation of members and value for the individual. Comments included:

From a personal point of view it is somehow difficult to determine, where exactly one can find the value added for tax administrations by this open, none secure Web site.

The ranking of the site suffers in many of the questions because of content. There is not a lot of participation so it reflects negatively on credibility. For example, the trade agreements search shows up the 2 same IRS documents for any country searched. Another weakness is the content provided often seems to be statements of intent or principal that provide no guidance or real insight. Other documents are of real interest however.

In principle the ideas are sound. However, I am not clear what knowledge is being exchanged, why or what it is hoped to get out of the site.

In dire need of cohesion, updating and a sense of purpose.

After site redesign

Once the new Web site had been completed, the comments were more upbeat, although it was evident that respondents still thought that there was considerable room for improvement. In terms of site design comments included:

Great site. Love the colours.

The structure, design, and format of the site is good; however, the crucial question is whether it will be maintained and kept up-to-date.

Much improved site.

Will use the site more frequently after this experience.

Site is much improved, and I expect it to continue to evolve and get better.

The design, organization and navigation of the site are good. With a little more exposure to it I feel I could very easily find what I need.

Overall, there were fewer negative comments. Those that were made emphasized the room for improvement in the visual elements and navigation links.

A great improvement since last time – but needs more coherence and better labelling of themes.

The globe of the Earth on the home page is not at the correct angle, it needs to tilt another 90 degrees.

I want the link in the FSMKE site to be more directly accessible to the contents related (e.g. not to the top page of homepage).

In terms of the quality of information, there was a general feeling that this had improved, but that more information was needed to create a really valuable resource. The translation engine was also mentioned as problematic for complex tax terminology. For example, respondents suggested:

The reason I assigned an overall poor mark to the site is because content is weak. There seems to be – from my limited perusing of the site – items which fall into several categories. Press release, conceptual papers, and program samples (for particular population subsections). Unfortunately the first two types are already widely distributed and there is limited value in them. The third type is more interesting (actual work being done) but navigating through the actual sites of the relevant home country provides better context and a more complete picture.

The quality of what I found was good, and useful, but only few countries are represented. Hope that that will improve. This was my first look at FSMKE; I will definitely be using it often in the future.

Great improvement from previous version. Translation engines are not sophisticated enough to translate tax terms.

Although service had improved on the EQI, some individuals still considered that there were significant differences regarding the offerings of individual member countries:

Noticeable that UK does not seem to have contributed much compared with Canada and Norway.

To be a credible source much more information is needed. Also better coverage. For example, in my own current work area (construction industry compliance/contract payments) there are numerous documents available from (amongst other countries) Australia, Germany, USA, Canada, UK, and other places, but only some of the Canadian material appears on the site. You might want to consider asking industry/functional specialists attached to particular fiscs to provide some sort of editorial support.

10.5 Recommendations for the FSMKE for e-Business improvement

User perceptions of the FSMKE Web site following the redesign project indicate that quality has improved significantly. The EQI has increased by 20 points from 58% to 78%. This quantitative improvement is supported by analysis of the comments made by respondents when completing the questionnaire. The comments provided richer insight into the assessment of the original site, fleshing out the quantitative evaluation in terms of the weaknesses in particular areas, such as site design and usability (especially broken links, difficult navigation, and aesthetics), information quality (especially volume, language translation, relevance, and currency) and service quality (especially purpose of the site, participation of members, and value for the individual). After redesign, the qualitative analysis provides strong support for the improvement of the site in the various areas of quality, and areas where further improvement is desirable.

The increase in the EQI from 58% to 78% is notably large. Is the increase in EQI due purely to improvements in the site or is there a Web site redesign Hawthorne effect at work? Perhaps users will greet with open arms any change to a site that looks tired and is cumbersome to use. It is quite possible that users who are unhappy with a site will over-compensate in their evaluation of a new site. The application of an earlier version of E-Qual to the Amazon bookstore produced an EQI of 82% (Barnes and Vidgen, 2001b). In a later study using E-Qual 4.0 (Barnes and Vidgen, 2002) Amazon again scored an EQI of 82%. Whether the FSMKE site is truly of Amazonian proportions needs to be tested by a re-application of E-Qual to FSMKE to see if there is indeed a Web Hawthorne effect and the extent to which it may erode over time.

The importance ratings assigned by respondents show that their primary concern is with accurate, believable, and relevant information from a Web site that is easy to use. However, information quality is the least improved dimension (15%) – this is an area for future development of the site that needs attention.

The site also ranked less highly in terms of empathy and community aspects. An area of development to be considered is personalization (e.g. user registration) and secure areas for download. This would have the added benefit of allowing more content to be made available and help to improve perceptions of information quality. Comments suggested that adequate availability of content from member countries and language translation was still a barrier.

Related to the last point, the third area for consideration is community and knowledge sharing. The site does not promote knowledge sharing other than at the level of document sharing, i.e. it is, strictly speaking, an FSM Data Exchange. Knowledge sharing could be enhanced through the building of an online community and the addition of facilities such as forums, promoting greater interaction between members and the sharing of best practices.

Regarding the limitations of this work, it is clear that a larger sample would provide a more sound basis for data analysis. As well as a larger sample size, it would also be useful to analyse the server logs of the FSMKE to determine which countries actually use the site and to what extent. This information would then help target sampling at a profile of desired countries and users. For example, the lack of participation from the United States, the Netherlands, Denmark, and Eire (Table 10.2) warrants further investigation – will the site redesign attract new users, or are the barriers political and organizational?

10.5.1 Further implications

Through the Web, expectations of the service levels that e-government sites must provide have been raised considerably. Online e-government organizations are becoming ever more aware of the need to improve their offerings. In this chapter we have shown how one cross-national e-government organization – an OECD forum for strategic tax policy and administration – has done just that. The analysis, using the E-Qual instrument, has shown how the organization's e-government operation has improved and also identified areas where there is still room for improvement. Such surveys are an important aspect of benchmarking. Indeed, they should be conducted regularly, especially when redesigns take place or major shifts in the environment occur which undermine the underlying basis for an e-Business offering (e.g. when a related site is launched or when a significant new technology appears).

Furthermore, e-Business operations often have multiple classes of user and a Web site redesign can affect many stakeholders. In our sample we collected data from a variety of FSMKE members. The multi-stakeholder analysis of the Web site redesign in this case has helped to enhance understanding on how quality is perceived differently among different groups rather than treating all site users as a homogeneous group. The perspectives of the range of international members emphasize the importance of a full understanding of how all users interact with the site when attempting redevelopment; an improvement for one group might be perceived as a lessening in quality for another group.

10.6 Summary

E-Qual has developed over several years from a tool for evaluating Web sites into a method for assessing the quality of the implementation of e-Business operations, where quality assessment is expressed through the voice of the customer. The Internet bookstore application presented here shows how E-Qual can be used to benchmark one organization's site against its competitors at a given point in time. The FSMKE application shows in detail the E-Qual method and illustrates the use of the instrument to provide a comparison of the same organization's e-Business offering at two different points in time, such as before and after a Web site redesign initiative. However sound the e-Business model might be, it must be implemented properly. Organizations need to address all three dimensions of E-Qual through initiatives such as Web site usability workshops (usability), Web content management strategies (information quality), and e-Business process integration (service interaction quality).

References and Further Reading

Bailey, J. E. and S. W. Pearson (1983). 'Development of a Tool for Measuring and Analysing User Satisfaction.' *Management Science* **29**(5): 530–545.

Barnes, S. J. and R. T. Vidgen (2000). WebQual: An Exploration of Web Site Quality. *ECIS 2000, A Cyberspace Odyssey*. H. R. Hansen, M. Bichler and H. Mahrer (eds). *Proceedings of the Eighth European Conference on Information Systems*, Vienna.

Barnes, S. J. and R. T. Vidgen (2001a). Assessing the Quality of Auction Web Sites. *Proceedings of the 34th Annual Hawaii International Conference on System Sciences*, Maui, Hawaii.

Barnes, S. J. and R. T. Vidgen (2001b). 'An Evaluation of Cyber-Bookshops: the WebQual Method.' *International Journal of Electronic Commerce* 6(1): 6–25.

Barnes, S. J. and R. T. Vidgen (2002). 'An Integrative Approach to the Assessment of e-Commerce Quality.' *Journal of Electronic Commerce Research* 3(3): 114–127.

Barnes, S. and R. Vidgen (2003). Assessing the Quality of a Cross-National e-Government Web Site: a Case Study of the Forum on Strategic Management Knowledge Exchange. *Proceedings of the 36th Hawaii International Conference on Information Systems*, Hawaii.

Bitner, M. J. (1990). 'Evaluating Service Encounters: The Effects of Physical Surroundings and Employee Responses.' *Journal of Marketing* (April): 69–82.

Bossert, J. L. (1991). *Quality Function Deployment: A Practitioner's Approach*. Wisconsin, ASQC Quality Press.

Cook, M. E. (2000). *What Citizens Want from e-Government*. [9 August], http://www.ctg.albany.edu/resources/htmlrpt/e-government/what_citizens_want.html.

Davis, F. (1989). 'Perceived Usefulness, Perceived Ease of Use, and User Acceptance of Information Technology.' *MIS Quarterly* 13(3): 340–391.

Davis, F. (1993). 'User Acceptance of Information Technology: System Characteristics, User Perceptions, and Behavioral Impacts.' *International Journal of Man–Machine Studies* 38: 475–487.

DeLone, W. H. and E. R. McLean (1992). 'Information Systems Success: the Quest for the Dependent Variable.' *Information Systems Research* 3(1): 60–95.

Economist (2000). *No Gain Without Pain* [24 June], http://www.economist.com/displayStory.cfm?Story_ID=80764.

Elmagarmid, A. K. and W. J. McIver (2001). 'The Ongoing March Toward Digital Government.' *IEEE Computer* 34(2): 32–38.

Gartner (2001). *e-Government: What are Citizens Really Looking For?* London, Gartner Research.

Kettinger, W. and C. Lee (1997). 'Pragmatic Perspectives on the Measurement of Information Systems Service Quality.' *MIS Quarterly* (June): 223–240.

King, R. (1989). *Better Designs in Half the Time: Implementing QFD*. MA: GOAL/QPC, Methuen.

Kubicek, H. and M. Hagen (2001). 'Integrating e-Commerce and e-Government: the Case of Bremen Online Services.' *Designing e-Government*. J. Prins (ed.). The Hague, Kluwer Law International.

La Porte, T., C. Demchak and C. Friis (2001). 'Webbing Governance: Global Trends Across National-level Public Agencies.' *Communications of the ACM* 44(1): 63–67.

Nielsen, J. (1993). *Usability Engineering*. CA: Morgan Kaufmann.

Nielsen, J. (1999). 'User Interface Directions for the Web.' *Communications of the ACM* 42(1): 65–72.

Nielsen, J. (2000). *Designing Web Usability*. IN, New Riders.

Parasuraman, A. (1995). Measuring and monitoring service quality. *Understanding Services Management*. W. Glynn and J. Barnes (eds). Chichester, Wiley: 143–177.

Parasuraman, A., V. A. Zeithaml and L. Berry (1985). 'A Conceptual Model of Service Quality and its Implications for Future Research.' *Journal of Marketing* **49**(Fall): 41–50.

Parasuraman, A., V. A. Zeithaml and L. Berry (1988). 'SERVQUAL: A Multiple-Item Scale for Measuring Consumer Perceptions of Service Quality.' *Journal of Retailing* **64**(1): 12–40.

Pitt, L., R. Watson and C. Kavan (1995). 'Service Quality: A Measure of Information Systems Effectiveness.' *MIS Quarterly* (June): 173–187.

Pitt, L., R. Watson and C. Kavan (1997). 'Measuring Information Systems Service Quality: Concerns for a Complete Canvas.' *MIS Quarterly* June (209–221): 173–187.

Shostack, G. 1985. Planning the Service Encounter. *The Service Encounter*. J. Czepiel, M. Solomon and C. Surprenant (eds). Lexington, MA, Lexington Books.

Slabey, R. (1990). QFD: A Basic Primer. *Transactions from the Second Symposium on Quality Function Deployment*. Novi, Michigan.

Spool, J. (1999). *Web Site Usability*. CA, Morgan Kaufmann.

Strong, D. M., Y. W. Lee and R. Y. Wang (1997). 'Data Quality in Context.' *Communications of the ACM* **40**(5): 103–110.

Van Dyke, T., L. Kappelman and V. Prybutok (1997). 'Measuring Information Systems Service Quality: Concerns on the Use of the SERVQUAL Questionnaire.' *MIS Quarterly* (June): 195–208.

Zeithaml, V., A. Parasuraman and L. Berry (1990). *Delivering Quality Service: Balancing Customer Perceptions and Expectations*. New York: The Free Press.

Zeithaml, V. A., L. Berry and A. Parasuraman (1993). 'The Nature and Determinants of Customer Expectations of Service.' *Journal of the Academy of Marketing Science* **21**(1): 1–12.

11 The e-sourcing opportunity: from projects and ASPs to value networks*

Leslie P. Willcocks and Robert Plant

11.1 Introduction

A careful examination of the business internet strategies of 78 case study organizations, during the period 1999–2002, identified that rather than strategy formulation driving corporate success, it was in fact 'strategy execution' that separated leaders from laggards. The leading issues preventing agile behaviour amongst 'bricks and mortar' organizations during this period, were actually traditional inhibitors of superior performance, namely cultural and political issues as well as those stemming from large-scale business process re-engineering such as problems in the areas of skill set, process and technology integration (Plant, 2000; Willcocks and Plant, 2001, 2002). Even such industry sector leaders as Charles Schwab, Dell and Cisco Systems were finding that a successful deployment and execution of an online business strategy could take two or more years (Dell, 1999; Bunnell and Brate, 2000; Pottruck and Pearce, 2000; see also Note 1).

Against this background, we have found that moves to e-Business have been marked by the need for speed in the face of volatile competition, but also, during most of the study period, by the relative scarcity of requisite expertise and capability. Both have led companies to consider sourcing externally. In the specific area of information technology (IT) the motive, even from mid-2000, has been to implement e-Business projects swiftly using externally available expertise rather than bear the costs of delay and of developing new expertise internally. More recently, from mid-2001, the logic changed again with organizations under pressure to outsource to achieve cost containment, sometimes by adopting offshore outsourcing, or utilizing 'off-shore' or 'near-shore' IT staff for specific projects. Leidner

---

*   This chapter has been developed from 'How Corporations e-Source: From Business Technology Projects to Value Networks.' *Information Systems Frontiers* 5(2): 175–193, 2003, and our work on Application Service Provision (ASP) represented in *Netsourcing: Renting Business Applications and Services Over Networks*, Prentice-Hall, NJ, and additional unpublished research carried out in 2003.

et al. (2003) also point to four observable approaches to managing IT during economic decline. Taking a short-term perspective some have chosen to 'maintain the legacy', that is squeeze what we have, while others have gone for 'house cleaning' (sharper prioritization, 'quick-win' projects). Others have taken a longer-term perspective: either 'extending the life cycle' – that is, retaining the strategic plan while extending the time taken to deliver it – thus spreading costs over a longer period, or 'bulletproofing the infrastructure'. Clearly the last three could be supported by forms of external sourcing, but with a sharper focus than before on cost-effectiveness of such external options. In particular we saw several organizations intent on 'bulletproofing the infrastructure' who were looking to the adoption of Web services by early 2003.

More generally, though, companies have been recognizing that strategic outsourcing of non-core activities such as logistics can be appropriately contracted to a specialist provider. From late 2000, we found economic downturn and renewed concern for cost containment reinforcing this conclusion in many of the corporations we researched. In the world of e-Business, where supply chain integration is becoming more common, such sourcing decisions have become a core activity of strategic management. In several respects then, e-sourcing can be a fundamental enabler of moves to e-Business, especially where it is about making the best use of the mix of internal and external suppliers throughout an organization's business processes.

However, our study finds that accomplishing effective e-sourcing is far from simple, and if not managed properly can result in competitive disadvantage. The problem set decomposes into two fundamental aspects we deal with in this chapter. The first is: how can organizations effectively leverage external service providers to get their Web-based and e-Business projects in place on suitable time scales to compete? The second aspect relates not to development but to utilizing e-sourcing principles for the strategic conduct of business, namely: how do we participate in strategic sourcing with business allies to more effectively compete on what has been called a 'co-opetition' or 'core capabilities' basis? In this final section we will look at the types of sourcing criteria successful corporations apply. We also present, as a summary of our findings, two decision-making matrices for strategic e-sourcing.

11.2 Research background

In order to obtain an understanding of what separated out the leaders from the laggards in terms of e-Business execution a wide variety of organizations, 78 in total, were studied in USA, Europe and Australasia throughout 1999–2002. The objective was to examine a variety of sectors in order to identify generic and sector-specific practices characteristic of those organizations that lead, lag or otherwise stand out in their use of Web-based technologies. The study covered car manufacturers and retailers, technology suppliers, biotechnology companies, financial services including credit card, stock broking, insurance and banking firms, airlines, information providers, pharmaceutical companies and energy utilities. It also included a range of retailers and service operations, for example Coles Myer, Levi Strauss, Dixons, UPS, Alamo, Ryder, Lennar and also manufacturers, for example Lockheed and ElectroComponents. Subsequently, we studied over 250 international customers of application service provision and carried out 10 major case studies of application service providers (ASPs) and their customers (Kern et al., 2002b). We use this second research base, and additional unpublished research carried out in 2003 to further inform the argument of the chapter throughout.

In our discussions with the executives and associates at the case organizations of the first study it was necessary to have determined, in advance, a criteria for the determination of being a 'leading' or 'lagging' organization. This determination was made in part based upon the degree to which a Web site applied across the customer resource life cycle, the degree to which business-to-customer (B2C) was achieving disproportionate market growth/profitability or moving to profitability; extent to which customers were being attracted and retained; size of spend and expected returns on marketing and e-development; business-to-business (B2B) and B2C position in sector and against competition. We gained some quantified measures of these in each case, but more often subjective judgements by respondents. It should be remembered that the sample was opportunistic and deliberately spread across sectors and across what we pre-judged as differently performing organizations, and deliberate over-representation of what we thought to be leaders. With these criteria and qualifications, we found some 26 'leaders', 20 'laggards' and 32 medium performing organizations.

11.2.1 Sourcing Internet implementation capability

To make a mark in e-Business it is essential to have access to Internet implementation capability. This usually means using some external sources for specific capabilities. This section focuses on securing such capability for Internet development projects. Invariably any specific sourcing choice involves trade-offs. For example, it has been found that large-scale, single supplier outsourcing is particularly risky when compared to shorter-term (3–4 year) contracts with several suppliers (Lacity and Hirschheim, 1993; Lacity and Willcocks, 1998, 2001). It has also been found that in some circumstances insourcing was also a more effective option (Lacity and Hirschheim, 1996; Willcocks and Lacity, 1998) and that outsourcing can lead to strategic inflexibility (Weill and Broadbent, 1998). Fortunately, the sourcing of previous rounds of technology, together with the outcomes of outsourcing arrangements has been heavily, and empirically, researched, several useful references are given in Appendix 11A.

The sourcing routes our organizations took consisted of one or a mix of four possible options:

■ *Internal development*: Corporations created their Internet systems within the boundary of their organization.

■ *External development*: Corporations largely outsourced to third party management their systems and Web site development.

■ *Selective sourcing*: Corporations combined partial outsourcing with some in-house development.

■ *Insourcing (or 'partnering')*: Corporations selectively sourced, contracting external skills to work under in-house management, alongside in-house resources. Respondents referred frequently to this as 'partnering' by which they meant close working relationships rather than the more classic definition of 'shared risk and reward based on win–win relationships' (Lacity and Hirschheim, 1993). This insourcing/partnering approach has been found to particularly appropriate where the technology or its application is new, and where experience with the particular technology and its applicability in a business is lacking (Feeny et al., 1997). As we shall see, this last approach proved particularly effective amongst several of the leaders we studied, who required fast implementation together with high internal learning and skills building.

11.2.2 Sourcing e-development: four routes

The central dilemmas for most organizations considering their sourcing options for e-Business development were the trade-offs between speed to market, cost and organizational learning. The seemingly fastest route to securing Internet presence and capability – outsourcing – may well undermine the organizational need to build up internal understanding. The concern to develop internal knowledge is driven by anxiety that Internet-based business processes will be fundamental in the future. As finances tightened, and the external labour market became less tight from mid-2000, the question as to what the cost implications were of different sourcing options also came much more to the fore. In this section, we look at how leading organizations, as we defined them (see above) dealt with these dilemmas.

Figure 11.1 provides a framework for selecting appropriate sourcing options based on the drivers of speed, cost and learning. In addition to these four options, companies may choose to mix their sourcing, either

Outsource	Insource/partner
Advantages	**Advantages**
• Taps into existing expertise • Variety of external services offered • Quickly get up to speed	• Taps into existing expertise • Wider variety of external services on offer • Quickly get up to speed • Share/build expertise with vendor • Facilitate internalization of learning • Organization can focus upon other, for example infrastructure issues
Disadvantages	
• Does not immediately facilitate internalization of learning • Builds vendor expertise, not yours • Vendors may not be skilled in organizational processes • Organization may lack basic infrastructure • Requires in-house skills to manage the supplier • Cost (includes vendor profit margin) • Ensuring technological alignment with strategic alignment • Coordination of content owners?	**Disadvantages** • Requires in-house skills to staff and manage the project – availability? • Requires business managers'commitment to achieve business and technology alignment • Contract management costs to coordinate project
'Cheap-source'	**Internal development**
Advantages	**Advantages**
• Low investment • Low internal effort and resources • Gains from a 'follower' Internet strategy	• Internalize organizational learning • Understanding of organization's processes and integration of issues • Understanding of internal IT infrastructure
Disadvantages	**Disadvantages**
• Little internal learning, or from market • Functional only in relation to a specific type of business strategy • Does 'followership' pay with Internet applications?	• Opportunity cost of mistakes • First mover expense • Scarce IT skills resources may inhibit development • Will the business side commit necessary resources?

Figure 11.1: Four sourcing options for e-development.

selectively sourcing or changing their sourcing options over time (see the Alamo example in the mixed-development paths below).

The in-house development path

In our research, companies going successfully down this route included UPS, Motorola, Direct Line, Citicorp, Meritanordbanken and Dow Jones. The primary determinant of internal development was a credible project champion, usually an executive officer or CIO, who oversaw the 'Internet development group'. Success via this route was assisted by high level project sponsors who created space, facilitated the necessary budget and resources to get off the ground, and protected the project at all times. Typically a project champion provided and sustained the vision and the motivation to the project, and the political influence needed to move it forward. Such projects were often dubbed 'skunk works' by their developers. Interestingly, there is strong support for this approach being effective in more traditional business technology projects, though organizations have frequently not adopted it (Feeny et al., 1997; Earl, 1998).

We found a clear example of the 'skunk works' internal development route at stockbroker Charles Schwab. Upon seeing a browser-based demonstration of the company's traditional trading system, the co-CEOs created, protected and nurtured a new stand-alone Internet development group in order to acquire, learn and adapt the technology to their needs. Ultimately recreating the company based upon Internet technologies, Charles Schwab became, by 2000, the largest online brokerage company in the world.

Early movers used the skunk works teams to focus initially on organizational learning, gathering experience with the new medium, assessing the costs of development, the nature of the technology and its platform. This tied in with the organization's ability to determine which technologies were worth pursuing early on, and which were not. Many of the skunk works projects were funded from R&D budgets, initially at low cost. A power utility executive also took this approach in 1995:

> we knew that we had to have a vanity page, the static stuff out there but we knew that we needed to understand from an IT perspective 'how do you make it more active?'

The second step on the internal development route was to build a strong technology infrastructure. Seen as the key to technological and organizational flexibility by many CIOs and executives, the IT infrastructure was critical to the successful transition of the Internet presence from the static to the dynamic. The correct infrastructure can be defined as one facilitating the implementation of value-added services through different organizational business drivers, so delivering a positive return on investment.

The executives and CIOs involved in our study indicated that in order to be successful, the infrastructure had to be designed to accommodate the major issues facing each company in its marketplace, in essence creating a market-space dimension of the organization. The creation of a strong yet flexible infrastructure was a precursor to the third element of the development – that of business process integration. This was the point at which companies had to leverage the organizational learning and experience acquired through the internal development route into customer-added value. Interestingly, a similar pattern of effective development has also been observed in parallel studies (Ware et al., 1998; Kalakota and Robinson, 2001).

Motorola provides an interesting case of effective internal development. They moved from skunk works experimental activities through process integration to highly market-focused value-adding e-Business. They then institutionalized their organizational learning through the creation of a specialist group. Their journey started in 1994 when a senior manager with a marketing background was searching for a communications vehicle to underpin the Motorola Online Channel Access concept to bring on board its supply chain partners. Emerging Web-based technologies provided opportunities that eventually resulted in an e-Business development plan as it became recognized across Motorola that the technologies had large-scale implications. By late 1994, 24 activities related to Web-based technologies had been grouped into four chronological phases; creating awareness through a technology presence; then coordinating the brand and how the company was represented on the Web; providing a service to customers and channel partners whilst achieving cost and labour reductions; finally moving to revenue generation and one-to-one marketing.

An initial Web presence was established in 1995, followed by 9 months spent integrating back-end systems. Through 1996 to 1999 the number of e-Business initiatives and groups grew across 10 business units. By 1999 an Architecture and Process group had been established consisting of a Director and eight technical developers responsible for back-end systems and Web presentation. Their role was to deal with the business units, keep Web content fresh and meet corporate guidelines. This centralized pool formed an organizational resource pool and also oversaw coordination and planning for all e-Business development initiatives into 2001.

The 'cheap-sourcing' path

An organization that is not pressured in its market-space to be at the leading edge of Internet presence would be advised to apply a 'cheap-sourcing' principle to its Internet development. We found this to often be the case with organizations occupying niche market positions, for example, a New York-based jeweller, whose site did not initially facilitate a direct sales model and that did not change with the frequency of a retail site, could be managed at relatively low cost. The primary driver for such organizations was the promotion of the brand; a direct sales channel would dilute potentially the overall corporate marketing position rather than reinforce it. However, due to the need for a sophisticated branding image to be maintained, the company may wish to outsource the sites graphic design work, marketing and site development to specialists. It may not be in the long-term plan of the organization to ever have a direct sales channel and therefore the need to internalize that learning is minimized. However, this may be to put a positive spin on what is in fact lagging practice. For example, by 2001, the jeweller mentioned above had developed its site for selling its products over the Web.

Another dimension to 'cheap-sourcing' since mid-2000 has been the reduced demand for e-Business development services and the slacker market for IT expertise, together with widespread requirement across the developed economies to reduce IT budgets (Fisher, 2001; London, 2001). In our sample we found some organizations responding to the latter by cutting back on e-Business initiatives, sometimes quite drastically. For example, UK retailer Safeway cancelled a number of pilot initiatives for online shopping in 2001. Other organizations have taken advantage of changed economic conditions to cheap-source e-Business developments, provided these were focused on low risk, internal productivity improvements; as we found, for example, at AirProducts and Office Depot.

The outsourcing path

Many organizations find themselves in the position of needing to rapidly develop a net presence; yet do not see any immediate economic advantage in extending its internal IT capability. In this situation, the most advantageous policy was to outsource the development. Here Internet use is developed by bringing in external consultants and service providers to inject the expertise otherwise gained through skunk works projects. Such external providers offer services in a variety of forms including Internet agencies, technical and ASPs, direct marketing agencies and relationship marketers. However, ownership responsibility for the development should still belong with the contracting organization and issues such as maintaining infrastructure and providing business leadership still necessitate internal attention and action. Actual Web development learning will be passed to the outsourcer, however, though internal learning on contract and supplier management skills still takes place. Some internal technology learning will also occur where the Net technologies and the existing infrastructure interface.

An organization in this situation was Lego. In March 1999 it was trying to establish its World Shop for its new children's game products. Competitively, speed was of the essence. As a result Lego outsourced its site and e-Business development to IBM, though it hired a separate independent consultancy to do Web site design work. Similarly, Jamjar, an online motoring information and car sale service, set up in May 2000 by UK-based insurer Direct Line. According to its IT Director:

> It's a major development, and we went for external hosting, because it's a huge system, with huge volumes, running 24 hours a day seven days a week.

The Jamjar application was developed by Quidnunc and hosted by SiteHost a Computacenter e-Business outsourcing service. In turn SiteHost uses the data centre facilities of Web host Exodus where it has its own service operations centre.

The insourcing/partnering path

Should the rate of change in an industry be rapid and the resources of the organization become stretched too far then competitive edge can be lost. This is counter-productive from an organizational learning perspective and requires 'insourcing' to become the primary development practice. Thus in several corporations infrastructure building, balancing and development, were performed by an internal group. Graphical Internet site design or other specialized tasks were externally sourced, and business process consultants were engaged to integrate the new channels created through the Internet with existing processes in the most effective way possible. American Express provides a successful example of this approach:

> It goes to our basic philosophy which is we do not have to build everything. The question is how do we get our products and services integrated into Internet interactive commerce. And you do it through people who are already working on it. (Amex senior executive).

Mixed development paths

We found organizations adopting different sourcing options at different times, or for different purposes, in their moves to the Internet. As we saw above, insurer Direct Line took the outsourcing route for its Jamjar online business. Direct Line was set up in the late 1980s to sell motor insurance direct via the phone. The business expanded into other types of insurance during the 1990s. In the late 1990s it also set up Directline.com to sell insurance services via the net. However, this was developed in-house for less than £500 000. According to its IT director:

> Directline.com is very much at the heart of our insurance business. It's totally and tightly integrated with our core systems. We couldn't have done it so quickly had it been outsourced.

Interestingly here, not only was the application seen as core business, but also, because internal expertise and business-specific knowledge were higher than that available on the market, the necessary speed could actually be achieved by in-house sourcing. Tesco, the UK's leading food retailer, adopted another mixed approach. In 1998 Tesco piloted its online shopping business, Tesco Direct (subsequently Tesco.com), with 20 000 grocery products and six trial sites. By March 2000 Tesco.com was part of multi-channel strategy, with some 100 stores involved and looking to gain more than half its online revenues from non-grocery items. In 1999 it made losses of £11.2 million on sales of £125 million but by end of FY 2003 Tesco.com had gained a 65% share of the UK Internet grocery market with 110 000 orders in the UK each week. This generated a £12.2 million profit on sales of £447 million a 26% increase in sales year over year. It had spent

£21 million on developing its Internet offering in-house, and in mid-2000 invested another £35 million. However, in early 2000 Tesco also entered a less familiar, but faster moving market – online banking – in which it planned to leverage the power of its brand. The Tesco Personal Finance service was developed in 3 months through utilizing technology developed by its partner, the Royal Bank of Scotland (RBS), only needing to modify the software to allow customers to transfer money to and from their accounts at other banks. Both partners invested in a series of Compaq 3000 servers, running internally developed software, allowing Tesco customers to link in with the RBS IBM9672 mainframe, which holds account details. Here the need for speed, and the availability of a complementary partner in an unfamiliar business became the key determinants of the sourcing decision. In 2003 Tesco.com also extended their reach to the customer through technology, providing a service that facilitates the download to PDA's of the details of Tesco's 20 000 grocery items, which can then be accessed, and orders forwarded to the Tesco.com site for processing. By late 2003 Tesco was also demonstrating its maturity in leveraging outsourcing by entering the retail telecoms service business with three partners. While Tesco provided the brand and customer list, Cable and Wireless provided telecommunications capability, Serista billing and support and Vertex Customer Management offered customer service competence.

An example that brings together much of this discussion is the development route pictured in Figure 11.2. Figure 11.2 shows how a corporation may well evolve through different parts of Figure 11.1, depending on circumstances and different perceptions of the relative importance of cost, organizational learning and speed to the Net. The path taken between 1995 and 2001 by Alamo, the US-based car hire company can be described in these terms.

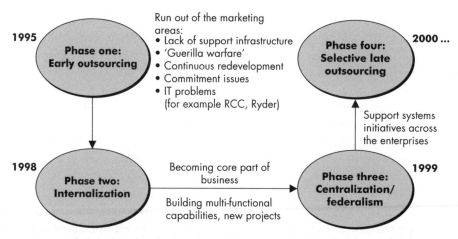

Figure 11.2: Alamo: evolving through a four-phase mixed sourcing path. Adapted from Forester Research Model.

Alamo outsourced its early Internet development. It ran into a number of problems. The Web site was too stand-alone and not linked back into the technology infrastructure. It suffered a number of technical hitches and required continuous redevelopment. It also experienced some supplier commitment issues:

> *The one issue I had was ownership. An internal group, if I call them and say our Web site is down, they feel it like I feel it; it is hitting profitability. A contractor does not have the same level of business commitment … and if they are not enamoured with this particular arrangement they might not give you quite as good service. Whereas with an internal service you would have clearly defined roles and responsibilities … (Alamo marketing executive).*

By 1998 Alamo began internalizing Internet development, realizing that Web-based technologies were becoming a core part of the business. A series of Web projects were launched and in 1999 a central group was developed to provide enterprise-wide service, support and control of business units' Internet initiatives.

This pattern – of early outsourcing to gain the advantages of speed to the net, followed by internalization due to the rising business importance of the Internet and the need for internal learning and capability – was frequently repeated in other organizations we studied, for example at Ryder Systems Inc. and P&O. The pattern also seemed to reflect those organizations' own increased learning about the advantages and disadvantages of different sourcing options. This learning also sharpened their ability to make more selective and precise sourcing decisions during phases two and three of Figure 11.2, and also undertake selective late outsourcing of development and Web operations in a fourth phase, on criteria we shall look at in the next section. Figure 11.1 provides a summary of the issues that leading organizations tended to take into account when attempting to achieve trade-offs and mitigate risks in the choice and management of their sourcing options.

11.3 e-Sourcing: from projects and technology to strategic partnering

So far this chapter has focused on sourcing technical development for e-Business projects. But e-Business sourcing is not solely about balancing learning and early use of new technology. It is also about making best use of the mix of internal and external suppliers throughout the organization's business processes. This involves understanding who has what core competences. In this section we examine the possibilities for more strategic forms of external sourcing as they emerged in many of the researched organizations – throughout the customer resource life cycle, in supply chains and through value networks. Two examples from our study organizations are then used to illustrate leading sourcing practice when partnering strategically. Here 'strategic partnering' can be distinguished from the insourcing form of partnering described above which here is restricted to e-development activities (see also Figure 11.1). Strategic partnering involves a much more long-term commitment to work together to underpin each other's strategies, as complementors in a competitive arena. Levels of dependence and trust need to be much higher, especially as each party will often be responsible for integrated, strategically critical activities of the other. We start by looking at two notions central to these forms of strategic partnering – those of core competence and 'co-opetition' – and see how these concepts have been applied in our research sample within the e-Business arena, notably around the customer resource life cycle, supply chain and in forming value networks.

During the 1990s there was a move in many organizations to focus upon core competencies as a business strategy. Commentators such as Pralahad and Hamel (1990, 1994), and Quinn (1992) argued that an organization can only be effective at relatively few core activities, and should concentrate on developing these to world class. Anything else should be eliminated, minimized or outsourced. Within this work we refer to core competence in relation to a distinctive, not easily replicable assembly of skills, techniques, ways of organizing, technologies and know-how that enable an organization to acquire, deploy and leverage positioning and resources, including relationships, in pursuit of business advantage (Feeny and Willcocks, 1998).

Debates about a specific firm's core competence are invariably bedevilled by two issues which both apply to e-Business. Firstly, it is frequently not easy to distinguish between a core and a non-core competence. For example, what is the scope of a core competence, and for how long can it remain a competitively differentiating factor? In our sample, Federal Express and UPS would recognize some of their core competence as lying in parcel logistics, but how do they differentiate themselves from each other, and what implications does the Internet have for redefining core and non-core in these firms? Below we will see Dell and Cisco effectively achieving distinctive definitions of core and non-core activities in the context of doing business over the Internet. Secondly, and relatedly, core competences, built over time as ways of dealing with problems and achieving stakeholder value, can create rigidities and resistances to value shifts in the competitive arena. This can be especially damaging in the fast-moving Internet-based business environment, where survival will often, according to many sources, belong to the fast and focused (Willcocks and Plant, 2000; Bornheim, 2001; Chen, 2001; Seybold, 2001). Again we will use illustrative examples to show such dangers, and how some organizations have avoided them.

In our research we found three notable areas where sample organizations adopted 'strategic partnering' sourcing principles in their moves to e-Business. These were in externally sourcing at points around the customer resource life cycle, in the supply chain, and through virtual integration and the creation of value networks.

11.3.1 Strategic partnering[2] in the customer resource life cycle

In order to exploit the e-opportunity, many researchers have stressed the criticality of gaining re-purchase decisions by managing the customer's total experience in such ways that the customer would regularly prefer the organization's products/services (Seybold and Marshak, 1998; Schwarz, 1999; Mahadevan, 2000; Feeny, 2001).

If the customer resource life cycle of an online business is broken down into eight major activity areas, as suggested by Feeny (2001) it is clear that the technical means and businesses exist for each area to be adequately sourced by an external service provider.

1 *Attracting customers*: Many companies basically provide technologies and services that attract and deliver targeted audiences to an e-Business. Services that we observed being used by sampled organizations, for example, Link Exchange and Befree, can provide fully developed customer affiliate programmes. We found DoubleClick offering targeted advertising.

2 *Informing customers*: We found organizations like OnDisplay.com and Cardonet.com acting as content mediators, serving up-to-date, relevant content to a Web site. Consider one of our researched organizations W. W. Grainger, in the maintenance, repair and operations business. It offers hard goods supplies to US businesses. Traditionally this has been done by printing 2.6 million catalogues and operating over 500 physical stores. In 1998 it partnered with OnDisplay, which then proceeded to utilize the information from 2000 plus supplier databases to develop online interactive catalogues for Grainger's three Web sites. Grainger's online sales exceeded US$150 million in 2000, though it pulled back from some of its Web site exposure during 2001.

3 *Customizing (self) service*: We found companies like Firepond.com, Selectica.com and Calico.com build configuration software that is such a strong feature of the Dell site offering build-to-order computers, and the Cisco Systems and Cabletron Systems sites selling routers and networking gear. Calico provides Cabletron with a configuration workbench that prompts a customer as a salesperson would. It showed product features, analyses the customer's needs, budget and time constraints, identifies compatible components, suggests options and generated price quotes. It also generated an

order that automatically passed to Cabletron's fulfilment systems that in turn updated stock, shipping and accounting databases.

4   *Transacting*: We found many companies, notably Ariba, Commerce One, Oracle, Moai Technologies offering market-making platforms. Ariba offered shared commerce services in B2B marketplaces. Several of Ariba's 142 major customers in 2003 were included in our sample included American Express, Cisco Systems, Charles Schwab and Chevron. Commerce One offered Web-based B2B procurement and platforms for creating vertical trading communities. Customers included British Telecom and Booz-Allen Hamilton. Moai Technologies provided B2B exchanges and auction platforms.

5   *Securing payment*: We found many organizations and customers having concerns over the security of payments over the Web. These concerns have encouraged the development of companies to look after the payment and financing functions of online transactions. Thus we found eCredit.com providing real-time credit underwriting engines, while Paylinx offered systems that support credit and debit card transactions.

6   *Customer support*: Many organizations new to e-Business felt unable to provide the necessary level of information, problem resolution, advice and order tracking for their customers. As a result external service providers have developed offerings for, for example, call centre facilities, live online services and the checking of order status.

7   *e-Fulfilment*: This represents a major potential area for new and fast growing e-Businesses to outsource. By 2001, in B2B, we saw many businesses outsourcing supply chain management systems that facilitated order fulfilment and supply and demand forecasting. We found many examples of companies providing such services included Celarix, Manugistics and i2. In addition many e-fulfilment companies had developed for the B2C market. As one example, Entertainment UK in the Kingfisher Group developed for its own use an internal warehousing and e-fulfilment capability for items such as CDs and videos. During 2000 they also set up as an e-fulfilment business for the end-customers of other supplier companies such as radio channels making special offers to listeners.

8   *Adaptive customer profiling*: Rather than developing the necessary software and internal capability, some companies were hiring collaborative filtering and data mining services from providers such as Verbind.com, Datasage.com and E-piphany.com. Verbind, for example, was providing sample corporation American Express with its LifeTime product. This analysed up to one year's online transaction data, establishes each customer's buying pattern, and enables e-mail and interactive messaging to customers and one-to-one marketing[3].

At one level these would appear to be exciting and highly functional developments. However, outsourcing extensively throughout the customer resource life cycle raised a number of issues for our researched organizations. Handing over control of activities creates exposure to risk. What level of exposure is judicious, and how can the risks be mitigated? Does increased dependence on suppliers mean that deeper relationships are required? At what stage might cooperators become competitors? In answering these questions one conclusion is clear as we shall see in the Cisco and Dell illustrative cases below – whatever the line of business, extensive fee-for-service outsourcing, and the treatment of every activity as a commodity to be outsourced is rarely appropriate.

A particularly profound problem occurs. How important is firm's ownership of the relationship with its end-customers? In practice, if this relationship is compromized through outsourcing, then so is a potential source of competitive advantage. Consider one company (A) we studied. Throughout 2000 it employed an e-fulfilment firm (B) to deliver goods but insisted that these be delivered to A's warehouse and not to the end-customer. At no time did B know who the end-customer was; it was only given enough information to deliver goods in the right quantity and at the right time to A. These goods were then relabelled by A and delivered to the end-customer. In this scenario, conditioned by previous experiences, A's behaviour was designed to protect its customer database and customer relationships. In these situations a company must be very careful to follow the examples of Cisco and Dell (described below) and delineate its core competencies (and how these may shift over time), but also put in suitable financial, information and managerial control processes, while developing strong co-dependent relationships with its complementor suppliers.

11.3.2 Strategic partnering[2] developments in the supply chain

Sourcing issues also arose from extensive use of third parties in the e-supply chain. By 2001 we found most firms investing over 10 times more in this area than in their B2C initiatives. By that date 'bricks and mortar' companies moving to the Web still had plenty of scope for radical improvements, further enabled by newer applications and external suppliers entering the arena. Many amongst our study organizations were to be found into late 2001 still developing supply chain management, enterprise resource planning and customer relationship management systems, often with external assistance. All had built electronic links with their suppliers and with their retail outlets, and were at different points down the road of making these Web-enabled. Rather fewer were doing this in a more sophisticated fashion, for example using auctions and exchanges in order to deal directly and more efficiently with suppliers and also with customers. This was especially the case during 2001.

As indicated above, some had also moved to handing over much of the e-fulfilment to external parties, while companies like Sun and Cisco

Systems had handed over most of their manufacturing and delivery to other parties. In all this, few had developed the suite of highly integrated synchronized production scheduling, collaborative product design and development, logistics and demand planning systems that enabled value networks to develop such as those at Dell and Cisco Systems (see below). Given this variety, we will look at the implications of strategic partnering for just one e-application that gained popularity during 2000 – that of Web-enabled exchanges in the supply chain. We will use the specific example of one of the more developed in our sample – that of Covisint.

In November 1999, Ford and General Motors announced separate Internet-based trading exchanges for their supply chains. Ford would partner with Oracle on AutoXchange, and General Motors with Commerce One on TradeXchange. By February 2000 a superior model had emerged. A single exchange would establish a global standard, and also be much more efficient. Ford, General Motors and DaimlerChrysler agreed to collaborate on a single automotive-parts exchange run through the Internet. The technology partners would be Commerce One and Oracle. The exchange was expected to deal with over US$300 billion in transactions annually, and achieve significant cost reductions for the car companies. Ford claimed, for example, a US$10 million saving on a US$75 million purchase on its first full use of AutoXchange. Other carmakers, like Toyota, Renault and Honda also considered joining the exchange. At the same time Ford was updating its customer-oriented Web sites for new and second-hand cars, announcing a joint venture with software developer Trilogy. By Autumn 2000 Covisint as the exchange became called had processed its first live transactions. These developments are shown in Figure 11.3. During 2001 Covisint was actively engaged in managing live transactions for its constituent suppliers and car manufacturer customers. By 2003 it was busily achieving significant cost savings for its purchasers.

During 2000 many such exchanges were announced across industries, though their development slowed markedly during 2001. However, although these developments sounded attractive, they do hide a number of complexities. Focusing on just the Ford/GM/DC example, the substantial cost savings for the car manufacturers also implied downward pressure on supplier prices and some switch of bargaining power from suppliers to the manufacturers. The auto exchange would also charge up to 0.5% commission on transactions. This amount would go to the manufacturers and technology developers running the exchange. So, how neutral would this joint venture be? Would other car manufacturers using the exchange feel excluded from influence and access to certain benefits? Clearly, the exchange represents considerable migration of value and power in the supply chain. Not surprisingly, therefore, by April 2000 Volkswagen had announced its own marketplace for procurement,

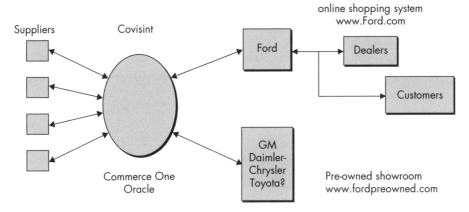

Suppliers   Covisint

online shopping system
www.Ford.com

Ford → Dealers

Customers

GM
Daimler-
Chrysler
Toyota?

Commerce One
Oracle

Pre-owned showroom
www.fordpreowned.com

Potential: US$500 billion trading annually

Issues
- Supplier cooperation
- Pressure on supplier prices
- Commission for transactions (¼–½%)

- Competitive edge information/concerns
- Relationships with suppliers
- Threat to dealers/links to retail side

Figure 11.3: Covisint: remodelling supply and delivery (early 2001).

forming a strategic partnership with IBM, i2 Technologies and Ariba. In the face of such proliferation of markets, six of the largest automotive-parts suppliers themselves announced that they would work together on joint technology solutions because of the problem of 'repetitive costs'.

The trading exchange also raised competitive edge concerns amongst some potential participants. As early as March 2000, Toyota suggested that it would restrict its participation to trading only in basic commodity items and office supplies. The company had several concerns about the exchange, centring on quality assurance and security on an open network. For Taadaki Jagawa, vice president of procurement: *the other companies are our rivals and we are competing on parts. We do not share information about our components*, including information about the price of core parts. Moreover: *our parts are not purchased through a bidding process. We buy them by building a relationship with suppliers over time.* Essentially Toyota saw its suppliers more as partners, and believed the close relationships with them gave a competitive edge in quality assurance but also in lead time on new car development. The spot pricing encouraged by a more transparent market could erode such relationships.

Further developments in e-Business on the customer side could also threaten the role of dealers in the distribution chain – a notoriously sensitive area, analogous with Web-enabled disintermediation in the travel agency and insurance broking industries. Meanwhile in the supply chain there may well be a number of more technical problems. One is non-repudiation – where an online company must be able to guarantee to a supplier that it can legally prove a purchaser's identity and activities in a court of law. A second is establishing standards for information exchange. XML on its own is as broad as data itself. Moreover technology suppliers are still much more enthusiastic about it than the majority of users, who typically will have different starting points on data protocols. All the issues considered in this section make clear that external 'strategic partnering' in remodelled supply and distribution chains can be a lot more complicated than they first seem. Once again we will see in the Dell and Cisco cases below the foundations of effective e-sourcing practice. We also need to acknowledge that the principles gleaned from more traditional forms of IT outsourcing (see Note 3), and also learned form implementing e-Business projects (as described above), still directly apply.

11.3.3 Strategic partnering[2] towards virtual integration

As organizations move to e-Business we have also seen new forms of organizing, such as the 'M' form and syndication (Moore, 1998; Werbach, 2000), as well as a resurgence of more familiar ideas. Thus concepts such as 'co-opetition' and the virtual organization have considerable salience in the e-Business world, and imply considerable use of external allies and service providers (Nalebuff and Brandenburger, 1996; Child and Faulkner, 1998). Co-opetition is about collaborating to compete, by allying with firms with complementary capabilities to mutual competitive advantage. In a schema that translates immediately into the e-world, Nalebuff and Brandenburger (1996) posit a value network consisting of the company, its customers, suppliers, competitors and complementors. A player is your complementor if customers value your product/service more when they also have the other player's offering than when they have your product/service alone. Organizations have multiple roles in a value network. For example, in our sample, on any given day AT&T might find, for different parts of their businesses, Motorola might be a supplier, customer, competitor or complementor.

A related concept is that of the virtual organization. As Child and Faulkner (1998) point out, few companies are excellent at all functions. Therefore greater value can be created if each concentrates on only the functions it does best, and relies on cooperating partners to carry out the other functions. In the value network, this requires cooperative attitudes; clear understanding of central objectives, electronic (increasingly Web-enabled) coordination and communication, and flexible modules, cultures and workforces.

In our research, Cisco Systems and Dell provided clear examples of virtual integration. Cisco's strategy was found to be threefold: do what it's best at, make acquisitions (81 in the period between 1993 and 2003), and secure alliances. By mid-2000 it had outsourced most of its production to 37 factories. Suppliers made all components, and carried out 55% of sub-assembly work and 55% of final assembly. All factories were linked via the Net, and an intranet was used for most internal work at Cisco.

The internal pages received 28 million hits a month. Use of the Web was saving Cisco an estimated US$500–800 million a year during 2000. Eighty-four per cent of sales were through the Web site, which allowed customized configuring and checking by customers. Eight-five per cent of customer queries were handled online.

All this enabled a high degree of virtuality. According to one respondent: 'we can go from quote to cash without ever touching a physical asset or piece of paper. You've heard of JIT manufacturing, well this is not-at-all manufacturing.' However, Cisco has been careful to control and dominate the value network. Thus it has maintained three factories itself to understand and give flexibility to its manufacturing base. Cisco designs production methods and uses the Internet to monitor operations closely. It also controls research and development. So for new production methods, for example: 'the source code is developed here and maintained here. So the innovation is all at Cisco.'

Dell has explicitly described its strategy as that of virtual integration. In 2000 it made more than US$40 million a day (over 50% of total sales) via the Internet. Its success is invariably put down to its customer focus. However, an underlying vital component, especially into the difficult marketplace of 2001, has been sourcing strategy and management. According to the CEO: 'I don't think we could have created a $12 billion business in 13 years if we had tried to be vertically integrated.' With fewer physical assets and people it has had fewer things to manage and fewer barriers to change. Through IT-enabled coordination and control of its value network of suppliers and partners, Dell can operate with less than a 20 000 rather than an 80 000 workforce. In the supply arena it has focused on making long-term deals and commitments with as few leading suppliers as possible. Datalinks measure and feed back supplier performance in real-time. Close ties with suppliers ('their engineers are part of our design and implementation teams') mean that Dell buys in innovation from its suppliers. Information technologies allow speed and information sharing and much more intense forms of collaboration. It also means that suppliers can be notified precisely of Dell's daily product requirements. This has also allowed Dell to focus on inventory velocity, and keeping inventory levels very low.

Dell has also sought strong partnering relationships with key customers. Seen as complementors, customers are often involved in research and development, where Dell's focus is on relevant, easy-to-use technology, improvements in the customer buying process, keeping costs down and superior quality in manufacturing. Dell also offers service centres in large organizations to be close to the customer. Thus in 2001 Boeing had over 100 000 Dell PCs and 30 dedicated Dell staff on the premises.

For present purposes, the criteria these companies are using to make sourcing decisions are particularly pertinent, showing ways of avoiding the strategic partnering dangers flagged above. Clearly Cisco has adopted practices that leverage complementors and suppliers whilst enabling Cisco to dominate the value network it has created. On our analysis, the Dell criteria for what are core competencies, and what can be safely outsourced, but under a strong regime of financial, managerial and information control, would seem to be sixfold:

1 Dell focuses its attention on all activities that create value for the customer. This includes R&D involving 1500 people and a budget of US $250 million that focuses on customer-facing activity and the identification of 'relevant' technology. It tends to outsource as much as possible all other activities that need to get done.

2 Dell carefully defines its core capability as a solutions provider and technology navigator. It uses partners/suppliers as much as possible to deal with such matters as products, components, technology development, assembly.

3 A key core task is coordination as against 'doing' tasks such as manufacturing and delivery.

4 Dell takes responsibility for seeking and improving all arrangements that give it speed and focus in the marketplace and in its organizational arrangements.

5 A key core capability is control of the value network through financial and informational means to ensure requisite speed, cost and quality. What does Dell control? Basically the company appoints and monitors reliable, responsive, leading edge suppliers of technology and quality.

This last point is worth developing because informational control emerges as a cardinal external sourcing risk mitigator in our study. Dell treats information management and orchestration as a core capability. This is an outcome of two strategic moves on its part. The first is to convert as much of the physical assets ('atoms') it manages into digital form ('bytes'). The second move is to outsource as much as possible of the remaining physical tasks and assets, while rendering management of the digital world a core set of tasks.

In Dell's and Cisco's external sourcing practices we found strong examples of what other researched organizations were discovering as the more effective ways of managing suppliers and complementors. In particular, Dell revealed itself as having massive clarity about what was core, and what was not. This enabled it to place 'non-core' activities as candidates for external sourcing, and make decisions on the best type of external sourcing. A further lesson from Dell and Cisco, especially where strategic partnering was being undertaken, was the critical importance of maintaining financial, managerial and information control in the relationship with any external supplier/partner thus offsetting many of the risks identified above. In the final section, to assist e-sourcing decisions, we bring together such learning from our study into two linked, summary matrices.

11.4 Bringing IT together: management implications for e-sourcing

Our research has made clear that, whether at the IT, project or strategic partnering level, fortunately, we can apply to e-Business sourcing many of the principles learned in other contexts in the 1980s and 1990s. Cisco and Dell are not so far removed from what has been called the original virtual organization, clothing manufacturer/retailer Benetton (Camuffo et al., 2001). Moreover many of the practices observed in IT sourcing over the last decade can apply directly to the e-world (Lacity and Hirschheim, 1995; Garner, 1998; Kern et al., 2002a). The purpose here is to build on this knowledge and focus on bringing the effective e-sourcing principles we have observed in action in our study organizations together. As such the two matrices we now develop incorporate the learning from studying the sourcing of e-Business development (including that identified in Figure 11.1), and the varieties of strategic partnering identified above.

Our research suggests that e-Business sourcing must start with the business imperative. In Figure 11.4 we identify two dimensions of business activities. The first is in terms of its contribution to competitive positioning. In IT, mainframes and payroll applications are frequently perceived as commodities, while British Airways' yield management system gives the company a competitive edge in ticket pricing and is regarded as a differentiator. The second is in terms of the underpinning

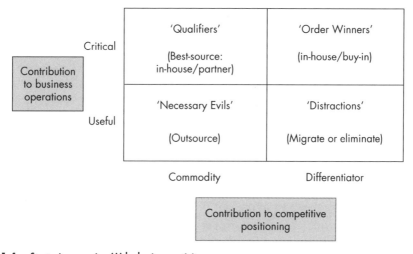

Figure 11.4: Strategic e-sourcing (A) by business activity.

it provides to business operations. As a broad example one Web site might be critical – as is the case for Amazon (no Web site and no business) – or it could be merely useful – for example the New York jeweller cited earlier. These two dimensions create four quadrants.

Let us use the Dell example to illustrate the thinking here. 'Order Winners' are those business activities that critically and advantageously differentiate a firm from its competitors. The five Dell items listed first in the previous section fall here. The strong message here is to carry out these core activities in-house, buying in resources to work under internal control where expertise is lacking and a build-up of internal learning is required. 'Qualifiers' are business activities that must be carried out as a necessary minimum entry requirement to compete in a specific sector. Historically, for airlines, aircraft maintenance systems are critical, but generally do not differentiate the airlines from each other – though of course the basis of competition may change over time. Thus in 1996 the CEO of British Airways argued that the brand, routes and the yield management system were 'core' – in principle all else could be outsourced. Often critical differentiators can become commodities and move to this quadrant. Thus, were Dell's excellent customer service ever to become an industry standard, it would be redefined as a 'Qualifier'. As at 2001, assembly, manufacturing and delivery are being defined by Dell as 'Qualifiers'. These should be best sourced and can be done by third parties, where they meet the right cost and competence criteria (see below).

'Necessary Evils' (a respondent's phrase, not ours) are tasks that have to be done but are not core activity and gain no strategic purchase from their fulfilment. Dell has tended to cut down on administration, inventory and payroll tasks, for example, and would seek to outsource as much of these sorts of activities as possible. 'Distractions' are failed or failing attempts to differentiate the organization from its competitors. The goal here must be to eliminate the activity or migrate it to another quadrant. Thus in 1989 Dell opened retail outlets, but soon discovered this development was not going to be successful, and fell back on its direct business model. It also during the early 1990s suffered from 'functionality creep' in its notebook designs, a practice ended when it was realised that this attempt to differentiate meant little to customers. A more profound mistake is not to notice until too late the value shifts in a specific competitive arena, for example IBM against Microsoft and Intel in the late 1980s/early 1990s PC market. Up to 2001, Dell had made few mistakes in this area. In fact we found its low cost Web-based distribution strategy giving it a critical competitive edge on pricing during 2001. Perhaps this resulted from its CEO's explicit recognition that 'looking for value shifts is probably the most important dimension of leadership'[4].

It is not enough, however, to identify a potential use for service providers or business allies. What is available on the market also requires detailed analysis. If the market is not cheap, capable or mature

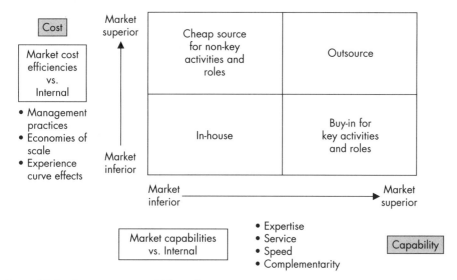

Figure 11.5: Strategic e-sourcing (B) by market comparison.

enough, then the organization will need to seek a largely in-house solution. Therefore the business activity analysis of Figure 11.4 needs to be supplemented by a second matrix to fully capture the major elements for consideration when utilizing the market.

In Figure 11.5 we plot the cost-efficiencies and the capabilities the market can offer against carrying out tasks internally. Where the market can carry out a task cheaper and better, then outsourcing is the obvious decision but only for 'Qualifiers' and 'Necessary Evils'. An example is Federal Express providing customer delivery for Dell. Where the market offers an inferior cost and capability then in-house sourcing will be the better alternative (assuming that 'Distractions' are best not sourced at all). Where the market offers a better-cost deal, then this should be taken, but only for non-key activities ('Necessary Evils'). Where the market offers superior capability but at a premium price above what the in-house cost might be, then there may still be good reasons for insourcing or strategic partnering with the third party, not least to leverage and learn from their expertise, and apply it to 'Qualifying' and 'Order Winning' tasks.

11.5 Conclusion: developments

Thus Figures 11.4 and 11.5 help to summarize the main criteria that can be used for making e-sourcing, and, in fact, many other business sourcing decisions. The matrices illustrate the decision criteria we uncovered that mitigate the often-significant risks that arise when attempting to leverage external parties for organizational advantage.

But, as this chapter illustrates, making the right sourcing decisions does not guarantee their successful implementation. As in the cases of Dell and Cisco, internal capabilities must be developed to manage the risks, relationships and performance issues inherent in the extensive use of external service providers and business allies[5]. This too endorses the relevance of findings elsewhere on outsourcing implementation practices in the more traditional IT world (Earl, 1996; Feeny and Willcocks, 1998; Garner, 1998; Klepper and Jones, 1998).

At the time of writing, prospects for e-sourcing were interesting. Hagel (2002) and Kern et al. (2002b) make a positive case for much greater use of external services over the Net, but both point to the false start 'Netsourcing' has experienced in the 2000–3003 period. As ever the issues are only partly technological. There is also the supplier issue of finding customers and viable business models in a period of economic decline, and of customer's ability to mature their handling of the realities and risks of taking these options (Kern et al., 2002c). Meanwhile organizations have variously taken on board the offshore and nearshore outsourcing opportunities being provided by many developing countries, as indeed have suppliers themselves. IBM and Accenture are not alone in having their own large offshore sites in India, for example, as customer cost pressures drive suppliers themselves to cheaper alternatives. Finally, the biggest potential growth area seemed to be in business process outsourcing (BPO), where a supplier takes over the commodity aspects of a business process (for example claims handling) (or of a function for example human resources and procurement). This implied taking over any related moves to the Internet, as for example occurred where BAE Systems outsourced its HR function to Xchanging, and Lloyds of London and the London Markets outsourced their back-offices to the same company (Feeny et al., 2003). On some projections the European BPO market will rise from €27.6 billion in 2002 to €72 billion in 2005. Our own work points to the need to manage the increased risks of outsourcing business processes or functions that connect in multiple ways with other suppliers, technologies and parts of the business. A more partnering style of external sourcing may well be needed, as we found in our own case studies in insurance and aerospace.

Appendix 11A

Details of the 78 corporations studied throughout 1999–2002

Note: The companies have been anonymized throughout at their request. The judgements on Performance and Development Path are those of the authors, arrived at by applying the criteria described in the paper. The assessments have been updated to the end of 2001.

Table 11.1: Case study organizations performance assessment

Company sector	Country	Performance	Development path
1. Computer hardware	USA	Leader	Internal
2. Banks-M.C.	USA	Leader	Internal
3. Transportation services	USA	Leader	Internal
4. Financial Division	USA	Leader	Insource then selective partnering
5. Comm. Equip	USA	Leader	Internal
6. Utilities	USA	Mid level	Internal
7. Computers hardware	USA	Leader	Selective partnering
8. Chem. –Spec	USA	Laggard	Internal
9. Non-metalic minerals	USA	Laggard	Internal
10. Biotec	USA	Leader	Internal
11. Manf. specialized	USA	Mid level	Internal then selective partnering
12. Entertainment	Japan	Leader	Internal
13. Online retail	USA	Mid level	Internal then selective partnering
14. Automotive	UK	Laggard	Internal
15. Automotive	Germany	Mid level	Internal then selective partnering
16. Svcs. Comm	USA	Mid level	Outsourced then internalized then selective outsourcing
17. Logistics	USA	Laggard	Internal
18. Internet services	USA	Laggard	Internal
19. Travel	USA	Mid level	Selective partnering
20. Healthcare services	USA	Mid level	Internal
21. Financial	USA	Laggard	Internal
22. Insurance carrier	Swiss	Mid level	Internal
23. Finance	USA	Leader	Internal then selective partnering
24. Energy	France	Leader	Internal
25. Defense	USA	Leader	Internal
26. Finance	USA	Leader	Internal then selective partnering
27. Finance	USA	Leader	Selective partnering
28. Automotive	USA	Leader	Selective partnering
29. Internet service provider	USA	Leader	Internal
30. Retailing	USA	Mid level	Selective partnering
31. Retailing	Australia	Laggard	Internal
32. Automotive	USA	Mid level	Selective partnering
33. Energy	USA	Mid level	Selective partnering
34. Transportation	USA	Leader	Selective partnering
35. Insurance	UK	Mid level	Internal
36. Banking and financial services	Finland	Leader	Internal
37. Basic materials	USA	Mid level	Internal
38. Retailing	UK	Laggard	Internal
39. Entertainment	Denmark	Mid level	Outsourced/external
40. Automotive	UK	Mid Level	Outsourced/external

(*continued*)

Table 11.1: (*continued*)

Company sector	Country	Performance	Development path
41. Retailing	UK	Leader	Mixed
42. Transportation	UK	Laggard	First outsourced then internalized
43. Telecommunications	UK	Mid level	Selective partnering
44. Consulting	USA	Mid level	Selective partnering
45. Telecommunications	USA	Leader	Selective partnering
46. Hi-tech supply/services	France	Mid level	Internal then selective partnering
47. Aerospace	USA	Laggard	Internal
48. Office supplies	USA	Leader	Internal
49. Medical manufacturing	USA	Leader	Internal then selective partnering
50. Communications equipment	USA	Leader	Internal
51. Utilities	USA	Leader	Internal
52. Rental and Lesing	USA	Laggard	First outsourced then internalized
53. Printing and publishing	USA	Leader	Internal
54. Recreational activitities	USA	Mid level	Internal then selective partnering
55. Construction services	USA	Laggard	Internal
56. Insurance	USA	Laggard	Internal
57. Miscellaneous capital goods supplies	USA	Mid level	Strategic partnering
58. Banking and financial services	UK	Mid level	Internal
59. Computer hardware	USA	Leader	Selective partnering
60. Computer hardware	USA	Mid level	Internal
61. Online travel industry	USA	Mid level	Strategic partnering
62. Electrical component manufacturer	UK	Mid level	Internal then selective outsourcing
63. Financial services	Australia	Mid level	Internal with limited selective outsourcing
64. Power utility	Australia	Mid level	Selective outsourcing
65. Retailing	UK	Laggard	Internal
66. Retailing	UK	Mid Level	Selective outsourcing
67. Online hi-tech service provider	USA	Mid level	Strategic partnering
68. Entertainment supplies	UK	Mid level	Internal then selective outsourcing
69. Engineering	Germany	Mid level	Internal plus technology partnering
70. Airline	USA	Mid level	Selective outsourcing
71. Insurance	USA	Laggard	Internal
72. Banking and financial services	UK	Laggard	Selective outsourcing
73. Online hi-tech security and services	UK	Leader	Internal
74. Water utility	UK	Laggard	Selective outsourcing
75. Apparel	UK	Laggard	Internal then selective outsourcing
76. Insurance	USA	Laggard	Total outsourcing
77. High street retailer	Australia	Mid level	Internal then selective outsourcing
78. High street conglomerate	UK	Laggard	Selective outsourcing

Notes

1 A more general study reinforcing this is by Kanter, R. (2001). 'The Ten Deadly Mistakes of Wanna-Dots.' *Harvard Business Review* January **79**(1): 91–105; See also Yoffe, D. and M. Cusumano (1999). 'Building a Company on Internet Time: Lessons from Netscape.' *California Management Review* **41**(3): 8–28.

2 For further examples see Davis, J. (ed.) (2000). *How IT Works*. Business 2.0, February, 112–140. The customer resource life cycle concept has a long history, in fact, and receives more detailed attention in Ives, B. and G. Learmonth (1984). 'The Information Systems as a Competitive Weapon.' *Communications of the ACM* **27**(12): 15–26. See also Vandermerwe, S. (1999). *Customer Capitalism*. Nicholas Brierley Publishing, London.

3 Two good overviews for these principles are Klepper and Jones (1998) op. cit. and Lacity and Willcocks (2001) op. cit. as cited in the References.

4 Quoted in Magretta, J. (1998). 'The Power of Virtual Integration: an Interview with Dell Computer's Michael Dell.' *Harvard Business Review* (March–April): 73–84.

5 For further reading on the risks of outsourcing see Earl (1996); Strassmann (1998), including that of strategic inflexibility (Weill and Broadbent, 1998). Researchers have also examined the conditions under which strategic outsourcing on a long-term basis might be effective (see, for example, McFarlan and Nolan, 1995; DiRomualdo and Gurbaxani, 1998; Kern and Willcocks, 2001). Economic and other rationales for IT outsourcing have been studied (for example, Loh and Venkatraman, 1992; Ang and Straub, 1998), while a range of theoretical perspectives have been offered that could be used for studying outsourcing arrangements (see Jurison, 1995; Hirscheim et al., 2002; Kern and Willcocks, 2002). There is also useful literature on effective practices for post contract management (for examples only, see Klepper, 1995; Sobol and Apte, 1995; Feeny and Willcocks, 1998; Klepper and Jones, 1998).

References and Further Reading

Ang, S. and D. Straub (1998). 'Production and Transaction Economics and IS Outsourcing: A Study of the US Banking Industry.' *MIS Quarterly,* December: 535–542.

Bornheim, S. (2001). *e-Roadmapping: Digital Strategizing for the New Economy*. London, Palgrave.

Bunnell, D. and A. Brate (2000). *Making the Cisco Connection*. New York, John Wiley and Son.

Camuffo, A., P. Romano and A. Vinelli (2001). 'Back to the Future: Benetton Transforms Its Global Network.' *Sloan Management Review,* Fall: 46–52.

Chen, S. (2001). *Strategic Management of eBusiness*. Chichester, Wiley.

Child, J. and D. Faulkner (1998). *Strategies of Cooperation. Managing Alliances, Networks and Joint Ventures*. Oxford, Oxford University Press.

Dell, M. (1999). *Direct from Dell: Strategies that Revolutionized an Industry*. London, HarperCollins Business.

DiRomualdo, A. and V. Gurbaxani (1998). 'Strategic Intent for IT Outsourcing.' *Sloan Management Review* 39(4): 1–26.

Earl, M. (1996). 'The Risks of Outsourcing IT.' *Sloan Management Review* 37(3): 26–32.

Earl, M. (1998). *Information Management: the Organizational Dimension*. Oxford, Oxford University Press.

Feeny, D. (2001). 'Making Business Sense of the e-Opportunity.' *MIT Sloan Management Review,* Winter: 41–51.

Feeny, D., M. Earl and B. Edwards (1997). Information Systems Organization: The Role of Users and Specialists. *Managing IT as A Strategic Resource.* L. Willcocks, D. Feeny, and G. Islei (eds). Maidenhead, McGraw-Hill.

Feeny, D. and L. Willcocks (1998). 'Core IS Capabilities for Exploiting IT.' *Sloan Management Review* 39(3): 9–21.

Feeny, D., L. Willcocks and M. Lacity (2003). *Business Process Outsourcing: The Promise of Enterprise Partnership*. Templeton Executive Briefing. Oxford: Templeton College.

Fisher, A. (2001). 'Investing in Information Technology.' *Financial Times IT Review* December 5: 8–9.

Garner, R. (1998). 'Strategic Outsourcing: It's Your Move.' *Datamation* February: 32–41.

Grover, V., M. Cheon, et al. (1998). Theoretical Perspectives on the Outsourcing of Information Technology. L. Willcocks and M. Lacity (eds) (1998) op. cit.

Hagel, J. (2002). *Out of the Box: Strategies for Achieving Profits Today and Growth Tomorrow through Web Services*. Boston, Harvard Business School Press.

Hamel, G. and C. Pralahad (1994). *Competing for the Future*. Boston, Harvard Business Press.

Hirscheim, R., A. Heinzl and J. Dibbern (eds) (2002). *Information Systems Outsourcing: Enduring Themes, Emergent Patterns, and Future Directions*. Berlin, Springer Verlag.

Jurison, J. (1995). 'The Role of Risk and Return in IT Outsourcing Decisions.' *Journal of Information Technology* 10(4): 239–247.

Kalakota, R. and M. Robinson (2001). *eBusiness: Roadmap to Success*, 2nd edition. Reading, MA, Addison-Wesley.

Kern, T. and L. Willcocks (2002). *The Relationship Advantage: Information Technology, Sourcing and Management*. Oxford, Oxford University Press.

Kern, T., J. Kreijger and L. Willcocks (2002a). 'Exploring ASP as Sourcing Strategy: Theoretical Perspectives, Propositions for Practice.' *Journal of Strategic Information Systems* 11: 153–177.

Kern, T., M. Lacity and L. Willcocks (2002b). *Netsourcing: Renting Business Applications and Services Over a Network*. NJ, Prentice-Hall.

Kern, T., L. Willcocks and M. Lacity (2002c). 'Application Service Provision: Risk Assessment and Mitigation.' *MISQ Executive* 1(2): 113–126.

Klepper, R. (1995). 'The Management of Partnering Development in IS Outsourcing.' *Journal of Information Technology* 10(4): 249–258.

Klepper, R. and W. Jones (1998). *Outsourcing Information Technology, Systems and Services*. NJ, Prentice-Hall.

Lacity, M. and R. Hirschheim (1995). *Beyond the Information Systems Outsourcing Bandwagon: The Insourcing Response*. Chichester, Wiley.

Lacity, M. C. and R. Hirschheim (1993). *Information Systems Outsourcing: Myths, Metaphors and Realities*. Chichester, John Wiley & Sons Ltd.

Lacity, M. and L. Willcocks (1998). 'An Empirical Investigation of Information Technology Sourcing Practices: Lessons from Experience.' *MIS Quarterly* 22(3): 363–408.

Lacity, M. and L. Willcocks (2001). *Global Information Technology Outsourcing: In Search of Business Advantage*. Chichester, Wiley.

Leidner, D., R. Beatty and J. Mackay (2003). 'How CIOs manage during decline'. *MISQ Executive* 2(1): 19–35.

Loh, L. and N. Venkatraman (1992). 'Determinants of Information Technology Outsourcing: A Cross Sectional Analysis.' *Journal of Management Information Systems* 9(1): 7–24.

London, S. (2001). 'Business Computing: Grind Replaces Glory.' *Financial Times* December 6: 14.

Mahadevan, D. (2000). 'Business Models for Internet-Based e-Commerce: An Anatomy.' *California Management Review* 42(4): 55–69.

McFarlan, W. and Nolan, R. (1995). 'How to Manage an IT Outsourcing Alliance.' *Sloan Management Review* Winter: 9–23.

Moore, J. (1998). The New Corporate Form. D. Tapscott, A. Lowy and D. Ticoll (eds). *Blueprint for the Digital Economy*. New York, McGraw-Hill.

Nalebuff, B. and Brandenburger, A. (1996). *Co-opetition*. London, HarperCollins Business.

Plant, R. (2000). *e-Commerce: Formulation of Strategy*. New York, Prentice-Hall.

Porter, M. (2001). 'Strategy And The Internet.' *Harvard Business Review* March: 63–78.

Pottruck, D. and T. Pearce (2000). *Clicks and Mortar: Passion Driven Growth in an Internet Driven World*. San Francisco, Jossey Bass.

Pralahad, C. and G. Hamel (1990). 'The Core Competence of the Corporation.' *Harvard Business Review* 68(3): 79–91.

Quinn, J. (1992). 'The Intelligent Enterprise: A New Paradigm.' *Academy of Management Executive* 6(4): 44–63.

Schwarz, E. (1999). *Digital Darwinism*. New York, Broadway Books.

Seybold, P. (2001). *The Customer Revolution*. New York, Random House.

Seybold, P. and R. Marshak (1998). *Customer.Com*. New York, Times Business Random House.

Sobol, M. and U. Apte (1995). 'Domestic and Global Outsourcing Practices of America's Most Effective IS Users.' *Journal of Information Technology* 10(4): 269–280.

Strassmann, P. (1998). *The Squandered Computer*. New Canaan, Information Economics Press.

Ware, J., J. Gebauer, A. Hartman and M. Roldan (1998). *The Search For Digital Excellence*. New York, McGraw-Hill.

Weill, P. and M. Broadbent (1998). *Leveraging the New IT Infrastructure*. Boston, Harvard Business Press.

Weill, P. and M. Vitale (2001). *Place to Space*. Boston, Harvard Business Press.

Werbach, K. (2000). 'Syndication: the Emerging Model for Business in the Internet Era.' *Harvard Business Review* May–June: 84–96.

Willcocks, L. and M. Lacity (eds) (1998). *The Strategic Sourcing of Information Systems*. Chichester, Wiley.

Willcocks, L. and R. Plant (2000). Business Internet Strategy: Moving to the Net. *Moving to e-Business*. L. Willcocks and C. Sauer (eds). London, Random House.

Willcocks, L. and R. Plant (2002). 'Pathways to eBusiness Leadership: Getting from Bricks to Clicks.' *Sloan Management Review* **42**(3): 50–59. Reproduced in Brynjolfsson and Urban, G. (eds) (2002). *Strategies for e-Business Success*, Chapter 5. San Francisco, Jossey Bass: 115–138.

12 Value creation in application outsourcing relationships: an international case study on ERP outsourcing

Erik Beulen and Pieter Ribbers

Abstract

Value creation in application outsourcing relationships is challenging. In this chapter an international case study on enterprise resource planning (ERP) outsourcing is presented to provide an insight in value creation. The capabilities of both the Service Recipient and the Service Providers are detailed. Furthermore the contracts and service level agreements (SLAs) are taken into account. Also the inter-organizational relationships between the Service Recipient and Service Providers are studied. This chapter contains an overview of the relevant theories including the resource-based view (RBV), the transaction cost theory, the incomplete contract theory and the relational view (RV). Analysing these theories and the case study resulted in a number of lessons learned. Recent developments in the ERP outsourcing market conclude this chapter. These developments will impact value creation in application outsourcing relationships.

12.1 Introduction

Outsourcing is still growing in the information technology (IT) and telecommunications technology sector. Corbett estimates a compounded annual growth rate of 20%, from 340 million US $ in 2001 to 490 million US $ in 2003 (Corbett, 2002). This is in line with the predictions of Gartner and IDC (Cox, 2002; Kennedy and Irshad, 2002). Also the enterprise resource planning (ERP) outsourcing is still growing from 27.4 billion US $ in 2003 to 32.4 billion US $ in 2005 (DeSouza, 2002). Klepper defined outsourcing as 'contracting of information systems hardware, software and systems functions or services to external vendors' (Klepper, 1995). The company that contracts information systems hardware, software and systems functions or services will be indicated as the

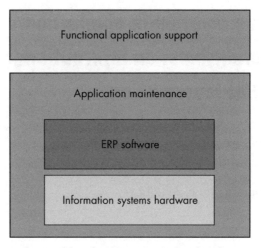

Figure 12.1:   Overview of responsibilities for ERP outsourcing (based on Klepper, 1995).

Service Recipient. The external vendors will be indicated as Service Providers. In ERP outsourcing the systems functions or services can be differentiated in application maintenance and functional application support. The application maintenance is responsible for running the application. Functional support is responsible for implementing changes as requested by the Service Recipient. This is detailed in Figure 12.1.

There are a large number of failures in outsourcing relationships due to the complexity of and inexperience with managing outsourcing relationships of both the Service Recipient and the Service Provider (Lacity and Hirschheim, 1993; Willcocks and Chio, 1995; Beulen, 2000; Cox, 2002). The Service Recipients have to consider the outsourcing alternative for ERP because '... hiring and retaining a quality operations and maintenance of staff for ERP applications is difficult ... .' (Travis and Bacon, 2003). This chapter will address the process of adding value in ERP outsourcing relationships by presenting the lessons learned from an ERP outsourcing case study in the consumer package goods sector. This will be detailed in addressing capabilities, contracts and service level agreements and inter-organizational relationships.

The second section contains the theoretical foundation, including outsourcing, resource-based view, transaction theory, incomplete contract theory and the relational view. The research model is detailed in Section 12.3. The case study description, in Section 12.4, is as an introduction to the model-based analysis in Section 12.5. This analysis will focus on capabilities, contracts and SLAs and inter-organizational relationships. The lessons learned are derived from the model-based analysis in Section 12.6. We conclude with a discussion section.

12.2 Theoretical foundation

In this section we discuss the theoretical background of our study. The first section defines outsourcing and ERP outsourcing. The second section focuses on the RBV of the firm. The RBV (Barney, 1991; Mata et al., 1995) focuses on resources and capabilities that companies need to have. These have to be detailed for both the Service Recipient and the Service Providers. The transaction cost theory (Coase, 1937; Williamson, 1975) discusses governance issues between the Service Recipient and the Service Providers. In the case of outsourcing this relationship is based on contracts and SLAs. As it is not possible to fully cover the relationship in contracts and SLAs, the incomplete contract theory applies to the relationship (Hart and Moore, 1990; Segal, 1995). These issues are dealt with in the third section. In order to find support for understanding how to create value in inter-organizational relationships, the last section finally discusses the RV.

12.2.1 Outsourcing and ERP outsourcing

Outsourcing is not a new phenomenon. Outsourcing options have existed since the dawn of data processing in the 1960s (Mason, 1990). Activities such as software programming, operation of large computers, timesharing and purchasing of packaged software have to some extent been outsourced since the 1960s (Hammersmith, 1989). In the 1990s outsourcing changed dramatically, expanded to multiple systems and represented a significant transfer of assets and staff to Service Providers (Eckerson, 1990). There is a considerable attention towards outsourcing in literature in the 1990s: Apte (1990), Buck-Lew (1992), Lacity and Hirschheim (1993), Willcocks and Fitzgerald (1994) and Currie and Willcocks (1998). As already mentioned in the introduction the outsourcing market and the ERP outsourcing market are still growing. To implement outsourcing contracts Service Recipients need additional capabilities to manage the Service Provider(s). This is only one of the critical success factors for outsourcing (Pinnington and Woolcock, 1995; Feeny and Willcocks, 1998). This will be discussed in the next section. This critical success factor is also related ERP outsourcing.

The ERP market started in the 1970s with material requirements planning (MRP). With this first version of ERP software (MRP-I) Service Recipients were able to calculate production and purchasing orders based on bill of material and a demand forecast. The successor of the MRP-I, MRP-II, was introduced in the 1980s. The additional functionality of the MRP-II includes integral planning tools and management concepts. Also the production capacity is taken into account in MRP-II. ERP started in the 1990s. ERP software contains in addition to the MRP-II functionalities, also functionalities such as finance, accounting, personnel, product flow and customers (Davenport, 1998). Major Service

Providers of ERP software are SAP, Oracle Cooperation, PeopleSoft, JD Edwards, IFS and BAAN. The application maintenance of an ERP software is often outsourced to Service Providers. Their investments in hardware platforms and the economies of scale they realize in managing and monitoring the ERP software, make outsourcing a feasible solution for client companies (DeSouza, 2002). The application maintenance of an ERP software is becoming a highly specialized commodity service (Travis and Bacon, 2003). Delivering the services still requires high-skilled employees and well-defined service delivery processes. Therefore only mature Service Providers are able to offer reliable ERP services (Anderson, 2003). The internal automation department of the Service Recipient often provides the functional application support. It is more difficult for an external Service Provider to achieve economies of scale in this domain. This service is much more connected to the business processes of the Service Recipient and thus highly specific, which results in a natural resistance towards outsourcing. Nevertheless, there are a large number of Service Recipients who have (partly) outsourced their ERP functional application support. The main argument for this is the absence of qualified staff within the internal automation department (DeSouza, 2002; Travis and Bacon, 2003).

12.2.2 RBV

In contrast to theories about firm performance, which emphasize the external strategic positioning, the RBV considers internal resources and capabilities as sources of potential competitive advantage. According to this view a firm can build a strategic position by picking the right resources and building the right capabilities. From an economic perspective, resources are stocks of factors of production owned or controlled by the firm (Armit and Schoemaker, 1993). Capabilities concern the capacity to deploy resources using organizational processes (Armit and Schoemaker, 1993), or stated differently, are socially complex routines that determine the efficiency with which the firm transforms inputs into outputs (Collis, 1991). Resources are considered the raw material for building capabilities (see also Ravichandran and Lertwongsatien, 2002).

In the literature a hierarchical distinction is made between (core) competencies and capabilities. Prahalad and Hamel (1990) define core competencies as the 'root system' of an organization 'that provides nourishment, sustenance and stability'; they are the collective learning in the organization how to coordinate diverse production skills and multiple streams of technology. Competencies are built on the foundation of functional and cross-functional capabilities (Grant, 1991). In analysing the case on ERP outsourcing we will focus on capabilities required from the Service Provider and Recipient to make the outsourcing relationship a success. In the case of IT, resources are defined as the tangible IT resources, the human IT resources, and the intangible IT-enabled resources (Grant, 1991).

Tangible IT resources

The tangible IT resources compromise the physical IT infrastructure component (information systems hardware and ERP software, see Figure 12.1). The IT infrastructure is a candidate for outsourcing. Information systems hardware has been a mature and commodity market for decades; the physical infrastructure can be duplicated fairly easy, and consequently physical IT infrastructure services will hardly serve as a source of competitive advantage (Mata et al., 1995). The ERP software market is different since it consists of only a few mature ERP software Service Providers. Integration is a key issue here. Non-integrated IT infrastructures limit Service Recipient's business choices (Keen, 1991). Integrating IT infrastructures requires considerable time and effort of the Service Recipient (Weill and Broadbent, 1998) and is a key capability of the Service Provider.

Human IT resources

The human IT resources comprise technical and managerial IT skills (application maintenance and functional application support, and management of the relationship between Service Providers and Service Recipient) (Capon and Glazer, 1987; Copeland and McKenney, 1988). Both the technical IT skills and the managerial IT skills include explicit and tacit knowledge (Nonaka, 1991; Mata et al., 1995). An example of tacit knowledge related to managerial skills is the insight into the cooperation between individuals in a project team. Furthermore the organizational structures and procedures facilitate the human IT resources (Laplante, 1997). The technical IT skills – application maintenance and functional application support – can be more easily outsourced to Service Providers than the managerial IT skills (Lacity and Hirschheim, 1993; Beulen, 2000). As a Service Recipient decides to outsource (ERP) the management IT skills need to be extended in order to be able to manage the IT supplier (Feeny and Willcocks, 1998; Pereira, 1999; Roy and Aubert, 2002; Anderson, 2003).

IT-enabled intangibles

According to Grant (1991), the intangible IT-enabled resources compromise knowledge assets, customer orientation and synergy. Other authors add know-how (Teece, 1998), corporate culture (Barney, 1991), corporate reputation (Vergin and Qoronflesh, 1998) and environmental reputation (Russo and Fouts, 1997). Especially in ERP outsourcing relations these IT-enabled intangibles contribute to the success of the outsourcing relationship (Pereira, 1999; Roy and Aubert, 2002; Travis and Bacon, 2003).

12.2.3 Contracts and SLAs

Contracts and SLAs are essential in managing (ERP) outsourcing relationships (Lacity and Hirschheim, 1993). In this section the transaction cost theory and the incomplete contract theory are detailed.

Transaction cost theory

Transaction cost theory distinguishes between executing transactions internally or externally. The hierarchy coordinates the internal transactions, so-called make-decisions. The market coordinates the external transactions, so-called buy-decisions (Coase, 1937; Williamson, 1975). ERP outsourcing is an external transaction.

Transaction costs are determined by transaction frequency and asset specificity (Williamson, 1979). With regard to frequency a distinction is made between occasional transactions and recurrent transactions. The degree of asset specificity can be either non-specific, mixed or idiosyncratic specificity. Klepper characterizes outsourcing as recurrent transactions with mixed or idiosyncratic asset specificity (1995). This is also valid for ERP outsourcing. The ERP outsourcing contracts have an average duration of over 36 months (Travis and Bacon, 2003), which leads to recurrent transactions. ERP outsourcing is based on the standard ERP software. This software is modified and customized towards the specific requirements of the Service Recipient, resulting in mixed or idiosyncratic asset specificity. As a consequence ERP outsourcing has to be contracted by relational contracting (Williamson, 1979). As a result of the asset specificity it is more difficult to predict the issues that will occur. By relational contracting the Service Recipient and the Service Provider agree on an approach to deal with unpredicted issues. In an escalation procedure all possible issue are open for discussion. Mutual trust will decrease the coordination costs for both the Service Recipient and the Service Providers.

Incomplete contract theory

Incomplete contract theory is closely linked to the transaction cost theory. Incomplete contract theory relates to situations in which the parties that want to enter into an agreement together are not able to predict all of the future situations that may occur as a result of the transaction they want to conclude (Hart and Moore, 1990; Segal, 1995; Maskin and Tirole, 1999). As a consequence, they are not able to describe all possible future scenarios as part of the contracts they wish to negotiate. The uncertainty is not related to the contracting parties involved, but to the transaction itself (Grossman and Hart, 1986; Tirole, 1989; Hart, 1995). In the IT outsourcing literature, the incomplete contract theory has been developed by Nam et al. (1996). The future information needs of the outsourcing organizations, driven by the dynamics of the marketplaces in which these organizations operate, or changes in strategies due to the emergence of new technologies, are elements, which cannot be defined when a contract is signed (Beulen, 2002).

This line of thinking is also applicable for ERP outsourcing. Future contingencies have to be addressed in contracts with ERP software vendors (Anderson and Disbrow, 2003). This is also applicable for information system hardware, however the implementation of future contingencies is more difficult due to the required investments. For application maintenance contracting, ERP seat prices contribute to adaptability to future contingencies. Of course the ERP seat prices are applicable within certain limited range of seats. Most of the functional application support is contracted on time × material basis and or on a project basis. The Service Recipient and the Service Provider agree on a certain number of hours and rates for the contracting period. This type of contracts minimizes the risks for the Service Providers but contribute to the adoption of future contingencies.

12.2.4 RV

The RBV is limited to resources that are housed within the firm. The RV incorporates the inter-organizational aspects (Dyer and Singh, 1998). The RV is based on the work of Asanuma (1989), Saxenian (1994), and Dyer (1996) and the transaction cost theory of Williamson (1975). The RV contains the following determinants: relation-specific assets, knowledge-sharing routines, complementary resources and capabilities, and effective governance (Dyer and Singh, 1998).

Relation-specific assets
If the Service Recipient or the Service Providers have to invest in relation-specific assets the duration of the safeguards and the volume of inter-firm transactions determine the coverage for these investments (Dyer and Singh, 1998). This is based on the transaction cost theory of Williamson (1975). The commitment to non-recoverable investments contributes to the inter-organizational relationship (Parkhe, 1993). In ERP outsourcing both the Service Recipient and the Service Provider have to invest in relation-specific assets. The design of the ERP software and hardware have to be made by the Service Providers and will not be charged separately to the Service Recipient. The Service Providers have to instruct their employees. These instructions are relation-specific and require considerable effort from both the Service Recipient and the Service Providers. If the inter-organizational relationship is terminated both the investment in the design and the instruction of employees are of no value to both the Service Recipient and the Service Providers. To cover these investments ERP outsourcing contracts have an average duration of over 36 months (Travis and Bacon, 2003).

Knowledge-sharing routines

To support knowledge sharing between the Service Recipient and the Service Provider the partner-specific absorptive capacity and the incentive to encourage transparency and discourage free riding are essential (Dyer and Singh, 1998). The partner-specific absorptive capacity is the understanding of ways of working together with a partner. Polanyi (1966) and Nonaka and Takeuchi (1995) differentiate explicit and tacit knowledge. The inter-organizational exchange of tacit knowledge is more difficult than the exchange of explicit knowledge. In ERP outsourcing the exchange of tacit knowledge is crucial. The implementation of ERP software and changes is always under great time pressure. There is limited time to make a proper documentation of the implementation and changes (Travis and Bacon, 2003). Furthermore the transparency between the responsibilities of the Service Providers is not always sparkling clear. Incidents in processing the ERP software can be related to the information systems hardware, the ERP software, the application maintenance or to the application functional support (Anderson and Disbrow, 2003).

Complementary resources and capabilities

Complementary resources and capabilities are the key factor for alliances (Harrigan, 1985; Teece, 1987). The effectiveness of leveraging complementary resources and capabilities depends on the ability to identify and evaluate potential complementarities and the role of organizational complementarities to access benefits of strategic resource complementarity (Dyer and Singh, 1998). In other words knowing the complementary resources results in competitive advantage. In ERP outsourcing most of the complementary resources and capabilities are present in the activities of functional application support and the application maintenance. Most of the Service Recipients do not have information systems hardware nor ERP software resources. The scope of the ERP outsourcing determines if the Service Recipient hands over the responsibility for the functional application support and the application maintenance to Service Providers.

Effective governance

To support the governance between the Service Recipient and the Service Providers the ability to employ self-enforcement rather than third-party enforcement governance mechanisms and the ability to employ informal self-enforcement mechanisms are essential (Dyer and Singh, 1998). Self-enforcement is defined as a governance structure that is not based on contracts. In ERP outsourcing third-party enforcement governance dominates over self-enforcement. But reputation, as mentioned by Weigelt and Camerer (1988) and Larson (1992), has an impact on third-party enforcement in ERP outsourcing relationships. Most of the Service Providers are not willing to damage their reputation in discussions with Service Recipients. On the other hand most Service Recipient are not willing to jeopardize the business continuity in discussions with Service Providers (Anderson and Disbrow, 2003).

12.3 Research approach

In this section the research model and the case study research will be detailed. The research model includes the research questions. The case study research explains the approach and the limitation of this research.

12.3.1 Research model

Our research addresses the value creation in application outsourcing relationships. In this chapter we focus on capabilities. The central research question of this chapter is: What kind of capabilities of Service Providers and Service Recipients are required to add value in an application outsourcing relationship?

This central research question will be detailed (Figure 12.2) in the following sub questions:

1 What are the capabilities of the Service Recipient to create value in an ERP outsourcing relationship?

2 What are the capabilities of the Service Providers to create value in an ERP outsourcing relationship?

3 What is the impact of contracts on an ERP outsourcing relationship?

4 What is the impact of inter-organizational relationships on an ERP outsourcing relationship?

12.3.2 Case study research

This chapter explores three specific areas of interest – capabilities, contracts and SLAs, and inter-organizational relationships – related to ERP outsourcing on the basis of RBV, Transaction cost theory, Incomplete contract theory and the literature on the RBV. Desk and field research involving a single ERP outsourcing case study was applied to develop these three areas further. The interviewees are detailed in Table 12.1.

The same research protocol was followed in all interviews conducted for the case study. The same analysis techniques for collecting data were used for all interviews. All interviews were recorded, fully transcribed

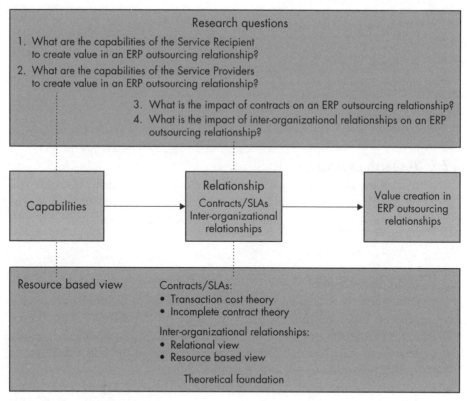

Figure 12.2: Research framework.

and further developed. The average interview was over an hour. The results were approved by the interviewees and constituted the basis for the analysis. In addition to the interviews, supporting documentation for the case study analysed was collected, including annual reports, organization charts and research reports on ERP outsourcing. The nature of this type of research is explorative. The case study method has been used, because it enables 'reality' to be captured in considerably greater detail than other methods, and it also allows for the analysis of a considerable greater number of variables.

In this case study the functional application support services and the ERP software licenses were addressed in all the four interviews. The Service Recipient did not allow us to interview the Service Provider, and the responsible manager of the internal automation department of the Service Recipient, which are mutually responsible for functional application support. The Service Provider responsible for the ERP software was not involved in the ERP outsourcing. This Service Provider has an independent relationship with the Service Recipient. This case study is presented anonymously, on request of the Service Recipient, to ensure the confidentiality of this ERP outsourcing relationship.

Table 12.1: Interviewees of the ERP outsourcing case study

No.	Job title	Service Recipient/ Service Provider	Responsibility
1	Chief information officer	Service Recipient	The chief information officer was involved in the contracting process. On behalf of the Service Recipient he holds a position in the partner board, responsible for the ERP outsourcing relationship. Furthermore he is responsible for the sourcing strategy of the Service Recipient.
2	Account manager	Service Provider (information systems hardware)	The account manager was responsible for contracting the supply of information systems hardware and supporting lifting of the information systems hardware from the premises of the Service Recipient to the data centre of the Service Provider responsible for the application maintenance. Furthermore he is end-responsible for managing the relationship with the Service Provider responsible with the Service Provider responsible for the application maintenance.
3	Sector director	Service Provider (application maintenance)	The sector director was responsible for acquiring the ERP outsourcing contract. Furthermore he is end-responsible for managing the ERP outsourcing relationship.
4	Technical manager	Service Provider (application maintenance)	The technical manager was responsible for the technical design of the architect in the contracting process. Furthermore he was responsible for lifting of the information systems hardware from the premises of the Service Recipient to the data centre of the Service Provider.

12.4 Case study description

The Service Recipient is a European-based global consumer package goods company. The total turnover is over 10 billion Euros. The Service Recipient faces strong market dynamics. The scope of the outsourcing relationship is Europe. This outsourcing relationship includes over 10 000 ERP seats. The Service Provider responsible for the Application Maintenance is implementing a rollout plan. The rollout plan is based on country-by-country approach. In Europe there are over 25 operating companies, which have profit and loss responsibility and are relatively autonomous.

The Service Recipient has outsourced the ERP application maintenance and partly the ERP functional application support. The relationship with the information systems hardware provider is extended. The ERP application maintenance and the ERP functional application support were no longer seen as part of the core business of the Service Recipient. Other arguments for outsourcing were the need to ensure business continuity and achieving cost savings.

Business continuity is ensured by the adoption of the twin data centre concept, as within this concept the data and hardware platforms are located on two separate physical locations which are able to take over the operations in the unlikely event of a disaster in a single location. Prior to the outsourcing the Service Recipient started the preparation of the implementation of the twin data centre concept. Also the application maintenance Service Provider has implemented the twin data centre concept at their data centres. The transition from the data centre of the Service Recipient to the data centre of the Service Provider was detailed in a project plan. This project plan was part of the ERP outsourcing contract. This was a business critical operation, which was carefully prepared and successfully executed by the application maintenance Service Provider and the information systems hardware Service Provider. Also the Service Recipient was involved in the execution of this project.

The costs saving are mainly achieved by optimizing the number of external consultants responsible for ERP. Prior to the outsourcing over 50% of the resources responsible for the ERP were external consultants. These consultants were hired from a large number of Service Providers. After the outsourcing the application maintenance Service Provider replaced all these external consultants by their own employees. Because of the volume the application maintenance Service Provider was able to reduce the total cost of ownership (TCO).

In the contracting process the Service Recipient have issued a request for information (RFI) and request for proposal (RFP); flexibility was one of the major selection criteria. The final negotiations resulted in a 3-year contract based on a seat price. On top of this contract a contract was signed for the transition project. The contract for ERP application maintenance and the ERP functional application support are signed less than 12 months ago. The capabilities and (contractual) relationships of the investigated ERP outsourcing relationship are detail in the text below and in Figure 12.3.

12.4.1 Capabilities

The Service Recipient is responsible for developing and implementing the IT strategy (corporate information office). The Service Recipient is also responsible for the implementation of the demand management (corporate information office and corporate IT services centre). The Service Recipient and the functional application support Service Provider are

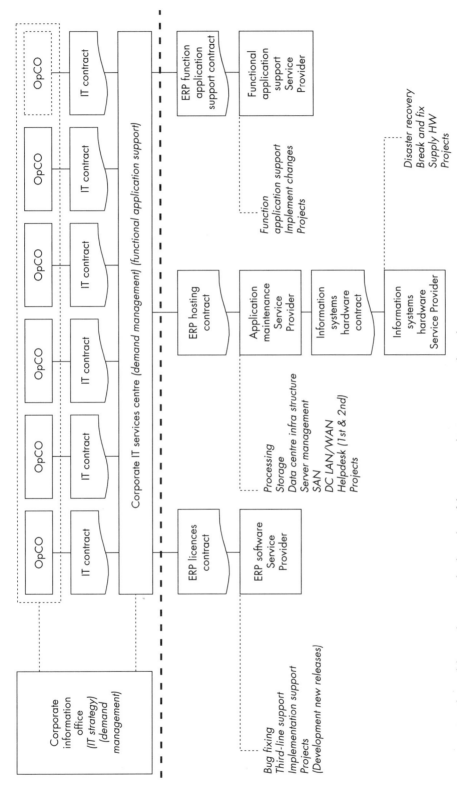

Figure 12.3: The capabilities and (contractual) relationships of the investigated ERP outsourcing relationship.

responsible for parts of the functional application support and the implementation of changes in the ERP software (corporate IT services centre).

The ERP software Service Provider is responsible for bug fixing, third-line support, implementation support and projects. Outside the scope of the ERP outsourcing relationship the ERP software Service Provider has to develop new releases of the ERP software.

The application maintenance Service Provider is responsible for processing of the ERP software. This includes managing the infrastructure environment and the helpdesk. The application maintenance Service Provider is also responsible for managing the information systems hardware Service Provider.

The information systems hardware Service Provider supplies the hardware. The information systems hardware Service Provider is also responsible for the disaster recovery and the break and fix services. All the Service Providers are involved in ERP projects.

12.4.2 Contracts and SLAs

The Service Recipient's corporate IT service centre is responsible for the IT supply to the operating companies. This is covered in internal contracts including a clear description of the service levels and settlement. To execute the services the corporate IT service centre has partly contracted services with Service Providers. The contracts with the Service Providers fully cover the contracts of the corporate IT service centre with the operating companies. The corporate IT service centre has a contractual relationship with the ERP software Service Provider, the application maintenance Service Provider and the functional application support Service Provider. Prior to the ERP outsourcing contract the corporate IT service centre had a direct contractual relationship with the information systems hardware Service Provider. This direct relationship has lasted for over 15 years. Now the information systems hardware Service Provider is a subcontractor of the application maintenance Service Provider. This increases flexibility and decreases management attention for the corporate IT service centre.

All the Service Providers are involved in ERP projects. The projects are on an average about 30% of the total IT spend related to ERP. Projects have to be additionally contracted. Projects are outside the scope of the ERP outsourcing contracts.

12.4.3 Inter-organizational relationships

Except for the functional application support Service Provider, the Service Providers have framework agreements. The framework agreements capture the investigated ERP outsourcing relationship. The framework agreements also support the co-operations between the Service Providers. The design of the software and hardware is not separately charged to the Service

Recipient. The relation-specific investments of the Service Providers have to be recovered during the execution of the service.

Furthermore a change control board is implemented by the Service Recipient to facilitate the discussions between Service Providers, and between the Service Recipient and the Service Providers. The change control board is a knowledge-sharing routine between the Service Recipient and the Service Providers.

By structuring the ERP services in clearly defined domains the Service Recipient has identified the complementary of resources and capabilities. The Service Recipient is only partly responsible for the functional application support. All the other ERP-related services are outsourced to Service Providers. Third-party enforcement is the most important to support the governance of the outsourcing relationship. Contracts are key in the investigated relationship. Self-enforcement is of minor importance.

12.5 Model-based analysis

12.5.1 Capabilities

In an outsourcing relationship not only the capabilities of the Service Providers but also the capabilities of the Service Recipient contribute to the success of the relationship (Pinnington and Woolcock, 1995; Feeny and Willcocks, 1998). The RBV differentiates between IT infrastructure, human IT resources and IT-enabled intangibles (Barney, 1991; Grant, 1991).

IT infrastructure

As detailed in Figure 12.1 the IT infrastructure consists of ERP software and information systems hardware. Based on a selection process the Service Provider has selected its ERP software. For the rollout of the ERP software the Service Recipient has chosen for a country-by-country approach. This approach supports the governance model of the Service Recipient. The operating companies of the Service Recipients are relatively independent and have a profit and loss responsibility. The implementation in each country is based on a central-defined core system. This core system is modified for the specific requirements of each country. This approach helped the acceptance of the ERP software by the operating companies and supported the speed of the implementation process (Schoo, 1999). There is also a limited need to adopt business processes to the ERP software (Conner, 1994). Thulin (1999) defines this approach as 'slim big bang'.

The Service Recipient has selected the information systems hardware Service Provider. Changing the hardware platform is a very costly process for the Service Recipient (Markus et al., 2000), and will take a substantial period of time to be implemented. In order to avoid the risk of business discontinuity changing the hardware platform has to be incorporated in the IT strategy and be gradually implemented (Davenport, 1993). In the investigated case there was no time to even consider such a change. By indirectly contracting the information systems hardware, the application maintenance Service Providers were challenged to present the most effective proposition, which had to include the information systems hardware. This approach stimulated competition between the current information systems hardware and their competitors.

Human IT resources

The Service Recipient has only partly outsourced the technical skills. The management skills are still part of the retained organization of the Service Recipient (the corporate information office and the corporate IT services centre) (Terdiman, 1991). As the latter are different they are new roles for the Service Recipient (Quinn and Hilmer, 1994; Beulen, 2000).

The technical skills are outsourced to four different Service Providers and detailed in the previous section. The Service Recipient expects a clear understanding of its business processes, and their markets, and of the way it deals with these issues (the internal politics). As the role of the Service Recipient is limited to the role of subcontractor of its corporate IT service centre, it is doubtful whether this is a realistic expectation. It is of greater importance that the Service Providers have outstanding service delivery processes and invest in building up knowledge of new technologies (Kitzis, 1998). The chief information officer confirmed that a global service delivery model was one of the selection criteria in the contracting process. The chief information officer stresses the importance of a global service delivery process to implement one way of working (standardization). The Service Provider spends substantial effort on training and educating their employees.

The Service Recipient started a change process to support remaining employees in finding a position in the retained organization. This change process includes additional training. The Service Provider will find a way to deal with remaining employees that are not suitable for their new role within the retained organization.

As for the managerial roles, in the investigated case, the Service Recipient has appointed a contract manager. The contract managers are responsible for managing the contracts with the Service Providers. In these roles are embedded the capabilities 'contract facilitation' and 'contract monitoring' defined by Feeny and Willcocks (1998). The corporate IT service centre of the Service Recipient executes these activities. This is due to subcontracting role of the Service Providers towards the corporate IT service centre. The capabilities 'informed buying of IT services' and 'vendor development' are more strategic capabilities of the retained organization. These activities are embedded in the corporate information office.

IT-enabled intangibles

Prior to this outsourcing relationship the Service Recipient has outsourced its central mainframe data centre. As perceived by the Service Recipient there was a cultural mismatch with the Service Provider, which eventually lead to the failure of that previous outsourcing relationship. The culture of the current Service Providers is perceived as complementary to the culture of the Service Recipient, which contributes to the success of the relationship (Grönroos, 1990). The culture of the Service Recipient is however rather informal. To achieve the benefits of the outsourcing relationship the culture of the Service Provider is and has to be more formal. None of the interviews mentioned corporate reputation as important in this ERP outsourcing relationship. This maybe has to do with the maturity of the organization of all the involved Service Providers and the Service Recipient.

12.5.2 Contracts and SLAs

In this analyses only the contractual relationship between the Service Recipient and the Service Providers is taken into account. All contractual relationships are relationships between the Service Recipient and a Service Provider except for the contract between the information

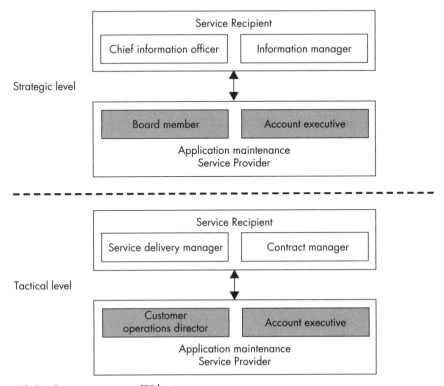

Figure 12.4: Governance structure ERP hosting.

systems hardware Service Provider and the application maintenance Service Provider. This is already detailed in Figure 12.4.

ERP licences contract

This contract is based on the number of used licences. Furthermore this contract covers the third-line support services. The Service Recipient and the helpdesk of the application maintenance Service Provider can put in additional service requests. Only limited information was collected in the interviews related to the ERP licences contract.

ERP hosting contract

The contract was negotiated in a relatively short time frame. For the ERP hosting contract, there is no framework agreement. However, as this is a 3-year contract the absence of a framework agreement does not enable flexibility. On the other hand there are exit clauses. Termination for conveniences at any time supports the required business flexibility. Market dynamics, like including mergers, acquisitions and divestments (MAD), require these kinds of clauses.

According to the chief information officer of the Service Recipient, ERP hosting services are commodity services. This reduces the need to have a layered contract structure (Baker and Faulkner, 1991). There is also a benchmark clause is part of the contract. The Service Provider has a slightly different view but confirms that there are components in the service delivery, which are commodity services.

The contract consists furthermore of a limited number of clauses. For example, how to deal with unforeseen occurrences. Unforeseen occurrences will be discussed at the strategic level in the relationship. Both the Service Recipient and the Service Provider perceive the relationship as a partnership, which supports the governance of the relationship (Willcocks and Chio, 1995; Currie and Willcocks, 1998). As the relationship is relatively young it is not able to benefit from company-based trust between the Service Recipient and the Service Provider. In the contract process however personal trust was an important success factor as mentioned by both the chief information officer and the sector director of the application maintenance service provider.

Information systems hardware contract

The information systems hardware Service Provider was already the preferred supplier prior to the ERP hosting contract. The costs of changing Service Provider for the application maintenance Service Provider are relatively high and the Service Recipient is not willing to pay for the transition.

The relationship between the information systems hardware Service Provider and the application maintenance Service Provider is based on an overall framework Agreement and on additional agreements for the relationship related to the investigated case. The additional agreements are documented in a limited way. This decreases the coordination costs related to this contract (Williamson, 1975; Willcocks and Chio, 1995). The information systems hardware Service Provider and the application maintenance Service Provider are also jointly provide service to other customers which supports trust and secures the interests of both Service Providers (Beulen, 2002). Trust is also an important element of the company culture of the information systems hardware Service Provider. In this specific relationship trust supports the required flexibility and speed. Trust compensates the more bureaucratic company culture of the application maintenance Service Provider. Their investment approval process hinders the required flexibility and speed. However informal communication starts prior to the formal approval.

ERP functional application support contract
This contract is based on a number of available hours to implement changes and requests from the Service Recipient. The change control board of the Service Recipient approves changes and requests. This approach prevents budget thresholds. Only limited information was collected in the interviews related to the ERP functional application support contract.

12.5.3 Inter-organizational relationship
In this analyses inter-organizational aspects of the RV of Dyer and Singh (1998) are taken into account.

Relation-specific assets
In ERP outsourcing relations Service Providers need to have an in-depth understanding of the business processes of the Service Recipient. These business processes are specific processes for the particular Service Recipient. Understanding these business processes is of no value for the Service Provider in other ERP outsourcing relations. In the investigated ERP hosting relationship the team of the application maintenance Service Provider has invested during the transition period over 4 man-months to understand application maintenance. These investments are non-recoverable investments that contribute to the inter-organizational relationship (Parkhe, 1993). Furthermore the application maintenance Service Provider has invested in dedicated hardware to offering the services. In the investigated case the deprecation of this hardware is linked to the contract period. The exit clauses of the contract cover the dedicated investments. The application maintenance Service Provider also leverages existing hardware platforms to offer the services to the Service Recipient, such as storage on demand. All the interviewees concluded that the impact of relation-specific assets in the investigated relationship was limited.

Knowledge-sharing routines

In the investigated case the Service Recipient and the involved Service Providers have regular meetings to discuss the projects and to be implemented changes. The discussions on projects and to be implemented changes go beyond the responsibilities of a single Service Provider. As projects and to be implemented changes are very dynamic the documentation in the investigated case is limited. This will result in an increased dependency between the Service Providers (Travis and Bacon, 2003). In the investigated case none of the interviews mentioned any issues on unclear responsibilities between the Service Recipient and the Service Providers or between Service Providers. This may be related to the toughness of the contracts, as the existing contracts of the corporate IT services centre with the operating companies was a clear starting point to draft contracts. Also the involvement of external lawyers might have contributed to the clarity of responsibilities.

Complementary resources and capabilities

In the investigated relationships there was clearly complementary of resources and capabilities. As the core business of the Service Recipient was not related to the development of ERP software and to the production of information systems hardware, these services were outsourced. In today's market dynamics most Service Recipient are no longer able to develop their software by themselves on time and within budget. Furthermore standard software packages, including MRP and ERP software packages, have been improved of the last decades (Markus et al., 2000). Prior to the ERP hosting relationship the Service Recipient had contracted a large number of external consultants. The only area with limited complementary of resources and capabilities is the functional application support. This is only partly outsourced to a Service Provider. The main argument to keep this activity partly in-house was the required business knowledge for executing these services. This is not unusual in outsourcing relations (Anderson and Disbrow, 2003).

Effective governance

In order to embed the contracts a multi-level governance-structure is implemented for ERP hosting, see Figure 12.4. Both the Service Recipient and the Service Providers representatives have their role in the governance-structure. Beside the operational level this is a two-level governance-structure. By implementing this multi-level approach all the issues can be resolved at the right level (KPMG, 1997).

On the tactical level the service delivery manager and the contract manager represent the Service Recipient. The customer operations director and the account executive are the representatives of application maintenance service supplier. The customer operations director is the contact person for the contract manager of the information systems hardware Service Provider. The information systems hardware Service Provider is not directly part of the ERP hosting. On the tactical level the overall performance is discussed. This is the escalation level for the operational level.

On the strategic level the chief information officer and the information manager represent the Service Recipient. A board member and the account executive are the representatives of application maintenance service supplier. On the strategic level the overall performance is discussed. Also the impact on the ERP outsourcing relation of developments in the business of the Service Recipient and the latest technological are discussed. This is the escalation level for the tactical level.

The interviews have resulted in only limited information on the function support and the ERP software relationships. Therefore only the ERP hosting governance structure is described.

12.6 Lessons learned

All the four interviewees perceive the investigated ERP outsourcing relationship as successful. Although the investigated relationship is successful, the model-based analysis has shown that creating value in ERP outsourcing relationships not easy. The lessons learned address the research questions.

12.6.1 Capabilities of the Service Recipient

The capabilities required of the Service Recipient to create value in an ERP outsourcing relationship concern the development and implementation of an IT strategy, management of the Service Providers, and provisioning of functional application support. Development and implementation of an IT strategy and management of Service Providers are undoubtedly the responsibility of the retained organization. In the investigated case study the functional application support was partly outsourced. Only if the Service Recipient is convinced of the capabilities of Service Provider the functional application support possibly can be fully outsourced. The Service Provider has to have business knowledge to successfully execute these services.

12.6.2 Capabilities of the Service Providers

The capabilities of the Service Providers to create value in an ERP outsourcing relationship concern technical and managerial skills. It is important that technical skills are properly maintained. Training and education are essential. Service Providers need to have a (global) service delivery model that has clearly defined interfaces with the service delivery models of other involved Service Providers. The service delivery model has to be integrated with the service delivery model of the Service Recipient.

In line with this, Service Providers have to implement supply management. The supply management is the interface to the retained organization of the Service Recipient. The supply management is responsible for managing the (ERP outsourcing) relationship and the contracts.

12.6.3 Impact of contracts

In this case study only the ERP hosting contract and the information systems hardware contract are investigated. The basis of these contracts is the set of contracts of the corporate IT service centre with the operating companies. This stipulates very clear requirements for the ERP hosting contract and the information systems hardware contract.

As ERP hosting is perceived as commodity services this contract is very straightforward with clearly set service levels. It also contains a clause on unforeseen circumstances and issues. A process is defined in the contract to solve these discussions. The exit clause ensures the required flexibility. If the Service Provider does not meet the agreed service levels the process of terminating the contract is clearly described.

The information systems hardware contract is based on generic framework agreement between the application maintenance Service Provider and the information systems hardware Service Provider. Additional conditions are agreed. Trust and reputation are of the greatest importance in this contractual relationship. As information systems hardware is a commodity service, this is rather remarkable. Trust and reputation are needed because of the lengthy purchasing process of the application maintenance Service Provider.

12.6.4 Impact of inter-organizational relationships

The dedicated investments are limited to creating understanding of the application maintenance environment and of limited dedicated hardware. Both investments of the application maintenance Service Provider are covered in the ERP outsourcing contract.

The knowledge-sharing routines are only applicable to the execution of projects and the implementation of changes. These are the only two activities in which the Service Providers have to cooperate. A change control board is implemented to discuss the impact of the changes. Also the Service Recipient is represented in the change control board. For special projects separate joint project teams are lined up. The complementarity of resources and capabilities is not really an issue in ERP outsourcing relationships. Except for the functional application support as already has been explained 'capabilities of the Service Recipient' in this section.

A multi-level governance structure to resolve the issues at the right level has been implemented in order to manage the ERP hosting relationship. The governance structure contains representatives of both the Service Recipient and the application maintenance Service Provider.

12.7 Discussion

In this section we discuss three future developments that will impact value creation in application outsourcing relations: the impact of market dynamics, the introduction of ERP software branch-specific modules and ERP software vendor consolidation. Future research is needed to investigate the impact of these developments.

12.7.1 The impact of market dynamics

In the early days of IT all the software was dedicated software. Over the decades more and more standard software packages became available on the market. Today a lot of Service Recipients buy these standard software packages, such as ERP software, to meet the demand of market dynamics. These standard software packages are tailored towards to business processes of the Service Recipients. These add-ons impact the maintenance and the future flexibility of the software.

The market dynamics are expected to increase in the years to come. In today's market the number of MAD is increasing. This impacts both the 'core business' discussion of IT and the need for standardized software within companies. The Service Recipients tend not to consider IT as their 'core business' anymore. This is also applicable for ERP services. So a growth in ERP outsourcing is expected. In order to meet the market dynamics the Service Recipient requires standardized software within its company in order to consolidate the required information to facilitate the decision-making process. There is no time and budget to customize standard software, such as ERP. Due to the market dynamics the scope of the standardization is expanded to the value chain of Service Recipients. Business units of the Service Recipient have to be easily added and disconnected from the IT systems. Non-standardized software is hindering the integration and disentanglement of business units.

12.7.2 The introduction of ERP software branch-specific modules

The introduction of branch-specific modules requires beside business knowledge also country-specific knowledge from the ERP software Service Provider. For example implementing an insurance module in France is due to country-specific regulations different from implementing this module in Germany. The availability of branch-specific modules supports the standardization ERP software, as add-ons to the ERP software itself are no longer necessary. This enables the maintenance and the future flexibility of the software and therefore contributes to the impact of market dynamics.

12.7.3 ERP software vendor consolidation

In today's market, ERP software market consolidates. Except of IFS no new ERP software Service Provider has entered the market successfully over the last decade. The current market position of IFS is very limited. IFS operated in niche markets such as aerospace and defence. BAAN is leveraging their installed base and is hardly acquiring any new customers. With the recent discussions between PeopleSoft and JD Edwards the ERP software market consolidates even further. The suggested take over of PeopleSoft by Oracle will even more turn the ERP software market towards an oligopoly. This will increase the dependency on the ERP software Service Providers, which is perceived as negative from the perspective of the Service Recipient. Furthermore this will facilitate the need for standardized ERP software in the value chain of Service Recipients and contributes to cost effective integration and disentanglement of IT in the case of MAD. This is perceived as positive from the perspective of the Service Recipient.

References and Further Reading

Al-Hawamdeh, S. (2002). 'Knowledge Management, Re-thinking Information Management and Facing the Challenge of Managing Tacit Knowledge.' *Information Research* 8(1 October).

Anderson, R. (2003). 'Q&A: How Midsize Businesses can Select and Deploy ERP.' *Research Note* QA-20-1090, 5 June.

Anderson, R and J. Disbrow (2003). 'Tips for Dealing with Large ERP vendors.' *Gartner Research Note* COM-19-8968, 1 May.

Andreu, R and C. Ciborra (1996). 'Organizational Learning and Core Capabilities Development: The Role of IT.' *Journal of Strategic Information Systems* 5: 111–127.

Apte, U. (1990). 'Global Outsourcing of Information Systems and Processing Services.' *The Information Society* 7: 287–303.

Armit, R. and P. Schoemaker (1993). 'Strategic and Organizational Rent.' *Strategic Management Journal* 14: 33–46.

Asanuma, B. (1989). 'Manufacturer–Supplier Relationships in Japan and the Concept of Relation Specific Skill.' *Journal of the Japanese and International Economies* 3: 1–30.

Aubert, B., S. Rivard and M. Party (1996). 'A Transaction Cost Approach to Outsourcing Behaviour: Some Experimental Evidence.' *Information & Management* 30(1): 51–64.

Baker, W. E. and R. R. Faulkner (1991). 'Strategies for Managing Suppliers of Professional Services.' *California Management Services*. 33(4 Summer): 33–45.

Barney, J. (1986). 'Strategic Factor Markets: Expectations, Luck, and Business Strategy.' *Management Science* 32: 1231–1241.

Barney, J. (1991). 'Firm Resources and Sustained Competitive Advantage.' *Journal of Management* 17: 99–120.

Beulen, E. (2000). *Governance of IT Outsourcing Relations*. Ph.D. Thesis. The Netherlands, Tilburg University (in Dutch).

Beulen, E. and P. Ribbers (2003). 'IT Outsourcing Contracts: Practical Implications of the Incomplete Contract Theory.' *Proceedings HICSS36 Conference, IEEE.* 0-7695-1874-5/03.

Bharadwaj, A. (2000). 'A Resource-based Perspective on Information Technology Capability and Firm Performance: An Empirical Investigation.' *MIS Quarterly* **24**(1 March): 169–196.

Buck-Lew, M. (1992). 'To Outsource or Not?' *International Journal of Information Management* **12**: 3–20.

Capon, N. and R. Glazer (1987). 'Marketing and Technology: A Strategic Coalignment.' *Journal of Marketing* **51**(3): 1–14.

Coase, R. (1937). 'The Nature of the Firm.' *Economica* **4**: 386–405.

Collis, D. (1991). 'A Resource-based Analysis of Global Competition: The Case of the Bearing Industry.' *Strategic Management Journal* **12**: 49–68.

Conner, D. (1994). *Managing the speed of change.* New York, Villard Books (Random House, Inc.).

Copeland, D. and J. McKenney (1988). 'Airline Reservation Systems: Lessons from History.' *MIS Quarterly* **12**(3): 353–370.

Corbett, M. (2002). *The Global Sourcing Market 2002.* Michael F. Corbett & Associates, Reasearch Report, June 2002.

Cox, R. (2002). *Gartner Service and Sourcing Scenario.* Conference European Symposium, Florence, Italy, 32A-SPR3 4/02, 8–10 April.

Currie, W. and L. Willcocks (1998). *New Strategies in IT Outsourcing: Major Trends and Global Best Practises.* London, British Intelligence.

Davenport, T. (1993). *Process Innovation, Reengineering Work Through Information Technology.* Boston, Harvard Business School press.

Davenport, T. (1998). 'Putting the Enterprise into the Enterprise System.' *Harvard Business Review* **76**(4): 121–131.

DeSouza, R. (2002). 'ERP Solutions for 2002–2005: Opportunities in a Mature Market, Research Brief.' *Gartner Dataquest*, 4 June.

Dyer, J. (1996). 'Specialized Supplier Networks as a Source of Competitive Advantage: Evidence from the Auto Industry.' *Strategic Management Journal* **17**: 271–292.

Dyer, J. and H. Singh (1998). 'The Relational View: Cooperative Strategy and Sources of Inter-organizational Competitive Advantage.' *Academy of Management Review* **23**(4): 660–679.

Eckerson, W. (1990). 'Workers Wage War Against Outsourcing by Filing.' *Network World* **7**(27), 2 July.

Feeny, D. and L. Willcocks (1998). 'Re-designing the IS Function Around Core Capabilities.' *Long Range Planning* **31**(3): 354–367.

Grant, R. (1991). 'The Resource-based Theory of Competitive Advantage.' *California Management review* **33**(3): 114–135.

Grönroos, C. (1990). *Service Management and Marketing, Managing the Moment of Truth in Services Competition.* Estados Unidos, Lexington books.

Grossman, S and O. Hart (1986). 'The Costs and Benefits: A Theory of Vertical and Lateral Integration.' *Journal of Politica Economy* **94**: 671–719.

Hammersmith, A. (1989). 'Slaying the IS Dragon with Outsourcery.' *Computerworld* **23**(38): 89–93, 18 September.

Harrigan, K. (1985). *Strategic Flexibility.* Lexington, MA, Lexington books.

Hart, O. (1995). *Contracts and Financial structure.* Oxford, Oxford University Press.

Hart, O. and J. Moore (1990). 'Property Right and the Nature of the Firm.' *Journal of Political Economy* **98**: 1119–1158.

Keen, P. (1991). *Shaping the Future: Business Design Through Information Technology.* Cambridge, MA, Harvard Business Press.

Kennedy, E. and K. Irshad (2002). 'IDC's 100 European Outsourcing Deals of 2001.' *IDC#RIO3J*, May.

Kitzis, E. (1998). *Market definitions and forecasts*. Gartner presentation: VENSvcsMkt498Ekitzis.

Klepper, R. (1995). 'The Management of Partnering Development in IS Outsourcing.' *Journal of Information Technology, Theme Issue Information Technology Outsourcing: Theory and Practice* **10**(4): 249–258.

KPMG (1997). *Service Level Agreements*. KPMG Management Consultants.

Lacity, M. and R. Hirschheim (1993). *Information Systems Outsourcing*. Wiley.

Laplante, A. (1997). 'Teamwork is Good Work: From Psychologist to Software Engineers, Web Development Groups aren't One-person Shows.' *Computerworld* (8 December): 8

Larson, A. (1992). 'Network Dyads in Entrepreneurial Settings: A Study on Governance of Exchange Relationships.' *Administrative Science Quarterly* **37**: 76–104.

Markus, L. et al. (2000). 'Learning from Early Adopters' Experiences with ERP: Problem Encountered and Succes Achieved.' *Journal of Information Technology* **15**(4): 245–265.

Marwick, A. (2001). 'Knowledge Management Technology.' *IBM Systems Journal* **40**(4): 814–830.

Maskin, L. and J. Tirole (1999). 'Unforeseen Contingencies and Incomplete Contracts.' *Review of Economic Studies* **66**: 83–114.

Mason, T. (1990). *Perot*. Homewood, Illinois, Dow Jones-Irwin.

Mata, F., W. Fuerst and J. Barney (1995). 'Information Technology and Sustained Competitive Advantage: A Resource-based Analysis.' *MIS Quarterly* (December): **9**(4): 487–505.

Mulligan, P. (2002). 'Specification of a Capability-based IT Classification Framework.' *Information and Management* **39**: 647–658.

Nam, K., S. Rajagopalan and H. Rao (1996). 'A Two-level Investigation of Information Systems Outsourcing.' *Ass. for comp. machinery. Com. of the ACM* **39**(7 July).

Nonaka, I. (1991). 'The Knowledge Creating Company.' *Harvard Business Review* **69**(November–December): 96–104.

Nonaka, I. and H. Takeuchi (1995). *The Knowledge Creating Company, How Japanese Companies Create the Dynasties of Innovation*.' Oxford, Oxford University Press.

Parkhe, A. (1993). 'Strategic Alliance Structuring: A Game Theoretic and Transaction Cost Examining of Interfirm Cooperation'. *Academy of Management Journal* **36**: 794–829.

Pereira, R. (1999). 'Resource View Theory Analysis of SAP as a Source of Competitive Advantage of Firms.' *Database for advances in Information Systems* **30**(1 Winter).

Peteraf, M. (1993). 'The Cornerstones of Competitive Advantage: A Resource-based View.' *Strategic Management Journal* **14**: 179–191.

Pinnington, A. and P. Woolcock (1995). 'How Far is IS/IT Outsourcing Enabling New Organizational Structure and Competences?' *International Journal of Information Management* **15**(5): 353–365.

Polanyi, M. (1966). *The Tacit Dimension*. New York, NY, Doubleday.

Prahalad, C. and G. Hamel (1990). 'The Core Competence of the Corporation.' *HBR* (May–June): 79–90.

Quinn, J. and J. Hilmer (1994). 'Strategic Sourcing.' *Sloan Management Review*, Summer 35(4): 43–56.

Ravichandran, T. and C. Lertwongsatien (2002). 'Impact of Information Systems Sources and Capabilities on Firm Performance: A Resource Based Perspective.' *Twenty-third International Conference on Information Systems* Barcelona: 577–583.

Ross, J., C. Beath and D. Goodhue (1996). 'Develop Long-term Competitiveness Through IT Assets.' *Sloan Management Review* 38(1): 31–45.

Roy, V. and B. Aubert (2002). 'A Resource-based Analysis of IT Sourcing.' *Database* 33(2 Spring): 29–40.

Russo, M. and P. Fouts (1997). 'A Resource-based Perspective on Corporate Environmental Performance and Profitability.' *Academy of management journal* 40(3): 543–549.

Saxenian, A. (1994). *Regional Advantages*. Cambridge, MA, Harvard University Press.

Schoo, K. (1999). 'Engineering Complex Software Implementation Programmes.' *Forschung-report*, PhD thesis, Tilburg University, The Netherlands, Berlin, VDE Verlag.

Segal, I. (1995). *Essays on Commitment, Renegotiation, and Incomplete Contracts*. Ph.D. Dissertation. Harvard University.

Teece, D. (1987). Profiting from technological innovation: implications for integration, collaboration, licensing and public policy. *The competitive challenge: strategies for industrial innovation and renewal*. D. Teece (ed.). Cambridge, MA, Ballinger: 185–219.

Teece, D. (1998). 'Capturing Value from Knowledge Assets: The New Economy, Markets for Know-how and Intangible Assets.' *California Management Review* 40(3 Spring): 55–79.

Terdiman, R. (1991). 'Outsourcing: Threat or Salvation.' *Gartner research report* IS: R-980-180, July.

Terdiman, R. and A. Young (2003). 'Management Update: Application Outsourcing Trends for 2003 and 2004.' *Gartner Article* IGG-02052003-03, 5 February.

Thurlin, N. (1999). *Partnerships for Power*. London, PriceWaterhouseCoopers.

Tirole, J. (1989). *The Theory of Industrial Organizations*. Cambridge, MIT Press (Chapter 1, pp. 15–61).

Travis, L. and A. Bacon (2003). 'Should My ERP Vendor be My Outsourcing Partner?' *AMR Research Report*, May.

Vergin, R. and M. Qoronflesh (1998). 'Corporate Reputation and the Stock Market.' *Business Horizons* 41(1 January/February): 19–26.

Weigelt, K. and C. Camerer (1988). Reputation and Corporate Strategy: A Review of Recent Theory and Applications.' *Strategic Management Journal* 9: 443–454.

Weill, P. and M. Broadbent (1998). *Leveraging the New Infrastructure: How Market Leaders Capitalize on Information Technology*. Cambridge, MA, Harvard Business School Press.

Willcocks, L. and C. Chio (1995). 'Co-operative Partnerships and "Total" IT Outsourcing: From Contractual Obligations to Strategic Alliance?' *European Management Journal* 13(1 March).

Willcocks, L. and G. Fitzgerald (1994). *A Business Guide to Outsourcing IT: A Study of European Best Practices in the Selection, Management and Use of External IT Services*. London, Business Intelligence.

Williamson, O. (1975). *Markets and Hierarchies*. New York, The Free Press.

Williamson, O. (1979). 'Transaction Cost Economies: The Governance of Contractual Relations.' *Journal of Law and Economics* **22**(2): 233–261.

Yin, R. K. (1989). *Case Study Research: Design and Methods,* Series: *Applied Social Methods*, Vol. 5. Beverly Hills, CA, Sage publications.

Part Four

---

e-Business Applications and Services

13 NHS information systems strategy, planning and implementation of primary service provision

Matthew W. Guah

13.1 Introduction

Many authors have written critiques concerning the use of Internet-dependent models for healthcare applications (Bender-Samuel, 1999; Bennett and Timbrell, 2000; Howcroft, 2001). However, before attempting a review of this work, it is perhaps appropriate to identify what constitutes the major characteristics of Software-as-a-Service to healthcare over the Internet. Some authors have referred to these characteristics as repeatability, reductionism and refutability (Planting, 2000; McCarthy, 2001; Kern et al., 2002). Others, for example Kreger (2003), refer to the strengths of Software-as-a-Service as including objectivity, rigour and respect for the end user and the overall focus of the exercise. Unfortunately, these key characteristics and strengths turn out to be weaknesses, or are at least problematic, when one considers what is presently available and appropriate for the healthcare industry.

The objective of this chapter is to show, using the National Health Service (NHS) case study, how a national healthcare organization can obtain value from Software-as-a-Service using Web services. The author will present an emerging application service provision (ASP) business model in the NHS – referred to as primary service provision (PSP). The PSP initiative is powered by Web services.

The chapter begins with a brief overview of the technology and business issues involving the delivery of applications over the Internet. It also discusses the existing literature on the NHS reform (Atkinson and Peel, 1998; DoH, 2000; Monro et al., 2000; Wanless, 2002), and the key factors that influence information systems (IS) strategic alignment with healthcare investment policy.

13.2 IS strategy, planning and implementation within the NHS

The structure of IS in the NHS has come under more scrutiny in recent years, due primarily to the frequency of changes this 55-year old organization is undergoing (Guah and Currie, 2002; Haines, 2002; Laycock, 2002). Markus (1983) describes the changes required in an organization as those of corporate culture, configuration and co-ordination, and in the way the organization deploys its human, technological and information resources. She describes such issues as culture – consisting of the shared values and beliefs that underlie and define corporate behaviours and objectives. Configurations refer to the physical and organizational structures that exist internally and externally to the NHS. Co-ordination includes the fundamental activities undertaken within the NHS. These activities include the management of healthcare processes and the flows of medical materials and records/health informatics throughout the NHS. It is also emphasized that if the NHS wishes to achieve organizational transformation, then change in one dimension of current strategy must be balanced within another.

For most organizations, the delivery of business applications over the Internet requires more than making the correct choice from the various technologies available. We summarize some of the key challenges facing the NHS as follows:

- Internet technology offers a cost effective means to deploy healthcare applications to various institutions and possibly all users both within and external to the NHS. Cost savings are anticipated to accrue principally from reduced deployment and support costs.

- Most healthcare applications can be Internet enabled today, yet care process support systems over the Internet show the technology is currently immature.

- Considering the quality of PCs in some of the NHS's remote facilities, it is worth noting that one does not need to use Java or other advanced object-oriented technologies to offer Internet access to existing applications. However, complex systems may not be appropriate. True object-oriented software based on either the DCOM or CORBA standards is required for robust healthcare processing systems using Internet technology (Brown and Venkatesh, 2003).

The important issue here is that almost all current applications within the NHS can be Internet enabled using existing and well-tried Internet technology. Any new application introduced to the NHS should offer user access via an Internet browser as a matter of course, taking advantage of Web services technology (Chatterjee et al., 2002).

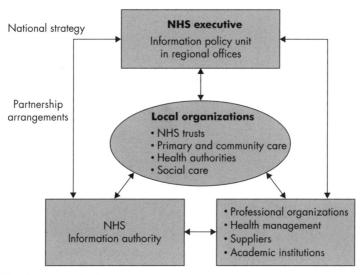

Figure 13.1: NHS structure for IS procurement.

13.2.1 The problem: delivering value from NHS IS strategy

Managers of NHS Trusts[1] are under pressure to meet strict performance targets to show that they are delivering best value for the taxpayers (Collins, 2003). In return for increased investment from the central government, the NHS is implementing root and branch reforms to ensure that the money is not squandered. The pre-PSP national strategy (see Figure 13.1) shows the current process of learning how to operate efficiently and cost effectively to deliver 'best value'. Within a rather monolithic organization, the difficult process by which investment into information technology (IT) is struggling to bring 'business benefit' into the NHS is shown in this chapter. This problem is clearly felt by the constant delays in IT procurement and deployment (see Figure 13.1), making it more difficult for the NHS to have better, faster and more consistent availability of healthcare data for practitioners (Laerum et al., 2001). It also affects up-to-date budget control and analysis as well as ease of technology implementation and use (Wanless, 2002).

Figure 13.1 depicts a complex IS organization within the NHS, composed of many disparate local and professional organizations, many with conflicting interests. To cope with pressures exerted within a more demanding population, of constantly evolving healthcare needs (Collins, 2003), the NHS continuously weighs all its available options, such as the development and maintenance of its own applications, or hiring them from

---

1. Organizational framework of the NHS is based around NHS Trusts, responsible for the provision of secondary services, health authorities and primary care groups/ trusts, responsible for commissioning healthcare services from NHS Trusts.

external suppliers (Kern et al., 2002). The NHS Information Authority (NHSIA) constantly assesses the impact of technology compatibility and the value of new investments in the perceived level of efficiency to NHS operations and management. Several studies into IS strategy and technology standards in the NHS have generated a number of theoretical models for optimizing investment in IT, leading to further expenditure on initiatives like PSP (Eccles et al., 2002; Robinson, 2002; Collins, 2003). PSP presents itself as a viable subset of the ASP business model.

New initiatives, however, must be observed against a background of previous ones within a centralized NHS IT organization, some of which have not always been a success. In the 1990s, several large ventures for hospital IS were disappointing, despite costing the NHS nearly $140 million. The reasons then were mainly due to a strategy of building the system locally, yet being managed centrally. A famous example was the Wessex Regional Health Authority experiment, which ended up with a financial loss to the NHS of around $88 million. A top-down approach, spearheaded by politicians, was at the heart of this project to computerize an entire regional authority. As PSP represents the government's largest-ever IT investment in healthcare, our interest in this chapter is to investigate NHS IS strategy, planning and implementation of PSP across the primary and secondary care systems.

For over a decade, the IS strategy for most organizations has been in a state of evolution toward a form of 'federal governance architecture' (Zmud, 1984; Avison and Fitzgerald, 2003). Within the context of the NHS, the authority for the management of IT infrastructure is vested with a central IT unit, such as the NHSIA, but the authority for the management of IT application and use is vested within individual business units (i.e. local IT management) or Regional Trusts. Such a situation has fuelled the growth of a variety of co-ordination mechanisms, such as IT councils, IT steering councils, service-level agreements (SLAs) and charge-back internal accounting systems, as structural overlays to supplement the hybrid federal governance architecture. With the emergence of e-Business models to enhance the remote delivery of software applications (Weill and Vitale, 2001), the NHS offers a fruitful source of new IT service contracts from external suppliers. In the next section, we discuss the feasibility of providing Software-as-a-Service to the NHS.

13.2.2 Software-as-a-Service to healthcare

The late 1990s saw a proliferation of Software-as-a-Service applications offerings across vertical (i.e. health, manufacturing and financial) and business-facing (i.e. enterprise resource planning (ERP), customer relationship management (CRM), supply-chain and financials) customers. This witnessed what became known as the ASP business model. ASP was marketed as a *revolution* in business computing, offering the potential to pay for software applications on a rental or subscription-pricing model

(Kern et al., 2002; Currie, 2003; Currie et al., 2004). The NHS was seen by many as a fruitful opportunity for suppliers, particularly as it had the reputation of a monolithic and old-fashioned institution with a poor record for developing and implementing technology.

An important debate surrounding the ASP model was the extent to which application outsourcing differs from traditional outsourcing (Kern et al., 2002; Currie, 2003). Probably the most noticeable difference between the two is the relationship between supplier and customer. Unlike traditional outsourcing, where the customer is likely to develop a close relationship with the supplier, the ASP model engenders a more distant, if not, completely remote relationship between the two groups. The issue of 'trust' therefore becomes critical, particularly where the customer deploys an ASP to host software applications containing sensitive and highly confidential data. In the context of the NHS, the issue of a third party becoming a repository for patient data is fraught with potential problems, particularly if the ASP has poor security policies.

13.2.3 Introducing the ASP model within the NHS: opportunity or threat?

As with previous IT initiatives offered to the NHS as a *silver bullet*, the ASP model is no exception. An 'ASP manages and delivers applications capabilities to multiple entities from data centres across a wide area network' (Currie, 2003). Various definitions of ASP are found in Table 13.1. Whilst the general thrust of the ASP model is to deliver software applications over the Internet, different varieties emerged in the form of enterprise, vertical, pure-play, horizontal and enabler ASPs. For example, ASPs targeting only the healthcare sector may market themselves as 'vertical ASPs'. Some examples emerged at the end of the 1990s. Others, offering ERP or CRM applications, were likely to use the term, 'enterprise ASP'. Such labels were useful as marketing tools, largely to help the ASP strategically differentiate itself from others. In addition to these labels, ASPs may claim to be 'the leading healthcare ASP' or 'the ASP for the high-technology equipment manufacturing sector' (Currie et al., 2004).

Within the NHS, the ASP business model offers the opportunity to become an intelligent informatics application, which can channel the flows of health information reaching patients and practitioners in various NHS organizations (Guah and Currie, 2003).

13.2.4 PSP strategy, planning and implementation

The scope of PSP implementation relies on the level of collaboration between a public sector NHS and various private sector service providers (Robertson and Powell, 2000). This process involves making a number of complex trade-offs between ad hoc and integrated system implementation and between accepting existing solutions from other industries and deriving new solutions using the latest available technology (Robertson and Powell, 2000). Horizontal division of the inner workings of the NHS

Table 13.1: Definitions of ASP

Definitions	Authors
An ASP is a third party service firm which deploys, manages and remotely hosts software applications through centrally located services in a rental or lease agreement	ASP Industry Consortium (2000)
An ASP facilitates a remote, centrally managed 'rent-an-application' service for the client	Cherry Tree & Co. (2000)
ASPs are firms that manage and deliver application capabilities to multiple entities from data centres across a wide area network	Currie and Seltsikas (2001)
An ASP is any company that offers specific business applications on a subscription and/or transaction basis via the Internet or other networked arrangements	Majority of ITAA Survey respondents; ITAA (2001)
An ASP is any company that delivers and manages applications and computer services to subscribers/ clients remotely via the Internet or a private network	ITAA and ASP Industry Consortium agreed consolidated definition; ITAA (2001)
ASPs represents the 1st wave to move beyond 'the firewall – key component of existing enterprise architectures – who take traditional enterprise applications like supply-chain management and human resource management and move them outside the firewall in an effort to serve small and medium-size enterprises	Hagel III (2002)
The concept of delivering business applications as a service, or 'apps on tap,' used to be called ASP	Kern, Lacity and Wilcocks (2002)
ASP model (used interchangeably with 'Software-as-a-Service) provides application software via the Internet, through dedicated network and/or through wireless, through an approach of one-to-many services, usually with standardized offerings, to numerous clients or through customizing offerings to a group of clients in particular markets, such as has already been provided to government and the financial sectors	Kakabadse and Kakabadse (2002)

is consistent with the 'push–pull' theory that says PSP is likely to succeed when a need and a means to resolve that need are simultaneously recognized (Zmud, 1984). One of the key challenges facing the NHS vis-a-vis PSP is the need for software applications integration. The expected innovation within PSP for the NHS signifies the adoption of a combination of internally generated and purchased devices, systems, policies, programmes, processes, products and services, which are new to the adopting organization. But for PSP to offer significant benefits to the NHS, it will need to exploit emerging technologies, such as Web services. As we saw with the majority of e-Business failures, and the poor adoption and diffusion of the ASP model (Hagel, 2002; Currie, 2003), most of the technology offerings did not deliver on their promises to enhance business processes and improve efficiency. Part of the reason for this was the lack of maturity in the technology, especially where ASPs were offering client-server systems and applications on a remote delivery model, often to customers who were already using a stand-alone version! In the next section, we explore some of the issues, which need to be addressed if Web services-based software applications are to be adopted by the NHS. We consider some of the software application areas which are likely to use Web services technology.

13.3 Types of applications and Web service technology

Existing literature on healthcare systems has distinguished between three basic types of applications detailed below (Pouloudi, 1999; Klecun-Dabrowska and Cornford, 2000; Laerum et al., 2001; Eccles et al., 2002). The fourth category, however, is a combination of one or more of the other types, but implemented using Internet technology: (1) group collaboration (or groupware), (2) healthcare support systems, (3) business intelligence and (4) e-Commerce.

1 *Group collaboration*: The original purpose of the Internet was essentially to enable (academic) group collaboration. Proprietary group collaboration applications in the NHS are consequently under great pressure from their low cost, tested and robust Internet equivalents (Pouloudi, 1999).

2 *Healthcare process systems*: Although the Internet does offer process systems capability, it is unsophisticated and unstable by comparison to the tried and trusted, but proprietary commercial equivalents. The Internet was never designed to offer more than a very basic transaction capability. Consequently more sophisticated systems require enhancements to today's Internet technology. We will discuss these differences further later on.

3 *Patient intelligence*: Patient intelligence usually involves looking for patterns within very large datasets, in the order of millions of individual data items. As long as the processing of the data happens on a central server, then the Internet forms a good means to deliver the finished results to anyone who requires the information. Viewing reports and simple graphics is easily supported, however complex manipulation of graphical information does not work well using today's Internet technology due to network capacity restraints.

4 *e-Commerce*: At its most basic e-Commerce is buying and selling over the Internet, whether to consumers or business to business. This can include taking payment electronically via a credit card, or it may be

restricted to qualified customers who pay by invoice. NHS systems may not require a financial transaction system, but the need to interact with patients is promoting e-Commerce type system to a higher position on NHSIA strategic agenda.

If we assume that an NHS Trust wants to allow patients to view their range of medical reports, test results and specify monitoring instructions, via the Internet, this is a relatively simple sequence of basic healthcare and can be implemented using today's Internet technology by 'bolting on' a Web server to your existing IT infrastructure with some additional code on the server. See Section 13.3.1.2 for more details.

Not only must Trust systems work together seamlessly, each must be integrated with Web technology, and the interactions will often require multiple steps in the correct order with a high degree of security. This is an advanced use of the Internet, and requires much more than a 'bolt on' solution.

13.3.1 Three generations of Internet technology

Internet technology is an implementation of a 2 tier 'thin client' architecture. Most of the processing is done on central server(s) and a Web browser essentially displays the results or information 'served up' by a Web server. More sophisticated applications which require significant local processing or complex transaction processing capabilities will see a move toward a 3 or '*n*' tier architecture. This will require the adoption of object-oriented-based technology if the NHS does not want to repeat the mistakes of the 1980s and early 1990s with the 'fat client' syndrome (MacIver, 2003).

Simple Web server technology

A Web server is a computer that transmits information in HTML formats across a TCP/IP network using the http protocol to the user's computer, which uses a Web browser to display the information. The browser can be a stand-alone executable program, for example Microsoft Internet Explorer or Netscape Navigator, or it can be a Browser widget (essentially a window with cut down browser capability) within another application. The Web server manages pages of HTML-formatted text, which contains references to graphics, other multimedia content and programs residing on the server. To view a smear result from the patient's home over the Internet involves animated graphics, video and audio, so the user will usually need to have a more advanced version of a specific browser or a plug-in installed. A plug-in typically must be downloaded over the Internet. For security reasons, the health authority must have policies forbidding installation of plug-ins on critical healthcare systems.

Where the information required is more dynamic, for example the results of a database query, the Web server extracts the information needed from one or more systems using a simple program (Kakabadse and

Kakabadse, 2002). For example, a cgi or VB script. A variant on this is where the application creates the relevant pages and passes them back to the Web server. For example, as the result of a database query by the diabetes patient or their carer, the application populates a page containing the table of results by using a template. Microsoft's active server pages technology is a popular means for performing this kind of simple requirement.

This type of Web server implementation basically supports simple single step transactions. Each time a request for information arrives, the Web server responds with the relevant information. It then waits for the next request for another user, but maintains no record of what it has done.

Technically the Web server maintains no state information. There is little or no security in this implementation with the exception of a firewall (software or hardware that blocks suspicious incoming network traffic), although there can be simple password/username protection implemented on the Web server. Performance and transaction integrity are not generally an issue in this sort of implementation. If a user's request is not answered, or the reply never reaches the user, then the user must re-send the request.

The typical health service use of this type of set-up is to offer information (Laycock, 2002). For example, a virus epidemic warning and alert notices for SARS, contact information and perhaps a simple e-mail facility for any patient in the country. On an Intranet, it might comprise the telephone list, HR policy manuals and the BMA or nursing newsletters.

Extended Web server technology

The extended Web server is an enhancement of the simple Web server. This is typical of e-Commerce applications implemented by many organizations today. The Web server has more complex scripting, and information is now usually partly or wholly password protected. Enhanced security, usually implemented using secure sockets layer (SSL) allows for the encryption of sensitive information, such as credit card payments. On an Intranet it might include interactive completion and validation of reporting forms, holiday applications and timesheets. The more robust password protection facility allows an Extranet to be created. The server is required to support multi-step transactions and so needs to maintain state information on the progress of the users' interaction. For example, at least five steps are required: input and validation of registration information, followed by the generation of a username, which then allows the patient to place an enquiry and confirm appointment. This is stretching the Internet technology beyond its original purpose, so there are a number of techniques that can be used. These divide into two main approaches: much enhanced server side scripting or downloading code to the browser. Sometimes a combination of both is used.

By using downloaded Cookies, Javascript, simple Java applets or Active X components, the functionality available on the user's computer can be considerably extended. For example, data input can be validated more easily and a more efficient connection can be established directly between the user and the ultimate application to offer improved transaction processing capabilities. Unfortunately, downloading code to the user's browser is controversial. Many companies expressly prevent this by installing their own firewall to block download of anything except HTML and simple graphics. Some consumers also block one or more of these technologies: the most disliked seem to be Cookies.

The other problem with using advanced coding options on the Web browser, or even some features of HTML, is that not all versions of browsers support those features. It is usually difficult to mandate a browser outside the organization, so you may inadvertently deny external customers access to your application if you use non-standard features.

On the server side cgi scripting capabilities can be extended using a proprietary application programming interfaces (APIs), ISAPI or NSAPI, from Microsoft and Netscape, respectively. Many tools vendors have now enhanced their standard coding tools to support both these standards, and to provide middleware to support management of state information, downloadable applets, the merging of data into Web pages and interfacing to application functions. Microsoft and Netscape spent considerable time warring over this arena in 1997 and 1998. The strength of this approach is that it can extend an existing investment and, with some effort, can be enhanced to the front of existing applications (Kakabadse and Kakabadse, 2002). However, it can be difficult to get good performance, and is likely to require considerable maintenance. This is a workable compromise for the NHS – especially if there are a number of legacy applications on the server side that cannot be replaced.

Advanced object-based Internet applications

The future of NHS applications (and the current situation for a few Trusts) is object-oriented technology, which is being fundamentally integrated with Web service technology. Typically part of the application is downloaded as required to the user's Web browser to create a true client–server application where significant processing can be performed on the user computer if required. Performance is much enhanced and multi-step transactions are much more easily supported. In this scenario the basic http protocol is only used to download the basic client side applet or component (such as a Java bean or an Active X component). Thereafter, more efficient protocols, such as DCOM, CORBA IIOP or Java's RMI, are used. There is research to show that these protocols are up to 200 times faster than the http/cgi technology used by basic Web servers (Gallivan, 2001).

The key technical issue is which object technology to use. There are two competing standards, DCOM and CORBA, supported by Microsoft and their commercial competitors, respectively. This is where Java comes into the picture. It is an object-oriented programming language with a number of built-in features that enable Internet application development and deployment. The 'pure Java' camp wants to use Java, in conjunction with CORBA, to bypass Microsoft's lock on the PC-operating system (DCOM is supported by Microsoft's-operating systems). Microsoft naturally opposes this strategy. The strength of this approach is that a robust application architecture can be implemented. Control continues to rest at the centre, as software is downloaded as required to the client side from an application server.

The major weakness of deploying Web services technology via the ASP model is its relative immaturity (Hagel, 2002). The technology is still evolving, so there is a risk that the NHS may adopt a risk-averse strategy by becoming a laggard as opposed to a leader. Like the corporate sector, the NHS raises some concerns about the safety of deploying software applications over the Internet. Any use of downloaded Java or Active X is still blocked by many Trusts. For patients, the lack of bandwidth on the public Internet will limit adoption. A set of Java beans or Active X components can easily exceed 2MB in size. In today's environment, that could take 30 min or more for a consumer to download. Despite these technical challenges, the development of Web services technology may generate a range of business benefits.

13.3.2 Key issues and benefits

Cost reduction

Cutting costs is a perennial issue and Web service technology offers the possibility to increase information flows and reduce or conjoin business processes. Firstly, the hardware and software is cheap and becoming cheaper. Furthermore existing network infrastructure (i.e. wiring) can probably be re-used. Secondly, less obvious costs of deployment and support can be reduced significantly by using this technology. Apart from the browser, there is no software to install on all those user machines.

Flexibility and speed

Given Web services technology, upgrades of applications can happen immediately, so it no longer takes one month to roll out 100 PCs in a single Trust. New users, for example temporary staff, can immediately be given access to the applications they need. E-mail is quicker and in many cases more convenient than the phone. Documents, drafts of contracts can be sent and patients can request information and receive an immediate reply. Patients can access information on scheduling and drugs availability, and information can be updated on a daily basis, not every few weeks. This makes it easier to reduce inventory and to manage those costs.

Patient care

The normal business hours of 9 to 5, Monday to Friday are obviously not applicable in a healthcare institution. The NHS system is a 24×7 organization. Also, not all users who use the NHS are UK based, so Web services applications can make resources and information available anytime and from anywhere. The convenience of a standard user interface should not be underestimated from the patient's viewpoint. As people become more familiar with e-Business, it becomes easier to use an online health check or general medical inquiry. Internet search engines (such as www.google.com, www.yahoo.com or www.Lycos.com) make it easier to locate the information required from the NHS Direct Web site (see Figure 13.3).

Patients and other users can be confident that they always have access to the latest information, and hence the Web service or ASP application will become their first port of call, before they pick use the phone to ask a physician to discuss a medical condition. A proviso is that software application may never satisfy all needs, and not all patients will be confident in using the application, at least in the next few years. This may result in a dual system where a qualified physician supports Web service (online) applications for patients.

Trust networking and strategic partnerships

The widespread use of networking and strategic partnerships in the NHS is a long established trend (Atkinson and Peel, 1998; Pouloudi, 1999; Wanless, 2002). The distributed nature of Web services technology makes it relatively easy to outsource parts, or even all, of the application and technology it runs on. Many ASP applications are built by 'bolting on' a Web server to existing applications. The Web server can be managed and run by a third party specialist. Taking as a basis an existing internal application, it is possible to have a third party design, develop, host and support an online service. This can be entirely transparent to patients, and many large Trusts are currently following this route with a range of applications.

Organizational impact

Web services applications raise some interesting organizational issues for the NHS. Many individuals, particularly those consultants with skills and experience that are in short supply, see private practice for 1 or 2 days a week as highly desirable. Other people want or need access to information in the evenings and/or at weekends. There are also the junior doctors and nurses who spend much of their time out and about with patients on the wards or at health centres. Web services technology can provide them with remote access to the specialist medical applications on demand. This sort of usage for NHS systems will continue to grow as the technology becomes ever more widespread.

The future

The use of Web services technology, both software and hardware, offers many new opportunities for the future of healthcare. IS suppliers, who have not yet Internet enabled their software, are watching this sector closely with a view to developing new Web-enabled offerings. The large suppliers are already working with this sector, but there are many new niche opportunities for smaller suppliers. The easy availability, cheap and ubiquitous Internet technology is forcing the long awaited integration of telephone and computer services. It will also cause a rapid growth in applications for personal use, such as personal organizers, pagers and data-enabled cellular phones. In the longer term, when the infrastructure can support it, entirely new services, such as individual patient treatment systems, will become established based on Internet technology.

13.3.3 Key suppliers

IBM

IBM, like its competitors, is an active player in the Web services arena. Nearly every technology they sell today is being Web services enabled, and their long-term commitment to Java is clear (Gottschalk et al., 2002). They also have a huge and lucrative software consultancy business, which has clearly targeted e-Business as an additional source of income. Traditionally IBM mainframes dominated the transaction systems market. Web services technology is both a potential threat and an opportunity. If IBM can get transaction systems working well in the NHS using Web services technology they can continue to dominate and expand this market area. Furthermore it may offer a challenge to Microsoft's dominance of the PC market.

Oracle

Oracle make their money from databases, sclling application development tools and business systems, such as Oracle Financials. They see Web services as a means to expand the business. Oracle is selling object-oriented applications to the NHS – based on Java technology – to perform the core services of taking and processing treatment-specific information gathering, disease monitoring, drugs ordering and management, etc. Their financial and other enterprise applications have Web services options for these purposes.

Sun

Sun sell hardware, associated operating systems, development software and services to the NHS. Their hardware servers are traditionally the workhorses of the Internet, but this business is under increasing pressure, both from other suppliers and the downward trend in Internet technology costs. One potential major source of income is Java. Whilst this is now being widely adopted, it remains to be seen as to what income Sun can derive from Java itself.

Microsoft

After initially dismissing the Internet, Microsoft are now very deeply involved in supporting Web services technology throughout their product range. They sell virtually all the software products and technology required to implement Web services applications, and hope to position their Windows-XP-operating system as the standard platform for Web services within and outside the healthcare industry. Key issues for Microsoft are to control how Java is used, and to subvert the technology/ commercial stance adopted by its major competitors.

ERP vendors

ERP vendors sell Enterprise Resource Planning software, the fundamental application suites on which most NHS Trusts now base their financial management. Traditionally this was a mainframe-based market that grew substantially as it adopted client–server technology. All of these suppliers have Internet enabled their applications.

13.4 ASP concerns and risks

The Internet era is information intensive involving many interlinked and interdependent business services and related transactions. With a move to the ASP model, such transactions are set to grow exponentially leading to fundamental changes in product and service delivery processes. Changes in technology act as a driving force for subsequent business process change (Scott Morton, 1991; Davenport, 1993; Orlikowski et al., 1994).

When the NHS uses one ASP for all applications, integration between health-critical applications is simple. However, if the NHS has multiple ASPs or only some applications in a hosted environment, the backend integration of these applications – allowing them to communicate – becomes very complicated.

Another issue is that individual Trusts with internal technology departments perceive surrendering control of the application to an ASP, as a vote of no confidence in IT. This is because there are risks in losing control of the application and the data if a third party is given control (Little, 1999; Currie, 2003). The relationship between your ASP and the system vendor can also be fraught with difficulties. Some of these risks are outlined as follows:

■ *Financial failure*: Many of the first phase of ASPs developed poor business models and subsequently went out of business (Hagel, 2002). Many ASPs targeting the health sector experienced difficulties in gaining access to the key decision makers (Currie et al., 2003). Whilst they believed their potential software applications would be of immense interest to healthcare professionals and IT managers, they found the many layers of bureaucracy and administration virtually impenetrable, finding that IT procurement is often done at the political (governmental) level, rather than at the individual NHS Trust level.

■ *Poor performance*: In general, an ASP should offer an SLA as part of the contract. The agreement will define mutual expectations as penalties for poor performance. Early ASPs and customers, alike, were often confused about how to develop an SLA. Some of the less ethical ASPs also ignored important criteria, such as data security controls, believing that potential customers would not seek to ask questions, preferring instead to focus upon price and application delivery.

■ *Software customization and integration issues*: Where the hosted software resides on a remote server controlled by the ASP, and the customer retains software locally, some form of integration may be necessary. One of the initial stumbling blocks of ASPs was the lack or importance they attached to customization and integration issues. The one-to-many offering from ASPs often proved unsuitable for those customers, which required at least some degree of customization and integration of their applications and data, respectively.

■ *Security breaches*: The use of an ASP is to place trust in a third party supplier. Many ASPs had poor external and internal security measures. A reputable ASP should be able to document and demonstrate their security provision in detail. The continued growth in the use of highly distributed networks supporting both Internet and mobile users is creating a continuous problem of ensuring that the appropriate person gets access to business information, without leaving the system vulnerable to attack from unauthorized users.

■ *Doubtful savings*: As ASP was depicted as an e-Business model to benefit small businesses, purchasing software on a subscription basis may offer cost advantages over locally installed and managed software. However, for a large customer, such as the NHS, caution must be followed as various 'hidden costs' may accrue, such as fluctuating broadband connection costs, and consultancy and support charges.

In the current economic climate the desire to take risks is diminished and the need to cut costs is paramount. The DoH and NHSIA are looking for technology propositions that are low risk and likely to deliver a high return quickly on the money invested (Whelan and McGrath, 2001).

13.5 Web services applications in the NHS

The NHSIA and IT service providers are constantly revising the principles that guide their collaboration. These principles are applied to the collaborative process generally and to the IS applications activities that are the object of the collaboration (Pouloudi, 1999). Although each example of successful public–private collaboration on health services in the UK is unique, certain characteristics are common to all.

Web services, in the case of NHS Direct, use e-messaging to share patient details with the out-of-hours services, wherein millions of messages have been recorded saving huge amounts of administrative resources for the NHS, which can be deployed elsewhere. Also realized here is the lesson that applying Web services to NHS Direct could have equal impact and is a real example of the benefits to be gained from sharing information. Other usage in the future could include future developments of the system to allow patients to book an appointment with their general practitioner (GP) practices via NHS Direct. Patient information sent electronically is protected by encryption and digital signature to ensure security and confidentiality.

The NHSIA sees Web services as a means of realizing its proclamation of a societal legitimacy for high quality health IS. The NHS Direct example provides a vehicle for an image of an empowered population – served by informational resources – shown to be making decisions about their own health and participating in the process of setting healthcare policy (Wanless, 2002). The integrated care records service (ICRS) example provides a means for operating-cost reduction, gross margin improvement and asset leverage through the more effective co-ordination of supply-chain processes across UK health sector.

13.5.1 ICRS

The twenty-first century NHS is a highly sophisticated and information intensive activity involving many interlinked and interdependent care and service-related transactions. Changes in technology act as a driving force for subsequent business process change (Orlikowski and Tyre, 1994; Porter, 1998). ICRS is a proposed national system that is intended to handle in excess of 3 million critical processes in the NHS facilities each day (see Figure 13.2). A comparison with the financial sector shows that it has gone beyond the point of processing even higher volume of bank transactions daily. Considering that the nature of health data is different from straightforward credit and debit items in various banks, the level of

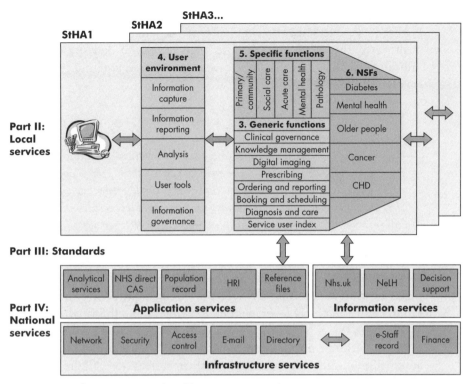

Figure 13.2: The ICRS structure (adapted from DoH, 2002).

system reliability would need to be higher (Uden, 2002). In a typical week, NHS laboratories and associated services can easily provide results on several millions of tests; 1.4 million people are expected to receive help in their home from the NHS system. Six million people visit their local surgeries (GP). While more than 800 thousand people are treated as hospital outpatients, pharmacists dispense about 8.5 million items on prescriptions (Collins, 2003).

Figure 13.2 shows the current flowchart layout for ICRS. A significant factor in the successful implementation of ICRS is the IT structure of the NHS which also affects the general health strategy by controlling resources for implementing the Twenty-first Century Strategy for Health, Medical records and the capabilities of the ICRS suppliers (DoH, 2000). It shows a complex organizational/contextual structure, where the current political agenda mediates organizational forms and performance with respect to the external environment.

In the case of ICRS, Web services integrate projects with many forms of heterogeneous IT components across the NHS. This protects old investments, which do not require the NHS to abandon the traditional IT infrastructure. This is because Web services have their roots in Internet-based open standards, component-based distributed computing and the software as a service model.

13.5.2 Delivering manageable applications

Whilst ASPs overstate the simplicity of the Web services solution in healthcare, the NHS must ensure that important key performance indicators, such as security policies and procedures, are built into SLAs. One NHS IT manager said:

> *Why do we implement clinical systems? Because they change peoples lives and even save lives. Any model underpinning IS in the NHS should: (i) provide clinicians with what they want like patient data, pathology results, etc.; (ii) be relevant to the medical consultant for physiology and must make treatment interactive; and (iii) provide patient with what they want like convenience and timely service, rapid test results and clear information. If anyone can guarantee me that in Web services, I'll take it any day.*

The ICRS project takes advantage of Web services as a significant new phase in the evolution of software development. It allows the NHS to rapidly and effectively leverage their existing IT and information assets.

The NHS Direct has shown how a Web services-based application can offer the NHS an unprecedented opportunity to increase the level of automation in their interactions with their patients (see Figure 13.3).

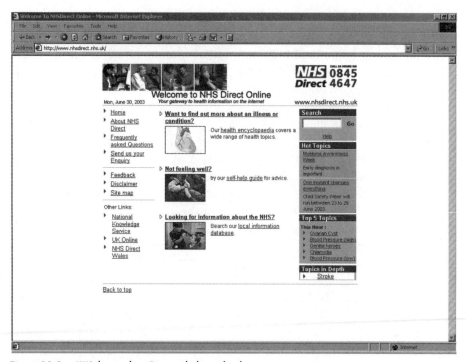

Figure 13.3:　NHS direct online @ www.nhsdirect.nhs.uk.

13.6 Conclusion

The discussion above has shown how the NHS uses the PSP model of providing software-as-a-service. This chapter has shown how the NHS considers many respects in which ASP business model seems to be logical extensions of a much broader outsourcing trend (Currie and Willcocks, 1998). The areas covered in this chapter bring forth the profound consequences of PSP for primary care. This initiative is as much about reshaping local services as it is about technology. PSP reflects a form of organization innovation diffusion that is a useful source to build a conceptual framework for ASP adoption and diffusion (Guah and Currie, 2002). Most existing applications in the NHS can be Web enabled using existing and relatively stable Web services technology. The need to interact with patients is promoting e-Business systems to a higher position on the NHSIA strategic agenda. Moreover, the NHS may benefit from the potential to cut costs and offer a 24×7 service. This will need to be seen as a result of the PSP scheme in conjunction with service provider/suppliers in a manner transparent to patients. Certain legacy systems in the NHS will require the adoption of object-oriented-based technology for the NHS to avoid a repeat of the 'fat client' problems of the 1980s and early 1990s. Some of the challenges facing the NHSIA in choosing Web services technology for deploying healthcare applications include:

1 The complexity of the application healthcare processing using Web services technology is not yet mature, and can therefore require considerable effort to implement.

2 It is difficult to predict the capabilities of the Web browser used by users external to the NHS. Many cannot run Java, Active X components or Javascript either because their PCs are not powerful enough or company policy forbids it. Others are using older versions of browsers which do not support the most recent HTML standard. It is advisable to be conservative in what one expects to do on the user's Web browser.

3 Complex Web services-based applications will require the use of object-oriented technology. There are essentially two choices: Microsoft's technology or that supported by their opponents at IBM, Sun, Oracle and Netscape.

4 Most existing NHS applications can be Web service enabled using existing and relatively well-tried Web services technology. Any new healthcare application should offer user access via an Internet browser as a matter of course.

The vision of NHS to maximize PSP potential will prove futile unless Web service architectures are embraced. This is due to the fact that the NHS is more likely to adopt Web services when the many disparate applications can be integrated.

References and Further Reading

Alter, S. (1996). *Information Systems: A Management Perspective*, 2nd edition. The Benjamin/Cummings Publishing Company.

ASP Industry Consortium (2000). *Industry News*. www.aspindustry.org. Accessed in December 2001.

Atkinson, C. J. and V. J. Peel (1998). 'Transforming a Hospital through Growing, not Building, an Electronic Patient Record System.' *Methods of Information in Medicine* 37: 285–293.

Avison, D. E. and G. Fitzgerald (2003). 'Where Now for Development Methodologies?' *Communications of the ACM*. January 46(1): 79–82.

Bender-Samuel, P. (1999). *A Fork in the Road for ASPs*. www.outsourcing-journal.com/issues/ Accessed in December 2001.

Bennett, C. and G. T. Timbrell (2000). 'Application Service Providers: Will They Succeed?' *Information Systems Frontiers* 2(2): 195–211.

Brown, S. A. and V. Venkatesh (2003). Bringing Non-Adopter Along: The Challenge Facing the PC Industry. *Communications of the ACM,* 46(4): 76–80.

Chatterjee, D., R. Grewal and V. Sambamurthy (2002). 'Shaping Up for e-Commerce: Institutional Enablers of the Organizational Assimilation of Web Technologies.' *MIS Quarterly* 26(2): 65–89.

Checkland, P. B. and J. Scholes (1990). *Soft Systems Methodology in Action*. Chichester, Wiley.

Collins, T. (2003). 'Doctors Attacks Health IT Codes.' *Computer Weekly*, February 6.

Currie, W. L. (2003). 'A Knowledge-Based Risk Assessment Framework for Evaluating Web-Enabled Application Outsourcing Projects.' *International Journal of Project Management* 21: 207–217.

Currie, W., B. Desai, and N. Khan (2004). Customer Evaluation of Application Service Provisioning in Five Vertical Sectors. *Journal of Information Technology*. (Forthcoming).

Currie, W. L. and P. Seltsikas (2001). 'Exploring the Supply-Side of IT Outsourcing: Evaluating the Emerging Role of Application Service Providers.' *European Journal of Information Systems* 10: 123–134.

Currie, W. L. and L. P. Willcocks (1998). 'Analysing Four Types of IT Sourcing Decisions in the Context of Size, Client/Supplier Interdependency and Risk Mitigation.' *Information Systems Journal* 8: 119–143.

Currie, W. L., B. Desai, N. Khan, X. Wang and V. Weerakkody (2003). Vendor Strategies for Business Process and Applications Outsourcing: Recent Findings from Field Research. *Proceedings: Hawaii International Conference on Systems Sciences*. Hawaii, January.

Davenport, T. H. (1993). *Process Innovation: Reengineering Work through Information Technology*. Boston, MA: Harvard Business School Press. Issue 337.

DoH (2000). *NHS Plan: An Information Strategy for the Modern NHS*. Department of Health, London.

DoH (2002). *NHS Plan: An information strategy for the modern NHS*, London.

Eccles, M., E. McColl, N. Steen, N. Rousseau, J. Grimshaw, D. Parkin and I. Purves (2002). 'Effect of Computerized Evidence Based Guidelines on Management of Asthma and Angina in Adults in Primary Care: Cluster Randomized Controlled Trial.' *British Medical Journal* 325(26 October): 941–944.

Gottschalk, K., S. Graham, H. Kreger and J. Snell (2002). 'Introduction to Web Services Architecture.' *IBM Systems Journal* 41(4): 170–177.

Gallivan, M.J. (2001). Striking a Balance Between Trust and Control in a Virtual Organization: a content analysis of open source software case studies. *Information Systems Journal*. Volume 11, pp. 277–304.

Guah, M. W. and W. L. Currie (2002). 'Evaluation of NHS Information Systems Strategy: Exploring the ASP Model.' *Issues of Information Systems Journal* III: 222–228.

Guah, M. W. and W. L. Currie (2003). 'ASP: A Technology and Working Tool for Intelligent Enterprises of the 21st Century'. *Intelligent Enterprises of the 21st Century*. J. N. D. Gupta and S. K. Sharma (eds). Summer. IGI Publications.

Hagel III, J. (2002). *Out of the Box: Strategies for Achieving Profits Today and Growth Tomorrow through Web Services*. Boston, MA, Harvard Business School Press.

Hagel, J. and J. S. Brown (2001). 'Your next IT strategy.' *Harvard Business Review* (October): 105–113.

Haines, M. (2002). *Knowledge Management in the NHS – Platform for Change*. www.healthknowledge.org.uk. Accessed in November 2002.

Howcroft, D. (2001). 'After the Goldrush: Deconstructing the Myths of the dot.com Market.' *Journal of Information Technology* 16(4): 195–204.

IBM, Microsoft (2002). *Security in a Web Services World: A Proposed Architecture and Roadmap*. www.106.ibm.com/developerworks/webservices/library/ws-secmap/. Accessed in November 2002.

Information Technology Association of America (2001). 'ITAA Survey of ASP Demand in the US Federal Market.' *GCN Magazine*. June.

Kakabadse, N. and Kakabadse (2002). 'A. Software as a Service via Application Service Providers (ASPs) Model of Sourcing: An Exploratory Study.' *Journal of Information Technology Cases and Applications* 4(2): 26–44.

Kern, T., M. Lacity and L. Willcocks (2002). Netsourcing: Renting Business Applications and Services Over a Network. New York, Prentice Hall.

Kettinger, W. J., J. T. C. Teng and S. Guha (1997). 'Business Process Change: A Study of Methodologies, Techniques, and Tools.' *MIS Quarterly* 21(1): 55–80.

Klecun-Dabrowska, E. and T. Cornford (2000). 'Telehealth Acquires Meanings: Information and Communication Technologies within Health Policy.' *Information Systems Journal* 10: 41–63.

Kreger, H. (2003). 'Fulfilling the Web Services Promise.' *Communications of the ACM* 46(6): 29–34.

Laerum, H., G. Ellingsen and A. Faxvaag (2001). 'Doctors' Use of Electronic Medical Records Systems in Hospitals@cross sectional survey.' *British Medical Journal* 323(8 December): 1344–1348.

Laycock, M. (2002). *Planning, Managing and Implementing Change. Health Knowledge*. www.healthknowledge.org.uk. Accessed in November 2002.

Little, G. R. (1999). *Paper 1: Theory of Perception*. www.grlphilosophy.co.nz. Accessed in June 2002.

MacIver, K. (2003). 'The UK's 10 Worst Web Application Failures … and What Could Have Been Done to Prevent Them.' *Information Age* (May): 36–40.

Majeed, A. (2003). 'Ten Ways to Improve Information Technology in the NHS.' *British Medical Journal* 326: 202–206.

Markus, M. L. (1983). 'Power, Politics and MIS Implementation.' *Communications of the ACM* **26**(6): 430–445.

McCarthy, T. (2001). 'Are ASPs for You?' *Financial Executive* 17(4): 45–48.

McGauran, A. (2002). 'Foundation Hospitals: Freeing the Best or Dividing the NHS?' *British Medical Journal* **324**(1 June): 1298.

Metters, J., M. Abrams, P. R. Greenfield, J. M. Parmar and C. E. Venn (1997). *Report to the Secretary of State for Health of the Professional Committee on the Appeal of Mr. D. R. Walker Under Paragraph 190 of the Terms and Conditions of Service of Hospital Medical and Dental Staff (England and Wales)*. London, Department of Health.

Monro, J., J. Nicholl, A. O'Cathain and E. Knowles (2000). 'Impact of NHS Direct on Demand for Immediate Care: Observational Study.' *British Medical Journal* **321**(15 July): 150–153.

Orlikowski, W. J. and M. J. Tyre (1994). 'Windows of Opportunity: Temporal Patterns of Technological Adaptation in Organizations.' *Organization Science* **5**(1 May): 98–118.

Planting, S. (2000). *The Internet is not the Automobile*. www.futurecompany. co.za/2000/07/07/featurec.htm. Accessed in December 2001.

Porter, M. E. (1998). *Michael E. Porter on Competition: A Harvard Business Review Book*. MA.

Pouloudi, A. (1999). 'Information Technology for Collaborative Advantage in Healthcare Revisited.' *Information and Management* **35**: 345–356.

Robertson, S. and P. Powell (2000). 'In Search of Flexibility: The Mercator Case.' *Journal of Information Technology Cases and Applications* **2**(1): 24–40.

Robinson, R. (2002). 'Gold for the NHS: Good News that Raises Questions on Consistency and Sustainability.' *British Medical Journal* **324**(27 April): 987–998.

Scott, M. M. (1991) *The Corporation of the 1990s. Information Technology and Organisational Transformation*. Oxford University Press: Oxford.

Subramani, M. and E. Walden (2000). 'The Dot Com Effect: The Impact of e-Commerce Announcements on the Market Value of Firms.' *International Conference on Information Systems* **2000**: 193–207.

Susarla, A., A. Barua, and A. B. Whinston (2003). 'Understanding the Service Component of Application Service Provision: An Empirical Analysis of Satisfaction with ASP Services.' *MIS Quarterly* **27**(1 March): 91–123.

Uden, L. (2002). 'Design Process for Web Applications.' *IEEE MultiMedia* (October–December): **9**(4): 47–55.

Walsham, G. (1993). *Interpreting Information Systems in Organizations*. Chichester, Wiley.

Wanless, D. (2002). Securing Our Future Health: Taking a Long-Term View. *Final Report of an Independent Review of the Long-Term Resource Requirement for the NHS. London, April*.

Weill, P. and M. R. Vitale (2001). *Place to Space – Migrating to eBusiness Models*, HBS Press.

Whelan, E. and F. McGrath (2001). '*A Study of the Total Life Cycle Costs of an e-Commerce Investment. A Research in Progress.*' Evaluation and Program Planning **25**(2): 191–196.

Yin, R. K. (1994). *Case Study Research: Design and Methods*. Sage Publications. CA.

Zmud, R. W. (1984). 'An Examination of Push–Pull Theory Applied to Process Innovation in Knowledge Work.' *Management Science* **30**(6): 727–738.

14 A framework of integrated models for supply chain e-Management[1]

Charu Chandra, Sameer Kumar and Alexander V. Smirnov

Abstract

The management of supply chain systems is one of the major tasks related to co-ordinating 'product–process–resource' logistics that a firm has to perform in this global economy. The purpose of this type of system is to disseminate information about the market and available capabilities into co-ordinated plans for production and replenishment of goods and services in the network formed by co-operating units. This (supply chain) network assumes different structures as it adapts to the evolving market dynamics. One of the primary goals of Internet-based management (e-Management) is to facilitate transfer and sharing of data and knowledge among the units, to support these supply chain structures. Knowledge-based modelling tools for supply chain management utilize reusable components and configure knowledge as needed, in order to assist users (agents) in decision-making. This chapter discusses a generic development methodology for e-Management of supply chain. It is based on the principles of domain-independent problem solving and modelling, and domain-dependent analysis and implementation. The purpose of such approach is to ascertain characteristics of the problem independent of the specific problem environment. Consequently, the approach delivers solution(s) or the solution method that are intrinsic to the problem and not its environment. For illustration, applications from the automotive industry have been utilized.

14.1 Introduction

The important traits of the emerging global digital economy are characterized as dynamic real-time decision-making, customer orientation,

---

1. This chapter is an adaptation of the paper by authors: Chandra C., S. Kumar and A. V. Smirnov (2002). 'e-Management of Supply Chain: General Models Taxonomy.' *Human Systems Management* 21(2): 95–113.

and speed in responding to market demands. e-Management has come to symbolize a management philosophy that reflects such traits. This topic has evinced interest among academics and researchers on various aspects of problems based on Internet technologies that implement e-Management strategies, viz. e-Commerce, e-Business, and e-Manufacturing. The structure of the organization employing e-Management strategies is characterized as a networking organization. Examples of such organizations are supply chain networks (SCNs); and virtual, extended and www-based enterprises. This chapter focuses on a crucial aspect of the e-Management problem. It deals with structural issues of the e-Management philosophy by offering a methodological construct, which is based on principles of:

■ Scalability of e-Management models in fulfilling customer orders.

■ Reconfigurability of networking organizations using e-Management models.

■ Reusability of e-Management information framework for applications in various domains.

Scalability is one of the major characteristics of a networking organization. Implementation of scalability enables achieving reconfigurability, reusability, and extensibility of organizational knowledge in the SCN. An SCN that embodies these traits in its operations is a scalable SCN. In designing an SCN, it is essential to concurrently manage its product, process, and resource characteristics efficiently. One of the growing requirements for product (goods and services) development is mass customization of custom orders. At the same time, it is also crucial to manage the product life cycle with minimum cost overlays and maximum resource utilization. In order to satisfy these conflicting objectives, reusable solutions, such as templates for configuration of: (i) custom-ordered product and (ii) scalable supply chain are utilized. The implementation of this approach is called reusable configuration engineering. It is a template approach for configuring scalable supply chains under dynamic market environment that uses conceptual models for intelligent support in decision-making.

These principles provide the motivation in proposing an innovative approach for e-Management of scalable supply chain. Its objective is to study the problem of e-Management with a fusion of: (a) integration of Internet-based communication technologies, (b) reusable configuration engineering, and (c) SCN management approaches. Implementation of e-Management methodology for decision-making in scalable SCNs would fundamentally change global business environment by enabling constructive collaboration among its network units to achieve shared objectives. This approach satisfies the need for increasingly complex business relationships and underlying technology infrastructure that firms are implementing to support their global strategies.

This chapter is organized as follows. In Section 14.2, concepts related to supply chain e-Management are explored. In Section 14.3, key business trends that have led up to enterprise integration and SCN are surveyed. Also in this section, research approaches on scalability in SCN are discussed. Following this, general framework and major technologies of e-Management are described in Section 14.4. In Section 14.5, related research on e-Management and associated topics is reviewed. Section 14.6 describes models taxonomy and major conceptual models for e-Management problem solving for scalable SCNs. Section 14.7 offers conclusion as well as future directions for this important research topic.

14.2 The concept of supply chain e-Management

In order to meet the challenges of growing global competition, manufacturing as well as service industries has fostered innovations in the design of products, processes, services, and organization structures. A sizable number of such innovations have targeted cost reductions in key functions, including logistics. These industries must develop a flexible delivery enterprise that is highly flexible and capable of efficient operations. This means effective management of a broad range of processes with diverse measures. The need to cut costs and compete has led to many mergers, acquisitions, and strategic partnerships across firms. Such consolidations have created new organizations made up of very different entities which are not as integrated as they should be. Due to competition, it has become imperative that enterprises seamlessly and efficiently provide and manage services (including purchase and delivery of supplies to the final user) across entities and continuum of services, both now and in the ever-changing future. One of the ways to achieve these objectives has been to facilitate establishment of supply networks, commonly known as a 'supply chain'.

Supply chain in the manufacturing context has been defined as a system of suppliers, manufacturers, distributors, retailers, and customers where material typically flows downstream from suppliers to customers (except for reverse logistics) and information flow in both directions. Supply chain management involves managing a connected series of activities, which is concerned with planning, co-ordinating, and controlling movement of material, parts, and finished goods from supplier to customer. For this to occur, material, financial, and information flows are managed as decisions are made at strategic, tactical, and operational levels throughout the supply chain.

One of the successful, yet practical ways supply chain management has been conducted is by exploiting the online availability of information in managing production and operation systems. The emergence of Web-based applications for these systems has opened up innovative ways for firms to manage their operations effectively and efficiently. Prominent among these are business-to-consumer, and business-to-business interfaces for goods and services, which have impacted the market substantially by driving costs down through, standardized networking technology, and creating entirely new enterprises and relationships with real-time interconnection of firms with their customers. e-Management of supply chain involves development and implementation of information-based operating policies for these dynamic business environments.

14.3   SCNs: trends, major issues, and e-Management processes

In order to understand the significance of changes taking place in enterprise integration initiatives, it is prudent to review trends in strategic, production, and operations management activities (Poirier and Reiter 1996; ISO TC, 1997; NIST 1999; Oak Ridge 1999; Sousa et al., 1999). These trends have emerged for various factors impacting an enterprise's performance, viz. global competition, process alignment, information technology, organization structure, co-operation, and synchronization among trading partners and problem-solving approaches.

Since 1990s, firms have had to compete in global markets. Strategic alliances among organizations have been growing steadily. Organization structures are starting to align with processes. Manufacturing systems are being enhanced with information technology tools, such as enterprise resource planning, distribution requirements planning, e-Commerce, virtual enterprises management, product data and knowledge management, collaborative engineering, multi-agent technology, etc. Design for disassembly, synchronous manufacturing, and agile manufacturing are some of the new paradigms adopted in manufacturing. There has been a growing appreciation in many firms of total life cycle cost focus for a product from its source to consumption, from the perspective of a supply chain as opposed to extracting lowest price from immediate vendor(s). Also, an increased reliance on purchased material and outside processing with a simultaneous reduction in the number of suppliers and greater sharing of information between vendors and customers is being placed. A noticeable shift has taken place in the marketplace from mass production to mass customization. This has resulted in the emphasis on greater organizational and process flexibility and co-ordination of processes across locations. Organizations are promoting employee empowerment and the need for knowledge-based, real-time decision support systems to attain organizational and process flexibility as well as to respond to competitive pressure to introduce new products more quickly, cheaply, and of improved quality.

Starting from the evaluation of existing enterprise integration architectures (CIMOSA, GRAI/GIM, and PERA), the IFAC/IFIP Task Force on Architectures for Enterprise Integration has developed an overall definition of a generalized architecture. The proposed framework was termed GERAM – generalized enterprise reference architecture and methodology (ISO TC, 1997). This approach could be implemented using a variety of enterprise modelling languages, such as ARIS, CIMOSA, GRAI/GIM, IEM, and IDEF.

The advent of e-Management utilizing Internet-based information technologies during the latter half of 1990s has witnessed the rise of co-operation among trading partners in integrating activities, as well as structuring and managing their organizations. New issues and problems have arisen as a result of this innovation that requires uniquely different approaches to problem solving. Some of these trends in the e-Management philosophy and their implications on problem-solving capabilities are discussed below through an example of an SCN.

The SCN is comprised of a group with more than one member. The supply chain is arranged in the order the flow of material, processes, and information occurs between its members. An effective SCN is characterized by: (i) increased connectivity between its units, (ii) alignment of its inter-organization support systems, and (iii) sharing of information resources among its units. Effective e-Management services required in support of an SCN are (i) local and shared data and knowledge maintenance, (ii) site maintenance, and (iii) content development. The common metric for an SCN is removing waste through highly co-ordinated decisions in order to reduce lead-time and inventory levels at various stages of the product life cycle.

A generic automotive supply chain has for its primary raw material vendors – chemical manufacturers, steel mills, aluminium plants, etc. Secondary raw material vendors are suppliers of accessories, such as nuts, bolts, batteries, tiers, etc. Original equipment manufacturers (OEMs) are engine manufacturers. Automobile manufacturers design, assemble, and market the automobile. Automobile dealers are retailers that consumers visit for buying and servicing their automobiles.

A classic problem encountered by a generic SCN is that of planning and co-ordinating SCN production to meet consumer demand while making effective use of resources and promoting co-operation among members so as to achieve lead-time (waste) reduction. In the automotive industry example, dealer to – automobile manufacturer, OEM, accessories manufacturer, and raw material vendor relays consumer demand. Similarly, flow of material occurs in transforming – raw material to automotive accessories by the tier-2 manufacturer, original automotive equipment by the OEM or tier-1 manufacturer, a name brand automobile by the automobile manufacturer, and a consumer product by the dealer. The interaction between members occurs as a consumer and a provider. Thus, an automobile manufacturer assumes the role of a provider (of automobiles) in its dealings with a dealer (a consumer of automobiles). However, it acts as a consumer of original equipment while dealing with an OEM (a provider of original equipment). Synchronization of the automotive SCN is achieved through co-ordination, primarily of: (a) replenishment schedules that have been passed on through the echelon, from dealer onwards to automobile manufacturer, OEM, accessories manufacturer, and raw material supplier and (b) commitments made on capacity utilization between various members in the supply chain echelon.

A customer order received by an SCN can be mapped on to distributed business processes (DBP). These are dynamic set of business processes (BP) that result in the end product of the SCN. DBP concept is an object-oriented model that encapsulates models of suppliers, orders, operations, etc. A BP is comprised of several business operations. These operations are performed in developing a unit. A unit is an individual and/or organization (user), such as customer, supplier, manufacturer, plant, regulatory agency, etc.

The customer order approach usually requires satisfying a priority of multiple criteria. These criteria may be different depending on the problem domain. Increasing evidence can be found for application of multi-criteria of common management objectives, such as agility, capacity, responsiveness, cost, quality assurance, risk, and reliability in problem solving. However, the nature and domain of problem determines which of these objectives are more suited for problem solving. As an example, for problems in defence, and environmental management sectors, risk and reliability are in majority of cases, classified as higher priority objectives than cost and agility. However, for problems in highly service-oriented industries (such as automotive), agility, capacity, responsiveness, cost, quality assurance have higher priority over risk, and reliability as objectives. As a result, different e-Management models could be developed and implemented for problem solving.

Different structures of an SCN can be derived based on a combination of its major essential characteristics, viz.

- *Location*: Single-site, multi-site.

- *Production philosophy*: Mass production, mass customization.

- *Planning orientation*: Centralized, decentralized, degrees of autonomy.

- *Management control orientation*: Negotiation, co-ordination, coalition.

Different levels of an SCN and its primary roles and responsibilities are:

■ *Management*: Strategic planning and control.

■ *Communication*: Location, architecture, protocol.

■ *Process/application*: Operational planning and control.

e-Management processes and their utility within an SCN can be described in the context of a product life cycle, viz.

■ Sourcing is the process for managing procurement of raw material and accessories required in the transformation of a concept to an end-product structure. One of the major activities in this process is order tracing which involves managing procurement of product structure mapped on to the production network.

■ Production is the process of transformation of raw material and/or components into an end product. Major activities for this process are capacity planning, order scheduling, and order fulfilment.

■ Inventory management (IM) is the process of mapping demand forecasts into stocks of inventory needed to support these demands. In managing the inventory, it is essential to plan stock levels in order to avoid stock outs and lost customer orders.

■ Dispatching is the process of warehousing an end product and shipping it to meet planned orders. Some of the activities performed in this process are sales forecasting, sales order processing, and inventory stock allocations.

■ Transportation is the logistics pertaining to shipping an end product to consumer. Activities carried out in this process are modes of transport, freight consolidation to maximally utilize carrier capacity, shipment tracing, and e-data-interchange of shipping details.

In view of the above trends and issues, the design and implementation of e-Management capabilities for a supply chain must incorporate development of models and methods for both macro and micro levels of decision-making. A key factor to consider for this purpose is scalability of enterprise (or the supply chain) in terms of its functions and operations.

14.3.1 Scalability in SCNs
Issues of scalability in an SCN are primarily due to focus on the problem, and scope of the system. Issues related to domain-dependent problems,

such as high inventory turns for a procure-to-stock item for a retailer are much narrower in focus than domain-independent problem of high inventory turns for the entire retail sector, which is broader in scope. However, the two problems may or may not be interdependent. For example, a retailer may achieve high inventory turns in its local market, but still may not be meeting the overall retail sector average inventory turns. Similarly, the scope of the above problem is localized at the retailer level and globalized at the retail sector level. Issues of scalability are different at different levels of this enterprise network.

Scalability can be classified into two broad categories: (1) operation scalability and (2) implementation scalability. These are described below:

- *Operation scalability* deals with operationalizing the enterprise for efficiency and effectiveness. This means adopting standards, procedures, and policies that enhance the performance of the enterprise. Issues encountered pertain to developing common – standards, procedures, methods, goals, policies, and objectives. For example, issues of operational scalability for the members of the US automotive industry may pertain to adopting common manufacturing standards across sectors represented by different OEMs, where manufacturing practices are as diverse as flow, cellular, and job shop manufacturing, respectively. Even within a sector, manufacturing practices can be diverse depending on the size and volume of operations.

- *Implementation scalability* deals with implementing concepts, such as flexibility, modularity, usability, and extensibility in the enterprise. Flexibility pertains to designing and modelling enterprise components to accommodate diverse structures that it may adopt in a changing market environment, such as virtual networks, alliances, value chains, supply chains, etc. Flexibility also pertains to the decision environment under which the network has to operate, e.g. batch vs. on-line, deterministic vs. stochastic, and optimal vs. pareto-optimal. Modularity implies that an enterprise can be modularized according to specialization of knowledge or technology. These modules can then be replicated throughout the enterprise, thus providing extensibility of knowledge. Extensibility also implies that information in the enterprise can be shared via Internet, Intranet, and Extranet for business-to-consumer, business-to-business service, and business-to-business goods transactions. Issues related to this category are – co-ordination, co-operation, negotiation and compromise, and synchronization throughout the enterprise echelon. For example, in the case of the large and diverse US automotive industry, co-ordination for sharing information related to demand forecasts, capacity allocation, or synchronization of actions among business partners is a problem.

The above categories of scalability are highly interdependent. For example, development of an operational standard, such as common order formats requires universal implementation standards for e-data-interchange or Internet communication. Yet, these categories are independent by themselves because of the nature and propensity of issues in each category that the system developer has to deal with in designing scalability in enterprises.

Scalability also deals with extensibility of organizational knowledge. Knowledge is assimilated for an activity (the lowest level of information) in a specific domain and aggregated for various decision-making levels in the enterprise. Main concepts in activity modelling in an SCN are briefly described below (Chandra, 1997b).

■ *Representation*: An activity represents the lowest level of interaction in the supply chain model. It is synonymous with a 'unit' for modelling business process, and an 'agent' for knowledge management environment. It is classified into various activity types depending on unique service(s) they provide. Activity(ies) is(are) used in relation to an aggregation. An activity possesses attribute(s), which describe its characteristics or features. An attribute assumes parametric values in relation to an aggregation model. Activities communicate with each other by exchanging message(s). Communication occurs based on a protocol whose boundaries are set by a control matrix prescribing level of resource(s) to be utilized by an activity, policies to be pursued, and objectives to be met in providing the service(s).

■ *Aggregation*: Aggregation represents a form of system. It has seven components – input, process sequence, output, mechanism, agent, environment, and function, which are defined by four matrices, viz. resource, performance, technology, and input/output (Nadler, 1970). Each aggregation (system) has its own control matrix to define relationships between its components. Aggregation can take on many forms, manifested by the orientation it is based upon, i.e. aggregation 'within' or 'between' systems. For example, material-life-cycle and order-life-cycle flows represent horizontal aggregation between systems. Building decision models across the enterprise represents a vertical aggregation between systems. Similarly, aggregating all activities within a system function represent, a 'within' systems integration.

■ *Protocol*: Protocols for each aggregation (system) describe conventions governing communication between activities, services rendered by activities to one another, and controls for that system. Communication between activities occurs in the form of message(s) exchanged to request a service. Service is of two types: resource and information (data and knowledge, and controls).

The approach put forth in this chapter utilizing SCN philosophy for enterprise integration, addresses issues of scalability by proposing domain-independent problem solving and modelling, and domain-dependent analysis and implementation. The purpose of the approach is to ascertain characteristics of the problem independent of the specific problem environment. Consequently, the approach delivers solution(s) or the solution method that are intrinsic to the problem and not its environment. Analysis methods help to understand characteristics of the solution methodology as well as provide specific guarantees of effectiveness. Invariably, insights gained from these analyses can be used to develop effective problem-solving tools and techniques for complex enterprise integration problems.

14.4 General framework of supply chain e-Management and supporting technologies

Enterprise integration issues have been addressed with a multi-disciplinary research focus. Techniques and approaches are being incorporated from economics, management science, industrial engineering and operations research, systems sciences, information sciences, and computer science and artificial intelligence fields. For the purposes of this chapter, research areas have been classified as those belonging to *systemic*, *reductionist*, and *analytic* approaches. Systemic approaches pertain to study of nature of systems. Reductionist approaches pertain to application of these systems in unique ways, capturing behaviours observed through systemic approaches. Analytic approaches describe how these systems can be utilized efficiently and effectively. This chapter offers insights into combining these approaches in order to advance system rooted constructs for developing an SCN. For purpose of illustration, Figure 14.1 depicts a template used in describing below the interconnectedness between above approaches and major technology areas to create the fusion necessary for scalability of SCN.

The existing relational data models coupled with Internet-based tools provide shared representation models/schemes for developing a kernel for an SCN. To accomplish this, however, the modeller has to overcome difficulties in integration of the enterprise due to incompatibility of conceptual models for enterprise resource planning with the above kernel. For this purpose, the methodology offered in this chapter incorporates above approaches. Research thrusts in these approaches are described

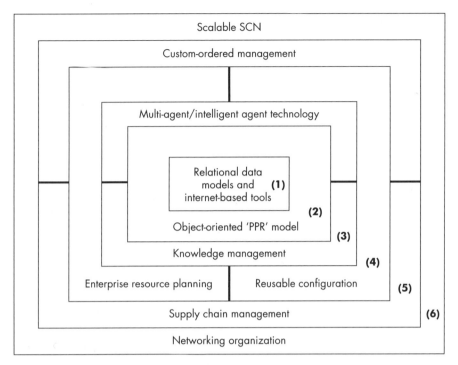

Figure 14.1: Interconnectedness of topics in enterprise integration research.

below with notation of level number marked (1) to (6). For this illustration, a bottom-up approach has been used. Systemic approach incorporates the abstract level and consists of relational data model (1), object-oriented 'product–process–resource' (PPR) model (2), and dynamic knowledge problem domain model (3). Reductionist approach incorporates the activity level and consists of dynamic knowledge problem domain model (3), internal state, and objectives of the enterprise units (4), and strategic management models (5). Analytic approach incorporates the implementation level and consists of internal state, and objectives of the enterprise units (4), strategic management models (5), and shared objectives of the SCN (6).

The proposed e-Management technologies are categorized into two groups: (i) problem solving and (ii) information support. For the first group, these are (1) custom-ordered (mass customization) management, (2) configuration management, and (3) constraint satisfaction and propagation. For the second group, these are (1) data and knowledge management, (2) multi-agent and intelligent agent, and (3) conceptual and information modelling. These technologies are described below.

Custom-ordered management. The purpose of custom-ordered management is to transform incomplete information about the market and available resources into co-ordinated plans for production and replenishment of goods and services in the network formed by co-operating units. One of the prominent techniques to deliver custom orders is mass customization, which is mass production of individually customized goods and services. The focus of this concept is on productivity, changing customer requirements, and structuring of products and processes. Mass customization operates with product configuration in order to adapt to customer requirements.

Configuration management. The objective of designing this organization utilizing configuration principle is to generate customized solutions based on standard components, such as templates, baselines, and models. There are two aspects to configuration management: (i) configuring/reconfiguring and (ii) configuration maintenance. Configuring deals with creating configuration solutions. Configuration maintenance deals with maintaining a consistent configuration under changing environment. This requires consistency among selected components and solutions. When a solution for selected component changes, configuration maintenance traces all related solutions and revises them, if necessary. Configuration management spanning the SCN is desired to implement appropriate configuration. The SCN configuration stage is represented by the following relationship:

configuring the product (product structure, bill of material) → *configuring the business process (process structure, operation types)* → *configuring the resource (structure of system, equipment, and staff types).*

This relationship is incorporated in a shared 'PPR' model, described later in this section.

Constraint satisfaction and propagation. Modern problem-solving strategies for manufacturing are based on a combination of techniques, such as constraint-based problem solving, constraint-based heuristic search, human decision-making, etc. Constraint satisfaction is a fundamental problem of design. Traditional constraint satisfaction procedures have been designed for the problem with one fixed set of constraints. In the design of an SCN, it is often necessary to solve a dynamic constraint satisfaction problem, where applicable constraints depend on various design aspects and time horizons.

An abstract PPR model is based on the concept of multi-criteria constraint network. The concept of multi-ontology classes of entities, the logic of attributes and the constraint satisfaction problem model represent the general idea of the network. A constraint network is a collection of constraints interconnected by virtue of variable sharing. A constraint satisfaction problem model can be used for problem solving as follows: (i) constraint satisfaction (searching for solution): finding – a solution, all solutions, and a pareto-optimal solution(s) for a given criterion and (ii) constraint propagation (modifying solutions): starting from a solution, this technique consists of finding a new solution, after having modified the value of one or more constraint variables.

Data and knowledge management. An important requirement for collaborative system is the ability to capture knowledge from multiple domains and store it in a form that facilitates reuse and sharing (Neches et al., 1991; Patil et al., 1992). The technology suggested in this framework is limited to designing SCN configurations for PPR systems and focused on using ontological descriptions. It is based on GERAM (ISO TC, 1997). Applying the GERAM enables forming the conceptual model of the scalable supply chain system. This is accomplished by knowledge modelling its product, process, and resource components to satisfy manufacturing constraints in its environment. The implementation of e-Management approach is based on the shared information environment that supports the PPR model, used for integration and co-ordination of user's (unit's) activity. This model is studied from different viewpoints of user (unit) groups.

Ontology. It is a form of representing knowledge applied in various domains. It is useful in creating unique models of an SCN by developing specialized knowledge bases, specific to various e-Management problem domains. Ontologies are managed by translation and mapping between different types of attributes and entities. These capture rules and constraints of the domain of interest, allowing useful inferences to be drawn, analyse, execute, cross check, and validate models. Ontological translation of an enterprise, such as an SCN is necessary because networks are multi-ontology classes of entities. Various ontologies for an entity describe its unique characteristics in context with the relationship acquired for a specific purpose or problem. For example, an entity 'automobile' may have a multi-ontology representation for a user with a marketing perspective, and for another user with a design perspective, respectively. For the user interested in the marketing perspective of an automobile, its attributes of size, shape, and style are important. However, size, quality, and precision may represent the same automobile's characteristics for the user interested in its design specifications. Obviously, each user works with its own ontology-based dynamic constraint network.

Multi-agent and intelligent agent. The implementation of the basic principle of co-operation in the SCN is based on distribution of procedures between different units/users (or different agents) concurrently in the common knowledge space. It is, therefore, natural to represent knowledge as a set of interacting autonomous agents in a multi-agent environment. Agent is a software tool that captures behavioural characteristics of the problem for a specific process or activity. Intelligent agent is an autonomous software entity that can navigate heterogeneous computing environment and, either alone or working with other agents, achieve some goals (Franklin, 1996).

Conceptual and information modelling.   In order to design and implement an SCN, it is important to explore and understand its structure and behaviour as a system under dynamic business environment. Conceptual and information modelling enable representation and evaluation of system entity: characteristics, relationships to other entities, and controls to achieve system goals and objectives. Some of the modelling techniques utilized are entity relationships modelling, object-oriented modelling, and computational modelling for evaluation of various enterprise configurations using enterprise-wide database.

In order to co-ordinate the flow of material within a multi-echelon SCN, it is important to synchronize activities within process both at inter- and intra-levels by sharing information. To accomplish this objective, it is imperative that activities between trading partners are based on a set of commercial and contractual rules that identify protocols necessary to guarantee co-operation and co-ordination. To support this objective, an information kernel in the form of an 'SCN conceptual model' is needed. This kernel describes following major components of an SCN:

- A set of objectives at strategic level.

- A set of SCN model attributes.

- A set of strategies.

- A set of SCN units.

- A set of constraints for every unit.

- A set of products for every unit.

- A set of unit resources.

- A set of contract relationships among units.

- A set of coefficients for bilateral relationships among units.

The proposed e-Management framework concerns theoretical foundations in the analysis, design and modelling of SCN and e-Management information support technologies. It has been guided by following common themes:

■ *Behavioural representations of a system*: The representation of a system must depict separation of its cognitive and physical behaviours. A flexible system must conform to basic principles of modularity, adaptability, and reconfigurability. That is, the physical implementation of such a system is amenable to separation from its logical and cognitive designs.

■ *Unification of models*: In order to realize the goal of integration in a system, it is necessary to unify its various sub-models in a spirit of co-operation. In a complex system, usually a cadre of sub-models are designed and developed to perform specialized tasks or implement specific policies. However, if these sub-models are not linked to one another as part of an overall strategic architecture, these may work against rather than with each other. The design of co-operative systems enables disparate models to function in unison to achieve common goals of the enterprise.

■ *Communication*: In order to achieve co-ordination between sub-models of an enterprise, these must communicate with one another. In a complex system, transactions between various sub-models are highly inter- and intra-dependent stemming from common objectives, goals and policies of the enterprise. Protocols governing transactions *within* and *between* system components enable effective communication.

■ *Measurement*: One of the primary means with which to gauge the success of transactions exchanged *within* and *between* system components is through common performance measures, i.e. various autonomous system entities guided by shared beliefs and preferences binding them together to a larger system. For example, generic measures of performance, such as flexibility, adaptability, reliability, risk, quality, cost, time, and service to promote a common knowledge of beliefs and preferences in the system.

■ *Standardization and proceduralization*: Standards and procedures, taxonomy, and classification enable generalizations of theories and hypotheses across diverse disciplines and problems, e.g. the notion of activity in a system has a generic meaning in information modelling, object-oriented modelling, enterprise modelling, process modelling, simulation modelling, and optimization. Thus, it is easy to implement common standards across above techniques by utilizing a generic representation of an activity. Therefore, a standard activity-based form representation of a complex systems enterprise has been proposed.

The related work in direct comparison to three research approaches described above is discussed next.

14.5 Related research review

At the systemic level, an SCN is a general class of system that exhibits a co-operative behaviour within its business and market environment (Klir, 1991). The foundation of this system is built on a network architecture that has various demand and supply nodes as it provides as well receives goods and services to and from its customers and suppliers, respectively (Lee and Billington, 1993; Chandra, 1997a; Swaminathan et al., 1998). An SCN framework describes general foundational elements of integration between its marketing and production functions. These are in the form of general theories, hypotheses, standards, procedures, and models that are based on well-founded principles in these disciplines (Drew, 1975; Graves, 1982; Younis and Mahmoud, 1986; Cohen and Lee, 1988, 1989; Hackman and Leachman, 1989; Deleersnyder et al., 1992; Tzafestas and Kapsiotis, 1994; Lee, 1996; Diks and Kok, 1998; NIST, 1999). Systems modelling deals with general modelling issues of this class of systems, such as how to represent, quantify, and measure co-operation, co-ordination, synchronization, and integration (Morris, 1967; Little, 1992; Pritsker, 1997). Systems engineering describes methodologies for structuring systems as these are implemented in various application domains (Blanchard and Fabrycky, 1990). System integration deals with achieving common interface *within* and *between* various components at various levels of hierarchy in an enterprise (Shaw et al., 1992), as well as different architectures and methodologies (Hirsch, 1995; ISO TC, 1997; Pawlak et al., 1997; Beyer et al., 1999; Oak Ridge, 1999; Scherer and Katranuschkov, 1999; CE NET, 1999) using distributed artificial intelligence and intelligent agents (Gruber, 1995; Wooldridge and Jennings, 1995; Fischer et al., 1996; Stumptner, 1997; Bussmann, 1998; Sandholm, 1998; Hendler, 1999; Lesser, 1999; Wooldridge et al., 1999).

At the reductionist level, an SCN configuration is based on its local as well as global environmental constraints (Tsang, 1991; Giachetti et al., 1997; Fleischanderl et al., 1998). These constraints are imposed as the supply chain negotiates and compromises to adapt to its co-operative behaviour (Jennings, 1994). Enterprise modelling has been effectively used in decomposing complex enterprises, such as SCN. Knowledge modelling and ontologies describe unique system descriptions of supply chain that are relevant to specific application domains (Neches et al., 1991; Bradshaw et al., 1992; Patil et al., 1992; Bradshaw et al., 1993; Nadoli and

Biegel, 1993; Gruninger, 1997; Guarino, 1998; Fikes and Farquhar, 1999; Livelink). The classic problem for an SCN is an IM problem requiring co-ordination of product and information flows through a multi-echelon supply chain. This class of problem has been solved by integrating the front and back ends of the supply chain with costs and lead times as key measures of its performance (Clark and Scarf, 1960; Clark, 1972; Pyke and Cohen, 1990; Hariharan and Zipkin, 1995; Diks et al., 1996; Diks and Kok, 1997, 1998).

Analytic approach for the general class of supply chains has their origins in economic models of supply and demand co-ordination. Game theory principles for payoffs among market competitors have been used very effectively to design competitive strategies for supply chains (Masahiko, 1984; Gupta and Loulou, 1998). Co-ordination dealing with interfaces between strategies, objectives, and policies for various functions of an enterprise has received much attention in optimizing the performance of a supply chain (Malone, 1987; Malone and Crowston, 1994; Whang, 1995; Thomas and Griffin, 1996). Various aspects of co-operation have been prescribed for effective management of an SCN (Jennings et al., 1996; Walsh and Wellman, 1998; Sousa et al., 1999).

14.6 Models of problem solving in supply chain e-Management

The main thrust of SCN system modelling is based on the principle that its architecture should be domain independent whereas its application domain dependent (specific). Such a strategy assures integration of disparate applications to a common, yet generic architecture. Some guidelines for implementing this strategy are:

1 The structure of the conceptual model of an SCN system must reflect inner workings of its global (group) and local (member) components.

2 The design of an application of SCN should be based on a conceptual model of the SCN system architecture, but specific to decision-making relevant to that application.

3 Realization of objectives of an SCN system must be achieved through implementation of a highly co-ordinated set of strategies and policies at the global and local echelons. These should be consistent with trends and directions pursued by the industry for which the system is being designed.

4 Implementation of an SCN system application model must balance the issue of scope vs. focus.

Based on these guiding principles, a two-level SCN modelling approach is utilized. At the first or conceptual/virtual level, modelling is performed by using macro information about SCN units and formal models (see Appendix) with optimization procedures. At the second or physical/application level, modelling is performed using detailed (or micro) information about SCN units (real constraints of equipment, layout, etc.) and knowledge-based models with constraints satisfaction/propagation procedures.

14.6.1 General framework of SCN systems development

As noted earlier, an SCN is a complex network of systems, sub-systems, operations, activities, and relationships between one another. Modelling of such a system, therefore, can be a difficult task, unless various parts of it are cohesively tied to the whole. For this reason, a general framework of SCN systems development is proposed. Such framework enables retaining abstract ideas of modelling an SCN throughout the hierarchy of models that together comprise the SCN system. The proposed framework is a meta-model of an SCN. It identifies abstract model elements or building blocks and relationships between elements that are required in a mathematical representation of an SCN. When models of SCN are expressed in terms of these elements, extensions and generalizations become apparent. Moreover, the mathematical language and structure of the framework provide a foundation to compare and contrast seemingly unrelated models arising in diverse environments. The purpose in introducing this general framework is to: (1) assess the validity or accuracy of the representation of a particular SCN given by various optimization models and (2) guide the development of more accurate SCN optimization models when existing models provide inadequate representation of the SCN.

The proposed systems development framework adapts an integrated approach to couple research on issues, problem-solving strategies, methodological constructs, and tools and techniques in the supply chain. Its basic feature is to provide a suite of models and methods that integrate: (a) structural forms, (b) information flow, (c) decision-making processes, and (d) provide incentives for enhanced efficiency and effectiveness of the enterprise. Figure 14.2 depicts an integrated 'supply chain management systems development framework'. Its various elements are described below.

Theory. The theoretical underpinnings of this framework are embedded in: (a) the focus of this research on enterprise integration and (b) five guiding principles for an SCN, enunciated by this research. These are: (1) an SCN is a co-operative system, (2) an SCN exists on group dynamics of its members, (3) negotiations and compromise are norms of operation in an SCN, (4) SCN system solutions are pareto-optimal (satisfiying), not optimizing, and (5) integration in an SCN is achieved through synchronization.

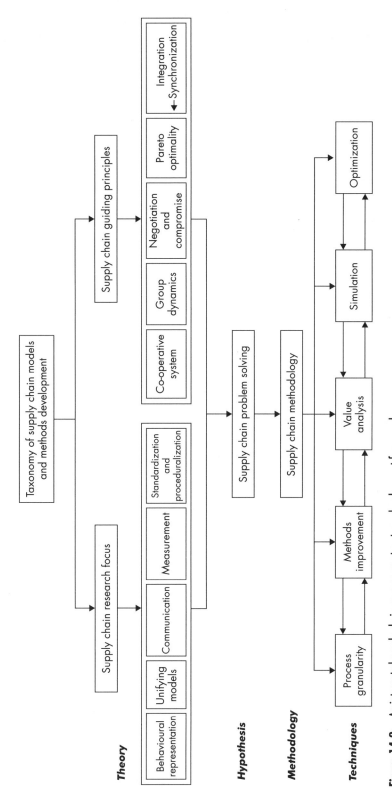

Figure 14.2: An integrated supply chain management systems development framework.

These guiding principles implicitly and explicitly impact designs, models, and analysis techniques for SCN management systems utilizing the framework proposed in this chapter.

Problem-solving strategies. To solve the SCN problems, following categories of optimization policies are examined:

- The manufacturer optimizes its own cost and imposes its policies on suppliers. In this case, no co-operation among members is forthcoming (centralized).

- Global cost of the supply chain is minimized by co-operation among members at various levels (autonomy in some form).

- Each level optimizes its local cost objective that may or may not optimize the global cost objective of the SCN. In this case, co-operation among members is opportunistic (decentralized).

- A combination of above three policies (combined).

Methodologies are intended to improve analyses of SCNs being developed, based upon functional elements identified for the analysis tool (Oakes et al., 1997). A combination of methods and tools for SCN analysis comprises the proposed SCN analysis methodology. Briefly, this methodology is designed to help the analyst 'create an (analysis) structure, install proper controls, and implement principles of optimization to synchronize the supply chain' (Chandra, 1997a).

Techniques are employed in this framework for the purpose of SCN analyses. These are classified into following general categories (Chandra et al., 1997):

- *Process granularity*: Techniques to decompose the SCN in its functional, process, and activity forms.

- *Methods engineering*: Characterizes the SCN as a collection of standard activities. As such, standard activity nomenclature and definitions are utilized to standardize and proceduralize the SCN.

- *Value analysis*: Utilizes various techniques to improve the performance of the SCN by minimizing the non-value-added component of its activities.

- *Simulation*: The SCN is simulated for its product life to analyse various forms (structures) that it can adapt to.

■ *Optimization*: Various problem specific optimization techniques for the integrated production planning and control (IPPC) problem (described in Section 14.6.3), such as forecasting, capacity planning and production scheduling are applied to optimize the SCN.

14.6.2 Taxonomy of domain-independent models

The concept of an SCN is about managing co-ordinated information and material flows, plant operations, and logistics. It provides flexibility and agility in responding to consumer demand shifts with minimum cost overlays in resource utilization. The fundamental premise of this philosophy is activity synchronization among multiple autonomous business units represented in it, i.e. improved co-ordination *within* and *between* various SCN units (members). Co-ordination is achieved within the framework of commitments made by members to each other. Members negotiate and compromise in a spirit of co-operation in order to meet these commitments. Increased co-ordination can lead to reduction in lead times and costs, alignment of interdependent decision-making processes and improvement in the overall performance of each member, as well as the SCN (group) (Chandra, 1997b).

An SCN management system (S) describes members (T) in an SCN and their relationship (R) to one another. Using notation, $S = (T, R)$, where $T = (t_1, t_2, \ldots, t_n)$, and $R = [\{(t_1, t_2)\ (r_1, r_2, \ldots, r_n)\}, \ldots, \{(t_1, t_n)\ (r_1, r_2, \ldots, r_n)\}]$. Likewise, such a relationship can also be expressed for components of a member (t_i); at a function (or business) $t_i(b_i)$; process $\{(t_i, b_i)\ (p_i)\}$; and activity $\{(t_i, b_i, p_i)\ (a_i)\}$; $i = 1, 2, \ldots, n$. Relationships in an SCN management system describe: (a) actions between its members (and their components – sub-units, users) involving exchange of data and knowledge, controls, and resources and (b) meta (or logical) systems (that is members and their components), decentralization, and specialization of autonomous members (Bond and Gasser, 1988; Gasser, 1991; Moulin and Chaib-Draa, 1996).

In this framework, the SCN is modelled as a system (or collection of systems) that possesses its four primary characteristics – structure, representation, diagnosis, and prescription. A taxonomic representation of models in an SCN system are based on the following categorization:

■ *Structural model*: Provides the basic structure to the SCN. Essentially, it defines the maxim $S = (T, R)$ for the SCN, that is, entities (members) and their relationships to one another. Such a structure provides the basis for defining further sub-relationships throughout the network via this primary relationship.

■ *Representation model*: Provides the architecture within which SCN can be represented. Thus, one may choose to represent the network, so as to offer a centralized, decentralized, or a quasi-centralized control. It is based on a standard linear programming decomposition model (Dantzig, 1963) and a continuous dynamic process flow model in the literature (Chandra, 1997a). Each model highlights different abstract model elements of the framework.

■ *Diagnostic model*: Provides the framework within which SCN problems can be diagnosed to establish their root causes. Models to minimize systemic waste in the SCN fall in this category. Four categories of waste have been identified – product waste, process waste, waste due to inefficient logistics, and waste due to general system inefficiencies.

■ *Prescriptive model*: Provides the application framework within which prescriptive solutions to problems diagnosed in the SCN can be applied. Models to minimize lead time and costs belong to this category.

The above modelling approach is further elaborated by two major representations of an SCN system model at a conceptual level:

1   An SCN system decomposition model is depicted in Figure 14.3, with notations in the Appendix (Taha, 1987). The technology matrix D_j and corresponding resource vector b_j represent the independent structure of the member. The technology matrix A_j and the objective function vector C_j denote the common structure of the group derived from the

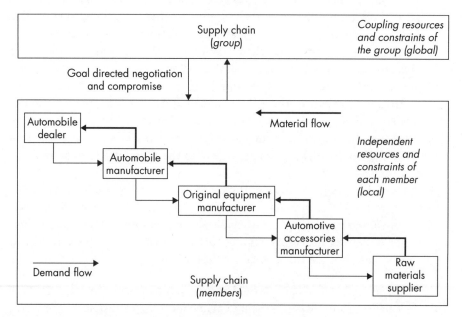

Figure 14.3:   An automotive supply chain enterprise decomposition model.

homogeneity of members. Controls embedded in the technology matrix constitute relationships between various strategies, such as marketing, production planning, warehouse operations, etc., in regards to their goals, objectives, and policies. These controls are propagated as constraint equations represented by the technology matrix. A similar approach is applicable for gathering group information.

2   An SCN system dynamic process flow model, with notations in the Appendix (Hillier and Lieberman, 1990) is depicted in Figure 14.4. It signifies the structure of a member. It has source S (supply) and sink N (demand) nodes with trans-shipment L acting as an intermediary node. Controls in this network are implemented by modulating (managing discrepancies) inputs (activity flow rates) based on strategies identified for marketing, production planning, and warehouse operations, in order to support goals, policies, and objectives. Linking of member networks through common control strategies produces the structure for the group.

For both models, coefficients for various decision variables in the technology matrix are derived by the application of various optimization techniques, such as methods engineering and value engineering on different operations of the enterprise across the value chain.

14.6.3 Taxonomy of domain-dependent models
A general domain-dependent model of SCN that incorporates workings of the SCN models taxonomy described above is presented. It is described in the context of an IPPC problem in a specific domain for forecasting and IM.

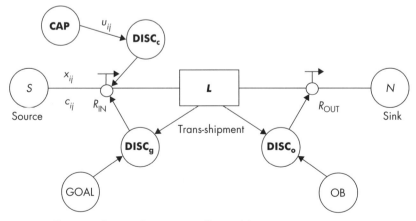

Figure 14.4:   Illustration of an SCN dynamic process flow model.

IPPC is a combination of philosophies, concepts, and tools and techniques to manage deviations in expectations of the demand and supply functions of a productive system. It is an integrated material-flow-based information system whose planning and control is based on feedback loop of control theory. Main approaches to IPPC are push, pull, and synchronous flow production systems (Sipper and Bulfin, 1997).

A generic modelling approach that creates a fundamental pattern (or cell) that contains all the components needed to make up an enterprise is utilized. The individual expression of these patterns and how these aggregate, determines the behaviour, performance, and functionality of the system being modelled. This model is utilized to create three main modules of an IPPC system: IM, capacity management (CM), and production management (PM).

The fundamental pattern. The primary objective of any enterprise modelling effort is to find efficient ways for the enterprise to consume time and resources, as it strives to attain its goals within its environment. Resources are defined as anything a system may utilize that facilitates goal achievement, e.g. labour, machines, and material. As resources move through a system, they attain only one of two states: storage and transformation. If the system in question possesses intelligence, it has the ability to control the flow of resources through these states. Consequently, only three building blocks are needed to model system behaviour. The triangle for storage, the circle for transformation, and the rectangle for control represent these. This abstract simplification is the basis from which generic activities are built. The structure of the generic activity (GA) is presented in Figure 14.5. It is a left-to-right directional pattern representing material flow through storage–transformation–storage. Control spans the entire cell, regulating the consumption of time and resources. One instantiation of the fundamental pattern, also known as GA can be used to model one operation in an enterprise, such as move or

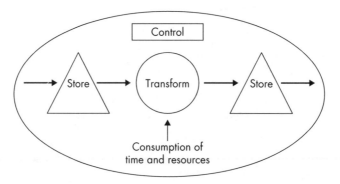

Figure 14.5: The fundamental pattern.

make, or it can represent an aggregation of operations for an entire assembly line, or even an enterprise. Thus, the fundamental pattern represented by the GA is completely fluid both horizontally and vertically. This functionality is accomplished through parameterization of the GA's variable set (Chandra et al., 2000).

The triangle is where resources of any type are stored. A triangle consists of an input valve, an output valve, and an ability to open and close these valves selectively. This means that the flow of resources into and out of the triangle may be controlled across time and resource type. Since the triangle's valves are controlled by the rectangle, intelligent algorithms can be used to selectively provide the system with those resources that have been scheduled for consumption. Also, since the rectangle is responsible for triangle's behaviour, dynamic changes in storage policy can 'easily' be modelled through the use of plug and play algorithms in the rectangle.

The circle is the abstract location, where the potential for trans-formations exists and consequently is the place where resources and time may be consumed. A transformation is defined as any activity that results in the alteration of a resource's physical attributes. This could be anything from the final assembly of an automobile to the transportation of fabric. The circle can also be viewed as a point of interaction between system resources. Interactions of the form raw material–workers–machines, workers–machines, workers–workers, etc., are modelled using the circle. The circle has input and output valves (similar to the triangle) that are controlled by the rectangle. Based on some recipe and a scheduling algorithm, the rectangle orchestrates the arrival of appropriate resources needed to initiate a transformation job.

The rectangle is where the behaviour of the circle and triangle may be intelligently planned and controlled. This component of the fundamental pattern has been broken down into three sub-components of the IPPC problem: IM, CM, and PM. The interaction between these three components of control is depicted in Figure 14.6.

IM generates long-, intermediate-, and short-term raw material and end-item requirement plans under conditions of uncertainty in supply and demand. In order to manage this task, IM consists of three sub-components: forecasting, inventory control (IC), and material management. CM plans the long-, intermediate-, and short-term capacity and utilization

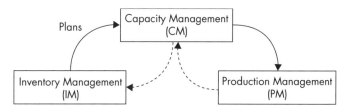

Figure 14.6: Elements and interactions of control.

requirements. Its three sub-components are capacity planning, production planning, and production sequencing. PM uses the IM and CM plans to control the daily operations of the fundamental pattern via triangle and circle valve control. The three sub-components required to manage this task are inbound logistics, production sequencing, and outbound logistics.

Since the fundamental pattern is completely fluid both horizontally and vertically, it can be used to represent different kinds of low-level operations, such as move or make, while at the same time it can also be used to represent high-level operations, such as an entire enterprise. Integration can be defined in terms of valve control scope. The broader the scope of valve control assigned to any one rectangle, the more integrated the system becomes.

Supply chain management concept is modelled as an industrial network enterprise creation and reuse that considers enterprises as assemblies of reusable units defined on shared 'PPR' domain knowledge model. Each object of above model represents knowledge about an agent charged with delivering a specialized technology. For example, the SCN agent is composed of one or more enterprise agents. Enterprise agent is composed of one each of inventory manager, capacity manager, and production manager agents. Similarly, IM agent is composed of one each of forecast management (FM), IC, and raw material management (RMM) agents. This relationship between agents signifies co-ordination of strategies, policies, goals, and objectives among them for problem solving in specific domain. Figure 14.7, depicts an object-oriented domain model for the IM agent. Its main components are IC, FM, and RMM agents, each of which carries specialized knowledge about these expertise areas/topics. For the automotive industry SCN described earlier, the object-oriented domain descriptions are as follows:

- Object 'SCN' describes the specific automotive product supply chain agent.

- Object 'enterprise' describes various member agents for this particular automotive supply chain, i.e. dealer and different OEMs.

- Objects inventory, capacity, and production describe agents with specialized knowledge in these fields.

- Objects FM, IC, and RMM describe agents with domain knowledge in the areas of forecasting management, inventory control, and raw material IM, specific to IM.

The primary purpose of modelling SCN is to improve integration of clusters represented by various memberships formed by its agent components while maintaining their independent identities. By

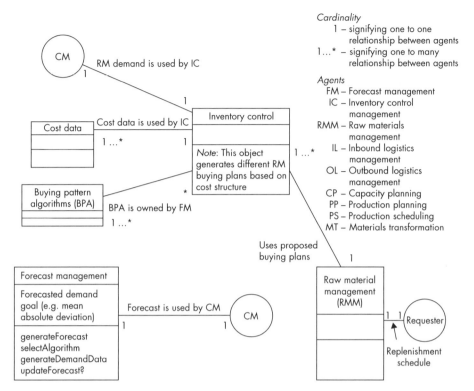

Figure 14.7: IM domain object model.

performing an object-oriented analysis, every agent object in the SCN system is accounted for because a complete enumeration of the enterprise is performed. In this manner, the contribution of each agent object in modelling the system is recognized. Furthermore, the knowledge captured is exhaustive.

14.7 Summary and conclusions

e-Management of SCN based on the principles of scalability offers flexible alternatives for enterprise integration through shared modelling and information infrastructure for problem solving. This chapter focuses on a crucial and as yet not much explored aspect of the e-Management problems, viz. structural issues of e-Management based on the development of a methodological construct. Major objectives of e-Management of custom-ordered scalable SCN configuration are to study the problem of e-Management with a fusion of: (a) integration of Internet-based communication technologies, (b) reusable configuration engineering, and (c) networking organization management approaches. The proposed e-Management technologies are categorized into two groups: (i) problem solving and (ii) information support. For the first group, these are (1) custom-ordered (mass customization) management, (2) configuration management, and (3) constraint satisfaction and propagation. For the second group, these are (1) data and knowledge management, (2) multi-agent and intelligent agent, and (3) conceptual and information modelling.

A general modelling framework of e-Management for scalable SCN systems utilizing above technologies offers an integrated approach to knowledge-based modelling of customer-responsive systems. The proposed framework offers a mechanism to experiment various types of behaviour patterns that may emerge through interaction of scalable SCN members and apply lessons learned in developing robust e-Management models for scalable SCNs. Main components of this proposed to be developed approach are:

■ *Macro-level enterprise models*: Development of macro-level manufacturing enterprise models and tools to address enterprise-level needs supported by different levels of source information using enterprise integration tools, such as SAP R/3 and 'mysap.com'.

■ *Capability representation models*: Development of manufacturing enterprise models to represent capabilities and core competencies at the enterprise and an extended enterprise level.

■ *Enterprise model library*: Development of a library of manufacturing enterprise models that can be selected and tailored based on a user dialogue with the system.

Areas of possible extensions of this research are as follows:

1 Models of integrated life cycle for customer order in scalable SCNs.

2 Taxonomies of e-Management models to support these life cycles.

3 Methods for knowledge-based configuration of e-Management models to fit a customer order.

4 Integrated information framework to support e-Management models under dynamic environments.

Appendix 14A A co-operative supply chain system decomposition model

14A.1 Notation

A_j: technology matrix of the jth member representing common constraints.

b_0: resource vector for the jth member with respect to common constraints.

D_j: technology matrix of the jth member representing independent constraints.

b_j: resource vector for the jth member with respect to independent constraints.

C_j: vector of the objective function coefficients for the jth member.

X_j: vector of decision variables corresponding to jth member.

14A.2 Problem formulation

Common objective

Maximize, $z = C_1 X_1 + C_2 X_2 + \cdots + C_n X_n$

subject to (constraints):

Common constraints

$A_1 X_1 + A_2 X_2 + \cdots + A_n X_n = b_0$

Independent constraints

$D_1 X_1 = b_1$
$D_2 X_2 = b_2$
$\vdots$
$D_n X_n = b_n$

Non-negativity constraints

$X_j \geqslant 0, \quad \forall j$

Appendix 14B A co-operative supply chain system dynamic process flow model

14B.1 Notation

Variables

L: level (stock) in the trans-shipment node, denoted by a ▢

R: flow (rate) per unit of time t, denoted by a ⌀

R_{IN}:   flow rate 'in' through feedback

R_{OUT}: flow rate 'out' as feed forward

t: time (period)

Δt: change at time t

x_{ij}:   average flow through arc $i \rightarrow j$

c_{ij}:   cost per unit flow through arc $i \rightarrow j$

u_{ij}:   arc capacity for arc $i \rightarrow j$

b_i: average net flow generated at node i

$b_i > 0$, if node i is a source (supply node)

$b_i < 0$, if node i is a sink (demand node)

$b_i = 0$, if node i is a trans-shipment (intermediary node)

Auxiliary variables, denoted by a $\bigcirc$

GOAL: desired level

CAP: designed capacity

$DISC_c$: discrepancy with respect to capacity

$DISC_g$: discrepancy with respect to a goal

$DISC_o$: discrepancy with respect to an objective

OB: desired objective

1 Problem statement:
   Set up the flow model as a minimum cost flow problem, i.e.

$$\text{Minimize} \sum_{i=1}^{n} \sum_{j=1}^{n} c_{ij} x_{ij}$$

   subject to (constraints):

$$\sum_{j=1}^{n} x_{ij} - \sum_{j=1}^{n} x_{ji} = b_i, \quad \text{for each node } i$$

   and $0 \leqslant x_{ij} \leqslant u_{ij}$,   for each arc $i \rightarrow j$

2 Components of a system, represented as a flow model:
   Stocks (levels), rate of input/output, source (S), sink (N), system
   boundary, feedback/feedforward, goals, objectives, policies.
   'Intra'-flow: System boundary, capacity, feedback/feed forward
   'Inter'-flow: System boundary, capacity, feedback/feed forward

3 Conservation equations:
   $L(t + \Delta t) = L(t) + (R_{IN} - R_{OUT})\Delta t$ [level (stock) equation]
   $R_{IN}(t) = F(L(t))$ (rate equations)

   and

   $R_{OUT}(t) = G(L(t))$

   where F and G are some functions.

References and Further Reading

Beyer, N., W. Frithjof, J. Arrault and F. Rodrigues (1999). An Approach for a Practical Communication System for Supporting and Managing Concurrent Product Development. *Proceedings of the Fifth International Conference on Concurrent Enterprising 'The Concurrent Enterprise in Operation'*. N. Wognum, K. -D. Thoben and K. S. Pawar (eds). The Hague, The Netherlands, 317–324.

Bond, A. H. and L. Gasser (eds) (1988). *Readings in Distributed Artificial Intelligence*. San Mateo, California, Morgan Kaufmann.

Blanchard, B. S. and W. J. Fabrycky (1990). *Systems Engineering and Analysis*. New Jersey, Prentice Hall.

Bradshaw, J. M., P. D. Holm, J. H. Boose, D. Skuce and T. C. Lethbridge (1992). Sharable Ontologies as a Basis for Communication and Collaboration in Conceptual Modelling. *Proceedings of the Seventh Knowledge Acquisition for Knowledge-Based Systems Workshop*, Banff, Alta., Canada, 3.1–3.25.

Bradshaw, J. M., K. M. Ford, J. R. Adams-Webber and J. H. Boose (1993). Beyond the Repertory Grid: New Approaches to Constructivist Knowledge Acquisition Tool Development. *Knowledge Acquisition as Modeling*. K. M. Ford and J. M. Bradshaw (eds). New York, John Wiley: 287–333.

Bussmann, S. (1998). Agent-oriented Programming of Manufacturing Control Tasks. *Proceedings of the International Conference on Multi agent Systems*. Paris, France, 57–63.

CE NET White Paper on Concurrent Enterprising. Version 1.1. http://esoce. pl.ecp.fr/ce-net/CENET/XeditCENET

Chandra, C. (1997a). Enterprise Architectural Framework for Supply-chain Integration. *Proceedings of the Sixth Annual Industrial Engineering Research Conference*. Miami Beach, Florida, (May 17–18), 873–878.

Chandra, C. (1997b). A Formal System Analysis Methodology for a Cooperative Supply Chain. *Proceedings of the Second Annual International Conference on Industrial Engineering Applications and Practice*. San Diego, California.

Chandra, C., A. Nastasi, D. Powell and J. Ostic (1997). Enterprise Simulation Analysis of the Nylon Jacket Pipeline. *Technical Report LA-UR-97-154*, Los Alamos National Laboratory. Los Alamos, New Mexico.

Chandra, C., A. Nastasi, T. Norris and P. Tag (2000). Enterprise Modeling for Capacity Management in Supply Chain Simulation. *Proceedings of the Industrial Engineering Research Conference*. Cleveland, Ohio, May.

Clark, A. J. (1972). 'An Informal Survey of Multiechelon Inventory.' *Naval Research Logistics Quarterly* **19**: 621–650.

Clark, A. J. and H. Scarf (1960). 'Optimal Policies for a Multi-echelon Inventory Problem.' *Management Science* **6**: 475–490.

Cohen, M. A. and H. L. Lee (1988). 'Strategic Analysis of Integration Production–Distribution Systems: Models and Methods.' *Operations Research* **36**(2): 216–228.

Cohen, M. A. and H. L. Lee (1989). 'Resource Deployment Analysis of Global Manufacturing and Distribution Networks.' *Journal of Manufacturing and Operations Management* **2**(2): 81–104.

Dantzig, G. B. (1963). *Linear Programming and Extensions*. New Jersey, Princeton University Press.

Deleersnyder, J. -L., T. J. Hodgson, R. E. King, P. J. O'Grady and A. Savva (1992). 'Integrating Kanban Type Pull Systems and MRP Type Push Systems: Insights from a Markovian Model.' *IIE Transactions* **24**(3): 43–56.

Diks, E. B. and A. G. de Kok (1997). 'Optimal Control of a Divergent Multi-echelon Inventory System.' *European Journal of Operations Research,* October.

Diks, E. B. and A. G. de Kok (1999). 'Computational Results for the Control of a Divergent n-echelon Inventory System.' *International Journal of Production Economics* **56**(1–3): 327–336.

Diks, E. B., A. G. de Kok and A. G. Logodimos (1996). 'Multi-echelon Systems: A Service Measure Perspective.' *European Journal of Operational Research* **95**: 241–263.

Drew, S. A. W. (1975). 'The Application of Hierarchical Control Methods to a Managerial Problem.' *International Journal of Systems Science* **6**(4): 371–395.

Fleischanderl, G., G. Friedrich, A. Haselbouck, H. Schrener and M. Stumptner (1998). 'Configuring Large Systems using Generative Constraint Satisfaction.' *IEEE Intelligent Systems and their Application* **13**(4): 59–68.

Fikes, R. and A. Farquhar (1999). 'Distributed Repositories of Highly Expressive Reusable Ontologies.' *IEEE Intelligent Systems,* **14**(2 March/April): 73–79.

Fischer, K., J. P. Müller, H. Heimig and A. -W. Scheer (1996). Intelligent Agents in Virtual Enterprises. *Proceedings of the First International Conference and Exhibition on the Practical Application of Intelligent Agents and Multi-agent Technology.* London, UK, 205–223.

Franklin, S. (1996). Is it an Agent, or Just a Program?: A Taxonomy for Autonomous Agents. *Proceedings of the Third International Workshop on Agent Theories, Architectures, and Languages.* Springer-Verlag.

Gasser, L. (1991). 'Social Conceptions of Knowledge and Action: DAI Foundations and Open Systems Semantics.' *Artificial Intelligence* **47**: 107–138.

Giachetti, R. E., R. E. Young, A. Roggatz, W. Eversheim and G. Perrone (1997). 'A Methodology for the Reduction of Imprecision in the Engineering Process.' *European Journal of Operational Research* **100**: 277–292.

Graves, S. (1982). 'Using Lagrangean Techniques to Solve Hierarchical Production Planning Problems.' *Management Science* **28**(3).

Gruber, T. (1995). 'Toward Principles for the Design of Ontologies Used for Knowledge Sharing.' *International Journal of Human and Computer Studies* **43**(5/6): 907–928.

Gruninger, M. (1997). Integrated Ontologies for Enterprise Modelling. *Enterprise Engineering and Integration: Building International Consensus.* K. Kosanke and J. Nell (eds). Springer, 368–377.

Guarino, N. (1998). Formal Ontology and Information Systems. *Proceedings of FOIS'98.* Trento, Italy, (6–8 June). http://www.ladseb.pd.cnr.it/

Gupta, S. and R. Loulou (1998). 'Process Innovation, Product Differentiation, and Channel Structure: Strategic Incentives in a Duopoly.' *Marketing Science* **17**(4): 301–316.

Hackman, S. and R. Leachman (1989). 'A General Framework for Modeling Production.' *Management Science* **35**(4): 478–495.

Hariharan, R. and P. Zipkin (1995). 'Customer-order Information, Leadtimes, and Inventories.' *Management Science* **41**(10): 1599–1607.

Hendler, J. (1999). 'Making Sense Out of Agents.' *IEEE Intelligent Systems* **14**(2 March/April): 32–37.

Hillier, F. S. and G. J. Lieberman (1990). *Introduction to Operations Research.* New York, McGraw-Hill Publishing Company.

Hirsch, B. (1995). 'Information System Concept for the Management of Distributed Production.' *Computers in Industry* **26**: 229–241.

ISO TC 184/SC 5WG 1 (1997). Requirements for Enterprise Reference Architectures and Methodologies. http://www.mel.nist.gov/sc5wg1/gera-std/ger-anxs.html

Jennings, N., P. Faratin, M. Johnson, P. Brien and M. Wiegand (1996). Using Intelligent Agents to Manage Business Processes. *Proceedings of International Conference on The Practical Application of Intelliagents and Multi-agent Technology.* London, (22–24 April), 345–360.

Jennings, N. R. (1994). *Cooperation in Industrial Multi-agent Systems*, Vol. 43. World Scientific Series in Computer Science. World Scientific Publishing Co. Inc.

Klir, G. J. (1991). *Facets of Systems Science.* New York, Plenum Press.

Lee, H. L. (1996). 'Effective Inventory and Service Management Through Product and Process Redesign.' *Operations Research* **44**(1): 151–159.

Lee, H. L. and C. Billington (1993). 'Material Management in Decentralized Supply Chains.' *Operations Research* **41**(5): 835–847.

Lesser, V. R. (1999). 'Cooperative Multiagent Systems: A Personal View of the State of the Art.' *IEEE Transactions on Knowledge and Data Engineering* **11**(1): 133–142.

Little, J. D. C. (1992). 'Tautologies, Models and Theories: Can We Find "Laws" of Manufacturing?' *IIE Transactions* **24**(3): 7–13.

Livelink: Collaborative Knowledge Management, http://www.opentext.com/livelink/knowledge_management.html

Malone, T. (1987). 'Modeling, Co-ordination in Organizations and Markets.' *Management Science* **33**(10): 1317–1332.

Malone, T. W. and K. Crowston (1994). 'The Interdisciplinary Study of Coordination.' *ACM Computing Surveys* **26**(1 March): 87–119.

Manufacturing Enterprise Integration Program (1999), National Institute of Standards and Technology, Gaithersburg, Maryland, November (URL: HTTP://WWW.ATP.NIST.GOV).

Masahiko, A. (1984). *The Co-operative Game Theory of the Firm.* Oxford, UK, Oxford University Press.

Morris, W. T. (1967). 'On the Art of Modeling.' *Management Science* **13**(12 August): B-707–B-717.

Moulin, B. and B. Chaib-Draa (1996). An Overview of Distributed Artificial Intelligence. *Foundations of Distributed Artificial Intelligence.* G. M. P. O'Hare and N. R. Jennings (eds). New York, John Wiley and Sons: 3–55.

Nadler, G. (1970). *Work Design: A Systems Concept.* Homewood, Ill, Richard D. Irwin.

Nadoli, G. and L. Biegel (1993). 'Intelligent Manufacturing-Simulation Agent Tool (IMSAT).' *ACM Transactions on Modeling and Computer Simulation* **3**(1): 42–65.

Neches, R., R. E. Fikes, T. Finin, T. Gruber, R. Patil, T. Senator and W. R. Swartout (1991). 'Enabling Technology for Knowledge Sharing.' *AI Magazine* **12**(3): 16–36.

Oakes, W. R., D. R. Powell, J. W. Jackson, J. H. Fasel III, J. K. Ostic and K. R. Burris (1997). *An Evaluation Framework for Supply Chain Analysis Methods and Tools.* Los Alamos National Laboratory Report LA-UR-97-246, Version 1.0, January.

Patil, R. S., R. E. Fikes, P. F. Patel-Schneider, D. MacKay, T. Finin, T. Gruber and R. Neches (1992). The DARPA Knowledge Sharing Effort: Progress Report. *The Proceedings of Annual International Conference on Knowledge Representation*, Cambridge, MA.

Pawlak, A., W. Cellary, A. Smirnov, X. Warzee and J. Willis (1997). Collaborative Engineering Based on the Web – How Far to Go? *Advances in Information Technologies: The Business Challenge*. J. -Y. Roger, B. Stanford-Smith and P. K. Kidd (eds). IOS Press: 434–441.

Poirier, C. C. and S. E. Reiter (1996). *Supply Chain Optimization*. San Francisco, CA, Berrett-Koehler Publishers.

Pritsker, A. A. B. (1997). 'Modeling in Performance-enhancing Processes.' *Operations Research* 45(6 November–December): 797–804.

Pyke, D. F. and M. A. Cohen (1990). 'Push and Pull in Manufacturing Distribution Systems.' *Journal of Operations Management* 9(1 January): 24–43.

Sandholm, T. (1998). Agents in Electronic Commerce: Component Technologies for Automated Negotiation and Coalition Formation. *Proceedings of the International Conference on Multi Agent Systems*. Paris, France, 10–11.

Scherer, R. J. and P. Katranuschkov (1999). Knowledge-based Enhancements to Product Data Server Technology for Concurrent Engineering. *Proceedings of the Fifth International Conference on Concurrent Enterprising 'The Concurrent Enterprise in Operation'*. N. Wognum, K. -D. Thoben and K. S. Pawar (eds). The Hague, The Netherlands, 121–128.

Shaw, M. J., J. J. Solberg and T. C. Woo (1992). 'System Integration in Intelligent Manufacturing: An Introduction.' *IIE Transactions* 24(3 July): 2–6.

Sipper, D. and R. L. Bulfin Jr. (1997). *Production: Planning, Control, and Integration*. New York, McGraw-Hill, Inc.

Sousa, P., T. Heikkila, M. Kollingbaum and P. Valckenaers (1999). Aspects of Co-operation in Distributed Manufacturing Systems. *Proceedings of the Second International Workshop on Intelligent Manufacturing Systems*, September. Leuven, Belgium, 685–717.

Stumptner, M. (1997). 'An Overview of Knowledge-based Configuration.' *AI Communications* 10(2): 111–125.

Swaminathan, J. M., S. F. Smith and N. M. Sadeh (1998). 'Modeling Supply Chain Dynamics: A Multiagent Approach.' *Decision Sciences* 29(3): 607–632.

Taha, H. A. (1987). *Operations Research: An Introduction*. New York, Macmillan Publishing Company.

Technologies for Enterprise Integration, Rev 3.1 (1999). Integrated Manufacturing Technology Roadmapping Project, Oak Ridge Centers for Manufacturing Technology, Oak Ridge, Tennessee, (October) (URL: HTTP:// IMTI21.ORG).

Thomas, D. and P. Griffin (1996). 'Coordinated Supply Chain Management.' *European Journal of Operational Research* 94: 1–15.

Tsang, J. P. (1991). Constraint Propagation Issues in Automated Design. *Expert Systems in Engineering: Principles and Applications*. G. Gettlob and W. Nejdl (eds). Berlin, Springer-Verlag: 135–151.

Tzafestas, S. and G. Kapsiotis (1994). 'Coordinated Control of Manufacturing/ Supply Chains Using Multi-level Techniques.' *Computer Integrated Manufacturing Systems* 73(3): 206–212.

Walsh, W. and M. Wellman (1998). A Market Protocol for Decentralized Task Allocation. *Proceedings of International Conference on Multi agent Systems*, Paris. (July 3–7), 325–332.

Whang, S. (1995). 'Coordination in Operations: A Taxonomy.' *Journal of Operations Management* **12**: 413–422.

Wooldridge, M. and N. R. Jennings (eds) (1995). *Intelligent Agents – Theories, Architectures, and Languages*. 403 Lecture Notes in Artificial Intelligence. Springer-Verlag, 890.

Wooldridge, M., N. Jennings and D. Kinny (1999). A Methodology for Agent-oriented Analysis and Design. *Proceedings of International Conference On Autonomous Agents*. Seattle, 69–76.

Younis, M. and M. Mahmoud (1986). 'Optimal Inventory for Unpredicted Production Capacity and Raw Material Supply.' *Large Scale Systems* **11**: 1–17.

15 Building out the Web services architecture: the challenge of software applications integration

Wendy L. Currie

15.1 Introduction

The economic downturn of the last few years has witnessed the demise of thousands of dot.com or Internet businesses worldwide (Cassidy, 2002). Despite the promises of value creation from *e-Business, the digital economy* (Department of Commerce, 1999) and *the networked society* (Castells, 2000), e-Business models have been poorly designed and executed (Quinn-Mills, 2001). If we remind ourselves of the 'hype' which surrounded e-Business in the recent past, the 'irrational exuberance' which suggested that 'If you're not an e-Business, you're out of business!'. This led many established firms in the technology sector to develop new e-Business ventures. In parallel, numerous start-up firms emerged having gained first-round venture capital funding to develop their various business models. In 1999, 3957 US firms received a total of $59.5 billion. The average venture capital deal in 1999 was $15 million (Cassidy, 2002, p. 240). Many of these firms adopted a 'get big fast' (GBF) strategy (Oliva et al., 2003) by forming strategic alliances and partnerships to compete in the high velocity technology market (Eisenhardt and Martin, 2000). Yet many of these strategic alliances and partnerships proved unstable, characterized by a lack of commitment from one partner (usually an established industry player) leading to the demise of another (usually the start-up firm) (Hagel and Seely-Brown, 2001; Currie et al., 2004).

Against a backdrop of dot.com failure, our interest in the growth and diffusion of the Internet and e-Business models as a unit of analysis (Amit and Zott, 2000) persists. This has led some to ask: 'What fundamentally new or revitalized research questions of importance to managers are arising from the emerging digital economy?' (Geoffrion and Khrisnan, 2003a, p. 1278). Or perhaps more importantly: 'How is business value created from the digital economy?' and, 'What performance measures and metrics can we used to evaluate and measure e-Business models?'. Some writers suggest that only by creating *on-demand business models* can firms fully exploit the potential of *on-demand computing* (Haeckel, 2002, p. 405).

This chapter completes this volume by discussing some of the results from a 5-year research project on the deployment, hosting and integration of an *on-demand* business model, which came to be known as application service provision (ASP). ASP was one of the most popular acronyms during the height of the dot.com era (IDC, 1999). As an e-Business model targeted largely at small and medium enterprises, ASP is a form of application outsourcing, designed to offer customers a hosted (remote) software delivery option, priced on a subscription, or pay-as-you-go model (Kern et al., 2002). Within a short time period, numerous firms labelled themselves, ASPs. Firms ranged from telecommunications providers (offering infrastructure capabilities); independent software vendors (ISVs); data centre and co-location firms (offering data hosting/warehousing services), and an assortment of other firms including large and small management consultancies, specialist data security and networking firms (IDC, 2000). But despite the initial euphoria about ASP, largely confined to the technology sector, most ASPs went out of business within a couple of years (Hagel, 2002). More recently, the ASP business model, or at least the hype, which surrounded it, has been replaced by the Web services business model (Hagel, 2002). Unlike ASP, which concentrated largely on applications delivery and enablement, emphasizing the importance of 24×7 software applications availability (among other performance benefits); Web services aims to provide the 'missing link' which is software applications integration (Currie et al., 2004). Research findings from the earlier ASP era suggested that few customers were satisfied with the ASP model, largely because they required some form of customization and integration (Susarla et al., 2003). With Web services, the perennial problem of lack of integration is expected to disappear (Hagel and Seely-Brown, 2001).

In this chapter, we present our findings from research on ASP and review current literature on Web services. Our research question is: Will the Web services business model succeed where ASP failed? Whilst past disappointment and shortcomings from the first phase of e-Business does not determine nor predict future success or failure, our argument is that potential customers of information technology (IT) service provider firms need to identify a more rigorous approach to evaluating the benefits and risks from e-Business models such as ASP and Web services. As this chapter will demonstrate, empirical research on the ASP market identified a mismatch between service provider (vendor) marketing literature on the potential business benefits (i.e. value proposition) from a hosted (ASP) solution, and customer requirements from their existing and planned investment in Web-enabled software applications. While vendor hype and overselling is part and parcel of the technology sector, suggesting that each new IT artefact is the new *silver bullet*, the level of investment from venture capital firms in supporting start-up ASP ventures was evident of a commitment to the likelihood that this business model would succeed. Our research findings, however, point to the need for technology firms to engage more closely with their existing and potential customers, particularly in the light of the broken promises and poor results from e-Business.

This chapter is divided into five parts. First, we discuss the recent history and evolution of software applications targeted at the business community. We briefly discuss the service provider or xSP landscape. Our main interest here is to explicate the reasoning behind the proliferation of ASP firms and, more recently, the growth in Web services. Second, we discuss the potential of Web services in the context of software applications integration. The topic of integration is central to the Web services value proposition. Here, we suggest that integrating software applications will prove to be a major challenge for Web service providers and customers. Next, we present two short case studies from the UK financial services industry on the challenge of integrating disparate software applications. We ask whether Web services will resolve this challenge. This follows another short case study on how Amazon.com are using Web services in their business. Finally, we broaden our discussion by considering how Web services may provide the impetus for business process outsourcing (BPO).

15.2 The evolution of software applications: a recent history

The commercial use of software applications over a 40-year period has undergone significant change (Shanks et al., 2003), largely with the development of microelectronics (Forrester, 1980). Back in the 1960s and 1970s, very few firms developed their own IT systems, as the majority of 'office work' was paper based. Accounting and finance used ledgers and double-entry bookkeeping. Personnel (not human resources management!) similarly used paper-based methods and techniques for the storage of personnel records. With the development of mainframe computing, firms which needed to store large amounts of data were offered the option of using a *service bureau*. To some extent, this marked the birth of IT outsourcing, as service bureau providers sold 'space' on their mainframe computers to their customers for a rental/subscription fee. In many regards, this 'era' was 'technology centric', since the service bureaus did little else but provide a technology-based data repository service. Within firms, IT was also centralized. For example, banks and insurance firms set up their IT departments, having invested large sums of money in mainframe computers. Clearly, the IT departments of the 1960s and 1970s, with the 'punch-cards' are a different world from the highly automated offices of today!

As business computing developed throughout the 1980s and 1990s, new opportunities existed for technology sector firms to develop client server software applications. Customers demanded 'off-the-shelf' packaged applications. Firms like J. D. Edwards, Baan (now Invensys), Oracle, Peoplesoft and SAP all competed in the enterprise resource planning (ERP) marketspace. ERP systems for supply chain management, logistics, finance and accounting, etc., proved highly popular, as customers preferred purchasing software products and services rather than developing them in-house. Although, in the case of ERP, several writers have demonstrated that the variable costs of implementation (i.e. involving significant customization) completely outweighs the initial cost of the software license fee (Sumner, 2003). Alongside the ERP systems, developed ostensibly for the larger firm, numerous other software vendors developed packaged applications for the small-to-medium business (SMB).

During this period, the proliferation of software applications products and services fuelled the growth of the IT department. Whereas IT had usually fallen under the remit of accounting and finance, many firms developed the role of the chief information officer (CIO). In the UK, this position was usually referred to as the IT director (Grindley, 1991; Currie, 1995). Calls for the CIO or IT director to become a 'board level' position were common (Earl, 1988), usually accompanied by the argument that IT was now critical to the business (Earl, 1989). As a consequence of increasing adoption and diffusion of IT, management consultancies further developed their IT outsourcing businesses throughout this period. Firms like EDS, IBM, CSC, Anderson Consulting and others, won large IT outsourcing contracts, some of which were for the management the entire IT portfolio of their customers (Lacity and Hirschheim, 1993).

With the commercial development of the Internet and World Wide Web (WWW) during the 1990s, new possibilities for software applications emerged. The Internet would become a new delivery channel, spawning new online businesses such as banking, travel, shopping and auctions, to name only a few. Investors rushed to become part of what is now known as the dot.com bubble (Quinn-Mills, 2001). Unlike previous decades where firms negotiated with single or multiple service providers to resource their IT capability (i.e. purchasing ERP, contracting out systems development work, hiring space on a mainframe, etc.), the Internet era would become a virtual marketplace or marketspace (Weill and Vitale, 2001) offering numerous product and service choices. In the new, 'Internet era', service providers would develop new, or reconfigure existing, packaged software applications to sell and deliver over the Internet. Figure 15.1 depicts the three stages of software applications development and IT outsourcing. This representation was used by a Silicon Valley firm to secure first-round

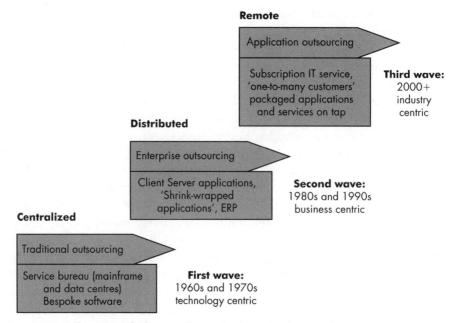

Figure 15.1: Three stages of software applications development and IT outsourcing.

venture capital funding to become an ASP targeted at the high-technology equipment manufacturing sector (Currie, 2003b). As the Figure suggests, in parallel with the changes in software applications development, IT outsourcing has further undergone changes from its initial 'traditional' mainframe outsourcing, moving through enterprise (ERP) outsourcing to the current application outsourcing (ASP and Web services). However, the latter 'era' where outsourcing is depicted by service providers offering software applications on a subscription-based pricing model is yet to be realized.

15.2.1 The xSP landscape

Since the 1960s, the technology sector has changed rapidly, where market leaders in hardware technology (i.e. IBM) have been joined by a multitude of software applications developers. Even IBM recognized the poor prospects of sustaining profitability from hardware and therefore set up a successful IT outsourcing business (i.e. IBM Global Services). IBM is currently spearheading Web services. In an environment of constant change, the high velocity and dynamic technology sector comprises numerous service providers or xSPs.[1] The xSP landscape

---

1. The generic term for service providers is xSPs. This incorporates service providers such as application service providers (ASPs) managed service providers (MSPs), Web Service providers (WSPs), independent software vendors (ISVs), telecommunications firm, networking and datacentre providers, and many others.

comprises established and new firms. With the advent of the Internet, xSPs undertake one of four main activities: resell capacity, infrastructure management, outsourcing and Internet services. For example, in the category of firms offering resell capacity, large established telecommunications firms such as Cable & Wireless, AT&T and BT all offer data centre capacity. In the case of Cable & Wireless, the acquisitions of Digital Island and Exodus served to reinforce this capability. Coupled with this, other firms provide infrastructure management under the labels, managed service providers (MSPs), infrastructure platform providers and managed components providers. Customers wishing to access their data on a remote model may utilize the services of an MSP to save time and effort in managing the software infrastructure. As part of this service, they will receive software upgrades, security checks, maintenance and other services which enable the seamless delivery of the software application.

The category of ASP is depicted as providing an outsourcing service. In this regard, ASPs offer application outsourcing, and are unlikely to extend this activity to infrastructure management (although some do). In the same category, ISVs may also offer outsourcing services. At the height of the dot.com era, numerous ISVs with an established customer base and channel to market investigated the possibility of offering their software applications on a remote delivery model. Large ERP vendors like Peoplesoft and SAP set up e-Businesses, largely to penetrate new customer markets such as SMBs. In the case of SAP, mySAP.com™ was created to offer SMBs the opportunity to purchase ERP software over the Internet, priced on a subscription basis. Whilst the value proposition of these initiatives looked interesting, the reality of developing a new customer base proved to be more difficult than originally expected.

The category of Internet services comprises largely those businesses which are developed as 'pure-plays', ones which develop products and services entirely for the Internet. This differs from some ASPs, which simply host the software applications of established ISVs. Another category of activity is ASP aggregators. These firms aggregate and integrate the services from multiple xSP and ISV partners. For example, firms like Jamcracker™ were set up to provide a portfolio of software applications to customers. This *pick-and-mix* approach was a novel idea aimed to offer customers choice and flexibility. But like many ASPs, even ASP aggregators found it difficult to generate revenues in a tight technology market. Table 15.1 gives a breakdown of the various categories and types of xSPs.

The lessons learned from the dot.com shakeout show that xSPs largely failed to develop an adequate customer base to remain viable (Currie, 2003b). Was this because xSPs failed to 'educate' potential customers about the value proposition of purchasing Software-as-a-Service? Or is it

Table 15.1: xSP categories

Type of xSP	Capacity service providers (CAPs)	Managed service providers (MSPs)	Application service providers (ASPs)	Internet business service providers (IBSPs)
	Co-location providers	Infrastructure platform providers	Managed applications providers (ISV or third party)	Develop and deliver Net-native application services
	Telcos Wholesale service providers	Managed components providers		
Main activity	Resell capacity	Infrastructure management	Outsourcing	Internet services
ASP integrators				
Aggregate and integrate services from multiple SP and ISV partners.				

Source: Adapted from Summit Strategies, Inc.

the case that xSPs developed poor or faulty e-Business models? Or a mixture of the two or neither?

Our research findings from the 5-year research programme suggest that the answer to the first two questions is 'yes'. In short, xSPs tended to be a self-serving community, attending numerous conferences and trade fair events, yet communicating only with each other! Within the wider business community, few customers (particularly those outside the technology sector) knew what it meant to have their software applications *delivered over the Internet*. The term ASP was relatively unknown within hospitals, schools, retail outlets, etc. Coupled with this, ASPs tended to overstate the ease with which they could establish a new market. Simply because everything was pre-fixed with 'e' did not guarantee that people wanted to pay for remote software, particularly when so much free software was already available on the Internet (whether legally or otherwise!). Added to this, the lack of broadband technology contributed to the failure of many xSPs in offering products and services over the Internet. Clearly, unless a software application is immediately usable, it is unviable. The general public and businesses in particular will not accept Internet downtime when they wish to use an application.

In recent years, software and platform vendors have brought Web-optimized applications and new generations of scalable, reliable middleware platforms to market. The rise of XML-based Web services potentially offers xSPs more flexibility to develop differentiated products and services to generate new revenue streams. If the promises of *on-demand* business models are fully realized, the software-as-a-service model could change the shape of the technology industry (Gottschalk et al., 2002). In the following two sections, we seek to explain the value proposition surrounding the beleaguered ASP model, and the more recent growth in interest in Web services. We position our discussion in the context of a 'buyer-beware' or sceptical approach to e-Business, particularly in the light of the demise of so many e-Business firms.

15.2.2 ASP

The ASP business model emerged during the late 1990s as a 'revolutionary' approach to delivering and enabling software applications. Large technology analyst firms (IDC, Forrester, Gartner, etc.) all championed the ASP business model. This section is divided into three parts. First, we consider some definitions of ASP. Second, we investigate the first phase of the ASP market from 1999 to 2001. Third, we discuss the reasons behind the decline in the ASP market, which Hagel (2002) has described as 'a flawed business model'.

Definitions of ASP

In parallel with other forms of *e-Business* (i.e. business-to-business (B2B), business-to-consumer, etc.), ASP was spearheaded by several groups with a vested interest. Large technology sector firms mobilized themselves to set up various special interest groups and membership organizations. The ASP Industry Consortium (ASPic) was established in May 1999 by twenty-five[2] technology sector firms. Its mission was to *promote the ASP industry by sponsoring research, fostering standards, and articulating the measurable benefits of this evolving delivery model.* ASPic members defined an ASP as a firm that, *manages and delivers application capabilities to multiple entities from data centers across a wide area network. An ASP may be a commercial entity, providing a paid service to customers or, conversely, a not-for-profit or government organization supporting end-users.* Another definition was that, *ASPs are service firms that provide a contractual service offering to deploy, host, manage and rent access to an application from a centrally-managed facility. ASPs directly, or indirectly with business partners, provide all of the specific activities and expertise aimed at managing the software application or set of applications* (IDC, 1999).

Despite the notion that ASP was perceived as a new *e-Business model* to provide SMBs with opportunities to deploy, host and manage their

---

2. The ASP Industry Consortium (ASPic) founding members were: AT&T, AristaSoft, Boundless Technologies, Cisco Systems, Citrix Systems, Compaq, Cylex, Ernst & Young, LLP, Exodus, FutureLink, GTE, Great Plains Software, IBM, Interpath, JAWS Technogies, Marimba, Onyx Software, SaskTel, Sharp Electronics, Sun Microsystems, The Taylor Group, Telecomputing ASA, UUNet, Verio, Wyse Technology.

software applications, the majority of ASPic founding members were themselves, large firms. Yet within a year, the membership base of ASPic grew to over 600 firms, many of which were start-up, self-styled ASPs (others were telecommunications firms, hardware manufacturers, ISVs, database and networking firms, large and small management consultancies, among others). For the established industry players, ASP was perceived as a way to generate new business opportunities. Yet one industry analyst commented that, '... serious opportunities still exist for start-up and emerging players' (Durlacher, 1999). Large firms saw their role as setting an example for their smaller counterparts, by promoting a new information system (IS) innovation.

Other outlets to promote ASP emerged in the form of Internet reference or news sites. For example, WebHarbor.com described itself as, *The ASP Industry Portal*. Others were *aspnews.com* and *aspindustrynews.com*, with the mission to, *cover the ASP marketplace*. All these sites served to *'educate'* potential customers by providing market analysis on the latest Software-as-a-Service product offerings, markets trends and surveys, mergers and acquisitions between industry players, ASP customer reference sites, gossip and industry/business analysis.

The ASP market

One quote from 1999 which provided a boost to the ASP market was from the chief executive officer (CEO) of Sun Microsystems, Scott McNealy:

Five years from now, if you're a CIO with a head for business, you won't be buying computers anymore. You won't be buying software either. You will rent all your resources from an Application Service Provider (*Source*: Scott McNealy, CEO, Sun Microsystems). Indeed, the backing from market leaders (notwithstanding their own self-interest) provided the impetus for large investment from venture capital firms to fund start-up ASPs.

In addition to this, various business analyst firms predicted that the ASP market would grow to $18 billion (Gartner Group) or $24 billion (IDC Group) both by 2005. Others also predicted similar growth rates (i.e. Forrester $23 billion, Dataquest $22.7 billion and Yankee Group $19 billion). These revenues would be derived mainly from the delivery of Software-as-a-Service. Customers would pay for their software on a subscription, pricing model which was a move away from paying for software as a product. Thus, the *utility model* of software delivery was born. Customers would therefore pay for their software as they pay for gas, electricity, telephone and other utilities.

By 2000, ASPs had emerged in various guises. Enterprise ASPs offered vanilla-ERP software to SMBs; vertical ASPs targeted specific industry sectors (i.e. health, finance and manufacturing); horizontal ASPs offered business software applications (i.e. payroll, HR, travel and expenses, etc.); pure-play ASPs dealt only in software applications designed to be Web-enabled (these firms were largely Internet start-ups); finally,

ASP-enablers comprised largely technology sector firms which provided the IT infrastructure (i.e. telecos, etc.) (Currie and Seltsikas, 2001). Indeed, the proliferation of ASPs followed a trend to offer *something for everyone*. So by the end of 2000, the ASP market comprised of firms of all shapes and sizes, offering a wide range of Web-enabled software applications, yet mainly undifferentiated, commodity products and services.

Poor adoption and diffusion of ASP

Supported by much hype surrounding the ASP business model, it was interesting to observe the rapid decline in the fortunes of numerous ASPs by mid-2001. Despite spending vast amounts of money on advertising and marketing, SMBs (the target customer market) remained unconvinced about the value of using ASPs, especially as procuring commodity applications (e-mail) on a price per seat/per month basis offered them few business benefits (Ekanayaka et al., 2002). But using ASPs for more complex software applications hosting exposed the customer to additional risks such as data security infringement and theft (Currie, 2003a). The first phase of the ASP market was therefore characterized by flawed and failed e-Business models (Hagel, 2002), with few paying customers, resulting in the demise of numerous ASPs. One by one, ASPs went out of business. Cable & Wireless a-Services™, a subsidiary of the parent firm which began by offering Microsoft Office/Exchange™ products and services on a hosted delivery model closed in November 2001. Similarly, Aristasoft, a Silicon Valley-based ASP, serving the high-technology equipment manufacturing sector closed. Pandesic, e-Carisma, Futurelink, also went out of business. USinternetworking, considered to be one of the major ASPs, went into Chapter 11 in the USA. All these firms shared the same problem of failing to build a sufficient customer base to generate enough revenues for a sustainable business.

Our research study identified five key performance areas (KPAs) which business value could be created for the customer (Currie, 2003). They are: delivery and enablement, management and operations, integration, client/vendor relationships and business transformation. Whilst it is outside the scope of the present chapter to discuss the findings of this study, the key reasons behind the poor adoption and diffusion of the ASP model are as follows. First, few ASPs clearly understood the customer requirements of their targeted product/service and/or sector. Many ASPs adopted the position that customers would pay for a hosted software application given their need for 24×7 delivery and enablement. This was clearly misguided. Findings suggest that few customers were concerned about the *anytime, anyplace, anywhere* (the Martini) approach to software delivery and access. Rather, customers were more concerned about their data security and integrity. Trusting their data to a third party was not a simple matter, particularly a start-up firm with few customer reference sites. Second, few ASPs offered mission-critical software applications. Most offered simple collaboration tools (i.e. e-mail and office suites). Potential customers could not see any additional business value in paying for a hosted office suite, particularly when the leading ISV charged extra for this service even where the customer was already using the suppliers' products! Indeed, the one-to-many model simply became same-for-all, with no discernable benefits. Third, ASPs found that collaboration tools were not sufficient to generate revenues, unless they could scale the application to adequate numbers (i.e. thousands of paying customers). Few managed to achieve this. To the extent that some ASPs managed to offer simple collaboration tools to customers who did not wish to manage this particular technology in-house, the revenue streams flowing from this service were poor. But more customers meant more staff for the ASP, and more staff increased costs. Coupled with this, it was not easy for ASPs to convince potential customers about the advantages of ASP. Whilst the IT industry could easily engage in a dialogue among itself about the intricacies of the ASP solution, the average small, non-IT firm was often confused about e-Business offerings, and few had even heard of the term ASP. In fact, one SMB IT manager believed that the ASP acronym stood for 'Active Server Pages!'.

As ASPs continued to go out of business, service provider firms that survived the fallout re-positioned themselves within the technology sector. To some extent, ASP became synonymous with dot.com failure. As a result, 'ASPs' re-labelled themselves using terms like: managed service providers, application infrastructure providers and Web service providers.[3] The proliferation of ASPs by the end of the 1990s was clearly unsustainable. Too many ASPs in an immature industry dictated that only a few, with convincing business models, having achieved first mover advantage, would survive. But like most industries, increasing maturity leads to consolidation, with only a few market leaders (Marks and Werrell, 2003).

Recognizing the need to add value to the customer, the second phase of the ASP market must address important issues from resolving data security problems to offering integrated and interoperable e-Business solutions. Web services are one of the latest developments from the technology sector claiming to offer a *new paradigm* for connecting business processes independent of their underlying implementation. Unlike the first phase of the ASP market, Web services are designed to extend the life of legacy systems. They represent a new approach to the perennial problem of integrating disparate applications within or between organizations. The next section introduces the concept of Web services, in the context of their potential to provide the 'missing link' in the drive to create on-demand e-Business models.

---

3. See http://www.aspnews.com/trends/article

15.2.3 Web services

The current proliferation of Web service vendors provides some interesting comparisons with the first phase of the ASP market. Whereas ASPs were predominently start-up firms, many of which forming strategic partnerships with ISVs to host their software applications on a pay-as-you-go model, Web services have the backing of several technology market leaders: i.e. Microsoft and Sun Microsystems. With their competing technology platforms (Microsoft .NET and J2EE), these firms are engaged in serious competition within the Web services arena. But what are Web services?

Web services are emerging as a systematic and extensible framework for application-to-application integration. Built upon existing Web protocols and open XML standards (Curbera et al., 2002) information can be seamlessly passed between remote applications running in different environments. This architecture heralds the way for Web services, promising to provide real business delivery mechanisms, system integration and strategic opportunities for firms. This new distributed computing model is described as the next generation of service-oriented Internet applications.

In the past, consistent implementation was necessary to enable distributed application integration. But with Web services, the playing field may be levelled, enabling the construction of new composite applications using business functions from other internal or external applications without being dependent on an implementation. This services-orientated approach aims to integrate applications within and across firms. The key difference between a traditional Web application and a Web service is that the data and information returned can be easily integrated into Intranet, server, or desktop applications.

Definitions of Web services

Definitions of Web services vary, with some pundits focusing on the technical features and others, on the business benefits. Table 15.2 captures some of the current definitions of Web services.

The Web services market

The drive towards Web services is built upon the premise that significant benefits will arise from integrating software applications across heterogeneous organizations, sites and departments. One of the failings of the dot.com era of the late 1990s and early 2000s was the implicit message that firms should move towards e-Business, by abandoning their traditional business! For CIOs and IT directors, the implication was that *legacy* software applications and infrastructure needed to be replaced, or at least reinforced with *Web-enabled* technology. For banks, insurance firms and many others having invested

Table 15.2: Definitions of Web services

A Web service is a software application that is identified by a URL whose interfaces and bindings are capable of being defined, described, and discovered by XML artefacts, and supports direct interactions with other software application using XML-based messages via Internet-based protocols.	W3C Web Services Architecture Group (http://www.w3.org/-TR/wsa-reqs)
A collection of business functions or capabilities taken from a single or multiple software applications that, when bundled together, can be published to a network using standard XML-based protocols for use by other applications. Each Web service is a bundling block that enables the sharing of software functionality with other applications residing outside of the Web service's native IT environment.	*Source*: Triple Tree
Web services are loosely coupled software components delivered over Internet standard technologies. A Web service represents a business function or business service and can be accessed by another application … over public networks using generally available protocols …	*Source*: Gartner Group
The promise and hype of Web services is that … applications will begin to function as services that can be identified, located, accessed, compiled, and assembled in pre-specified configurations, dynamically, in real time.	*Source*: IDC
Discrete software components that run on top of the Internet as if it – along with the diverse systems it connects – constituted a huge distributed operating system … Web services are analogous to software components such as Enterprise Java Beans, which make up the elements of a full application that runs on a single-server operating system.	Summit Strategies
Web services are a set of standards and protocols, embraced by all major technology providers, that allow software resources to be shared, combined, used an re-used within and between organisations.	Jyoti Banerjee, CEO, MyBusiness.net
Web services are loosely-coupled, self-describing services that are accessed programmatically across a distributed network, and exchange data using vendor, platform, and language-neutral protocols.	Marks and Werrill, 2003, p. 27.

heavily in IT, the prospect of Web-enabled 'add-ons' was insignificant in the context of their overall IT infrastructure and human capabilities. Investing further sums of money with no discernable business benefits was both impractical and undesirable. The key issue for these industries was not only to replace IT, but instead to explore ways to better integrate existing systems. Yet the cost of integrating numerous disparate systems (e.g. compliance, order management, reconciliation, data attribution, performance analysis, treasury, etc.) requires a large commitment in terms of money, time and skill.

So what is the impetus for the perceived growth in Web services? Clearly, large firms having invested millions (even billions) of dollars in their IT infrastructure over many decades are now faced with a significant business and technology challenge: the need for integration.

According to Gartner Group,

> *The need for e-Commerce, collaborative commerce (c-Commerce) and involvement with other divisions or departments is pushing vendors to honour enterprises' requests for easy integration, if not out-of-the-box then certainly without having to rely on extraordinary resources... Through 2006, service-orientated development will change the way software is built, packaged and sold by more than 80 per cent of ISVs. By 2005, new licences for software that use Web services standards will represent £21 billion in sales. (Gartner 13 November 2002, p. 2)*

Unlike ASP, which Hagel describes as a *'false start'*, Web services promise to resolve the problems of lack of applications integration and poor flexibility. Some believe that Web services will create new, and transform existing, business and customer-facing software applications. Unlike traditional applications, which are stand-alone and self-contained, deployed in fixed locations like thick-client desktop machines or centralized application servers, Web services are not tied to specific technology platforms and operating systems. Applications based on delivery via Web services will benefit the customer through its simplicity of use within a single IT structure.

According to Hagel,

> *Out of the ashes of the first wave of e-Commerce experimentation, a new technology architecture is emerging. This technology architecture, known as Web services architecture, responds to major challenges that previous generations of technology have been unable to address. Despite its name, the focus of Web services architecture is not to connect people with Web sites. Instead, it focuses on connecting applications and data directly with each other, automating connections that might otherwise have required human intervention. The architecture is designed to ensure that applications and data can be accessed by authorised entities, regardless of location or underlying technology platforms (Hagel, 2003, p. 24).*

The business requirement for integration is expected to become a multi-billion dollar market. The Aberdeen Group estimated that new enterprise information integration technology would become a $7.5 billion market in 2003.

A new e-Business model or 'more hype'?

Like ASP, Web services may be treated as a new e-Business model to be exploited by IT service providers. The new business and technical opportunities provided by leading industry players (see below) enable Web service vendors to offer customers the ability to collaborate with their customers and suppliers. If we consider the development of software applications over a 20-year period, the emergence of ERP systems was seen as a revolutionary step in providing customers with the tools and techniques to transform their business processes (Ross et al., 2003). ERP systems were expensive and engaged the customer and supplier in a closely-coupled relationship. Whilst ERP systems offered many benefits in terms of providing a structure to a firm's business processes, they equally created enterprise silos. Observations of ERP implementation further confirmed that the firm's business processes were invariably adapted to fit the supplier's business process design (Shanks et al., 2003).

With the emergence of the Internet as a software delivery channel, ERP vendors saw fresh business opportunities to offer vanilla-ERP to SMBs. Ignoring the many pitfalls of ERP implementations, Enterprise-ASPs partnered with leading ERP vendors to build a new channel to market by targeting SMBs. Rather than a one-to-one model of delivery and enablement, where an ERP implementation would be customized for a specific customer, the ASP model would offer the same software application to all (on a one-to-many basis). However, ASPs found that many potential customers required some form of customization and integration, so this restricted their potential customer base. With Web services, the thorny problems of integration are expected to be resolved. According to Hagel (2003, p. 19), *What makes Web services technology so powerful is its distinctive ability to help managers operate more flexibly and collaborate more successfully with business partners.*

Table 15.3 compares the software applications of ERP, ASP and Web services in five KPAs. Despite substantial investment in ERP, firms have found such implementations have imposed rigidity to their business operations, restricting them to change business processes and IS to meet emerging requirements. ERP implementations resulted in a business architecture based on internal operations versus interactions with customers and suppliers. The difficulty of integrating ERP-centric backbones with other organization's ERP backbones persists and has created a substantial market for B2B integration tools such as enterprise application integration (EAI), messaging software and other middleware solutions (Marks and Werrell, 2003, pp. 9–10).

More recently customer relationship management (CRM) software packages are premised on the basis that firms should develop a *relationship* with their customers to encourage loyalty, which may generate additional revenues (Dowling, 2002). Hosted CRM packages are currently gaining some ground within the ASP market, which is interesting given that *customer–relationship–management* in this context is remote (distant). The success of forming close customer–supplier

Table 15.3: Types of software application and KPA

KPA	Customized ERP 1980s–1990s	Commodity ASP 1990s	Web Services 2000+
Delivery and enablement	One-to-one End-to-end solution Restricted availability Low scalability	One-to-many Point solution 24 × 7 availability High scalability	Many-to-many Enterprise-wide 24 × 7 availability Unlimited scalability
Management and operations	Economies of scope Effectiveness (of business processes) Team performance improvement Competitive advantage Market driven pricing models	Economies of scale Efficiency (of business applications) Individual performance improvement Operational advantage Utility pricing models	Economies of scale and scope Adaptiveness (to business change) Enterprise-wide improvement Industry advantage Multiple, fluctuating pricing models
Integration	Bespoke applications Processual data/information Process integration	Packaged 'stand-alone' applications Functional data/information Application integration	Component-based applications Business intelligence Synergy through combination of applications
Client/vendor partnerships	Closely-coupled client/vendor relationship Project management outsourcing Shared risk and reward Strategic partnership	Remote client/vendor relationship Application outsourcing Service level agreement (SLA) Service contract	Loosely-coupled client/vendor relationship Business process outsourcing Multiple SLAs Market opportunity
Business transformation	Business centric Business process innovation Inter-organizational change Technology core to business Seamless processes	Application centric Continuous improvement Inter-departmental change Technology peripheral to core business Silo effect	Industry centric Changing industry/market dynamics Industry-wide change Mixed technology portfolio Synergistic (more than the sum of the parts)

relationships using a hosted model of business computing remains the subject of some debate.

Web services based on the service-orientated architecture (SOA) framework provide a technical foundation for making business processes accessible within enterprises and across enterprises (Leymann et al., 2002). The maturity of Web services is expected to move through four distinct phases: integration, collaboration, innovation and domination (Marks and Werrell, 2003, p. 19). In the first phase of Web services adoption, firms will engage in internal system integration projects. This requirement is driven by the myriad of information silos created by proprietary enterprise applications implemented to support various activities (i.e. general ledger, accounts payable, accounts receivable for financial management; and costing systems, order management, procurement and production scheduling more generally). These enterprise applications are likely to be large, client–server implementations built with an internal organization-facing view of the world, and orientated toward internal efficiency and controls. The second phase of Web services is expected to drive process and operational improvements in many business areas, provided that the integration hurdles can be overcome and that the tools and technologies are mature enough to enable collaboration. The third phase is innovation. This will see firms devising new ways of doing business using Web services. These firms will leverage what they have learned in previous (integration and collaboration) phases with outside customers, partners and suppliers. The fourth phase, domination, is the culmination of the three previous stages. Market leaders will emerge, which drive superior business value through the use of Web services in distributed business process execution (DBPE). The four phases are presented in Table 15.4.

The use of 'phases', 'stages' and 'eras' to depict the progress of e-Business, in this case, Web services, is not new. From our discussion about ASP, we can discern different phases in which this market underwent. For example, the first phase comprised of market hype about the possibilities of ASP, as a new (some argued, 'revolutionary') way of accessing software applications. Following a rush by venture capital firms to invest in ASP, the market quickly became overcrowded with ASPs of all shapes and sizes. This followed by a rush to win customers, mainly in the SMB sector. The inability to achieve this led to the collapse of numerous ASPs, and a post-mortem of what went wrong. Similarly, Web services are now discussed in the light of moving through various phases. Currently, the promise of Web services is yet to be realized (Bradbury, 2004). Like ASP, Web services is receiving similar hype. However, leading industry players are investing large amounts to develop this market. In the next section, we explore some of the technical and business issues facing Web services vendors and customers. In particular, we ask: How will Web service providers meet the challenge of integration?

Table 15.4: Phases of Web service adoption

Integration
- Experimentation with Web services with small, internal integration projects
- SOAP enablement of legacy applications and ERP, CRM systems
- Fast cycles of learning reach the limits of early Web services, unprepared IT architectures
- Increase in shared information across the business

Collaboration
- Experimentation with Web services outside firewalls
- Increasing interaction with trading partners and customers
- Close trading partners implement Web services to drive shared value
- External trading partners begin sharing information to drive industry value chain benefits

Innovation
- Lessons from integration and collaboration applied to new processes and business models
- New distributed Web service processes and applications drive business change
- Dramatic business results are achieved as Web service are applied in many ways, driving new value propositions

Domination
- First movers begin to assert their dominance over respective markets and industries
- Industry dominance achieved by innovating new business models as well as out-executing competitors
- Web services leaders win through rapid innovation and cycles of learning
- Web services mastery creates new company and industry structures as boundaries are redefined

---

15.3 Integration: the challenge for Web services?

15.3.1 Web services: a technical overview

Rather than being developed in a vacuum, divorced from any practical application, Web services must be seen as a natural evolution to the commercial application of the Internet. The Internet has evolved from other computing paradigms, integrating the approaches and standards that can be seen to exist for electronic data interchange, EAI, distributed object computing and of course the Internet protocol (Aoyama et al., 2002).

From object-orientated component computing to Web services

Technically, Web services have been developed from object-orientated and component computing, inheriting several advantages from both technologies. These can be seen as shorter development time, more reliable code and more efficient use of development resources. Both object-orientated and component computing cannot solve the interoperability issue among heterogeneous IT systems (Orfali et al., 1999). For object-orientated computing, the classical objects only live within a single program, which impedes the communication between the 'objects' implemented in other programmed applications (Lim, 1996). For component computing, the plug-and-play middleware capability has never been guaranteed. For instance, EAI implemented in component computing cannot provide a common solution because it attempts to solve the problem using an incomplete set of proprietary technologies. When multiple firms integrate systems that are themselves integrated using different EAI products, developers face the recursive problem of integrating 'integration' solutions. Therefore, it is necessary to establish holistic, commonly accepted and standardized Web services, instead of proprietary solutions (Samtani and Sadhwani, 2002; Stal, 2002).

EAI, ASP and Web services

Enterprise IS have evolved over the last 30 years. While EAI has been successful in point-to-point integration, it has frequently failed because of complexity and cost (Samtani and Sadhwani, 2002). EAI heavily relies on proprietary technology, which is not only expensive to acquire, operate and maintain, but is complex to implement. As an integrated solution for individual application, EAI creates vendor dependence, or 'lock-in', where it is difficult to switch service providers. EAI focuses on data level integration and communication, rather than the application level. For a particular enterprise IS, the customized EAI is quite efficient, but it never creates generic, flexible and reusable processes in a variety of different, higher-level applications. Initially, ASP was supposed to resolve this problem by promoting software-as-a-service (Currie and Seltsikas, 2002). Yet the delivery and integration of ASP offerings proved difficult, especially for complex systems (unlike collaboration tools such as e-mail).

The promise of Web services

Evolving from object and component computing and implementing the *object-orientated* (OO) middleware concept, Web services promise to bridge the gap between previous computing technologies. Web services are emerging to provide a systematic and extensible framework for application-to-application interaction; built on top of existing Web protocols and based on open XML standards (Curbera et al., 2002). The communication problem in *objects* and *components* computing can be addressed by the standard interface mechanisms of Web services, instead of individual EAI solutions. For instance, currently, the communication between the COBRA architecture and Microsoft COM architecture is almost impossible since it needs a very complicated interface mapping approach to bridge the CORBA object and COM object

(Pope, 1998). Moreover, there is no common standard interface except expensive proprietary EAI solutions. It has already been mentioned that Web services are in effect Web sites for computers to use. However, unlike the human centred applications that need to consider presentation as well as content, these Web services only exchange information. This is known as a Simple Object Access Protocol (SOAP) document. This document is transmitted across the Internet using the standard HTTP protocol, and it is constructed with XML.

The structure of SOAs

The Web services standard comprises of four key technologies:

- XML, the universal format for structured data.

- Universal Description, Discovery and Integration (UDDI, www. uddi.org), a service description level that describes the network and eventually publishes and distributes this into the UDI.

- Web Services Description Language (WSDL, www.w3.org).

- Simple Object Access Protocol (SOAP), the application message protocol.

A typical SOA procedure as shown in Figure 15.2 consists of the following interactions:

- A Web service advertises its WSDL definition into a UDDI registry (Step 1).

- The client looks up the service's definition in the registry and retrieves the WSDL link from UDDI (Step 2 and 3).

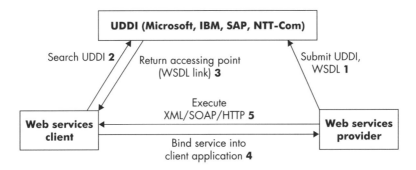

Figure 15.2: Description and discovery processes in Web service architecture. *Source:* Vinoski (2002).

■ The client binds the service by the WSDL definition to sends messages or requests directly to the service via SOAP (Step 4 and 5).

A comparison between Microsoft's .NET and Sun's J2EE platforms

The Microsoft .NET[4] platform and Web services are tightly integrated, which has given .NET an initial lead as a Web services platform. In contrast to the J2EE[5] framework which is a set of open standards, the Microsoft .NET framework is a product suite. Some of its offerings have been built on standards, others have extended these standards in a proprietary way. J2EE was designed to simplify complex problems with the development, deployment and management of multi-tier enterprise solutions. J2EE is an industry standard, and is the result of a large industry initiative led by Sun Microsystems. Figure 15.3 details some key differences in features between these two mainstream technologies (Chappell and Jewell, 2002; Lee and Geralds, 2002; Samtani and Sadhwani, 2002).

Fundamental design and support for Web services. .NET provides runtime support for SOAP, WSDL and UDDI as native .NET protocols. Tightly integrated it allows the building of XML-based Web services, and all Web services that communicate to each other via using ASP.NET. Support for Web services in Java is implementing through many application programming interfaces (APIs) such as Java API for XML Messaging (JAXM), Java API for XML Processing (JAXP), Java API for XML Registries (JAXR) and Java API for XML-based RPC (JAX-RPC). The EJB + Servlet/JSP container will be the interpreter for J2EE's version Web services.

Business process management and e-Commerce. .NET provides business process management (BPM) and e-Commerce capabilities in its BizTalk server. These capabilities are not provided in a J2EE specification, but can be acquired from other Java technology vendors.

Support for existing systems. .NET offers legacy integration through the Host Integration Server 2000 or BizTalk server 2000. This can use the Window DNA architecture to communicate to the mainframe

---

4. Microsoft .NET is a set of Microsoft software technologies for connecting your world of information, people, systems, and devices. It enables an unprecedented level of software integration through the use of XML Web Services: small, discrete, building-block applications that connect to each other – as well as to other, larger applications – via the Internet. (http://www.microsoft.com/net/basics/whatis.asp)

5. The Java™ 2 Platform, Enterprise Edition (J2EE) defines the standard for developing multi-tier enterprise applications. (http://java.sun.com/j2ee/overview.html)

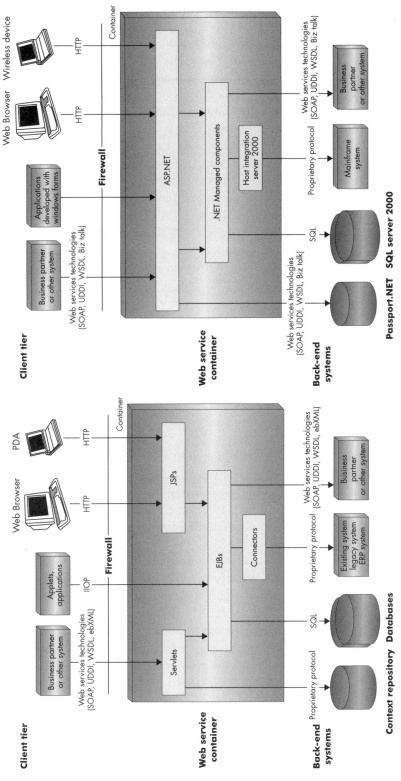

Figure 15.3: The Web services structure of J2EE and .NET. (*Source:* Vawter and Roman, theserverside.com)

system. Supporting and integrating packaged applications and legacy systems (e.g. Siebel, Oracle, or SAP) will be easier with J2EE and J2EE Connector Architecture (JCA) rather than .NET.

Implementation.   .NET claims to target an application integration between platforms using XML. All program code in .NET is compiled down to MS Intermediate Language (MSIL), regardless of whatever development language is chosen. This is not × 86 machine instruction code, because if it were it would only run on processors that support this language. The MSIL is not dependent on any processor and needs to be further compiled into the native code that the processor understands. This is called the Common Language Runtime (CLR). Unlike .NET which does not target a specific platform, J2EE has been created to focus on application portability and connectivity between platforms supporting Java. All Java Codes are compiled into bytecode, run by Java Runtime Environment (JRE). Thus, the implementation of Web services in J2EE will typically be done through Enterprise JavaBeans (EJBs).

Tools and server.   Microsoft's cornerstone development tool, the Integrated Development Environment (IDE) for Web services is Visual Studio.NET (VS.NET). The Web services enabled servers from Microsoft including BizTalk 2002 and SQL Server 2000. In contrast to .NET, there are multiple firms that have built IDEs and application servers based on J2EE. Products such as Sun ONE Web Services Platform, IBM WebSphere serials.

Maturity of platform.   Although .NET inherits a lot of features from the Window DNA architecture, it is still relatively new and has to prove itself to be able to offer an enterprise-wide framework. J2EE has proven to be a robust, scalable and a mature platform over the last 4 years. The addition of support for Web services is just another feature for this platform.

Drivers of platform.   Software firms are more likely to favour J2EE because it can run on a variety of different platforms. But users may prefer .NET because software can be developed in several programming languages, even though it only runs on Microsoft technology.

Both of these technologies have advantages and disadvantages. As a new Microsoft technology supported by its integrated development toolset VS.NET, it comprises the requirements for the development of the next generation of Web services. However, from a service providers' perspective, .NET is still relatively immature, particularly in regard to the integration with legacy systems. The adoption of .NET has also been restricted as most services' applications were developed by the J2EE standard, which is not supported by .NET. The technical challenge for Web services will therefore depend upon the issue of standards, and how legacy systems can be fully integrated with these new technology platforms and architectures.

The technical challenge for Web service vendors, according to Gartner (13 November 2002, p. 2) is to provide:

■ Service-orientated necessities such as the ability to expose functionality as a service.

■ XML-based APIs, if not fully fledged SOAP APIs. Some of these features will come only with version upgrades. In rare cases, vendors will provide bonus functionality or new software through the use of Web services.

15.3.2 Web services: the business benefits

The fallout from the first phase of ASPs provides a salutary lesson for the market readiness of Web services. The biggest single factor, which led to the demise of start-up ASPs, was the lack of attention to how business value would be created for the customer (Currie, 2003a). Many ASPs simply believed that potential customers would be convinced about the benefits of accessing their business software using a remote delivery model. But on closer analysis, it is difficult to see what benefits would be realized from a change in usage. For example, the notion that all customers would benefit from being able to access their software applications on a 24 × 7 basis, was unfounded (Currie et al., 2004). Many customers had little need for 99.999% uptime, and were more concerned about data security and integrity than simply access. Empirical findings from a recent study on customer satisfaction from ASPs indicated *a need for ASPs to facilitate integration with existing IT client organizations, ensure superior performance delivery, emphasize rigorous enforcement of SLAs, and ensure that their applications meets standards of software capability* (Susarla et al., 2003, p. 111).

These findings confirm the need for xSPs to provide significant business value to customers, manifested through EAI and possibly BPO initiatives. Web services vendors, with their promises of integration, may therefore succeed where ASPs largely failed. But the hype surrounding Web services echoes that of ASPs a few years before.

The benefits of accessing software applications across multiple entities and heterogeneous technology platforms, at an affordable cost, are perceived as the key business benefit of Web services. The loose coupling of resources means that the connections can be established without being tailored to the specific functionality embedded in the applications to be connected.

Integration: the challenge for Web services?

One of the most cited business and technical challenges for firms in the twenty-first century concerning their IT infrastructure is integration.

The challenges in achieving integration are financial, commercial and technical. On the financial side, firms constantly seek business value from their IT investment, largely to address the productivity-paradox, where IT expenditure increases without any identifiable financial benefits (Hitt and Brynjolfsson, 1996). On the commercial side, firms realize that, whilst technology to a large extent is a commodity (Carr, 2003), it can also have strategic benefits if it is aligned with the business objectives (Keen and Smith, 1996). The information management issues are therefore imperative. On the technical side, firms recognize that technology is no *silver bullet*, and that the proliferation of new IT products and services does not automatically lead to business advantage. However, the vast financial investment in IT, coupled with the commercial benefits, encourage managers to consider new offerings such as Web services. But unlike ASP, which did not fully address the need to maximize existing IT investment, Web services treats integration as central to its value proposition. Integration is further seen as a perennial consideration of CIOs and IT directors. Thus,

> *Integration is the driving force of this decade of IT spending. As enterprises buy more and more packaged applications, it is estimated that the task of combining these application 'silos' results in over 40% of IT spending, even though the amount of code written for integration is significantly smaller than 40%. This is because integration projects tend to be one-of-a-kind, and complex to write. The question for software and services vendors is this: 'Can the cost of integration be reduced to be more in line with that of packaged applications?' (Jhingran et al., 2002, p. 555).*

This author identifies four distinct forms of integration:

■ Portals (or 'at-the-glass') integration is the shallowest form, bringing potentially disparate applications together in a (typically Web) single entry point.

■ Business process integration orchestrates processes across application and possibly enterprise boundaries such as those involved in a supply–chain relationship. Web services and their derivatives are becoming important here.

■ Application integration, in which applications that do similar or complementary things communicate with each other, is typically focused on data transformation and message queuing, increasingly in the Extensible Markup Language (XML) domain.

■ Information integration, wherein complementary data are either physically (through warehousing tools) or logically brought together, makes it possible for applications to be written to and make use of all the relevant data in the enterprise, even if the data are not directly under their control. A typical examples of this would be a new customer relationship application that combines the relational call log with the speech-to-text translated call itself (Jhingran, 2002, p. 555).

The following section considers two case study examples of the challenges of integrating disparate software applications.

15.4 Integration: two case studies in the financial services industry

15.4.1 Firm A

This firm was initially an independent UK fund management company, managing funds totalling over $20 billion. It was bought by one of the largest investment management companies in the world at the end of the 1990s (providing a combined fund management value of almost $600 billion). It trades traditional securities such as unit trusts, common stock and government debt. It manages portfolios for individuals (ISA's and PEP's), pensions for numerous companies (local authorities and private companies) and accounts for wealthy investors. It had been looking to buy an order management system (OMS) for many years prior to the take-over. This new parent company added an additional layer of complexity, as all of the IT systems had to be integrated and not just those of firm A. This increased the difficulty and scope of the project. The final system was one of the largest implementations of its type.

15.4.2 Firm B

This firm has specialized in managing funds in the emerging markets (e.g. South America and Asia). Initially, it was part of a large banking group, but became independent following a management buyout in the mid-1990s. When it first started it had almost $20 million under management. This has now grown to nearly $8 billion. Predominantly it manages high-risk debt securities that have defaulted or are not recognized by institutions such as Bloomberg. It has managed spectacular growth, increasing profitability year after year, despite the downturn in the financial markets over the past few years. Due to its increasing internal complexity, it felt that the time was right to buy an OMS to help manage the business.

15.4.3 The OMS

These case study examples contrast the implementation of an OMS within two very different firms. Both firms are fund management houses located in central London. Each day, the OMS system was uploaded with information from the accounting system. For example: account details, securities held, ratings, indices, exchange rates and models. This information was used to help the fund managers develop a long-term investment strategy. All of the orders made within the system are checked for compliance breaches prior to being forwarded onto the dealers. At the end of the day, compliance tests are executed on every account to ensure that none of the rules are breached (e.g. a passive breach caused by a recent large price change). The OMS can be seen as in integral part of a straight-through-process, removing the need to key data in more than once while providing interfaces to existing systems (using API and/or Web services). The two firms described here, each traded a wide variety of securities across global markets. Both were seen as being above their respective industry benchmark for performance and investor returns. However, they had many differences, a few of which can be summarized in Table 15.5.

As can be seen from Table 15.5, the firms were very different in both character and size. Nevertheless, the same OMS was implemented at both sites. The drivers that were used to justify the cost of implementing the new system were almost the same. These are given below:

■ Improved scalability of the investment process.

■ Reduction in client mandate breaches.

Table 15.5: Differences between the two firms used in the study

Attribute	Firm A	Firm B
Existing system	Four different systems that could not connect with each other	Excel spread sheets and paper-based deal tickets
Size	Part of a group that employed 22 000. The 120 users managed corporate pension plans, private clients and wealthy individual investors. Twelve dealers.	Thirty employees, the four fund managers also dealt their own trades
Infrastructure	Windows NT, LAN and WAN. All Oracle and SQLServer database systems in US	Windows XP. SQLServer database
In-house skills	Expert DBA, network teams, 24 h help desk, in-house training	No expert IT skills
Implementation team	Over 20 at its peak (1 external)	2 core people (both external)
Compliance rules	Over 5000	Over 350
Accounts	15 000	35
Securities traded	Debt (10%) Equity (60%) Unit trusts (10%) Money market (10%) Foreign exchange (10%)	Debt (60%) Derivative (35%) Equity (5%)
Time to implement	3 years	6 months

- Improved operational efficiency, capacity and control.

- Reduction in business risk.

- Improved support for the investment decision-making process.

- Reduced business risk through improved compliance monitoring, management information and auditing.

- More timely and accurate portfolio data available to fund managers.

- Automated loading of transaction data into the accounting system would leading to improved data quality and enabling shorter lead times for the production of periodic client reports.

- The creation of capacity for future business growth.

Firm A had never purchased an OMS. It had grown from a management buyout of part of a firm. The four fund managers also acted as traders. They were skilled at spreadsheet manipulation and so ran the firm from a collection of macro driven Excel worksheets. They took Bloomberg data feeds and index calculations to develop their strategy. The problem was clearly the dependency upon a tool that was not adequate for order management. They could not use any electronic trading, run real-time modelling or apply any compliance rules to their orders. Whilst they currently only had a few accounts, they needed to have a better way of modelling if they were to increase the number of accounts they held. What rules they had were limited to the functionality provided by the accounting system, which was seen as the centre of all the data that is used by the firm. It provided both the start of day portfolio valuations, together with the end of day reconciliation. Expecting any functionality to help calculate mandate breaches for complex derivative options and futures trading was unrealistic. Since the fund managers and compliance users were eager to have a 'proper' system that would ease their job, there were no obstacles in getting them to use it. As with firm A, problems over scalability and compliance management led the search for a single solution capable of satisfying all areas.

Prior to the full installation of the OMS at firm B, the four existing 'legacy systems' had to be replaced. These applications were all DOS based and had been used for many years. The systems appeared to satisfy their varied trading requirements, ranging from the 15 000 private clients (small value ISA's and PEPS) to the 300+ large segregated and retail accounts. The existing systems led to one of the problems in the implementation of the project: Would the new system be able to offer at least the same functionality? Some of the senior fund managers could not see the benefit for them in having to learn any new system if the shortcomings of the existing system would not be addressed by a new system. They were only concerned with managing their portfolios. The reality was that having separate systems for different fund managers and dealers has caused several trade errors. These ranged from typing 'SELL' rather than 'BUY' for 500000 shares to holding a tobacco stock for one account that had expressly stated that they should be excluded! A top level decision had been made that in order for the business two grow in a sustainable manor, a single system had to be used.

Whilst firms A and B have many differences, they shared a fundamental problem: the complexity of integrating the OMS with all of the other in-house systems. The diagram below shows an overview of how the OMS was going to sit within each organization. Both firms strived for the same final solution. This can be simply stated as the import of reference data and matched orders into the accounting system, followed by its export to other system. Clearly they had different attribution systems, index suppliers and universe of fixed income securities. The brokers and custodians were different as were the order matching systems. However, the Figure 15.4 can illustrate them both.

Neither firms A and B had the in-house expertise to develop an OMS. Even if they had, the he drawback to this approach is the cost, timescale and risk involved in such a large-scale development. Although firm B could have attempted to integrate and enhance its existing systems, it would still have been left with old technology, limited support and

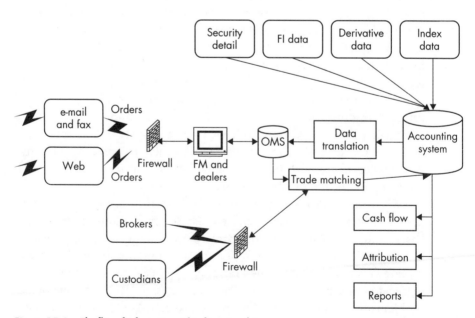

Figure 15.4: The flow of information within firms A and B.

unable, e.g. to reap the benefits of new developments such as Web technologies. Both firms chose to purchase an off-the-shelf system. Such an approach has the disadvantage of an imperfect functional fit but the advantage of a proven system, relatively low cost and short implementation timescales. Clearly, the timescale is relative to the scope and complexity of what has to be delivered.

The biggest factor in implementing this OMS was its integration into the existing environment within both firms. The system was used to extract data from the accounting system, apply specific translations to it in the middleware, then import it into the target system. But core to all of this, was the quality of the data itself. For example, even though a value may exist within the accounting system, it may not be correct. Data fields can be missing, incorrect or simply be represented by a number (e.g. 14). Also, payment frequencies and accrual types may be incorrect.

The greatest source of problems is in matching fixed income data from one system into the other. Different types of calculation, need different data items. For example, a corporate bond needs a coupon. However, there may be a call date for this bond that affects the yield calculation. If this information is not used, then the firm could make a loss on holding the security longer than it should (one firm had a $1 million loss because it held a bond for too long, simply because of incorrect data). There is also a need for the OMS to match the analytics delivered by Bloomberg. If the two systems produce different duration values, it is unlikely that they will assume Bloomberg is wrong. Whilst data needed for these calculations might be held in the accounting system, it is not always possible to use it. The two accounting systems used by these firms did not have an open architecture. Thus, even if the data was available it could not be accessed without paying for the service. Security coupon payments and bond maturity payments provided another challenge for cash flow forecasting. It was not enough to get the basic information on a bond correct, how it was processed had to be considered.

Once data integrity has been validated and the information can be imported into the system in a repeatable way, the next challenge lies in the order workflow. Exporting all of the trade information out of the OMS and back into the accounting system is just as important as getting the data out at the start. Here, the reverse of the translations need to take place (the accounting system could use ISO 2 for countries (e.g. US), yet the OMS ISO 3 (US) in order that the data's integrity is maintained. The final element to this process is the reconciliation that happens at the start of business. Here, the OMS will validate that all of the data that was exported the previous day, matches exactly the data that is imported from the accounting system. Once done, the daily trading process can begin.

The case examples presented here illustrate the complexity of the data and information contained within a single system. This complexity is reinforced with the implementation of new technology such as the OMS. Even with the best efforts to avoid implementation problems, through good project planning and execution, problems will always arise, some of which are unforeseen.

15.4.4 Complex systems and data

The issue of systems and data complexity is highlighted in the following example, which considers data in three different contexts: heterogeneity, federation/distribution and competitive advantage. This author suggests that, 'While centralization of data operations was a significant driving force of the growth in the database business (both transaction processing and for decision support) it is clear that decentralized tendencies in the growth of data have accelerated in the recent past' (Jhingran, 2002, p. 558).

The heterogeneity of data. Data are no longer just records that sit in well-defined tables (typically referred to as 'structured' data). Increasingly, an enterprise has to deal with unstructured content such as text (in e-mails, Web pages, etc.), audio (call centre logs) and video (employee broadcast). In addition, data are beginning to emerge in XML format, which in some ways is the bridge between the structured and unstructured worlds, through that is an oversimplification in the sense that a perfect solution for XML is often a less-than-perfect solution for the two extremes.

The 'federation' and distribution of data. Data are no longer on one logical server (such as in a well-architectured warehouse), but distributed across multiple machines in different organizations (some within and some across enterprises). This is in the classic sense of distributed databases, except that the scale could be as large as billions of databases (whereas classic databases have handled distribution at the scale of around 10). In addition, federation (who own and controls the data and access to the data) is a new problem that distributed database technology has typically not addressed. In federation scenarios, one typically cannot assume full SQL or its equivalent access to distributed data sources. In addition, privacy and security issues need to be solved.

Using data for competitive advantage. The data need to be manipulated, aggregated, transformed, analysed in increasingly complex ways to produce business intelligence. And the speed of access and analysis is becoming closer to real time. A large fraction of the growth in relational databases in the early to mid-1990s was fuelled by 'business intelligence' – a term for a collection of tasks ranging from decision support through complex SQL queries, to online analytical processing (OLAP), and all the way to data mining – wherein the system automatically discovered and told the users about what it had found. With the increase in data, the ability for the decision makers to sift through the data is falling ever behind, and therefore data analysis that works across all the modalities of data is becoming increasingly important. (Jhingran, 2002, p. 556).

15.5 A case study on Web services at Amazon.com

In order to examine the ubiquitously adopted potential of Web services worldwide, we discuss a case study using Amazon Web service as a cooperated associate. Whilst Web services are still immature, lessons may be learned about the development and deployment of the client side Amazon Web service. In this section, we discuss the two steps of consuming a Web service, *discovery and execution* and illustrate how to create an Internet-based customer client application to acquire the information from Amazon Web service provider.

According to recent research results (Baker, 2002) three clear steps are needed for Web services integration: (1) Internal integration, (2) Going outside the enterprise and (3) the collaborative agile business on the Internet. Most of Web services today are remaining largely under the inside-the-firewall phenomenon. A big exception to this trend is Amazon Web services, which has initiated a public Web services program that lets Web site owners and developers to include Amazon features and information on their sites (Gralla, 2002). Amazon's Web service efforts are a result of its popular associates program, in which Web site owners earn 15% sale commission for each transaction they send back to Amazon. Initially, Amazon supported some static links containing the associate's ID which can be embedded in the associates' Web site. Although this program was quite successful, associates wanted more functionality from Amazon. For instance, instead of leaving the associates' Web site for searching and purchasing, they required more flexibility to complete those transactions staying in their own Web site.

Web services have emerged as an explicit way to solve the above issue. Either by using simple XML formats transacted over HTTP protocol, or embedding XML data into SOAP, associates can retrieve data from Amazon's Web service provider that can then be formatted to display Amazon's product information on their site. Furthermore, it translates shopping cart transactions within the associates site. Associates can use XML 'heavy' or XML 'lite' documents when creating their Web services. The 'heavy' documents give access to everything displayed on Amazon's product page, including customer reviews, images of the items to be purchased and more, while the 'lite' document gives only a stripped-down number of features.

15.5.1 Discovery and integration of the online Amazon Web service

The discovery of a Web service will typically be done on a B2B level. In other words, two businesses will agree to exchange the data using Web services, and the provider of the service will inform the consumer about the way to find the service. The process to discover Web services will be dealt on the UDDI (http://www.uddi.org) and its four member firms, Microsoft, IBM, SAP and NTT-Com, which provide the search engine services. Registered business members can publish their available Web services in WSDL format on UDDI for those potential customers.

In order to explore the appropriate service in our project, we searched Microsoft and IBM UDDI with the provider's keyword 'Amazon'. It would then respond with a WSDL document link (http://soap.amazon.com/schemas/AmazonWebServices.wsdl) containing the URL for invoking the XML Web service, the Web methods, input arguments and the output data type. As a built-in XML Web service development environment, Microsoft VS.NET allows the developer to reference other Web services without any obvious complications. For instance, developers utilize Web service listener automatically mapping classes and functions of Web services providers instead of creating a proxy class manually as needed in other Web service development platforms. Using 'add Web reference' function in VS.NET, the platform itself will create all related classes and functions. Therefore, developers can browse the Web methods and parameters simply from 'Class View' option, which speeds up the whole development process.

To retrieve the information from the Amazon Web service provider, a Dataset object has been used to deliver the information in ASP.NET, the process of creating and filling Dataset object easily simplifies complex transactions between database server and remotes client application. Binding the filled Dataset object into a DataGrid (a special format to display information in HML page in the presentation layer), the client's application can illustrate all information by users' querying.

15.5.2 Lessons learned as Amazon Web services' client

Several important lessons have been learnt from this case. Together with quality criterions used to judge a Web service these can be summarized into three areas: maintainability, copyright and quality of service.

Maintainability.   Although all elements to build up the Web services are not totally new technologies and these primary technologies have emerged as worldwide standards, Amazon Web Service cannot afford a robust service due to multi-supporting needed for .NET developers, J2EE developers and open source world PHP/Perl developers. Seamless interoperability across heterogeneous systems, platforms, applications and programming languages is not an easy task to be conquered. For instance, it may take several days for a support team to figure out the problems caused by .NET version Amazon Web service.

Copyright and business model.   There are not many appropriated business models and business laws for Web services. Amazon Web service appears more as an extended service for its online shop. In terms of services level, it is not a pure service provider who credits its benefits upon its service transactions. Therefore, the business model of Web services is still immature. On the other hand, most existed Web services' clients are depending on the same Web services resource. However, the solution to avoid infringing each other's copyright could become a serious issue that needs to be resolved in the near future. A 'Google-ish' layout used for searching Web application which deploys Amazon Web service has been banned based on similar issue (Amazon lite, http://www.kokogiak.com/amazon/).

Quality of network service (QoS) in UDDI.   Unlike normal Internet search engines, UDDI offers four search solution for users (Siddiqui, 2002). Hence, users can query UDDI Business Registry by business name, business location, business identifier, industry sector, service type and other categories. However, the quality of results are not all of a similar standard (Zhang et al., 2002). For example, a business search for 'Online book store' in a popular search engine may respond with more than hundred online bookshop services, but may return nothing on Microsoft and IBM UDDI. On the other hand, the UDDI is only a basic directory. It is a simple database-like mechanism that lets participants insert descriptions of services they offer and query for services offered by other participants. There is not a brokering or facility service that is fully qualified to answer the customer's query intelligently (Huhns, 2002). For instance, in Amazon Web service, the shopping cart facility can be easily integrated in the Web application, however eventually the customer needs to finish the payment transaction on Amazon's Web site, but not on client's (associate) site. If a brokerage service could use knowledge about the requirements and capabilities of registered service to decide an appropriate payment service, the whole process would be much appreciated by associates, and it also can help keeping the customers' loyalty on the associates' Web site, not Web service providers'.

15.6 Conclusion

This chapter has explored some of the technical and business issues and concerns in relation to building out the Web services architecture. From a backdrop of disappointing value creation from e-Business models, notably, the first phase of the ASP market, questions must be asked about the emerging Web services model. Although ASP was, and remains, ostensibly a remote software application delivery and enablement option, Web services extends this activity by offering a new technology platform for integrating disparate software applications across multiple environments. Yet the notion that Web services offers 'agility' and 'flexibility' through the re-use of existing code is still to be fully realized (Bradbury, 2004). Web services has the backing of the major industry players like Microsoft, Sun Microsystems, BEA and others, yet the ease with which firms will be able to deploy Web services offers a major challenge. However, the recognition that CIOs wish to maximize existing IT investment is one, which was almost lost during the dot.com downturn. As we saw in the first phase of the ASP market, products and services were targeted to potential customers without any understanding of their requirements. As a result, the adoption and diffusion of ASP remained low. If Web services vendors are to avoid the same mistakes, they, and the industry in general, will need to ensure that Web services provides seamless integration between software applications and platforms to avoid enterprise silos. Otherwise, customers will be reluctant to extend their investment in Web services. At the time of writing, SOAs promise to resolve the data silo problem, but achieving this will take considerably more time than some of the pundits predict. What is certain, however, is that further 'false starts' in the IT industry will only result in caution and lack of investment, particularly as many senior managers now perceive IT as little more than serving a commodity to their business (Carr, 2003) than a strategic differentiator or *silver bullet*.

References and Further Reading

Adams, H., D. Gisolfi et al. (2002). *Best Practices for Web Services: Back to the Basics*, Part 1. IBM developerWorks.

Amit, R. and C. Zott (2000). Value Creation in E-Commerce Business Models. Presentation, *the Wharton Conference of Winners and Losers in the E-Commerce Shakeout*, The Wharton School, October 2000.

Anderson, R., B. Francis et al. (2001). *Professional ASP.NET*. Birmingham, Wrox Press Ltd.

Aoyama, M., S. Weerawarana et al. (2002). Web Services Engineering: Promises and Challenges. *24th International Conference on Software Engineering*, Orlando, Florida.

Baker, S. (2002). *The Three Steps to Web Service Integration*. IONA.

Bichler, M., J. Kalagnanam, K. Katircioglu, A. J. King, R. D. Lawrence, H. S. Lee, G. Y. Lin and Y. Lu (2002). 'Applications of Flexible Pricing in Business-to-Business Electronic Commerce.' *IBM Systems Journal* **41**(2): 287–302.

Bradbury, D. (2004) 'Service Orientated Architectures Will Deliver Eventually, but Don't Hold Your Breath.' *Computer Weekly*: 20. www.computerweekly.com.

Carr, N. G. (2003). 'It Doesn't Matter.' *Harvard Business Review* **81**(5 May), 41–51.

Castells, M. (2000). *The Rise of the Network Society*. Blackwell Publishers.

Cassidy, J. (2002). *Dot.con: How America Lost its Mind and Money in the Internet Era*. Perennial, HarperCollins.

Chappell, D. A. and T. Jewell (2002). *Java Web Services*. Sebastopol, O'Reilly & Associates.

Curbera, F., M. Duftler et al. (2002). 'Unraveling the Web Services Web, An Introduction to SOAP, WSDL, and UDDI.' *IEEE Internet*: 86–93.

Currie, W. (1995). *Management Strategy for IT*. Pitman Publishing.

Currie, W. (2003a). 'A Knowledge-based Risk Assessment System for Evaluating Web-enabled Application Outsourcing Projects.' *International Journal of Project Management* **21**(3 March).

Currie, W. (2003b). 'Value Creation from Application Services Provisioning: Lessons from Four Vendor Firms.' *International Conference on Information Systems*, 14–17 December. Seattle, WA, USA.

Currie, W. (2004). 'Value Creation from Application Service Provider e-Business Models: the Experience of Four Firms.' *Enterprise Information Management* (forthcoming).

Currie, W. and P. Seltsikas (2001). 'Delivering Business Critical Information Systems though Application Service Providers: the Need for a Market Segmentation Strategy.' *International Journal of Innovation Management* **5**(3): 323–349.

Currie, W. and P. Seltsikas (2002). Evaluation the Application Service Provider(ASP) Business Model: The Challenge of Integration. *35th Hawaii International Conference System Sciences*. Hawaii.

Currie, W., X. Wang and V. Weerakkody (2004). 'Developing Web Services Using the Microsoft .Net Platform: Technical and Business Challenges.' *Journal of Enterprise Information Management* **17**(4).

Earl, M. (ed.) (1988). *Information Management: the Strategic Dimension*. Oxford, Clarendon Press.

Earl, M. (1989). *Managerial Strategies for IT*. Prentice Hall.

Department of Commerce (1999) *Understanding the Digital Economy*. Report by the US Department of Commerce, http://mitpress.mit.edu/ude.html.

Devaraj, S. and R. Kohli (2003). 'Performance Impacts of Information Technology: Is Actual Usage the Missing Link?' *Management Science* **49**(3): 273–289.

Dewan, R., B. Jing and A. Seidmann (2003). 'Product Customization and Price Competition on the Internet.' *Management Science* **49**(8): 1055–1070.

Dowling, G. (2002). 'Customer Relationship Management: In B2B Markets, Often Less is More.' *California Management Review* **44**(3): 87–104.

Durlacher (1999). *Application Service Providers: A Report by Durlacher Research*, July, Durlacher Inc.

Ekanayaka, Y., W. Currie and P. Seltsikas (2002). 'Delivering Enterprise Resource Planning Systems through Application Service Providers.' *Journal of Logistics and Information Management* **15**(3): 192–203.

Eisenhardt, K. and J. A. Martin (2000). 'Dynamic Capabilities: What are They?' *Strategic Management Journal* (21): 1105–1121.

Farrell, J. A. and H. Kreger (2002). 'Web Services Management Approaches.' *IBM Systems Journal* **41**(2): 212–227.

Forrester, T. (1980). *The Micro-Electronics Revolution*. Blackwell.

Geoffrion, A. M. and R. Khrisnan (2003a). 'e-Business and Management Science: Mutual Impacts (Part 1 of 2).' *Management Science* **49**(10): 1275–1286.

Geoffrion, A. M. and R. Khrisnan (2003b) 'e-Business and Management Science: Mutual Impacts (Part 2 of 2).' *Management Science* **49**(11): 1445–1456.

Glass, G. (2000). *The Web Services (R)evolution, Applying Web Services to Applications.* IMB developerWorks, Web Services library.

Gottschalk, K., S. Graham, H. Kreger and J. Snell (2002). 'Introduction to Web Services Architecture.' *IBM Systems Journal* **41**(2): 170–177.

Gralla, P. (2002). Lessons from the Front: How Amazon is using Web Services, searchwebservices.

Grindley, K. (1991). *Managing IT at Board Level.* Pitman Publishing.

Haeckel, S. H. (2002). 'Leading on Demand Businesses – Executives as Architects.' *IBM Systems Journal* **42**(3): 405–413.

Hagel, J. (2002). *Out of the Box: Strategies for Achieving Profits Today and Growth Tomorrow Through Web Services.* Harvard Business School Press.

Hagel, J. (2003). *Out of the Box: Strategies for Achieving Profits Today and Growth Tomorrow through Web Services.* Boston, Harvard Business School Press.

Hagel, J. and J. Seely-Brown (2001). 'Your Next IT Strategy.' *Harvard Business Review* **79**(9): 105–115.

Hitt, L. M. and E. Brynjolfsson (1996). 'Productivity, Business Profitability, and Consumer Surplus: Three Different Measures of Information Technology Value.' *MIS Quarterly* **20**(2 June) : 121–142.

Huhns, M. (2002). 'Agents as Web Services.' *IEEE Internet* 93–95.

IDC (1999) 'Understanding the ASP Food Chain and Application Hosting Environments.' Presentation given by Euan Davis, European Services Industry Research, International Data Corporation, at *Conference on Application Service Provision: Outlook for Growth and Product Development in 2000,* (14–15 December). Café Royal, London.

Jhingran, A.D., N. Mattos and H. Pirahesh (2002). 'Information Integration: A Research Agenda.' *IBM Systems Journal* **41**(4): 555–562.

Keen, J. D. and H. A. Smith (1996). *Management Challenges in IS.* Chichester, Wiley.

Kern, T., L. Willcocks and M.C. Lacity (2002). *Application Service Provision: Risk Assessment and Mitigation.* MIS Quarterly Executive, Vol. 1, Issue 2, June, pp. 113–126.

Knight, A. and N. Dai (2002). 'Objects and the Web.' *IEEE Software*: 51–58.

Knott, A. M., D. J. Bruce and H. E. Posen (2003). 'On the Strategic Accumulation of Intangible Assets.' *Management Science* **14**(2): 192–207.

Lacity, M. and R. Hirschheim (1993). *Information Systems Outsourcing,* Wiley, UK.

Leyermann, F., D. Roller and M. T. Schmidt (2002). 'Web Services and Business Process Management.' *IBM Systems Journal* **41**(2): 198–211.

Lee, C. and J. Geralds (2002). Web Services Wins Customers at Last. *Computing.* London: 14.

Lim, B. B. L. (1996). Component Computing and Objects: Is There Any Common Ground? *Tenth Annual Midwest Computer Conference.* Loyola University Chicago, US.

Malaika, S., C. J. Nelin, R. Qu, B. Reinwald and D. C. Wolfson (2002). 'DB2 and Web Services.' *IBM Systems Journal* **41**(4): 666–685.

Marks, E. and M. J. Werrell (2003). *Executive's Guide to Web Services.* Chichester, Wiley.

Nerkar, A. (2003). 'Old is Gold? The Value of Temporal Exploration in the Creation of New Knowledge.' *Management Science* **49**(2): 211–229.

Offutt, J. (2002). 'Quality Attributes of Web Software Applications.' *IEEE Software*: 25–32.

Oliva, R., J. D. Sterman and M. Giese (2003) 'Limits to growth in the New Economy: Exploring the '*Get Big Fast*' Strategy in e-Commerce.' *System Dynamics Review* **19**(2): 83–118.

Orfali, R., D. Harkey et al. (1999). *Client/Server Survival Guide*. New York, John Wiley & Sons Inc.

Pope, A. (1998). *The CORBA Reference Guide*. Reading, Massachusetts, Addison Wesley Longman Inc.

Quinn-Mills, D. (2001). 'Who's to blame for the Bubble?' *Harvard Business Review* **79**(5): 22–23.

Ross, J., M. Vitale, and L. Willcocks (2003). 'The Continuing ERP Revolution: Sustainable Lessons, New Modes of Delivery.' *Second-Wave Enterprise Resource Planning Systems*. G. Shanks, P. B. Seddon, L. P. Willcocks (eds). Cambridge University Press: 102–134.

Samtani, G. and D. Sadhwani (2002). *Enterprise Application Integration (EAI) and Web Sevices. Web Services Business Strategies and Architectures*. P. F. a. M. Waterhouse, Birmingham, Expert Press Ltd: 39–54.

Samtani, G. and D. Sadhwani (2002). *Web Services and Application Frameworks (.NET and J2EE). Web Services Business Strategies and Architectures*. Birmingham, UK, Expert Press Ltd.

Shanks, G., P. B. Seddon and L. P. Willcocks (eds) (2003). *Second-Wave Enterprise Resource Planning Systems*. Cambridge University Press.

Siddiqui, B. (2002). UDDI-based Electronic Marketplaces. *Web Services Business Strategies and Architectures*. P. Fletcher and M. Waterhouse (eds). Birmingham, UK, Expert Press Ltd.

Stal, M. (2002). 'Web Services: Beyond Component-based Computing.' *Communications of the ACM* **45**(10): 71–76.

Sumner, M. (2003) Risk Factors in Enterprise-Wide/ERP Projects. *Second-Wave Enterprise Resource Planning Systems*. G. Shanks, P. B. Seddon, L. P. Willcocks (eds). Cambridge University Press: 157–179.

Suslarla, A., A. Barua and A. B. Whinston. 'Understanding the Service Component of Application Service Provision: An Empirical Analysis of Satisfaction with ASP Services.' *Management Information Systems Quarterly* **27**(1): 91–118.

Thornhill, S. and R. Amit (2003) 'Learning About Failure: Bankruptcy, Firm Age, and Resource-based View.' *Management Science* **14**(5): 497–509.

Varian, H. and P. Lyman (2002) 'How Much Information?' http://www.sims. berekley.edu/research/projects/how-much-info/.

Vinoski, S. (2002). 'Web Services Interaction Models. Part 1: Current Practice.' *IEEE Internet Computing*: 89–91.

Weill, P. and M. R. Vitale (2001). *Place to Space – Migrating to e-Business Models*, HBS Press.

Zhang, L. -J., H. Li et al. (2002). XML-based Advanced UDDI Search Mechanism for B2B Integration. *Fourth IEEE International Workshop on Advanced Issues of e-Commerce and Web-Based Information Systems (WECWIS'02)*. Newport Beach, California.

About the authors

Currie, Wendy L. is a Professor in Information Systems at Warwick Business School. She is a Principal Investigator of EPSRC and ESRC (Paccit/Link) funded research projects into e-Business models and emerging technologies. Currently, she is an Associate Editor of *MIS Quarterly*, and Member of the Editorial Boards of *Journal of Strategic IS* and *Journal of Information Technology*; European, Middle East and African representative for the Association of Information Systems; Joint Program Chair for *ICIS* 2006; Track Chair for *ICIS* 2004; and Mini-track Chair for *AMCIS* and *HICSS Conferences*. Research interests include information management, e-Business models and emerging technologies. She has also held position as Professor at Brunel and Sheffield Universities.

Barnes, Stuart is an Associate Professor at Victoria University of Wellington, New Zealand. From 2005, he will take up a Chair in Management at the University of East Anglia, UK. Stuart has been teaching and researching in the information systems (IS) field for over a decade. He holds a PhD from Manchester Business School. He has published more than 70 articles in journals, such as *Communications of the ACM*, the *International Journal of Electronic Commerce*, the *e-Service Journal*, *Electronic Markets* and the *Journal of Electronic Commerce Research*. He has published three books – most recently M-Business in 2003.

Beulen, Erik PhD is associated with Tilburg University in the Netherlands, and is employed as an international business development manager with Atos origin. He obtained his PhD from Tilburg University. His research concentrates on outsourcing, offshore outsourcing and the management of outsourcing relationships. His papers have been published in journals and the proceedings of the *HICSS* and *International Conference on Information Systems (ICIS)*. He is the author and co-author of various books on the subject of outsourcing.

Chandra, Charu is an Associate Professor in Industrial and Manufacturing Systems Engineering at the University of Michigan–Dearborn, Dearborn, Michigan, USA (charu@umich.edu). His research focus is on *Supply Chain Informatics*, which deals with integration of operational and information models for supply chain management. Professor Chandra is widely published in the areas of supply chain management, and information design and modelling.

Freeman, Phillip is a Senior Lecturer at Swinburne University, Melbourne, Australia. Phillip has over 20 years experience consulting and working in the information technology (IT) industry. Prior to joining Swinburne, Phillip was the e-Business Principal for the IBM Consulting Group and IT strategy competency leader for IBM and IBM Global Services in Australia. In these roles, Phillip has assisted many global and local corporations develop and implement their IT strategies and solutions to achieve value from their IT investment. Phillip has also held senior IT technical and product management positions servicing clients both within and outside Australia.

Gordijn, Jaap is an Assistant Professor in e-Business at the Free University Amsterdam – Faculty of Exact Sciences. His research interest is innovative e-Business applications. He is a key developer of and has internationally published on e-Business modelling methodology (called e^3-value) addressing the integration of strategic e-Business decision making with ICT requirements and systems engineering. Also, he is a frequent speaker on international conferences. In the recent past, he was a Member of Cisco's Internet Business Solution Group and he was employed by Deloitte and Touche as a Senior Manager of D&T's e-Business group. As such, he was especially involved in rolling out e-Business applications in the banking and insurance domains and in the digital content industry.

Grandón, Elizabeth E. is an Assistant Professor at Emporia State University, Kansas. She is currently a Doctoral Candidate at Southern Illinois University at Carbondale, where she received her MBA in MIS with the support of a Fulbright scholarship and the University of Bío-Bío, Chile. Her research has been published in *Information and Management, Communications of the AIS, Journal of Computer Information Systems, Journal of Global Information Technology Management, Journal of Computing Sciences in Colleges* and various national and international conference proceedings. Her research interests include e-Commerce, technology acceptance, IT adoption in small businesses and database management.

Guah, Matthew is a Doctoral Candidate with the Department of Information Systems and Computing at Brunel University. His research looks at emerging technologies in healthcare, fusing specifically on the use of application service provisioning within National Health Service (NHS) trusts in UK. Prior to this, he worked in IS development for Merrill Lynch. He has over 15 years professional experience. Matthew has already published his research at international conferences: *AMCIS, HICSS* and *ECIS*.

Huang, Jimmy C. is a Lecturer in the IT and Strategy Group at Nottingham University Business School, UK. Prior to joining Nottingham University he was a Lecturer in the Department of Management Studies at the University of Aberdeen. He is also a Member of the IKON research group based at the University of Warwick. His research focuses on the process of cross-functional knowledge integration underlying organization-wide project implementation. He has published articles on this subject in journals, such as *Communications of the ACM, European Journal of Information Systems, Journal of Decision Support Systems* and *Journal of Information Technology Management.*

Joyce, Philip is a Lecturer at Swinburne University of Technology, Melbourne, Australia. He was previously at Deakin University, Geelong, Australia. Philip holds degrees in Electrical/Electronic Engineering from the University of Melbourne, and Computer Science, with Hons, from Deakin University. He is currently completing a doctoral thesis at Deakin University. Philip has previously worked as an Engineer with the Department of Defence. His research interests are wide ranging and include the adoption and usage of e-Commerce and IS, and the development and implementation of distributed systems and Web-based grid systems, and strategic visioning and process visualization using systems dynamics.

Kumar, Sameer is a Professor and Qwest Endowed Chair in Global Communications and Technology Management in the College of Business, University of St. Thomas, Minneapolis, Minnesota, USA (skumar@ stthomas.edu). His major areas of research interests include optimization concepts applied to various aspects of global supply chain management, IS, technology management, product and process innovation, and capital investment justifications. Professor Kumar has published extensively in inventory management, supply chain management, new product development, product design, IS and technology management.

Lewis, Geoffrey is a Professorial Fellow at the Melbourne Business School, University of Melbourne. After completing a PhD at the London Business School, Geoff joined the faculty at the International Management Institute, Geneva. Three years later, he returned to Australia and joined the faculty of Melbourne Business School. In 1988 Geoff joined the faculty at the Darden School, where he taught strategy on the MBA programme and executive education courses. In 1992, he returned to Australia to take up his position at Melbourne Business School, where he teaches Business Strategy and Corporate Strategy. Geoff returned to the Darden School as Visiting Professor during 2000–2002.

Madeja, Nils is a Research Associate and Doctoral Candidate at the Otto-Beisheim Graduate School of Management (WHU). His research and teaching activities include success factors in electronic and mobile business. His research has been published in journals, such as the *JECR*, and presented at international conferences, such as the *HICSS* and *ICEB*. Prior to joining the department, he spent 2 years in Japan, where he worked in the semiconductor industry and for an e-Commerce system vendor. He also gained professional experience in the semiconductor and telecommunications industry in Germany. Nils Madeja holds an advanced degree in electrical engineering (Dipl.-Ing.) from the University of Kiel, Germany.

Moon, Jon is Director of the World Class Finance Practice of Ernst & Young LLP. He holds a doctorate from Henley Management College. He has extensive international operational and professional services experience and combines this with academic interests. His doctoral research was focused on e-market (EM) business models using causal network analysis and some of the results of this work are presented in this book.

Newell, Sue is a Trustee Professor in the Department of Management at Bentley College, USA. She has previously worked in UK at Aston and Birmingham Universities, Warwick and Nottingham Business Schools, and Royal Holloway, University of London. She gradated with a PhD in psychology from Cardiff University. She is one of the founding Members of IKON (the innovation, knowledge and organization networking research centre, based at Warwick University). This research centre reflects her main research interest, which focuses on exploring innovation processes from a knowledge perspective, looking at the networks through which knowledge is shared and created. Sue has published extensively in a wide variety of management, IS and organizational behaviour journals including *Journal of Management Studies, Human Relations, Organization Studies and Information Systems Journal.*

Osterwalder, Alexander is a Research and Teaching Fellow at the Business School of the University of Lausanne in Switzerland (Ecole des HEC), where he earned his PhD. His research specializes in e-Business, IT and strategy. Recently, he started studying the opportunities and risks of Information and Communication Technology in developing countries. His current research investigates the relationship between information and communication technology, international trade and development in West Africa.

Pearson, J. Michael is an Associate Professor at Southern Illinois University at Carbondale. Dr Pearson's articles appear in *Communications of the ACM, Information and Management, Journal of Strategic Information Systems, Decision Support Systems, Review of Business, Journal of Internet Commerce, Information Resources Management Journal* and *Public*

Administration Quarterly. His primary research interests are in project management, technology acceptance, e-Commerce, management of quality and IT productivity measures.

Pigneur, Dr Yves is a Professor and Head of the Information Systems Department of the Business School (HEC) of the University of Lausanne. He has a PhD from the University of Namur in Belgium in the field of computer-aided requirement engineering. In 1994, he was a Visiting Professor in the IS Department of Georgia State University (Atlanta) and the Hong Kong University of Science and Technology. In 2004, he is a Visiting Professor in the IS Department of the University of British Columbia in Vancouver. His interests cover IS design, requirement engineering, management of IT and e-Business.

Plant, Robert is an Associate Professor in the Department of Computer Information Systems at the University of Miami. He obtained his PhD in computer science at the University of Liverpool, England. Previously he studied Computation at the Programming Research Group, Oxford University, England and Wadham College, Oxford. His research interests are in the area of strategy and IS having published over 30 journal articles. Dr Plant is a Microsoft Certified Systems Engineer, a Chartered Engineer (UK), an European Engineer and a Fellow of the British Computer Society. Dr Plant is a Research Affiliate of Templeton College, Oxford University, England; Visiting Professor of Information Systems and Strategy at Universidad Gabriela Mistral, Santiago de Chile; and Visiting Fellow at Victoria University, New Zealand.

Ribbers, Pieter is Professor of Information Management at Tilburg University, School of Economics and Business Administration, the Netherlands, where he is head of the department of Information Management. At Tias, the school for executive education of Tilburg University, he also chairs the Executive Master of Information Management program. From 1991 till 1995 he held a position as affiliated Professor in Information Management at the Washington University in St. Louis MO. His interests span management of information technology (in particular questions related to alignment and information economics), inter-organizational systems (in particular e-Business), and the strategic and organizational consequences of the use of Information Technology. He is active as a researcher, lecturer and consultant. He has contributed articles in this field to professional, national and international journals and has (co-)authored several books. He is an active speaker at conferences in both Europe and the United States. As a consultant he worked for companies like Brunel and ING-group especially in outsourcing, scenario development and information economics.

Schoder, Detlef has recently been appointed as a Professor at the University of Cologne, after serving as Professor at the Otto-Beisheim Graduate School of Management (WHU). His research and teaching focuses on e-Commerce/e-Business, mass customization, peer-to-peer, ubiquitous computing and media management. Detlef Schoder has over 130 reviewed publications, including articles in leading international and German journals. He also acts as a reviewer for several international journals and conferences and is a member of numerous academic committees and editorial boards. Detlef Schoder holds an MBA degree and a DBA degree. He has worked in Germany, USA, the Republic of Kazakhstan and Japan.

Seddon, Peter B. is an Associate Professor in the Department of Information Systems at the University of Melbourne, Australia. His teaching and research interests focus on helping people and organizations gain greater benefits from the use of IT. His major publications have been in the areas of evaluation of IS success, packaged enterprise application software, IT outsourcing and accounting IS. Peter is an Associate Editor for the *Journal of Information Technology*, and has recently retired as an Associate Editor for *MIS Quarterly*.

Shanks, Graeme is a Professor in the School of Business Systems at Monash University, Australia. He has also held academic positions at the University of Melbourne and Chisholm Institute of Technology. Before becoming an academic, Graeme worked for a number of private and government organizations as a programmer, systems analysts and project leader. His teaching and research interests include information quality, conceptual modelling, implementation and impact of enterprise systems, and decision support systems. Graeme has published the results of his research in over 100 refereed journal and conference papers. He is on the editorial boards of various journals, a Member of the College of Experts of the Australian Research Council, and a Fellow of the Australian Computer Society.

Smirnov, Alexander Victorovitch is Head of the Laboratory of Computer-Aided Integrated Systems and Deputy Director for Research of St. Petersburg Institute for Informatics and Automation of Russian Academy of Sciences (smir@iias.spb.su). He has been involved in various European and Russian projects in areas of advanced manufacturing systems, business process re-engineering and concurrent enterprising. For the past several years, he has been a participant of a research project group in the area of production network configuration at Ford Motor Company both in Europe and USA. Professor Smirnov has published in journals, books and manuals, as well as proceedings of international conferences.

Vidgen, Richard is a Reader in Information Systems in the School of Management at the University of Bath. He has 15 years' industrial experience of IS development and holds a first degree in Computer Science and Accounting, an MSc in Accounting and a PhD in Information System Quality. His research interests include IS development methods and systems theory, e-Commerce quality and e-Business transformation. He has published the books *Data Modelling for Information Systems* (1996) and *Developing Web Information Systems* (September, 2002) as well as many book chapters and journal papers.

Willcocks, Leslie is a Professor of Information Management and e-Business at Warwick Business School, UK. He has an international reputation for his work on e-Business, information management, IT evaluation and IS outsourcing. He is also an Associate Fellow at Templeton College, Oxford; Visiting Professor in Information Systems at Erasmus University, Rotterdam; Professorial Associate at the University of Melbourne and Distinguished Visitor at the Australian Graduate School of Management. He holds a Doctorate in Information Systems from the University of Cambridge, and has been for the last 12 years Editor-in-Chief of the *Journal of Information Technology*. He has published 23 books and over 140 papers in journals, such as *Harvard Business Review, Sloan Management Review, California Management Review, MIS Quarterly, MISQ Executive, Journal of Management Studies, Communications of the ACM* and *Journal of Strategic Information Systems*.

Winch, Graham holds a BSc in Industrial Chemistry and PhD in Business Administration, and is presently a Research Professor in Business Analysis at the University of Plymouth Business School. Previously he lectured for 9 years at Durham University, and has worked in the chemical industry and in market research in Germany and UK. He has also held consulting posts in USA including serving as Vice President and Board Director of Federal Group Inc., the Boston-based strategy consulting subsidiary of a New York investment bank. He has published widely in System Modelling and Visualization, and has been Editor-in-Chief of the System Dynamics Review. He is currently the President Elect of the System Dynamics Society.

Glossary of terms

AIAI	Artificial Intelligence Applications Institute
API	application programming interface
ASP	application service provider
ASPic	ASP industry consortium
B2B	business-to-business
B2C	business-to-consumer
BM_3	business model 3
BOL	Bertelsmann Online
BP	business processes
BPA	buying pattern algorithms
BPM	business process management
BPO	business process outsourcing
BPR	business process re-engineering
C2B	consumer-to-business
C2C	consumer-to-consumer
CAP	capacity service provider
CASE	computer-aided software engineering
CEO	chief executive officer
CIO	chief information officer
CLR	common language runtime
CM	capacity management
CRM	customer relationship management
CyPRG	Cyberspace policy research group
DBP	distributed business processes
DBPE	Distributed business process execution
DIY	do-it-yourself
ECCRM	Electronic commercial customer relationship management
ECR	efficient customer response
EDI	E-Data Interchange
EJB	Enterprise JavaBeans
EM	e-markets
EMH	e-market hypothesis
EQI	E-Qual Index
ERP	enterprise resource planning
FAXM	Java API for XML messaging
FM	forecast management
FS	full service
FSMKE	forum on strategic management knowledge exchange

GA	generic activity
GBF	get big fast
GSS	group support systems
IBS	Internet Bookshop
IBSP	internet business service provider
IC	inventory control
ICRS	integrated care records service
ICT	information and communication technologies
IDE	integrated development environment
ILS	inventory locator system
IM	inventory management
IOE	industrial organization economics
IPPC	integrated production planning and control
IS	information service
ISV	independent software vendors
IT	information technology
JAXP	Java API for XML processing
JAXR	Java API for XML registries
JAX-RPC	Java API for XML-based RPC
JRE	Java runtime environment
MAD	mergers, acquisitions and divestments
MIS	management information systems
MSP	managed service provider
NHSIA	NHS information service
OE	organizational economics
OECD	organization for economic cooperation and development
OEM	original equipment manufacturers
OLAP	online analytical processing
OMS	order management systems
OO	object-orientated
OS	open standard
PBIT	profit before tax
PM	production management
PPR	product-process-resource
PSP	primary service provision
QFD	quality function deployment
QoS	quality of network service
R&D	research and development
RBV	resource-based view
REA	resource event agent
RFI	request for information
RFP	request for proposal
RIO	return on investment
RMM	raw material management
ROA	returns on assets

ROCE	return on capital employed
ROE	returns on equity
RV	relational view
SBU	strategic business unit
SCM	supply chain management
SCN	supply chain networks
SD	standard deviation
SE	standard error
SLA	service level agreement
SMB	small-to-medium business
SMEs	small to medium enterprises
SOA	service-orientated architecture
SOAP	simple object access protocol
SSL	secure socket layer
SWOT	strengths, weaknesses, opportunities and threats
TAM	technology acceptance model
TCE	transaction cost economics
TCO	total cost of ownership
TOVE	TOronto Virtual Enterprise
TPB	theory of planned behavior
UCM	use case map
UDDI	universal description, discovery and integration
UML	unified modelling language
UoD	universe of discourse
VMI	vendor managed inventory
WSDL	web services description language
WSP	web service provider
WTO	world trade organization
WWW	world wide web
XML	extensible markup language

Index

Abstractions of strategy 6, 13, 18, 22, 25–6, 28
Acquisitions and divestments 300
Activity system map 18–19, 23, 26, 28, 30–1
Adam Smith 46
Add-on selling 79
AIAI enterprise ontology 123
Alamo 255, 257, 262–3
Amazon.com 3, 5, 44, 50, 79, 159–61, 372, 401
American Express 22, 31, 261, 266
Application programming interfaces (API) 322, 390, 393, 396
Application service providers (ASP) 3, 5–6, 9, 10, 137, 140, 142–4, 253, 280, 313, 316–19, 323–4, 326–7, 331–4, 371–2, 374–81, 383–4, 386, 388, 390, 394, 402–7
Architecture 95, 259, 332, 339, 347, 370, 390, 405
Atomic e-Business model 4, 23–4, 26, 31, 67
AUCNET 134–5
Automatic teller machine (ATM) 162
Automotive industry 9, 335, 339, 342, 360

B2B 4, 75, 94, 132, 135, 159–62, 223–6, 255, 384, 405, 407
B2C 75, 159–60, 162, 171, 220, 223–5, 230, 233, 255, 267
Balanced scorecard 146
Best practice 246, 249
BPR 44
Bricks and mortar 4, 5, 8, 231, 253, 267
Business model (unit of analysis; murky; taxonomies) 3–5, 11, 13, 21–6, 31, 35, 37, 45, 47, 66–7, 84, 91–3, 144, 160, 178–9, 408

Business performance 208
Business process management 390
Business process model (BPM) 390
Business process outsourcing (BPO) 276, 280, 372, 393
Business strategy 33, 93
Business value of IT 219

C2C 159–60
Causal network analysis 136, 140–2
CEO 35, 94, 135–6, 181, 188, 271, 274, 378
Charles Schwab 253, 258, 266
Cheap-sourcing path 259–60
Chile 198
CIO 181, 257, 373, 378
Client server 322, 326, 373
ColourPlaza value configuration 88
Community membership 170
Competitive focus 6, 11–12, 28–30
Competitive positioning 6, 11–12, 23, 27–8, 30–2, 273
Complementary resources 290
Complex systems and data 400
Computer aided software engineering 183–4, 208
Conceptual modelling 7, 54, 98, 365
Conceptualization of strategy 14, 15
Configuration management 345–6, 362
Connectivity 215, 220, 339, 392
Contingency approach 168, 173
Co-opetition 91, 254, 264, 270
Core competencies 48, 84, 264, 267, 272, 286, 362
Corporate strategy 42–3, 309
Corporate Web sites 8, 183
Critical success factors 285
Culture 36, 48, 156, 177, 203, 207, 245, 287, 299, 301, 314

Customer equity and relationship 78, 79, 82
Customer relationship management (CRM) 267, 316, 384, 405
Customization 72–3, 218, 220, 226, 371, 405
Custom-ordered management 345

Data processing 285
Data warehousing 168
Degree of integration 90–2
Dell 5, 12, 22, 31, 56–7, 84, 253, 264–5, 264–8, 270–6, 279–80
Detailed actor 102–3, 111–12, 114–15, 119–20
Differentiation (strategic differentiation) 27, 29, 40, 44, 168, 173, 175, 366
Direct-to-customer 4, 56, 58
Distribution channels 76
Domain-dependent models 357–60
Domain-independent models 355–7
dot.com 370
Dynamic knowledge problem model 345
Dynamic process flow model 356, 357, 363
Dynamic process model 54

Easyjet.com 173
e-bay 3
e-Business development 256, 257
e-Business markets and strategies 131–210
e-Business models (definitions, unit of analysis, taxonomies) 3–7, 23–4, 31, 48–9, 61, 65, 67–9, 92, 100–1, 125, 316
e-Business models (diffusion/flawed/proliferation/successful) 3–7, 23–4, 31, 48–9, 61, 65, 67–9, 92, 100–1, 125, 316
e-Commerce 4, 155, 158–77, 179, 186, 189–90, 206, 390
E-Data Interchange (EDI) 183, 184, 187
e-government 8, 229, 235–36, 249, 250
e-learning 170

e-management 6, 9, 335–41, 344–5, 347–8, 351, 361–2
e-market business models 131–57
e-procurement 4, 48, 85
E-Qual 8, 229–37, 241–4, 248–50
e-sourcing 254, 263, 266, 270, 273, 275–6
e³-value e-Business model 7, 98, 113, 117–27
Economic value 17, 44
Edinburgh Group 69
Efficient customer response 85
Electronic commerce customer relationship management 213
Electronic data interchange 92, 94, 183–5, 206–7, 227
Electronic markets (EM) 7–8, 131–7, 140–6
EM hypothesis (EMH) 132
EM paradox model 146
Emergent strategy formulation 38
Enterprise application integration (EAI) 384, 387–8, 393, 407
Enterprise information systems 388
Enterprise ontologies 7, 65, 123
Enterprise resource planning (ERP) 267, 283–309, 316–17, 326, 344, 373, 375, 378, 384, 405–6, 408
Environmental models of competitive advantage 40
Epistemologies 163–4, 167, 176
Exchange 8, 25, 108, 156, 229, 235–6, 249–50, 265, 379
Executive information systems 207

Firm performance 4, 180–1, 208–10, 221, 286, 307
Firm specificity 12, 27, 29
First mover advantage 380
Five-forces model 15, 50
Forester Research Model 262
Free internet services 111, 112, 116
FSMKE 8, 229, 235–8, 241, 244–5, 247–50
Fulfilment modelling 51
Full-service (FS) provider 58, 59

Gartner Group 378, 383
Generic development methodology 9, 54, 335
Generic strategy 36
Global actor 102–4, 111, 113, 115, 119, 120
Group support systems (GSS) 183, 184, 187

Harvard School 12, 14, 29
Human IT resources 287

IBM 43, 175, 260, 269, 274, 276, 308, 325, 331–3, 373–4, 392, 402–6
IDC 10, 283, 308, 371, 377–8, 406
Immediacy, 215
Inbound logistics 85–6, 360
Incomplete contract theory 8, 285, 288, 289, 291
Independent software vendors (ISV) 375, 380
Individualization 218
Industry competition 36
Information and communication technologies 61–2, 70, 73, 75, 79–82, 92–3, 100, 159–60, 162, 165, 171, 175
Information and communication technology (ICT) 159–62
Infrastructure management 66, 124
Insourcing/partnering path 261
Intangible IT resources 287
Integrated production planning and control (IPPC) 355, 357, 358, 359
Integration 287, 307, 339, 350, 360, 362, 366–8, 370, 384, 387–90, 393–5, 401–2, 405, 407
Integration care records service (ICRS) 328–30
Intelligent agent 348, 366, 369
Interactivity 214
Internet implication capability 255
Internet service provider 112
Inter-organizational relationship 296, 301

Interview variables 154
Investment 45, 95, 181
iThink 54, 55

J2EE 381, 390–2, 402, 407

Key performance areas (KPA) 379, 384
Key performance indicator 330
Knowledge management 7, 158, 163–73, 175–7, 209, 306, 308, 333, 343–5, 362
Knowledge sharing 165, 236, 249, 290, 366–7
Knowledge-sharing routines 290

Laggards 8, 253–5
Leaders 8, 10, 14, 73, 91, 253–6, 309, 374, 378, 380–1, 386
Low cost 40, 48, 173–4, 258–9, 274, 319, 399

Managed service provider 380
Management information systems 64, 176, 183, 187, 194, 205–7, 209, 219, 227, 251–2, 279, 281, 308, 332–4, 406–7
Market conditions 7, 131, 135, 137
Market segment 40, 75, 105, 110–11, 179, 405
Mergers, acquisitions and divestments (MAD) 300, 305, 306
Microsoft .NET 381, 390
Mined sourcing path (MSP) 375
Mixed development path 261–3
Multi-agent 347, 367

New economy 41, 63, 309
New management tools 7, 65
NHS 9, 313–17, 319–20, 322–34
NHS Information Authority (NHSIA) 316, 320, 327–8, 331
NHS Trust networking 324

Object-based internet applications 322
Object-oriented domain model 360

Object-orientated component computing 387
OEM 339
Old economy 4
Ontology 7, 34, 65–9, 93–4, 98–102, 112–13, 115, 117–19, 123–6, 208, 346–7, 366
Orange 81, 83
Order management systems (OMS) 395–400
Organizational economics (OE) 16
Organizational learning 177
Osterwalder and Pigneur ontology 124
Outsourcing 94, 260, 279–81, 283, 285, 306, 308–9
Outsourcing path 260

Partnerships and alliances 87, 90
Perceived strategic value 8, 188, 194–7, 200–4
Personalization 74, 165, 167–9, 241, 243, 249
Personalized market 134, 144
Priceline 3
Primary Service Provisioning 9, 313, 316–17, 331
Problem-solving strategies 354
Process flow model 52
Process model 151, 152, 153
Product and information flows 23, 351
Product innovation 70–3
Product–process–resource 335, 345, 346, 347
Profitability sheets 121–2

Quality function deployment 229

REA ontology 124
Relational data model 345
Relational view (RV) 8, 283–4, 307
Requirements, engineering 99, 126
Research methodology 135–6
Resource based view (RBV) 8, 40–1, 48, 50, 283, 285–6, 289, 291
Return of equity (ROE) 16
Return on assets (ROA) 16, 180
Return on investment (ROI) 180

SAP 286, 308, 362, 373, 375, 392, 402
Scalability 336, 341–43
Service level agreements 283, 284, 285, 296, 299–301
Service oriented architectures (SOA) 386, 389, 404
Simple object access protocol (SOAP) 389, 390, 391, 401
Small medium enterprise (SME) 192, 217
Software applications integration 370–404
Statistical procedure 194–5
Strategic business units 14
Strategic investment 45
Strategic partnering 264–5, 267–73, 275
Strategic value 178–205
Strategy perspective 38
Substitutability 41
Supply chain activities 36, 267, 335–64
Supply chain management 337
Supply chain networks (SCN) 56, 336
SupplyGenie.com 26
SWOT analysis 14, 15
System dynamics 54

Tacit knowledge 164
Tangible IT resources 287
Target customer 66, 74, 124, 379
Technology acceptance model (TAM) 156, 180, 183, 203, 207, 209, 219
Technology arrangements and factors 46
Technology-mediated exchanges 159
Tesco.com 261
Theoretical framework 8, 179–80, 183, 186, 188–9, 192, 194, 196, 198, 201–2, 204
TOVE ontology 123
Transaction cost economics (TCE) 134
Transaction cost theory 8, 283, 285, 288, 289, 291
Triple pair process flow model 52, 55, 57

Unit circle model 133
Universal description discovery and integration (UDDI) 389

Use case maps (UCMs) 117–21
User acceptance 6, 7, 131–2, 135, 137,
    147, 155, 183, 206, 218, 227, 251

Value activity 101–3, 115–17, 123–4
Value chain 16, 30, 36, 38, 40, 45, 48,
    51, 84–5, 126, 305–6, 342
Value configuration 86, 87
Value creation 205, 283, 405
Value exchange 108, 109, 114
Value interface 107–8
Value networks 253
Value object 105
Value offers 106–7
Value port 106
Value proposition 21, 25, 26, 65–6,
    70–5, 79, 82, 86, 93, 98, 100, 169,
    171, 173–5, 179, 371–2, 375, 377,
    394
Value shop 87

Value transaction 108–9
Vendor management inventory 92
Virtual integration 265, 270–1

Web features 8, 213–14, 218, 220–1,
    224, 225–6
Web service description language
    (WSDL) 389
Web services 3, 6, 9, 313–14, 318,
    323–6, 328–31, 333, 371–2, 374,
    377, 380–4, 386–7, 389–90, 392–4,
    401–3, 405–7
World Wide Web (WWW) 47, 183,
    185, 206, 214, 222–3, 226,
    367, 373

Xerox 44, 63, 166
XML 270, 376, 381, 388–90, 392–3,
    400–2, 407
xSP 372, 374–5